WITHDRAWN

Playing to the Camera

Edited by Bert Cardullo, Harry Geduld, Ronald Gottesman, and Leigh Woods

Playing to the Camera

Yale University Press *New Haven and London*

Film Actors Discuss Their Craft

Published with assistance from the foundation established in memory of Philip Hamilton McMillan of the Class of 1894, Yale College.

Film stills courtesy of the Museum of Modern Art, New York, N.Y., and the British Film Institute Stills Archive, London. The photograph of Charles Graham is reproduced courtesy of the Raymond Mander and Joe Michenson Theatre Collection, Kent, England.

Designed by Sonia L. Scanlon
Set in Bulmer type by The Composing Room of Michigan, Inc.

Printed in the United States of America by Bookcrafters, Inc., Chelsea, Michigan.
Library of Congress Cataloging-in-Publication Data
Playing to the camera : Film actors discuss their craft / edited by Bert Cardullo . . . [et al.].
p.   cm.
Includes bibliographical references and index.
ISBN 0-300-06983-9 (cloth).
1. Motion picture acting.   2. Motion picture actors and actresses—Interviews.
I. Cardullo, Bert.
PN1995.9.A26P63 1997
791.43′028—dc21   97-1644
                                                CIP

A catalogue record for this book is available from the British Library.

The paper in this book meets the guidelines for permanence and durability of the Committee on Production Guidelines for Book Longevity of the Council on Library Resources.

10 9 8 7 6 5 4 3 2 1

Contents

Foreword

This book is a prize for all who care about film. Open it anywhere and it gleams with insight, experience, professional knowledge. Read it through and an odd truth comes clear: this is a history, informal but vivid, of the most famous of the film arts—yet one that has not been as thoroughly explored as some others. The editors, with phenomenal research, with an instinct for relevance, have done what could be done in one volume of this kind to amend that lack. The result is a treasury.

Obviously, this is not to say that every piece in the collection is a pearl of wisdom. But every piece is quarried from the experience of a working professional. Not many of the pieces are without prejudices—how could they be?— and some are most interesting as curios. Still, through this book one can view from the inside the growth of the particularities of film acting, as it becomes distinct from theater acting. We can see the achievements and adjustments, the vanities and generosities in this growth. Adding viewpoint to viewpoint through the past century, this book gives us the mapping of a new territory in art.

From the beginning, a chief concern of actors in the new medium was that it was different from the theater, especially that there was no audience. Remembering his work in 1912, Charles Graham says: "One thing the shadow people of the screen can never know is the joy that comes from feeling the audience begin to play their part." In 1916 the Shakespearean star E. H. Sothern says, "One of the strangest experiences in this posing for the 'movies' is the absence of the audience." But by 1938 Lionel Barrymore, a theater veteran who had become a screen eminence, opines that "the stage actor has an audience trained to contribute to the dramatic illusion. . . . The film audience is not so trained. . . . So the [screen] actor has to compete with reality." In other words, Barrymore thinks that film acting, instead of being shrunken by an audience's absence, is spurred to contribute even more: collaboration between actor and audience still exists, but a greater share devolves upon the actor.

Yet no matter how sophisticated the views of film acting become, comparisons with the theater do not cease. Albert Finney, much later than the people cited above, misses the "sense of space and time" of the theater but is glad to be rid of the burdensome realization that in a long-run play, he'll "be putting the same glass down in the same place at the same time four months from now." On the other hand, he says, film acting brings the sobering thought that "the first-day's shooting is intended to be part of the film"—unlike in the theater, the actor virtually begins work with the finished product. Against a widespread view, Mai Zetterling argues that though screen acting is fragmentary, done in bits and pieces, the view of theater acting as unitary is false: scene breaks and act breaks fragment stage performances, too. She feels that sufficient rehearsal time for films would eliminate the much-mooted differences in continuity between film and theater acting. Rod Steiger refutes the argument that film actors don't have enough time to prepare. In "On the Actor," he says he has seen them "while they sit around for two and a half hours waiting for a technician to light a candle thirty blocks away."

It's notable that, from the start, actors believe that screen acting involves personality much more than theater acting does. This view, in itself debatable, was possibly promoted by the proximity of the film audience: the camera is much closer most of the time than any theater spectator is. Sothern says, "In the moving picture art you are never your hero [your character] for one moment, you are always yourself intensely interested in showing through your expression what kind of man your hero was." Eric Portman, decades later, suggests, rather oddly, to the screen aspirant "that you can test your audience projection in ordinary life. The next time you go into a crowded room, see if you can project your personality. See if people stop talking when you enter, look at you, rise quickly to give you a drink, a cigarette." This unique screen test would not appeal to Marcello Mastroianni, who loves to change roles because, he says, either mistakenly or modestly, "changing helped me overcome the problem of not having a strong personality."

The last section of this anthology centers on the Method, which is just, considering the importance that the Method has had, one way or another, for actors in this century. In fact, the subject appears before we get to that section. Liv Ullmann is blunt in her opinion of the Method but adds that "it's for bad actors that the Method can be dangerous." Laurence Olivier is equally blunt about Lee Strasberg, high priest of the Method, but he is strongly for Stanislavsky, whose teachings were the origin of the Method and whom he calls "an intensely practical man." Vsevolod Pudovkin, the actor-director, speaks even earlier of the relevance of Stanislavsky to the screen; and Elia Kazan, who was a Method actor before he became a Method director, has said (in *Kazan on Kazan*), "There's a basic element in the Stanislavsky system that has always helped me a lot in directing actors in the movies. The key word, if I had to pick one, is 'to want.'" We are left with the feeling that Stanislavsky and the Method will continue to be debated as warmly in regard to film acting as to theater acting.

One of the reasons that film acting has had insufficient attention in film studies is that ultimately, film is the director's medium—at any rate, the filmmaker's medium. The director, usually joined later by the editor and producer, chooses what the audience will look at and how it is to be seen. Charles Chaplin and Buster Keaton, successful theater clowns before they made films, were among the first to understand that they had to control the whole process if their performances were to be seen as they intended. But not many actors have had complete control of films, or therefore of their performances, and they deplore it all through the decades of film's existence.

Yet though these matters of execution are fixed, there is a paradox. If the film is the director's work, then, when we think of good films, why do we think of actors as often as of directors? When I remember *Way Down East,* certainly I recall Griffith's mastery, but equally I think of Lillian Gish's body language as her life and status change. With *Mother,* Pudovkin, yes, but at the crucial moment, it is Vera Baranovskaya who picks up the flag, not Pudovkin. *The Passion of Joan of Arc* is exalted by Dreyer's genius, but Dreyer's work would have come to little without the consecration of Falconetti's performance.

In the sound era, the paradox is even more striking. With *Twentieth Century,* it's not Howard Hawks I think of first but John Barrymore, epitomizing nineteenth-century acting. With *The Grapes of Wrath,* not John Ford but Henry Fonda, speaking out of the heart of stricken America. With *Camille,* not George Cukor but Garbo, dying. With *The Organizer,* not Mario Monicelli but Marcello Mastroianni, rallying the strikers. With *Ikiru,* not Akira Kurosawa but Takashi Shimura, singing softly in the snow on the playground swing. With *The French Lieutenant's Woman,* not Karel Reisz but Meryl Streep waiting for her lover. With *Howards End,* not James Ivory but Vanessa Redgrave and Emma Thompson in their epoch-ending duet. With *The Verdict,* not Sidney Lumet but Paul Newman addressing the jury. Certainly directors touched all those performances, to one degree or another, but it was the actors whose talents fulfilled the films.

Actors, in a profession not noted for reticence, tend to underrate their importance to film. To put it quite personally, I have immense debts to some theater actors for what they have given me, but the blessings of film acting have flowed more copiously. When Bernard Shaw was a theater critic in London, he said that he liked going to a certain theater because it specialized in "good acting and plenty of it." For me, to an agreeably surprising measure, this has been true of films.

That is why I'm especially happy to welcome this book and to hail its abundant recognition of an art to which so many of us filmgoers owe so much.

Stanley Kauffmann

Preface

Everybody in the world is an actor. Conversation is acting. Man as a social animal is an actor; everything we do is some sort of a performance. But the actor whose profession it is to act is then something else again. . . . I don't understand what a picture is if there is bad acting. I don't understand how movies exist independently of the actor—I truly don't.

Orson Welles, This Is Orson Welles, *pp. 262–263*

The seeds of the Arctic lupine are said to be viable for 10,000 years, those of the Indian lotus for 400 years. It should not seem so shocking, then, that the present volume has incubated for twenty-five years. The original seed was planted by Harry Geduld and Ronald Gottesman in the form of a voluminous collection of materials—letters, interviews, essays, selections from autobiographies, and the like—in which screen actors variously described, interpreted, and explained what they believed they had contributed to the famously collaborative process of filmmaking. Geduld had edited anthologies on the contributions made by writers and directors to filmmaking, and he and Gottesman reasoned that it was time for actors to have their say, particularly at a moment in the history of cinema when actors were becoming something more than stars or even celebrities and were beginning to control the studios, just as, until the early 1950s, the studios had controlled them. By 1975 Geduld and Gottesman had gathered enough selections for two volumes. The selections addressed in chronological fashion many aspects of acting for the camera—from the earliest days of silent movies to the 1960s, when the boundary between film acting and stage performance had begun to ossify. But the authors still didn't have a book.

For various reasons, the project gathered dust until they had the good fortune to encounter Bert Cardullo and Leigh Woods, who agreed to bring to bear on the project their formidable understanding of acting and of film history. They have in turn radically augmented, rearranged, updated, and contextualized the selections and shaped them into a valuable anthology that should be of interest to anyone interested in screen *or* stage acting.

Playing to the Camera should interest students of acting because theirs is still a relatively unexplored subject—not least because acting takes place in such a daunting variety of technological, material, and procedural circumstances. Screen acting is, moreover, perhaps even more puzzling in its essential mysteriousness of effect and affect than are older forms of acting, in which at least the "bare forked animals" are continually in view as they perform in real time. It may be startling to say so, but we know relatively little about the ancient practice of acting, in spite of the vast secondary literature on the subject and the abundant testimony of its practitioners. We do know for certain by now that the human voice can be—and has always been—a powerful instrument of ideology that enables destructive giants to come to power. We also know, in Wallace Stevens's words, that a voice can undo giants by whispering "heavenly labials in a world of gutturals." We understand that the body is a tongue that speaks to the unconscious as well as to more mediated forms of awareness. We know, in short, that performers and their witnesses are the tines of a tuning fork by means of which, at least for a time, human isolation can be breached and mortal fixity made to flow. A theater is a place where, paradoxically, we can become ourselves by becoming others. In a movie theater this may be even truer. And what actors for the camera have to say about such magic may more than reward our attention.

Ronald Gottesman

Introduction *Leigh Woods*

Acting, like drama itself, entails conflict, tension, and paradox. When we speak of acting, we have in mind the energy produced and released in performance — not only in mimetic compositions for stage and screen but also in the "acting" that manifests itself so often in real-life circumstances involving duress or potential but doubtful gain. At root, drama takes its definition from conflicts at the heart of society and of individuals, and acting shows us humanity in its moments of greatest tension or opposition. Thus, professional actors by the very nature of their work capture tension and indeed might be said to embody it.

Writing more than two centuries ago, Denis Diderot found it both marvelous and suspect that actors could exercise their art dispassionately while representing passion on the stage. In his "paradox of the actor" Diderot attributed to performers the enigmatic ability to render public a realm of experience more generally considered private. For hundreds of years before Diderot, actors had been regarded with suspicion because they did not recognize bourgeois distinctions between public and private. Thespians' odd routines, their irregular hours, and their endless sartorial transformations were viewed with mistrust in a time when transformation of any kind was considered insidious and potentially subversive. It is hardly surprising that actors showed themselves signally reticent to discuss their work. In the two hundred years since the era of Romanticism, actors have grown more forthcoming about themselves but less about their work. Their selective disclosures have steadily drawn charges of self-indulgence from people who suspect that a strict correspondence exists between the lives of the characters that actors play and the actors' own lives. This putative equivalence surfaces more persistently in discussions of acting than in discussions of any other art, because it is often so difficult to distinguish actors' bodies, voices, and imaginations from those of the characters they portray.

The advent of film a hundred years ago has in some respects exacerbated actors' longstanding reluctance to give away professional secrets for nothing. In the face of modern technology, actors have, if anything, grown more reluctant to compromise their effectiveness before an audience that they hope will watch what they do rather than how they do it. Meanwhile, actors have been subjected to greater scrutiny than before, ever since their enlarged images began to appear on motion picture screens. Such scrutiny, in turn, revived an old, largely unspoken challenge from actors to their audiences, which if it were voiced would go something like this: "If you want to know more about what I do, you can pay to watch me do it."

But over the last century such protective instincts have been severely tested. Acting, previously exercised onstage, in the flesh, before relatively small live audiences, has gained a new and more hermetic setting in film, where images are preserved in two dimensions only and projected, very often, in places remote from their creation. This development exposes a given performance to much larger numbers of viewers, while fostering less interaction among those viewers, and virtually none at all between viewers and the actors themselves. Film acting is now purveyed even more widely on television, where it is watched almost always by people in small groups or in utter solitude. In this sense, the consumption of drama has increased since the advent of film (and later, television), while at the same time growing less interactive and, in some senses, more private.

Viewers in almost every part of the world can witness acting in considerable variety and abundance. Now that they are exposed to performances in different formats, under varying conditions of reception, and at different times of day, audiences surely find their appreciation of acting altered, if not enhanced in every instance. Such broad accessibility has increased not only the number of those watching but the volume of questions about how actors do what the viewers see. In response to the outpouring of interest, some actors hold their techniques even closer to the chest than they did in the days before films, as a way of protecting their privacy, and their marketability at the same time. Others, while seeming to take the audience into their confidence, offer disclosures rooted in personal context or in particular material circumstances, to discourage strict imitation. Even actors willing and eager to discuss their work, as are most who do so in these pages, often speak about it elliptically or indirectly.

Accordingly, we have selected pieces that feature some of the most recurrent, vivid, and telling observations by professional film actors. We have organized the actors' reflections to point up the areas not only of consensus but of disagreement, too.

Readers will notice that the essays contain as great a range of writing and speaking styles as of opinions about film acting. Some actors' words seem to accord with the images conveyed in their films, whereas others' testimonies appear at odds with their acting. Reasons for this are not hard to find. Acting, particularly as it has been refined in film, communicates meaning through nuance of facial expression, intonation, or inflection in close-ups, and by means of posture, gesture, or gait in longer shots. To the extent that acting is a kinetic art, verbal accounts of it must necessarily be incomplete. In this connection, actors have always been resistant to encapsulation or even adequate description in writing. And their resistance may have been expedient, given that their profession has so often been marginalized, mythologized, or demonized.

The first conclusion readers might draw from the pieces in *Playing to the Camera* is that no single approach suits all actors, in all films, at all times. It is to their credit that actors, when they *do* speak or write about their work, so often acknowledge the material conditions that affect them. Most are either reluctant or unable to distinguish between their imaginative work and the apparently external factors that have led them to act in a particular film. Therefore, readers hungry for glimpses into the creative process will be frustrated by the tendency for actors' focus to fluctuate between sharp if scattered artistic insights and details that appear merely logistical. We have tried in our editing of the actors' essays to anticipate and ease such frustration; but it is a delicate matter to distinguish between concerns related to the "inside" of acting and those which may seem incidental or even extraneous, to an outsider. *Playing to the Camera* reveals that film actors generally have a more encompassing, though less glamorous, sense of what their work entails than their viewers do. In presenting this cross-section of actors' testimonies over time, which cuts across national boundaries, we propose to make apparent the surprisingly wide range of elements that have influenced the acting in films.

The layered, interwoven, or, to an outsider's eyes, often jumbled quality of the accounts gives some notion of how actors mingle personal and professional experience to constitute what viewers see on the screen. Actors take indications from the script and the director and combine them with their own experience and observation, including borrowings from other actors. What emerges is a synthesis of their responses to the demands of the moment and to odds and ends imported or resurrected from different times and places. This eclectic quality makes acting all the more difficult to judge and to discuss, even for its foremost practitioners.

Playing to the Camera contains four parts. The first two, "The Silent Performance" and "Finding a Voice," show how rapidly demands on film actors changed in the years before the Second World War. The shocks and crudity mentioned by early actors stand in contrast to the rather different set of concerns that dominates the last two parts in the book. The third part, "European Acting," chronicles the emergence of film as a separate, legitimate, and often distinguished pursuit for actors in nations with much stronger theatrical traditions than the United States. The last part, "Hollywood Acting," treats mainstream American filmmaking, with all its emphasis on commercial success and broad exposure.

"European Acting" is divided further into three subsections: "Stage and Screen: The British," "Acting and Ideology: The Soviets," and "Continental Alternatives." In these sections, ideological as well as geographical distinctions come to the fore, together with differences in the filmmaking of various European nations. "Hollywood Acting" is similarly divided into three sections: "The Golden Age of the Studios," "The Business of Acting," and "The Method Revisited and Matters of Style." Each group of actors' accounts is preceded by an introduction that lays out issues specific to the commentators and the contents of the part or section.

One consequence of our method of organization is that there are frequent lapses from strict chronology. The section on the Soviets, for example, contains pieces by actors who worked in silent films and so steps back in time from the section on British acting after the advent of sound. Furthermore, the book's later parts span longer periods of time than do the first two, and as a result, the later parts and subsections of the book are likely to encapsulate thirty or forty years of filmmaking rather than only ten or twenty. At the same time, our organization of the material recapitulates a conclusion readily drawn from the several accounts: film acting has always depended as much on the gifts and propensities of individual performers as it has on chronology, "progress," or national, technological, and economic factors. Moreover, a number of the actors represented in this collection proved difficult to categorize even under rubrics that we designed expressly to contain them. Charles Chaplin, for example, would have fit as easily into "The Business of Film Acting" or among his British compatriots in "Stage and Screen" as he does in "The Silent Performance," where we placed him. In Chaplin's case, as in other film actors', distinctions between Europe and America—and between past and present, for that matter—occasionally collapse in the context of these examinations of their work.

Chaplin is also typical in the way he interweaves the various elements in his narrative, including the manner in which he got the job in the first place, actors and directors' collaboration prior to filming, and his creative choices before the camera. Because this composite quality is characteristic of film actors' discussions of their work, we have had to make other tricky editorial choices, including where to locate Chaplin's countrymen Charles Graham and George Arliss, or continental expatriates Greta Garbo and Michael Chekhov. Like most non-American actors in this collection (except the more isolated Soviets), each of these four made films in more than one country. All except Graham also performed in both silents and sound films, and in more than one film genre.

The popularity Hollywood films have enjoyed abroad since Chaplin's film debut has, in some measure, promoted an international perspective among filmmakers stateside, mercenary and self-serving though their motives have often been. Thanks to this internationalism, fueled by marketing, noted foreign actors have continually been recruited to America, especially from the West European countries. Several international stars, including Chaplin, join the Americans in this collection in considering the influence that commercial imperatives exercise over acting. These discussions figure occasionally in the section featuring the British, and in "Continental Alternatives" and "The Method Revisited and Matters of Style." Still more searching inquiries into the role of commercialism in filmmaking lie at the heart of most commentaries included in "The Business of Acting."

The first two parts, those on silents and early sound films, manifest actors' early, and as it turns out, enduring, fondness for comparing acting in films with acting on the stage. This recurring theme—more like an obsession, really, given the frequency with which it figures in this book—points partly to the simple fact that most film actors, at least until very recently, began their careers in the theater. Recognition of their talent on stage often attracted film directors, producers, and (in nations where films have been heavily commercialized) casting agents. It is hard now to remember that film acting took several decades to establish itself, in the face of a subtle but relentless crusade by the theater people to discredit it. As late as 1940, traditionalists like George Arliss could still refer to filmmaking as a "holiday." Such attitudes reflect a disdain for film acting that surfaces with surprising consistency among some very noted actors.

A close and often jealous relationship between theater and film extends back to the inception of the younger form. Several of the Edison Company's films of the mid- and late-1890s captured scenes from then-familiar plays, musicals, and operettas. Since the days of its early and rather leechlike fealty to the stage, film has enjoyed a broad popularity that has been held against it by theater folk. Those who align themselves with high culture have often denigrated films in part at least to erase the theater's own historical lineage as a popular and therefore degraded entertainment, at least by the standards of the modern avant-garde. Partisans of the theater have done more than voice steady disapproval; they have sought to justify the tendency of the modern stage to reach smaller and presumably more sophisticated audiences. Films, by contrast, were drawing much larger and more inclusive audiences than the stage within a decade of their invention. This development was so rapid and so obvious, in fact, that by 1920 the theater conceded the commercial ascendancy to films, which films then conceded to television, in considerable measure, by the mid-1950s.

Largely because of the patronizing attitude on the part of adherents of the legitimate stage, there existed no serious criticism of film acting until the form was nearly twenty years old. This situation helps explain why the earliest account included in *Playing to the Camera* dates from shortly before the First World War. Whether performances on film could be considered acting at all in a legitimate theatrical sense remained problematic until the introduction of live sound recording for feature films in the late 1920s. Some of the earliest French films, by the Lumière brothers in the 1890s, used the directors' family members as performers, and many of the filmmakers who followed the Lumières evinced a similar indifference toward acting talent. With acrobatics, action sequences, travelogues, and trick photography so popular among the earliest film audiences, acting skill of the sort valued on the stage was largely moot. D. W. Griffith shifted the terms of the debate, though, when he advanced the view that acting before cameras posed challenges of its own. In part, Griffith's opinions gave a boost to film at a time when the form needed buttressing if it was to outlive the period of its sheer novelty. A former stage actor himself, Griffith explored means for suggesting and indeed for creating characters' subjective responses through his pioneering uses of the camera and of cross-cutting. His aim was to refine the previously crude narrative texture of cinema, but his innovations also helped increase the range of challenges for film actors.

Griffith accomplished this improvement, however, even as he chose to diminish the degree to which early film scripts mimicked those of the theater. That emulation of the theater included the appearance of stage stars to promote some of the earliest feature films, first in France and later in the United States and Great Britain; the slavish and clearly memorial spirit surrounding these borrowed stars' appearances in warmed-over stage productions on both sides of the Atlantic; the deferential and derivative ways in which film featured stars on the very same sets and even at times the same stages used for theatrical premieres or revivals; the dependence of early film actors on a set of gestures codified by the nineteenth-century French acting theorist François Delsarte; film actors' deployment to stock companies, in imitation of the preferred organization of theatrical production during the 1800s; and the dependence of early film narratives on a brand of melodrama that created an even starker opposition between good and evil than the theater had. This last tendency was a consequence of silent film's lack of audible dialogue and its reliance on typecasting more rigid than had ever been in force on the stage.

In light of the ascendancy film had enjoyed since the early decades, it is not surprising that Griffith's opinions on the distinctive qualities of film acting find support among most of the actors in *Playing to the Camera*. At the same time, though, many who have conducted the greater parts of their career in film believe that stage acting offers better training and still stands as the most rigorous test of their skill. A good many others are willing to give stage and film acting equal weight, in the belief that both make legitimate, if distinct, demands. But most of these actors also express a preference for one kind of acting over the other, with a surprising number (given their success in films) saying that they *prefer* stage to film. Many actors say they value the time for rehearsal and preparation the stage affords them, while even more actors miss the intimacy and the highly charged atmosphere they associate with performing before live audiences.

Actors who prefer the stage fall into two groups. There are those who assert that they feel greater freedom on the stage and those, by contrast, who contend that they feel greater *control* there. For some actors, however, "freedom" seems to derive precisely from their notion of control; and these antithetical values—or perhaps they are only nominally so—intertwine in a number of accounts. Although many actors believe that film acting has effectively supplanted stage acting in its influence on culture as a whole, only a small number assert that film acting entails a greater range and complexity in the demands it makes. The view that film and stage acting have maintained a dialogue for some time is gaining credibility, although not as steadily as might be expected.

Actors' compulsive need to compare stage to film is indicative of the difficulties they experience in describing either medium. The discourse about stage acting is much older, of course, and has lent film acting a stable and legitimate context. Yet stage and film acting seem to resist verbal description in equal measure. The common actorly inclination to define the one in terms of the other may show merely that actors find it easier to talk about what a particular kind of acting is *not* than about what it is or might be.

Several other issues that the actors raise relate to the debate about stage versus film. Foremost among these, in prevalence and theoretical significance, is the definition of audience as crucial to film acting. The most commonly held perception is that the camera functions as a kind of spectator, or, in more literal terms, as a viewer. Actors who advance such notions, though, differ in their views of the camera's nature. Some regard it as a foreign, relentless, and entirely mechanical presence, while others see it as a sort of friendly eye or even, as Michael Caine has written elsewhere, as a paramour. This last opinion is noteworthy in gainsaying, probably unwittingly, the contention advanced by Laura Mulvey and others in the late 1970s that the camera's gaze has, throughout the history of film, been decidedly "male." This is unavoidable, Mulvey and others have argued, so long as the camera has been wielded in a patriarchal society and largely at the discretion of male directors, producers, writers, and technicians.

Feminist film theorists mistrust the camera as a source of power; and indeed women and men film actors alike accord it respect. The very reverence actors of both sexes show the camera, however, seems to foster ambivalence toward the instrument recording their labor. Some actors recommend ignoring the camera entirely, to avoid a sense of pressure, particularly in close-ups, while others say that the camera should be acknowledged at the least, or even wooed. It is, again, paradoxical that as "presence" has come under attack in many poststructuralist theories of human agency, awareness of a mechanical presence—of the machine as almost a living being—has become customary in other quarters, for example, among actors, who attribute to the camera the ability to heighten or alter their own efforts.

Most actors regard the camera as either a stand-in or a synecdoche for a group of living spectators. A good many others, though, during the process of filming routinely envision a live audience, which they have apparently transposed in imagination from recollections of a screening or live venue. The feeling of obligation to hypothetical viewers may well be a legacy of the theater, where actors are used to performing for a body of sentient, engaged lay spectators.

Actors also regard their fellow actors, or more often still their crews, as their first and most consequential viewers. This response may seem exaggerated, but film actors are thrown together with crew members during the entire filming, whereas they usually see their fellow actors only during the shooting of shared scenes.

With film it is possible for performers to serve as their own audience, too, by watching *rushes,* or previews of filmed sequences. This is yet a further trait that distinguishes film acting from that practiced on the stage. Some actors, however, refuse to watch rushes of themselves, in the belief that though such self-observation might sharpen their critical faculties, it would diminish their intuitive ones.

Whom or what actors regard as their audience casts light on broader assumptions about the cultural and political authority they perceive their work to have. It can also reveal what actors crave, or fear, from criticism, and what influence they concede to the public as arbiters of their work.

Even more than they vary in their images of audience, film actors differ in whether they regard themselves as part of an ensemble or as individuals performing the histrionic equivalent of musical solos. This divergence is owing to a more fundamental disparity, between the actors who retain a sense of utter solitude before the cameras and those who feel themselves to be integrated within a collective enterprise. The actors who are most obviously and strongly politicized, such as those who appear in the Soviet section or in "Continental Alternatives," are more likely to view themselves as collaborators than as stars.

In several of the accounts originating before the mid-1960s, actors contend that the critical and nurturing capacities of their fellow actors are extended only to the film community, and still more narrowly in some cases—to the film colony located in and around Hollywood. This clannishness or esprit de corps has its roots in the history of the theatrical world. Actors have always led a life apart from the norm, whether the gypsylike existence of former times or the extreme celebrity that has, since the early years of this century, attached to the best known stars.

If film actors are in accord on any single issue, it is that film is a director's preserve, just as in their eyes the stage is incontestably the actor's realm. But oddly enough, actors' sense of the power that film directors exercise can feed feelings either of creative communion or of alienation. And which will prevail depends as much on how actors respond to particular directors as it does on how their directors deal with them. Both groups share responsibility for complex relationships that can change drastically from one film to the next, or even over the course of a single film. The process of transformation inevitably involves surprises, seldom all pleasant. Actors' general agreement about directors' right to the preeminent role in filmmaking in no way precludes expressions of frustration or even hostility toward directors, whom actors regard as their closest collaborators, and vice versa. Their collective sense of film directors' power may also explain actors' wish—granted increasingly often in recent years—to direct films in their own right.

Even so, some of the same actors who are eager to direct also welcome relinquishing a measure of freedom to their film directors, and with it a potentially crushing sense of responsibility for the success of the films in which they appear. Such actors are less likely to regard themselves as stars and more inclined to discuss their directors in detail than are actors who consider their film work as their own or who imply that they are autonomous, by mentioning only in passing (or not at all) the directors they have worked with. Some actors seem positively to relish the hurly-burly of film work, the technicians and the technology; and for every few actors who write of feeling distracted by the bustle, there is one who draws inspiration from the concentrated efforts of other professionals on the set.

Television acting does not figure as often in the accounts we have selected as one might expect. Its status as a sort of poor relation to theater and film is reminiscent of the lack of regard in which film acting was held for so long.

Television is mentioned only here and there in *Playing to the Camera,* a proof that acting for television has not yet attracted the volume of attention that film acting has.

Like its poor relation, television acting, film acting may have become professionalized over time, but it still failed to gain wide respect, even after having established itself in the 1910s as a potentially lucrative pursuit. Ungrudging respect has not always been forthcoming since then, either, particularly when nonprofessionals or fledgling actors figure prominently, as they do in the films of Soviet director Sergei M. Eisenstein or the Italian neorealists. Such noted filmmakers were convinced that editing could override and definitively shape any impressions actors could make on film. Early producers exploited nonprofessionals as a money-saving measure; over the succeeding decades, directors have come to rely on the acting of other amateurs, especially children, whose innocence and transparency can sometimes outshine more studied performances. This successful casting of amateurs has given some credence to doubts about the need for any trained acting skill at all in film.

Many well-established stage actors have bridled at the degree to which they are treated as commodities in the film world. Issues of marketing and consumption naturally figure in the utopian dream of a state-directed "people's art" invoked by the Soviets, but also in the ambivalence actors commonly express toward American filmmaking, whose moguls evince an often slavish regard for the marketplace. Successful actors' work is influenced, sometimes profoundly, by the ways their careers are funded. This is not to say that all actors view commercialism with a jaundiced eye. In fact, surprising numbers of them emerge from the accounts that follow as partisans of the old-style Hollywood studios, and many believe that with the studios' decline came a diminution in the quality of American films.

Not all actors take such a nostalgic view of the studios, though, or of the prerogative those studios exercised over actors' services. Some of the more onerous aspects of stardom are first voiced by Louise Brooks, who worked at a time when silents endowed film stars more heavily with mythic qualities than at any time since. The sort of spectacular stardom that dates from Theda Bara's heyday might be easier to understand if all the film stars who succeeded her had been great actors. But because that is not the case, it seems reasonable to interpret stardom as a commercial device that film borrowed from the stage and then expanded on in a way only a mass entertainment could. Most of the actors represented in this collection who have experienced stardom at first or second hand express mixed feelings about it. Latter-day versions of Diderot's distinction between public and private often seem to lie at the heart of their critiques of stardom; and men and women appear equally inclined to make that distinction.

Indeed, in general we as editors—all of us men, true enough—have found it difficult to generalize about actresses, or about actors, for that matter, on the basis of the accounts we have assembled. Actors of both sexes agree that casting and "character," as indicated in the pages of a screenplay, are crucial to them, and that character is almost always expressed in gender-specific ways. It may also be true that casting is so decisive in its effects on performers that its indications of gender render other matters of collaboration and characterization merely secondary for performers. But when it comes to cases, for every actress who discusses her sensitivity to her collaborators, at least one other displays steadfast independence. For every actress who feels objectified, at least one actor reports having felt the same way.

It will be interesting to see what, if anything, will change as the number of women grows in specialities other than acting within the world of filmmaking, as is already the case and will continue to be. Will actresses find themselves less objectified, or only *differently* objectified with change and over time? The same question applies to performers of color.

One way to escape objectification may be to follow the recommendation frequently articulated in *Playing to the Camera*—that actors produce and write screenplays, as well as direct, if they wish to exercise greater influence over their films. Broader and more diverse engagement in the work of production might furnish film actors with at least some recompense for the relentless objectification and commercialization they endure, and for their fans' volatile and sometimes destructive identification with them.

Mae Marsh, who acted in several of D. W. Griffith's films, considered the invention of "business" in film acting to be her most fundamental obligation. Her interest in "good business," as she puts it, underscores the conflation of art and commerce that has typified commercial filmmaking. In its most popular forms, film has not drawn on the religious and sacred origins of the stage but has instead often been conceived in and dedicated to the proposition that it should make money, and the more of it the better. Film acting, and to a still greater degree stardom in films, have been essential to this formula.

Some readers may find it strange, therefore, that film actors—and especially the stars—should feel tormented about how much they make. But the amount of money that most successful actors in film earn implicates them in the corporate mentality that has come to typify the entertainment industry in the United States and, increasingly, everywhere else. At the same time, these actors' agonizing over their complicity in a business that is so often crass and exploitative betokens the idealism that most here have brought to their work.

We hope that this book will thus hold some interest for working and aspiring film actors. Those who have dedicated themselves to performing in films, or who plan to, can draw their own conclusions about history, about techniques, and perhaps more important, about *values* from the judgments of these actors, who have assisted in the invention, promotion, and refinement of narrative film.

It has often been claimed or assumed, at least in academic circles, that any credit for the poststructuralist and postmodernist outlook should go directly to the theorists, or occasionally creative writers, who have given those movements shape in writing. *We* think that equal credit at least is due to film actors, who, in considering the disjointed qualities of filmmaking, have offered repeated testimonies to the mechanization, discontinuity, and lack of community now widely understood to plague modern life. Jack Nicholson recalls his dawning realization of the significance of film acting, which took place at the moment he "began to think that the finest modern writer was the screen actor." This remark signals the degree to which images, often speaking images, have come to challenge literature in the course of what has sometimes been called the Film Age.

Perhaps the Film Age has given way already to the Television Age, and more lately to the Video Age. In any case, actors on film, television, and video have embodied and in some ways helped usher in the postmodern moment. They have come to terms with shooting scenes out of narrative sequence, realized their roles in bits and pieces, reinvented themselves continually, and performed before machines that orient, frame, and finally absorb their efforts. Actors working in front of cameras have given the "post-" movements some substance by dealing in fragmented images of humanity. Over time, the very diversity of these images has posed a challenge to the notion that human behavior is cohesive, sustained, and "universal," which no longer seems credible or even desirable to many. In the pages that follow, it is striking how many actors refer to chance or accidents as propitious and even spiritually laden elements of their work.

When E. H. Sothern, as much a dyed-in-the-wool stage actor as any in the collection, called film a "new language," back while the First World War was still raging, he showed great prescience. The language that film actors have studied and in some measure coined over the last several generations has not always been euphonious, nor has its development been linear. Film portrayals have come to seem troubling, in part, through their enlargement on the longstanding affinity in the theater world for conflict, tension, and paradox. In many instances, a casual but persistent utopianism mingles in filmmaking with distinctly capitalist fervor, and ever more sophisticated technologies combine to enhance human agency. Most recently these technologies have permitted electronic, computerized, and digitized effects that at times threaten to supplant acting and writing in the forms in which we have come to know them.

Understanding of the history of film may contribute to an appreciation of actors' ability to help bring their audiences to terms with the present. Film actors can also afford us glimpses of the future—and a better future, we hope, not just a more superficial or corrupt one, as they have sometimes been accused of doing. When all is said and done, though, readers of this book may be still more interested in what film actors have *shown* us over the last hundred years than in what they have told us. It is our hope, finally, that *Playing to the Camera* will put images from the screen into a more complete and human context, even though they may appear no less enigmatic than ever.

Part I The Silent Performance

When viewers had their first exposure to film one hundred years ago, it is unlikely that they interpreted silence as loss. Then, motion pictures represented a striking novelty; the ability to convey photographic detail in motion produced images that on initial viewing must have seemed quite dramatic in themselves.

Oddly enough, filmmakers' earliest efforts to convey a story may have called attention to the unremitting silence of actors on the screen. Almost immediately, dramatic episodes adapted or drawn directly from the legitimate stage began to contend with more strictly documentary forms such as travelogues and newsreels. The simple sight of people's mouths moving—an alien one, given the stiffness of nineteenth-century photography—must have prompted audiences to wish for the same range of expression on the screen that they had grown accustomed to in live performances.

When stage actors first came to film, they moved and spoke as they had been used to doing before live audiences. In fact, when acting in screenplays adapted from the theatre, actors in silent films were sometimes called on to utter the very same lines of dialogue they had spoken on stage. Actors used speech in this way to protect themselves against the distractions endemic to filmmaking, even though they knew their words would not be heard from the screen. They were trying in part to maintain the energy necessary to command the stage and in part to bring the respectability of stage work to the rough-and-tumble of filmmaking.

It is not surprising, however, that many stage actors wondered whether film required techniques different from those they had refined before live audiences. Should they merely try to adapt stage methods to film, or did they need to take more drastic measures to meet the demands of the camera and those of the huge new audience that film had attracted? Actors posed such questions with increasing insistence over the generation spanned by this first part. In the opening piece by Charles Graham, the questions are still immediate; Mae Marsh, Lillian Gish, and Louise Brooks, by contrast, regard filmmaking as a given in their various accounts, written over nearly half a century. We have arranged the selections in rough chronological order, according to the dates when the films that the six actors we refer to were made, rather than the dates when their accounts were published. This ordering should help readers construct a time-lapse version of the debates that marked the earliest professional discussions of film acting.

15

The sometimes frivolous tone of commentaries in this part is attributable to the fundamental question actors posed during this period, especially early on: Was film even worth considering as an arena for serious acting? If esthetic concerns did not always settle this question, ever-larger salaries did as time went on. Taken in sequence, the accounts that follow show how lucrative film work quickly became. The First World War played an especially significant role in elevating Hollywood and its films over the films made by the ravaged, sobered, and in some ways culturally discredited European nations. Effects of this shift in culture, and in filmmaking, too, manifest themselves through the rest of this book.

Now to particular contributors. Charles Graham's piece was written more than a generation after his experiences before the camera, but his phrase *walking gent* evokes the nineteenth century, when that was the theatrical name for a male extra. Like many other Britons who entered film, especially in America, Graham regards it as only a pale imitation of the stage. Charles Chaplin shows film much greater respect, his British origins notwithstanding; and this is hardly surprising, given Chaplin's long perspective on film's development and his seasoning in British music halls and American vaudeville, less elitist forms than the legitimate stage. Chaplin is unusual among film actors in considering how the manner of his hiring influenced his first efforts before the camera. He also examines characterization in ways that seem quite contemporary; for example, he conceives of his famed tramp character in terms of visual and behavioral *contradictions* rather than consistencies.

E. H. Sothern enjoyed the major part of his stage success in America. Like Graham and Chaplin, however, he had a transatlantic career, his education and training having been completed in Great Britain. The recurrence in silent film of backgrounds such as Sothern's underscores the influence that British actors had on the American stage throughout the nineteenth century and have continued to exercise in the theatre as well as in Hollywood ever since.

Stage stars of comparable renown from the French company Film d'Art or its American counterpart, Famous Players, disdained to consider film at all and assumed that it was manifestly inferior to the stage. Sothern, however, showed himself willing to acknowledge new possibilities, in the belief that the sheer size of the film audience created a responsibility to use the form for educational purposes, in the service of humanity. This same conviction surfaces later among the Soviet actors whose accounts appear in this book.

Mae Marsh demonstrates an interest in acting that affiliates it more nearly with modeling than with characterization in the theatrical sense. Marsh's innocent good looks qualified her to play heroines in several of D. W. Griffith's films, and her story emphasizes the degree to which a debut role can determine an actor's future in films, and the often paramount importance of personal appearance in determining that future.

Griffith's authoritarian qualities were doubtless strengthened by his fondness for hiring, and then molding, actresses sometimes even younger and less experienced than Marsh. One of these was Lillian Gish, who began working with him while still a young girl and whose exposure to him influenced the rest of her career. In capturing Griffith's passion for demonstrating effects, Gish makes it clear in her narrative that he possessed a highly developed narrative sense, which he drilled into novices and seasoned professionals alike. By doing so, he helped her and others generate a full-bodied style, capable of expressing emotion without making it seem grotesque. This style, at its best, distinguishes acting in silent films from the acting in films with sound, which was typified by greater restraint.

Louise Brooks enjoyed a transatlantic career at the height of her fame, and unlike the other actors here, was "rediscovered" two generations after her most noted film appearances. As an older woman, long after the controversy surrounding her has died down, she speaks of the difficulty studios found in casting her, a concern expressed regularly by actors in the section on the golden age of the Hollywood studios. Brooks is particularly acute in identifying the degree to which directors and audiences together define sexuality on the screen. She is also surprisingly generous in crediting Josef von Sternberg, known generally as a tyrant and an autocrat, for his deftness in directing her and other actresses. Her tribute thus anticipates those of more recent actors who praise directors and technicians for the rigor and precision they bring to filmmaking—and for their technological expertise, as well.

Charles Graham Acting for the Films in 1912

Film Acting for the First Time

We joined a crowd of people amongst whom I recognised a couple of English actors; the rest were Americans. We had not said a word to a soul, and no one had questioned us, when a man in shirt sleeves and with a green shade over his eyes came into the room and scrutinised first one and then another. He picked out one or two and then came to Arundel and myself. "I can use you," said he, and handed each of us a card. My card bore a number and the mystic words "Walking Gent Card Scene." Arundel's card bore the same number and the same words. We learnt that the film would be known by this number till its name was revealed to a waiting public, that we were the "walking-gents" in a card playing scene which was to be shot that morning and that we were to take the card to the wardrobe room.

Here a man chewing a fat cigar took our cards, looked us over, and said, "Your clothes will do, but wear straw hats. What's your size?" A young and rather pessimistic fellow then took us off to the makeup room, where a stout gentleman of Italian extraction and redolent of garlic proceeded to make me up with black, white, grey and yellow till I looked like a black and white wash drawing on a cream tinted background. Panchromatic films were things of the future and healthy colours were taboo.

We were sent to studio number 6 where we were fated to come into a room which had three sides only and no ceiling, shake hands with no less a person than Clara Kimball Young, then fade away to a table at the side, sit down and play part of a hand of cards with two American women, one stout and fair, the other thin and dark.

Mr. Young, the beautiful Clara's husband, was the producer, and if he knew what he was producing I certainly did not. We came into that painted canvas room fifty times if we came into it once, we smiled the same smiles, we frowned the same frowns, we played the same cards and at last the big lights went on and we did it all again while the cameras shot the scene. "Come to-morrow at eleven," we were told, and we went back to the makeup room. Thus we earned our first money on the films, ten dollars apiece—not so bad for about three hours work.

Excerpt from Charles Graham, "Acting for the Films in 1912," *Sight and Sound* 4, no. 15 (Autumn 1935), 118–119. Reprinted by permission.

Next morning at eleven we presented ourselves again, but Young was not shooting. We were seen, however, by another producer. Again the same procedure, but this time I drew a dress suit, and Arundel an American navy seaman's uniform. The whole thing reminded me rather of a lucky dip. We spent three very pleasant weeks; we talked to beautiful ladies whom we had till then seen only on the screen; we were photographed going upstairs and going down, in the studio, in the country, in gardens, and on the deck and in the cabin of a fine ocean-going yacht on the Hudson.

And then Nemesis overtook me. The scene was a struggle for life in the engine room. True to the rehearsal I struggled last up the iron ladder, and just as I reached toward the top with the water nearly up to my neck the man above put his foot on my head and pushed me under the water. Whether he or I was the villain of the piece I did not know, and I have never found out. What the picture was, and whether it was ever released, I cannot say. That was the last of my experience of acting for the films in America.

Acting for the Films in England

. . .

The more I saw of these methods the more I was amazed that they could produce anything as coherent as were even those early films. The fact remains however that it was possible to produce thousands of films which were accepted by the public, and in which the majority of the cast probably knew as little as I did of the plot. The actor's part was thus reduced to the level of a puppet. But this cannot be true of a man like George Arliss, who exhibits logical growth of characterization in some, at all events, of the roles he plays; and that most thorough actor, Edmund Gwenn, lives in his part. The film gains every time when the art of the actor is recognised. I am sure that it is more like that now than in 1912, and I am sure too that it was like that in Charlie Chaplin's film *The Woman of Paris,* whose every part was a gem. It is good to think that acting as an art, and not as a system of mechanical registering of emotion to command, has come out of the slough in which it had at one time appeared to be its fate to be submerged.

Now, to what has that improvement been due? The years 1910–11 saw the birth of the star system and the beginning of the death of picture making on mass production lines. Stardom put the public in the "driver's seat," and from then on, the movie kings had to give what the public wanted. Stardom brought its evils, but on the whole it brought more benefits than drawbacks in its train. Mary Pickford was an actress and Charlie Chaplin a mummer born and bred. They knew what they were doing, and would not be suppressed. Soon the public were demanding something better than the mere appearance of a star, and so the level of film productions rose as the stars felt the urge of self-preservation.

Film versus Stage Acting

To me, the film never will replace the art of the stage.

The very insubstantiality of the figures on the screen has made for a wider, a more lasting and intimate appeal to the emotion of the audience than the art of the actor has achieved. Close ups of enormously magnified faces have permitted a change in mood to be grasped more clearly by the boy in the back of the cinema gallery than the actor can hope to achieve by his facial expression on the most impressionable young woman in the front row of the stalls in the theatre. It is not only because on the screen he can appear in fifty thousand cinemas at a time that Ronald Colman has his thousand devotees where Lewis Waller had one. It is because Ronald Colman's every eyelash can be seen, a full foot or more in length upon the screen, that his audience knows him as Waller's never knew their idol. They are so much larger than life these heroes of the screen they cannot fail to impress themselves on lesser mortals, and yet though it be held as heresy, I still would have you believe that it is more satisfying to the actor's soul to be the substance than the shadow.

In acting on the stage it is not the actor alone who has a part to play. The audience have theirs, and one thing the shadow people of the screen can never know is the joy that comes from feeling the audience begin to play their part and—catching fire in turn from them—to give just that little bit better show that night than before.

Charles Chaplin My Autobiography

Mr. Charles Kessel, one of the owners of the Keystone Company, said that Mr. Mack Sennett had seen me playing the drunk in the American Music Hall on Forty-second Street and if I were the same man he would like to engage me to take the place of Mr. Ford Sterling. I had often played with the idea of working in films, and had even offered to go into partnership with Reeves, our manager, to buy the rights of all Karno's sketches and make movies of them. But Reeves had been skeptical, and sensibly so, because we knew nothing about making them.

Had I seen a Keystone Comedy? asked Mr. Kessel. Of course, I had seen several, but I did not tell him that I thought they were a crude mélange of rough-and-tumble. . . .

When we played the Empress in Los Angeles, we were a howling success, thank God. It was a comedy called *A Night at the Club*. I played a decrepit old drunk and looked at least fifty years old. Mr. Sennett came round after the performance and congratulated me. In that short interview, I was aware of a heavy-set man with a beetling brow, a heavy, coarse mouth and a strong jaw, all of which impressed me. But I wondered how sympathetic he would be in our future relationship. All through that interview I was extremely nervous and was not sure whether he was pleased with me or not.

He asked casually when I would join them. I told him that I could start the first week in September, which would be the termination of my contract with the Karno Company. . . .

Eager and anxious, I arrived in Los Angeles and took a room at a small hotel, the Great Northern. The first evening, I took a busman's holiday and saw the second show at the Empress, where the Karno Company had worked. The attendant recognized me and came a few moments later to tell me that Mr. Sennett and Miss Mabel Normand were sitting two rows back and had asked if I would join them. I was thrilled, and after a hurried, whispered introduction we all watched the show together. When it was over, we walked a few paces down Main Street, and went to a rathskeller for a light supper and a drink. Mr. Sennett was shocked to see how young I looked. "I thought you were a much older man," he said. I could detect a tinge of concern, which made me

Excerpt from Charles Chaplin, *My Autobiography* (New York: Simon and Schuster, 1964), 141–142, 144–153, 258–260. Reprinted by permission.

Charles Chaplin (center) in *Kid Auto Races at Venice* (1914)

anxious, remembering that all Sennett's comedians were oldish-looking men. Fred Mace was over fifty and Ford Sterling in his forties. "I can make up as old as you like," I answered. Mabel Normand, however, was more reassuring. Whatever her reservations were about me, she did not reveal them. Mr. Sennett said that I would not start immediately, but should come to the studio in Edendale and get acquainted with the people. When we left the café, we bundled into Mr. Sennett's glamorous racing car and I was driven to my hotel. . . .

On another set was the great Ford Sterling, whom I was to replace. Mr. Sennett introduced me to him. Ford was leaving Keystone to form his own company with Universal. He was immensely popular with the public and with everyone in the studio. They surrounded his set and were laughing eagerly at him.

Sennett took me aside and explained their method of working. "We have no scenario—we get an idea, then follow the natural sequence of events until it leads up to a chase, which is the essence of our comedy."

This method was edifying but personally I hated chase. It dissipates one's personality; little as I knew about movies, I knew that nothing transcended personality.

That day I went from set to set watching the companies at work. They all seemed to be imitating Ford Sterling. This worried me, because his style did not suit me. He played a harassed Dutchman, ad-libbing through the scene with a Dutch accent, which was funny but was lost in silent pictures. I wondered what Sennett expected of me. He had seen my work and must have known that I was not suitable to play Ford's type of comedy; my style was just the opposite. Yet every story and situation conceived in the studio was consciously or unconsciously made for Sterling; even Roscoe Arbuckle was imitating Sterling. . . .

At last the moment came. Sennett was away on location with Mabel Normand as well as the Ford Sterling Company, so there was hardly anyone left in the studio. Mr. Henry Lehrman, Keystone's top director after Sennett, was to start a new picture and wanted me to play a newspaper reporter. Lehrman was a vain man and very conscious of the fact that he had made some successful comedies of a mechanical nature; he used to say that he didn't need personalities, that he got all his laughs from mechanical effects and film cutting.

We had no story. It was to be a documentary about the printing press done with a few comedy touches. I wore a light frock coat, a top hat and a handlebar mustache. When we started I could see that Lehrman was groping for ideas. And of course, being a newcomer at Keystone, I was anxious to make suggestions. This was where I created antagonism with Lehrman. In a scene in which I had an interview with an editor of a newspaper I crammed in every conceivable gag I could think of, even to suggesting business for others in the cast. Although the picture was completed in three days, I thought we contrived some very funny gags. But when I saw the finished film it broke my heart, for the cutter had butchered it beyond recognition, cutting into the middle of all my funny business. I was bewildered, and wondered why they had done this. Henry Lehrman confessed years later that he had deliberately done it, because, as he put it, he thought I knew too much.

The day after I finished with Lehrman, Sennett returned from location. Ford Sterling was on one set, Arbuckle on another; the whole stage was crowded with three companies at work. I was in my street clothes and had nothing to do, so I stood where Sennett could see me. He was standing with Mabel, looking into a hotel lobby set, biting the end of a cigar. "We need some gags here," he said, then turned to me. "Put on a comedy make-up. Anything will do."

I had no idea what make-up to put on. I did not like my getup as the press reporter. However, on the way to the wardrobe I thought I would dress in baggy pants, big shoes, a cane and a derby hat. I wanted everything a contradiction: the pants baggy, the coat tight, the hat small and the shoes large. I was undecided whether to look old or young, but remembering Sennett had expected me to be a much older man, I added a small mustache, which, I reasoned, would add age without hiding my expression.

I had no idea of the character. But the moment I was dressed, the clothes and the make-up made me feel the person he was. I began to know him, and by the time I walked onto the stage he was fully born. When I confronted Sennett I assumed the character and strutted about, swinging my cane and parading before him. Gags and comedy ideas went racing through my mind.

The secret of Mack Sennett's success was his enthusiasm. He was a great audience and laughed genuinely at what he thought funny. He stood and giggled until his body began to shake. This encouraged me and I began to explain the character: "You know this fellow is many-sided, a tramp, a gentleman, a poet, a dreamer, a lonely fellow, always hopeful of romance and adventure. He would have you believe he is a scientist, a musician, a duke, a polo player. However, he is not above picking up cigarette butts or robbing a baby of its candy. And, of course, if the occasion warrants it, he will kick a lady in the rear—but only in extreme anger!"

I carried on this way for ten minutes or more, keeping Sennett in continuous chuckles. "All right," said he, "get on the set and see what you can do there." As with the Lehrman film, I knew little of what the story was about, other than that Mabel Normand gets involved with her husband and a lover.

In all comedy business an attitude is most important, but it is not always easy to find an attitude. However, in the hotel lobby I felt I was an impostor posing as one of the guests, but in reality I was a tramp just wanting a little shelter. I entered and stumbled over the foot of a lady. I turned and raised my hat apologetically, then turned and stumbled over a cuspidor, then turned and raised my hat to the cuspidor. Behind the camera they began to laugh.

Quite a crowd had gathered there, not only the players of the other companies who left their sets to watch us, but also the stagehands, the carpenters and the wardrobe department. That indeed was a compliment. And by the time we had finished rehearsing we had quite a large audience laughing. Very soon I saw Ford Sterling peering over the shoulders of the others. When it was over I knew I had made good. . . .

Under Sennett's direction I felt comfortable, because everything was spontaneously worked out on the set. As no one was positive or sure of himself (not even the director), I concluded that I knew as much as the other fellow. This gave me confidence; I began to offer suggestions which Sennett readily accepted. Thus grew a belief in myself that I was creative and could write my own stories. Sennett indeed had inspired this belief. But although I had pleased Sennett I had yet to please the public.

In the next picture I was assigned to Lehrman again. He was leaving Sennett to join Sterling and to oblige Sennett was staying on two weeks longer than his contract called for. I still had abundant suggestions when I started working with him. He would listen and smile but would not accept any of them. "That may be funny in the theatre," he would say, "but in pictures we have no time for it. We must be on the go—comedy is an excuse for a chase."

I did not agree with this generality. "Humor is humor," I argued, "whether in films or on the stage." But he insisted on the same rigmarole, doing what Keystone had always done. All action had to be fast—which meant running and climbing on top of the roofs of houses and streetcars, jumping into rivers and diving off piers. In spite of his comedy theories I happened to get in one or two bits of individual funny business, but, as before, he managed to have them mutilated in the cutting room. . . .

Someone said that the art of acting is relaxing. Of course this basic principle can be applied to all the arts, but an actor especially must have restraint and an inner containment. No matter how frenzied the scene, the technician within the actor should be calm and relaxed, editing and guiding the rise and fall of his emotions—the outer man excited and the inner controlled. Only through relaxation can an actor achieve this. How does one relax? That is difficult. My own method is rather personal: before going on the stage, I am always extremely nervous and excited, and in this state I get so exhausted that by the time I make my entrance I am relaxed.

I do not believe acting can be taught. I have seen intelligent people fail at it and dullards act quite well. But acting essentially requires feeling. Wainwright, an authority on aesthetics, a friend of Charles Lamb and the literary lights of his time, was a ruthless, cold-blooded murderer who poisoned his cousin for mercenary reasons. Here is an example of an intelligent man who could never have been a good actor because he had little feeling.

All intellect and no feeling can be characteristic of the archcriminal, and all feeling and no intellect exemplify the harmless idiot. But when intellect and feeling are perfectly balanced, then we get the superlative actor.

The basic essential of a great actor is that he loves himself in acting. I do not mean it in a derogatory sense. Often I have heard an actor say, " How I'd love to play that part," meaning he would love himself in the part. This may be egocentric; but the great actor is mainly preoccupied with his own virtuosity: Irving in *The Bells*, Tree as Svengali, Martin Harvey in *A Cigarette Maker's Romance*, all three very ordinary plays, but very good parts. Just a fervent love of the theatre is not sufficient; there must also be a fervent love of and belief in oneself.

The Method school of acting I know little about. I understand it concentrates on development of personality—which could very well be less developed in some actors. After all, acting is pretending to be other people. Personality is an indefinable thing that shines through a performance in any case. But there is something to all methods. Stanislavsky, for example, strove for "inner truth," which, I understand, means "being it" instead of "acting it." This requires empathy, a feeling into things: one should be able to feel what it is like to be a lion or an eagle, also to feel a character's soul instinctively, to know under all circumstances what his reactions will be. This part of acting cannot be taught.

In instructing a true actor or actress about a character, a word or a phrase will often suffice: "This is Falstaffian," or "This is a modern Madame Bovary." Jed Harris is reported to have told an actress: "This character has the mobility of a weaving black tulip." This goes too far.

The theory that one must know a character's life story is unnecessary. No one could write into a play or a part those remarkable nuances that Duse conveyed to an audience. They must have been dimensions beyond the concept of the author. And Duse, I understand, was not an intellectual.

I abhor dramatic schools that indulge in reflections and introspections to evoke the right emotion. The mere fact that a student must be mentally operated upon is sufficient proof that he should give up acting.

As for that much-touted metaphysical word "truth," there are different forms of it and one truth is as good as another. The classical acting at the Comédie Française is as believable as the so-called realistic acting in an Ibsen play; both are in the realm of artificiality and designed to give the illusion of truth—after all, in all truth there is the seed of falsehood.

I have never studied acting, but as a boy I was fortunate in living in an era of great actors, and I acquired an extension of their knowledge and experience. Although I was gifted, I was surprised at rehearsals to find how much I had to learn about technique. Even the beginner with talent must be taught technique, for no matter how great his gifts, he must have the skill to make them effective.

I have found that orientation is the most important means of achieving this; that is, knowing where you are and what you're doing every moment you're on the stage. Walking into a scene one must have the authority of knowing where to stop; when to turn; where to stand; when and where to sit; whether to talk directly to a character or indirectly. Orientation gives authority and distinguishes the professional from the amateur. I have always insisted on this method of orientation with the cast when I'm directing my films.

E. H. Sothern The "New Art"

I have discovered a "new art" in posing for the moving pictures, an art that I can perhaps best describe as the concentrated essence of expressiveness. When I first decided to "act" in the various pictures for the Vitagraph Company, people said to me, "Oh, but it will be easy for you because you are an actor of experience and have the nuances of your profession." And this seemed very reasonable; but I found when I began posing that "acting for the movies" was a very different thing indeed from acting for a living audience, and that my work in the past, all the experience that I had acquired in years on the stage, the gesture, the voice, the expression, not only did not avail me, but rather stood in the way of the work I had prepared to do in my real farewell to the American public, for that is what I consider this work with the moving pictures. I am actually saying good-bye to all my friends all over the country simultaneously, and this is an inspiration to me in my acting, because I feel that I am acting before the largest audience I have ever known—for three million people is really a very large audience! . . .

. . . There is no limit whatever to the opportunity for the instruction of children through moving pictures. This, it seems to me, is the great power that the film will have in the future. I can see the opportunity of education through the film extending out in so many channels that it is absolutely limitless. Just as today so many people are getting their musical education through the machine, so I believe millions of people in the future will receive their education by pictures. There is the problem of whether or no education that comes so easily will not possibly deaden the capacity for creative thought. I doubt if this problem can be settled except after testing out the matter

Excerpt from E. H. Sothern, "The 'New Art' as Discovered by E. H. Sothern," *The Craftsman* 30 (September 1916), 572–579, 642–643.

through an entire generation of educational effort. While it really requires more mental effort to respond to the written word than to the picture, it is a well known fact that the pictures make a more indelible impression upon the memory, and this is an immense advantage for children in public schools, in any method of education that has a limited time and a varied curriculum, with children who have but a few years of educational opportunity. . . .

One of the strangest experiences in this posing for the "movies" is the absence of the audience. It is like acting in a continual rehearsal until you realize suddenly that you must become accustomed to doing without that wonderful stimulus which the audience offers to every actor who moves it. I am sure all actors like myself on the legitimate stage rely equally for producing emotional effects upon good scenery, the use of the voice and the response of the audience. Also on the legitimate stage we have an opportunity of testing effects again and again. We have an entire stage at our disposal, and if a "picture" is not satisfactory at one angle we may test it out at another; I am sure too that every actor relies upon certain modulation of the voice to infuse emotion not only in the audience, but into his acting. We do our acting before the moving camera absolutely denuded of such help as this, with even our gestures limited, with our space for moving about cut to the narrowest allowance. If we attempt to express some sudden violent emotion with a wide gesture we are told quickly that we are out of the picture, if we stride across the stage to express irritation, annoyance, we are out of the picture, if we glance away from the people with whom we are acting our glance is out of the picture. In fact, the first thing to learn in acting in the "movies" is to keep in the picture. Everything is limited for the actor except his facial expression, and that must be exaggerated beyond anything he has ever permitted himself on the legitimate stage. Frequently, every variety of emotion—anger, rage, pride, joy, sorrow—must be given out through the reel to the canvas and then to an audience solely by the varying expression of the eyes and the mouth. That is why I feel, as I said at the beginning of this article, that I had discovered a new art which was the essence of concentrated expression.

Another thing you find very quickly is that you have no opportunity of working up to your scene. In the play written for the legitimate stage usually an actor works up through his first and second act to the final culmination of emotional expression in the third. I shall always remember my bewilderment when I discovered one day that I was being called upon to pose my third act first of all because that scenery was ready and the lights were placed so that that particular part of the room could be best photographed. And it may be that in one moving play an actor will be photographed in various parts of a building or various parts of a town or various parts of a country, according as the director desires to make a particular play intensely and vividly realistic, so that there is no opportunity for putting yourself in a psychological state and living your part from hour to hour, of becoming the actual man you portray.

In the moving picture art you are never your hero for one moment, you are always yourself intensely interested in showing through your expression the kind of a man the hero was, for you see you are never with your audience. You are working for the screen, not for the people, and you are doing what the screen demands. That is why every expression must be intensified in moving pictures, because through the expression alone, most rapidly presented, will the people who have nothing to do with your personality, your voice, your gesture, receive an impression of the picture you are trying to convey. In the legitimate theater an actor sees a play as a whole. He is deeply affected, for instance, by the entire life and psychological development of Hamlet, his heart beats with Hamlet's sorrow, his pulse quickens with Hamlet's joy. If you were to put *Hamlet* on the screen none of these things would happen; you would tell the people by your expression only how Hamlet looked when he felt these emotions. In other words the moving picture portrays the emotion the character feels without the actor's feeling it at all.

On the stage a man is within the bonds of nature, he is persuading his audience as to the reality of his presentation. For instance, both Bernhardt and Booth would induce certain moods by the words uttered, by the voice in which they were uttered, by the surroundings of the stage. In the moving picture all these opportunities are wiped out. You stand in the corner of an immense room where three or four other plays are going on; you inhabit only a narrow strip of a corner where your own play is going on. Probably you have only the illusion of scenery on two sides of you. At first you even hear the stage directions given to the other actors and lights are going up and down all about you and people are passing everywhere. Occasionally to your astonishment, at least during rehearsal, they walk through your "set," and by chance the new hand may delay in the "set" when the reel starts so that you can no more count upon any outside illusion to help you with the development of your creation than you could if you were walking down Broadway. Your entire picture must come mechanically from your brain, you cannot acquire any inspiration, any stimulus. Either you have the face to express what you mentally recall of the plot, or you have not. In other words, either you are a good moving picture actor or you are not. A moving picture actor never tries to feel any emotion, only to help the audience to feel it.

It seems to me that really the successful moving picture actor is a man who can rise superior to his environment, who can become most completely absorbed in an idea. It is really a triumph of mind over matter, a reversal of all the methods employed for the most complete realization of dramatic achievement on the legitimate stage. While if you let yourself become conscious of the people, sounds, light or shadow about you it will be impossible to present anything through the moving picture camera except surprise, horror, disappointment and despair. It is the art of concentration, of self absorption developed to the highest degree.

Also one learns many lessons in discipline. All actors apparently are school-children under the "movie" school-master, called the director. No inspiration, no emotion, no relief, no desire to express beauty or grace counts at all against the order of the director "to keep in the picture, move this way, look in this direction, keep your hand down, stay in line." He is the man who knows the mechanics of the situation and the mechanics control everything in moving picture plays. You may express the most abounding beauty, the profoundest emotion, the richest gesture, but if the camera is not making a note of it you have not accomplished the task the director has set for you. Also he knows the expression that will carry on the canvas, he knows the look that the audience will answer; in other words, he knows the machine and the audience and he knows how to make the actor a satisfactory connecting link.

I have been told that already Mr. Edison or some other wizard of the moving picture world is devising a machine that will take down the actor's words as the reel takes his expression and that both will be reproduced simultaneously in the future moving-picture play. I am not sure whether this will render the actor's work simpler or more complex, whether the fact that his voice is to be reproduced will add to the mechanical difficulties or whether it will give him greater inspiration for his expressions. I question if any actor could tell until he had accomplished the feat and had heard himself talking to himself some yards away on the stage.

I have also been told though not in connection, naturally, with the moving pictures that wonderful instruments are being devised whereby records may be kept of all one's daily existence, every word, thought and gesture, so that in days or years to come one may have the horrible experience of seeing exactly how one appeared to the world in all one's daily relationships. The possibility seems too terrible to contemplate. As life is today we are mercifully permitted to let certain deeds and words grow hazy in our own memory. It seems to me that such an instrument as this would be a complete realization of the old story of Nemesis, more terrible than the power of any retributive Greek god. But these wonderful instruments are happily but visions of the future. . . .

So many people have asked me why, in "playing" for the "movies" I have not put on Shakespeare. The reason seems to me interesting enough to mention in this article. Unless a play can be copyrighted by the moving picture firm that is to produce it, it is no sooner presented to the public successfully than immediately a dozen people may produce it in their own way or in imitation of the original production, without hindrance, and this means, of course, a great loss to the original producer and as it is a little too late to copyright Shakespeare it would mean too great a financial risk for any film company to produce his plays with any degree of beauty and success. And so my work in the "movies" must be in such plays as may be presented exclusively by one firm. This is a matter of regret both to the firm and to myself as I would like nothing better than to speak to the vast film audience through those plays which have become most endeared to me in my work as an actor. On the other hand, I have had the fresh experience of working along new lines, developing new ideas and speaking this new language.

Mae Marsh Screen Acting

In any art or profession the ability to seize opportunity when it presents itself is important. This is especially true in motion pictures. Things move very fast there. It is like a game where the knack of doing the right thing at the right time determines one's value.

After the beginner has done his extra work, or small bits, if he is of the right stuff, he will some day be given a part. He may be unaware of it, but that will be the biggest moment of his screen career.

When doing extra work or small bits the critics, the public, and the profession have paid little attention to the beginner. But once the beginner secures a part he comes instantly into the eye of everyone interested in the screen. We are all diverted by new faces.

Thus the impression that the beginner will make in his first part is one that will for a long time endure. It comes very near making or breaking him. This may seem hard. Often it is unjust—a beginner may have a part forced upon him for which he is unfitted. But it is true. And we have to deal with conditions on the screen as we find them.

For that reason when the big moment comes, and the part is secured, the

Excerpt from Mae Marsh, *Screen Acting* (Los Angeles: Photo-Star Publishing, 1921), 51–87.

Mae Marsh in *The Birth of a Nation* (1915)

beginner must do everything within his or her power to be as well prepared as possible.

There are in this respect three important mechanical details that must be looked after. I should list them as follows:

1. Studying the story
2. Studying make-up
3. Studying costuming

The beginner will be given the story—or script—typewritten in continuity form. Continuity means the scene by scene action through which the story is told. Ordinarily there will be some three hundred scenes or "shots" to the average photoplay.

The beginner will first look to the plot and theme of the story. We want to know what the author is telling and how he is trying to tell it. We find the big situations and the action that precedes them. More important, we locate the why of it.

When I have established the idea of the play I immediately go over the script again with an eye alert for business. By business I mean the tricks, mannerisms, and the apparent unexpected or involuntary moves that help to sustain action.

The value of good business cannot be overrated. It goes a long way toward making up for the lack of voice. Without clever business any photoplay would drag. The two-reel comedy, which I have observed is popular with audiences of all ages, is usually but a sequence of business.

If the business that is planned upon seems natural to the character—the wiggling of a foot when excited, the inability to control the hands, the apparent unconscious raising of an eyebrow, etc.—I am sure there can be no real objection to it. The audience, who are the final critics, love it. . . .

Now while the audience may believe that these things are done on the spur of the moment the facts are very contrary. These bits of business must be planned in advance and it is only an evidence that they have been well planned when they appear to be done unconsciously.

While it is true that we have all discovered very telling bits of business during the actual photographing of a scene, we can count this as nothing but good fortune. To leave the matter of business until the director called "Camera!" would be fatal.

Thus in going over a script I look for business. I think of all the business I can, knowing that much of it will prove impracticable and will have to be discarded. Nor is that all. When the scenic sets upon which we are to work are erected at the studio or on location, I look them over very carefully in the hope that some article of furniture, etc., will suggest some attractive piece of business. An odd fan, a pillow, a door, in fact, anything may prove valuable.

I should suggest to my candidate that he or she be just as alert for good business as the star is. The good director is always open to suggestion. Business may make all the difference between a colorless and a vivid portrayal of a part. Thus for the beginner who, in obtaining a part, has reached the most vital moment of his career, the value of keeping an eye open to the possibilities of business is apparent.

Make-up, like much of everything else on the screen, is a personal matter. There are, however, some general rules that can be followed to advantage.

I should instruct my candidate not to make up too much. It seems to me that I have observed a tendency in this direction recently. . . .

Blonds, in motion pictures, are traditionally fluffy-haired. There is a very good reason for this, by the way. Some years ago Mr. Griffith—who usually does everything first—discovered that by leveling a back spotlight on Blanche Sweet's fluffy, blond hair it gave the appearance of sunlight showing through.

On the screen it was beautiful. Since that time the "back spot" has been worked to death. In spite of the fact that it is an old trick it is one that is still very much respected by the actress—or us blond actresses, as it were. . . .

As in the case of the ill-shaped nose there are stars who have succeeded in spite of an absence, or too great presence, of chin. They have learned the photographic angles at which they appear to the best advantage. In one way or another, when working close to the camera, they keep always within these angles. Thus they prove that there can be an exception to any rule.

If in the matter of make-up I can convince my candidate that he or she will be better off by using as little as possible of it, I shall be willing to pass on to the next topic. . . .

Whatever may be the case in everyday life clothes do make the man, or the woman, in motion pictures. They establish character even more swiftly than action or expression. No where so much as in motion pictures does the general public accept people at their clothes value. There are the over-dress of vulgarity, the shoddiness of poverty, the conservatism of decency and so on, each of them speaking as plainly as words of the person so attired.

Now if mere over-dress, shoddiness, conservatism, and so on, were all that were necessary the process would be quite simple. But the art of costuming is more subtle than that.

In each costume there must be something original and personal. In other words, something that is peculiarly suited to the precise character that is being portrayed. There must be also a color contrast or harmony that will be favorable to good motion picture photography.

In addition, the costume in a broader sense should harmonize with the scenic setting. The costume, more than anything else, will establish the fiction of age. To appear very young or middle-aged is to dress young or middle-aged.

In addition to its value in suggesting character the costume has attained a new importance in that the screen has become a sort of fashion magazine. The thousands of young ladies who live outside of New York, London or Paris have come to look more and more to the screen for the latest fashions, and are accordingly influenced. . . .

The beginner who learns the knack of dressing for the screen in a manner that is sharply expressive of the character being played, and, in a way to bring out what the actress herself has come to regard as her strong point, will find her pains rewarded. . . .

The matter of costumes, then, is one of the important things that the beginner must consider. On the screen clothes may be said to talk; even to act. The male artists, I am sure, also realize this. But the actress, particularly, must always dress in a manner to get the maximum of benefit from her clothes whether they be cheap or expensive.

In *The Birth of a Nation* during the famous cliff scene I experimented with a half dozen dresses until I hit upon one whose plainness was a guarantee that it would not divert from my expression in that which was a very vital moment.

The several qualities most likely to succeed upon the screen having been discussed, and the importance of knowing the story, make-up and costuming having been established, my candidate is now ready to go before the camera.

All that has been done before is but to build up to this vital moment. The camera tells at once and usually in no uncertain terms whether one is possessed of star possibilities.

It is a sort of court from which there is no appeal. For that reason every expression, every movement, every feeling and, I verily believe, every thought are important once the camera has begun to turn.

Now the actress or actor is standing entirely upon her or his own feet. Previously they have had the benefit of all the advice and help that the many departments of a studio could proffer. In a word they have been able to lean upon someone else and to correct mistakes at leisure.

It is different before the camera. The beginner will at once feel very much alone and terribly conspicuous. This tends toward self-consciousness, or camera-consciousness, which must be immediately overcome or success is impossible. Camera-consciousness is the bane of the beginner. I think most of us have suffered more or less from it. I have known actresses who possessed it to such a degree that, finding they could not rid themselves of it, they left the screen. By extreme good fortune this never happened to be one of my troubles.

Self-consciousness on the screen is much the same thing as stage fright in the spoken drama and proceeds, I suppose, from the same source, which is the inability to forget one's self.

When a dear friend of mine first began playing small parts she found that she suffered from it. She also saw that it would certainly be fatal if she didn't cure it.

"For that reason," she said to herself, "the best thing to do is to think so hard about the part that I am playing that I won't have time to think of anything else."

She gave herself good advice. Anyhow it worked and I am sure it will be successful in the case of the average beginner. If so, then camera-consciousness will really be a blessing in disguise, for it will have taught the actress concentration upon her part and concentration, in every fiber of one's being, I believe, is the big secret of screen success.

I remember the case of one young actress who came to me in tears saying that when she rehearsed her part in the privacy of her own home, or dressing room, she felt every inch of it, but once under the gaze of the director, the assistant director, the cameraman, possibly the author and perhaps a number of privileged persons about the studio, she seemed to wilt.

"Look at it this way," I advised. "When you are acting the director has his work to do and is doing it. So has the assistant director. Likewise the cameraman and the assistant cameraman have their work to do and are doing it. So are the other actors. As for the lookers-on, request that they leave. Then imagine you are in a big schoolroom where everyone is busy at his or her lessons. You have your lesson to get which is concentrating upon your part. Go ahead with it."

It helped the girl in question. She has become a very excellent and charming star and while she still prefers to work upon a secluded stage she does not find it positively necessary, as do some actresses. In any event there is no trace of camera-consciousness in her acting.

Camera-consciousness having been eliminated the beginner can now throw himself or herself entirely into the part being played. By throwing one's self into the part I do not mean forcing it. Nothing is quite so bad as that. I mean feeling it. If you do not feel the particular action being played then the result will certainly be a lack of sincerity. We have already decided that that is fatal.

Let me illustrate:

While we were playing *Intolerance,* one cycle of which is still being released as *The Mother and the Law,* I had to do a scene where, in the big city's slums, my father dies.

The night before I did this scene I went to the theater—something, by the way, I seldom do when working—to see Marjorie Rambeau in *Kindling.*

To my surprise and gratification she had to do a scene in this play that was somewhat similar to the one that I was scheduled to play in *Intolerance.* It made a deep impression upon me.

As a consequence, the next day before the camera in the scene depicting my sorrow and misery at the death of my father, I began to cry with the memory of Marjorie Rambeau's part uppermost in my mind. I thought, however, that it had been done quite well and was anxious to see it on the screen.

I was in for very much of a surprise. A few of us gathered in the projection room and the camera began humming. I saw myself enter with a fair semblance of misery. But there was something about it that was not convincing.

Mr. Griffith, who was closely studying the action, finally turned in his seat and said:

"I don't know what you were thinking about when you did that, but it is evident that it was not about the death of your father."

"That is true," I said. I did not admit what I was thinking about.

We began immediately upon the scene again. This time I thought of the death of my own father and the big tragedy to our little home, then in Texas. I could recall the deep sorrow of my mother, my sisters, my brother and myself.

This scene is said to be one of the most effective in *The Mother and the Law.*

The beginner may learn from that that it never pays to imitate anyone else's interpretation of any emotion. Each of us when we are pleased, injured, or affected in any way have our own way of showing our feelings. This is one thing that is our very own.

When before the camera, therefore, we must remember that when we feel great sorrow the audience wants to see our own sorrow and not an imitation of Miss Blanche Sweet's or Mme. Nazimova's. We must feel our own part and take heed of my favorite screen maxim, which is that thoughts do register.

It is true that we have good and bad days before the camera. There are times when to feel and to act are the easiest things imaginable and other occasions when it seems impossible to catch the spirit that we know is necessary. In this we are more fortunate than our brothers upon the spoken stage, for we can do it over again.

It is also very often true that even when we are entirely in the spirit of our part, and believe we have done a good day's work, that there will be some mechanical defect in the scenes taken which makes it necessary to do them over, possibly when we feel least like so doing.

In this event it is a good thing to remember that it doesn't pay to cry over spilt milk. We must learn to take the bitter with the sweet. Fortunately the mechanics of picture taking are constantly improving.

The hardest dramatic work I ever did was in the courtroom scenes in *Intolerance.* We retook these scenes on four different occasions. Each time I gave to the limit of my vitality and ability. I put everything into my portrayal that was in me. It certainly paid. Parts of each of the four takes—some of them done at two weeks' intervals—were assembled to make up those scenes which you, as the audience, finally beheld upon the screen.

Therefore, when first going before a camera it is well to resolve to put as much into one's performance as possible. We cannot too greatly concentrate upon our parts. If we do not feel them we can be very sure they will not convince our audiences.

Good screen acting consists of the ability to accurately portray a state of mind.

That sounds simple, yet how often upon the screen have you seen an important part played in a manner that made you, yourself, feel that you were passing through the experiences being unfolded in the plot. I imagine not often.

If a part is under-played or, worse, over-played—for there is nothing so depressing as a screen actress run amuck in a flood of sundry emotions—it exerts a definite influence upon you, the audience.

You begin to lose sympathy with the character itself. You are interested or irritated by the mannerisms—often hardly less than gymnastics—of the actor or actress. You never identify such an actor or actress with the part they are playing for the very good reason that they are not playing the part. They are playing their idea of acting *at* a part.

In any event your interest in the story crumbles. What the author intended as a subtle character development flattens out. An ingenious plot is ruined by its treatment. You index that particular evening as among those wasted. I know. I have done the same.

For those who would like to take up the screen as a career, however, such an evening may prove very profitable. For it is the learning what not to do that is important. There never was a character portrayal done upon the screen that could not have been spoiled without this knowledge. . . .

Whenever I study a scenario or story it is with an eye for the contrast of moods and the situations that call for emotional emphasis. I plan in advance of the actual camera work the pace at which I will play various stages in the development of the story. By shutting my eyes I can almost *see* how the part will look upon the screen. If there is a sufficient contrast of moods and opportunity for emphasis I feel that I shall, at least, be able to do all within my power to make the story a success.

The physical strain before a camera is a peculiar thing. At no time is the motion picture actress or actor called upon for a sustained performance such as is true on the spoken stage. For that reason we should theoretically be in condition to put forth our very best efforts on each of the short scenes or "shots"—averaging not over two minutes in photographing—that we are called upon to do. The ordinary director is well satisfied if he averages twenty "shots" a day during production.

But here, I should say, appearances are deceiving. Genius has been de-scribed as the ability to resume a mood. In the case of motion pictures it is necessary that a mood be resumed not once or twice, but possibly twenty times during a day.

This is no less important than it is at first difficult. There may be an hour or two hours' interval between scenes—often longer than that—and picking up the thread of the story where it was dropped, the actress must resume the mood of her characterization.

I can suggest no better aid to this undertaking than retiring to one's dressing room and remaining quiet. Absolute quiet is an excellent thing for the actress during the working day. It gives her a rest from the turmoil of the studio set. It provides her a chance to do a little mental bookkeeping on the part she is playing. I have found it a great help.

This ability to resume a mood, however, soon becomes something that is subconsciously accomplished and for that reason need not be too much worried over by the beginner.

Lillian Gish The Movies, Mr. Griffith, and Me

Before a movie was filmed a player would often get a chance to rehearse each part in the film under [D. W. Griffith's] supervision. As casting was not decided on until shortly before filming, we were obliged to be familiar with all the roles we had rehearsed. This system taught us range and flexibility. . . .

Once the parts were awarded, the real work would begin. At the initial rehearsal Mr. Griffith would sit on a wooden kitchen chair, the actors fanning out in front of him, and, as he called out the plot, they would react, supplying in their own words whatever was appropriate for the scene.

As rehearsals continued, Mr. Griffith would move around us like a referee in the ring, circling, bending, walking up to an actor, staring over his great beak of a nose, then turning away. By the time that we had run through the story several times, he had viewed the action from every conceivable camera angle. Then he would begin to concentrate on characterization. Often we would run through a scene dozens of times before he achieved the desired effect. If we still failed, he would act out the scene himself with exaggerated gestures that he would later moderate in us. . . .

In rehearsals we were expected to visualize the props—furniture where none stood, windows in blank walls, doors where there was only space. Our physical movements became automatic and our emotions completely involved.

Most rehearsals were open—that is, the whole staff, actors, workmen, and the men from the laboratory were free to come and watch. Often there would be visitors on the set. Mr. Griffith loved the presence of an audience while his company rehearsed—and rehearsed so effectively that at the end of the scene,

Excerpt from Lillian Gish, *The Movies, Mr. Griffith, and Me* (Englewood Cliffs, N.J.: Prentice-Hall, 1969), 84–86, 96–102, 279. Copyright © 1969 Lillian Gish and Ann Pinchot.

Lillian Gish with Richard Barthelmess (left) and Lowell Sherman in *Way Down East* (1920)

the onlookers would be in tears. Later, we learned to withhold, not to give as much as we would if the camera were operating. Film was expensive, and a scene was shot only once, so we conserved our strength for that one take. . . .

During lunch he would help those who happened to be eating with him. If an actor did not know what to do with a character, if he was baffled and could not get insight, Mr. Griffith would say: "Well, haven't you seen someone like this in your life? Go find him. Go get an idea from someone, and bring it back to me, and let me see if it's any good. I can't think of everything! I'm writing the whole story.

You have only one character to worry about, so you try to round it out and make it real and whole!" . . .

I would often be called in to rehearse parts for the more experienced actresses, who would sit by and watch me to see how the story unfolded. They thus gained perspective on their roles. Afterward I was allowed to stay while the more experienced players took over. Changing places in this way proved to be beneficial both to the craftsman and the novice. I often saw the scene again in the darkroom, thus learning how to correct my mistakes and profiting by the skill of the others. . . .

I won the role in *The Mothering Heart,* and it turned out to be a milestone in my career, primarily because, with two reels to work with, Mr. Griffith could concentrate more on the effects that he wanted and exercise more subtlety in his direction.

During the filming I worried that I was overplaying. But when I looked at the rushes during a lunch break, I asked Mr. Griffith why none of it showed on the screen. He explained: "The camera opens and shuts, opens and shuts with equal time—so half of everything you do isn't seen. Then take away the sound, and you lose another quarter. What's left on the screen is a quarter of what you felt or did—therefore, your expression must be four times as deep and true as it would be normally to come over with full effect to your audience."

He taught us that false emotions never move an audience, that you cannot make viewers cry with make-believe tears. "The first thing an actor needs is soul," he said. "The actor with soul feels his part, he is living his role, and the result is a good picture." . . .

He made it clear to us that acting required study. "No matter where you are, watch people," he told us. "Watch how they walk, how they move, how they turn around. If you're in a restaurant, watch them across the table or on the dance floor."

Whenever he saw some behavior pattern that intrigued him, he would use it at an appropriate moment in one of his pictures.

"Catch people off guard," he reminded us continually.

Sometimes, at the end of a shooting session, he would talk with those of us who remained to watch the rushes.

"Too many of us walk through life with blinders on our eyes. We see only what concerns us, instead of what goes on around us. Let's take a scene that is played again and again every day—one that we see and yet do not see. Let us imagine ourselves standing on a street corner. A pretty girl is waiting at the curb for a bus. A commonplace, undramatic event. Nearly every corner has a pretty girl waiting for a bus. But suppose we already know one fact—if the girl misses her bus, she'll be late for work. If she's late, she'll be fired. Let us begin then in the morning, when she comes awake abruptly in her room. We close in on the face of the clock to see the time. We watch her dressing with frantic haste. We see her drinking coffee. We show the hand holding the cup. It is trembling. We are becoming involved in the multitude of details which clothe every human event. When the girl leaves the house it is raining; she rushes back for an umbrella. Then we see her last-minute dash through the rain puddles for the bus. All of this, mind you, set against a montage of the hands of the clock moving and a backdrop of the office she is trying to reach. If we saw all this, we would be reliving our own tensions in similar circumstances, simply because we have been made to *see* it in all of its parts."

And he would repeat the familiar cry, "I am trying to make you *see!*"

To learn about human nature and to build our characterizations, we visited institutions normally closed to young people. At insane asylums, for example, we were escorted through wards by nurses or the doctors themselves. . . .

I sympathized deeply with all the patients. They may have been aware of my compassion, for one day when the nurse left the ward for a moment a young woman shuffled over to me. She whispered: "I'm no more insane than you are. My relative put me in here for a purpose. Here's my mother's telephone number. Call her and tell her to come and get me. I'm unjustly confined."

She sounded completely rational. Her appeal touched me, and I took the number. Just then the doctor entered and looked at her shrewdly.

"Mary, why did you break the window this morning," he asked, "and then take the glass and cut your leg?"

She regarded him innocently. "But I had no pen. And I had to write with *something.*"

Later, when I was faced in a film with a scene that required knowledge of insanity, I had seen enough of its physical manifestations to convey the necessary range of emotions.

During the filming of *The White Sister* many years afterward, I drew on my knowledge of epilepsy for one scene; it proved an effective way to register shock. Whenever I had doubts about the appropriate reactions to certain situations, I would consult an expert on the subject.

Mr. Griffith always emphasized that the way to tell a story was with one's body and facial expressions. "Expression without distortion," he always said. He meant, "Frown without frowning." Show disapproval without unsightly wrinkles. The only makeup he suggested was a golden tone, an idea he borrowed from Julia Marlowe, with whom he had acted and whom he admired tremendously.

I learned from him to use my body and face quite impersonally to create effects, much as a painter uses paint on canvas. Later on, when I worked with other directors, I would hang a mirror at the side of the camera, so that in a closeup I could see what effect I was producing.

Mr. Griffith kept constantly at his young players: "Let me see you walk with happiness. No, *not* gaiety, that's something else. That's better. Now, with sadness—*not* sorrow. Now—with comedy, tragedy, sickness, blindness.

Now, let me see you run in all these ways. Some of you move like wooden Indians. Must I open a dancing school to teach you flexibility?"

He and I used to have a constant argument on one point. When I played a young girl, he used to have me hop around as if I had St. Vitus' Dance.

"Young girls don't do that," I complained.

"How else can I get the contrast between you and older people, if you don't jump around like a frisky puppy?" he asked. Then, imitating a young girl, he would get up and hop about, shaking his balding head as if it had a wig of curls. A stranger would have thought him mad.

We were encouraged to train our bodies for acrobatic pantomime, which was particularly useful when the camera was shooting from a distance. We were also called upon to perform the most dangerous stunts. None of us ever objected; it did not occur to us to object.

I studied fencing with a teacher named Aldo Nadi. He approved of my good eyesight and long legs and told me that in two years he could have me ready for the Olympics. But I was interested in fencing only as an adjunct to acting.

I also joined the Denishawn Dancing School, studying with Ruth St. Denis and Ted Shawn, whose pupils—among them Martha Graham—have since won acclaim for their great talents. Their large living room had been converted into a studio with mirrors and practice bars, and later, while Miss Ruth and Mr. Ted were on tour, Mother rented it so that we could practice early in the morning and late at night. Within a few years my body was to show the effects of all this discipline; it was as trained and responsive as that of a dancer or an athlete.

Mr. Griffith also encouraged us to take voice lessons to develop strength and proper breath control. His studio was certainly no training camp for weaklings; the working hours were unlimited, the demands unpredictable.

Under Mr. Griffith's tutelage, some of the younger girls of the company also had a small, impromptu class. Strindberg, Schopenhauer, Nietzsche— we read them all with earnest, patient concentration. We might not have absorbed all the ideas, but we tried awfully hard. I myself was seldom on the set without a book under my arm. During that time I developed an admiration for anyone who knew more than I did, and I must confess that the feeling is still part of me.

We also were expected to search for possible story material, reading everything in the public domain. We would find promising stories, change the locales, and use the characters and situations in our films.

Mr. Griffith urged us to mingle with audiences in movie theaters to observe their reactions. "It doesn't matter how *you* feel when you're playing," he said. "I'm not interested in that. I'm interested in what you make an audience feel. You may be crying or having hysterics, but if you're not making the audience feel that way, you're not any use to my story. Go to a movie house and watch the audience. If they're held by what you're doing, you've succeeded as an actress."

I have often sat in the balcony, staring at faces to measure the effect of a scene. More than once I've put my face directly in front of a spectator's face; instead of being distracted, I found, he would move his head aside in order not to miss a second of what was happening on the screen. Then I would know that I had achieved what I was striving for. . . .

The essence of virginity—purity and goodness, with nobility of mind, heart, soul, and body—is the stuff out of which, under [Mr. Griffith's] prompting, I created heroines. He made me understand that only governments and boundaries change, that the human race remains the same. . . .

. . . Before Mr. Griffith would begin filming any production, he would rehearse the entire film from beginning to end. Other directors, I discovered, simply rehearsed each individual scene before it was filmed. I wanted full rehearsals on *La Bohème;* I had never worked without them. Through them an actor could develop his character, grow used to his partners, time his scenes, and set his tempo. This approach wasn't known at M.G.M., nor was my method of rehearsing. It didn't take me long to see that the other players were greatly amused by my actions—opening doors that weren't there, going up and down stairs that didn't exist. When they tried to imitate my actions, they simply became embarrassed. I could not impose my kind of rehearsal on the others, nor could I object when they wanted music for their scenes. I had never had music before, and I simply had to close my ears and continue working. The music was fine, of course, when I wasn't trying to concentrate on a scene.

Louise Brooks Dialogue with the Actress

J.K. I want to know how you felt about Hollywood then and now. . . .

L.B. You see, I just didn't fit into the Hollywood scheme at all. I was never, neither a fluffy heroine, nor a wicked vamp, nor a woman of the world. I just didn't fit into any category.

J.K. And yet you were increasingly popular at the time.

L.B. That was in spite of the studio. They didn't give a damn about me. They would just as soon put me in a bit. I played nothing more than a small part, for instance, in three or four pictures there. They didn't care. You see, I didn't interest them because I couldn't be typed. It's the very thing I was telling you about the Sternberg picture.* I wasn't Clara Bow, I wasn't Mary Pickford, I wasn't Lillian Gish and I wasn't anybody, and since they didn't know or care to analyze my personality and do something . . . You see, you had to have . . . a Dietrich has to have a Sternberg, and a Brooks has to have a Pabst to establish a personality once and for all, and at the time I made that picture with Pabst, I was just as unpopular in Germany as I was in Hollywood. That picture, *Lulu,* was a huge failure. They expected a *femme fatale,* a siren, a slinking woman with lascivious looks and leers. They expected a man-eater, a sex dynamo with a voracious appetite for men. And lots of people who see that film still insist on looking at it that way, although Lulu does nothing. She just dances through the film; she's a young girl, she leads a life she's always liked. She was a whore when she was twelve, and she dies a whore when she's about eighteen. How can an audience expect a girl at that age to reflect, to suffer?

J.K. But, Louise, you said that they didn't know how to type you, but yet when I saw *Love 'Em and Leave 'Em* and *A Girl in Every Port* and *Rolled Stockings* . . .

L.B. I never saw *A Girl in Every Port.* I have a very small part in that.†

J.K. But the moment you come on, it was sheer sexual force. . . .

Excerpt from a 1965 interview with Louise Brooks, in John Kobal, *People Will Talk* (New York: Aurum Press/A. Knopf, 1986), 71–97. Copyright © 1986 by The Kobal Collection, Ltd. Reprinted by permission of Alfred A. Knopf, Inc.

*A reference to her dissection of Von Sternberg's genius with women.

†She's the last in a succession of girls encountered by the two womanizing Hawks heroes, though she's the only woman who poses any threat to their male bonding.

Louise Brooks in *Diary of a Lost Girl* (1929)

L.B. I use no sex at all. I never had the feeling of sex. I never try to feel sexy, I simply . . . It's true in life that the people who try hardest to be sexy only fool other fools. But Howard Hawks admired me. He was the perfect director. He didn't do anything at all. He would sit, look very, very beautiful, tall and graceful, leaning against anything he could lean against, and watch the scene; and the person who did all the directing was that big ham Victor McLaglen. I mean, when we were shooting, diving into the tank, it was a freezing cold night on the Fox lot, and Howard was walking around in a very smart tweed jacket, and I was shivering with the cold coming out of this damn greasy tank, and he smiled at me and he said, "Is it cold?" [She laughs.] He was just someone who had wandered on the set and being sympathetic, but I liked him very much as a man and as a director. You see, Mal St. Clair was just the opposite and I hated the pictures I did with him, although Mal adored me as an actress and he was always plugging me. At the very end in Hollywood he was still trying to get me to come to the Fox studio when he was only an assistant to Zanuck then, and to make a test for a picture, and I wouldn't. But Mal came from the mugging school of Sennett and he did everything by making faces, and he would mug out a scene for me and then send me into the scene, and I would be so embarrassed. I tried my best to please him and yet not to make all these mugging faces that date so terribly, like Adolphe Menjou. You know, the old type of film acting in those days was because of the titles, to establish the emotions, let's say, a flirting leer at the girl, so Menjou would begin the scene by making this hideous, grim expression #7 of a grinning leer, and then he knew they were going to cut to some title and then his face would drop to nothing at all and he would go into his next emotion, and that was the kind of acting that Mal tried to direct. And I felt Mal was a really terrible director, although I thought he was a charming man, a lovely man. In those days anyone could become a director. As soon as the director got too tough and made too much money, they'd throw him out and give the job to an assistant, a writer, anyone who wandered on the stage and said he'd direct, because their pictures were all presold and it didn't make much difference whether they were good or bad, and so that was the way it was. Mal had become efficient then, he'd worked at Sennett as a carpenter and learned how to mug and make faces, and so they threw him into this picture, I think . . . *Our Children Are People* . . . or no, *Are Parents People?* . . . or something. . . .

J.K. Did you read Mae Murray's biography, *The Disenchanted* or *The Self-Enchanted?* . . . [It had just been published when I called Louise.]

L.B. No, I must get it. You know, it's so unfair. . . . Wait. [We pause for breath.] . . . It's so unfair the way they treat people. Now, for instance, Von Stroheim has become an idol, you see, and so Mae Murray just stinks all around, all over. Now, she was the most ridiculous woman, and a most ridiculous actress, and let us say insane. In a way. On the other hand, she was a great success, and anyone who made a success in the business has something, believe me. It is the roughest, toughest, most humiliating and degrading job in the world. So they will not allow her to be even barely good, let's say in *The Merry Widow*. It was the best performance she ever gave, and it is cruel, when she was an old woman, not to give her credit for what she had: a lovely body, a certain kind of grace, a kind of silly personality. The fact is, her pictures kept Old Man Mayer [Louis B.] going at Metro for a long time, so she must have had something, for in the end it is the public that matters with films. It was the same with Clara Bow. You know, I talked to Kevin [Brownlow] about her. I was so mad when he didn't go to see her in Hollywood. He said: "Well, I don't think she's so much." And in that year she died. 1965. She was born in 1905. And that was the last chance anyone had to interview her. And he didn't think she was much. And, my God, she was a terrific star! It isn't like great literature which very few people can understand and those few people had to pass it down from century to century. Anyone who goes to a movie can understand it; whether it catches them emotionally or not isn't the answer. All you have to have is an eye and an ear, to have lived, spoken, felt, eaten, drunk and so forth. That's the whole terrible thing about this movie cult, these movie curators [she curdles her voice on the word], these film archives . . . they go from cult to cult. This year they're mad about Japanese films and everything else stinks, and next year it's Ingmar Bergman and everything else stinks; and it's an idiotic, childish way to view . . . The films aren't art; it's like the public library, it's full of books from the beginning of printing, and it doesn't make any difference whether they're old or new. Some are good, some are bad, and to be a cult in reading is as idiotic as—well, to be a cult with film, I think, is equally idiotic. . . .

J.K. How did you feel suddenly about 1956–57 when this terrific resurgence in your popularity came about?

L.B. Oh, I got an enormous kick out of it. I was killed dead when *Pandora's Box* failed, so from that time on, I just didn't care. I lived for years and years with this terrible sense of failure . . . and to be suddenly reclaimed from the dead was marvelously exciting, and it made me enormously happy. Of course it did! If you lived for years thinking you were a perfect failure and then suddenly you have lived long enough . . . Most people die before things like that happen—to find that you are to a certain extent admired. It's a wonderful blessing. But I was always perfectly willing to face that I'd made my own particular hell. I never tried to push the blame on anybody but myself. I knew I'd done it all myself.

J.K. But it didn't provide you with an impetus to go back to films?

L.B. You know I never did go out anyplace in my life when I didn't have to do some kind of work. You cannot drag me out. I would still be in Kansas if my mother hadn't sent me off to Ruth St. Denis in New York.

J.K. That's right . . . you were with Ruth St. Denis.

L.B. And Ted Shawn. That's how I began. I'm a dancer.

J.K. Yes, of course, of course. And you danced with the Ziegfeld Follies too, right?

L.B. Well, yes, after I left St. Denis and Shawn. You know what burns me up? For years, John, my whole career as far as these charming United States of America are concerned has been a blank. Ted Shawn and Ruth St. Denis must have given thousands of lectures, and they've written between them fifteen books, and they have never found me worthy of so much as a *mention* of my name, ever having been with them, and it's the same thing with the Follies. Because Ziegfeld was going to star me in the Follies when I left, you know. I was supposed to do *Show Girl* and I wouldn't do it, so they gave it to Ruby Keeler. But in all the hundreds of books that have been written about the Follies or connected with the Follies or pictures of the Follies girls, my name, my picture, nothing. And if it hadn't been for the German films I made, and being advertised in Europe, my name would still never be mentioned in movies.

J.K. But I didn't discover you in your German films. I first saw you in *A Girl in Every Port.*

L.B. Yeah, but don't you see, all that was built up beforehand. By Pabst's *Pandora's Box* and *Prix de Beauté,* made in Paris, because before that no one could remember me. And it's just as . . . For instance, I was looking through [Richard] Griffith's book . . . what is it called? . . . *The Films.* No, *The Movies.* And do you know that there is not one picture of Betty Bronson? I mean, she was incomparable in *Peter Pan.* And not one picture of her. And so it goes, you see.

Well, now you can keep your mouth shut because I'm going into a monologue about Josef von Sternberg. So, quiet. I'm going to tell you about having read *Fun in a Chinese Laundry.* Well, you know the first thing I ask myself when I read a book is "Why that kind of book? Why did he write it?" Because all of us write because we have suffered some terrible humiliation and we've got to set the record straight and get even somehow. And of course I discovered that Sternberg wrote this and, instead of giving us that gag title from one of the first Edison pictures, he really should have called it "Why I Am Greater Than Marlene Dietrich." Because the whole thing is this argument to prove that he was a great director of genius and she was his puppet, manipulated and *created* by him. And it is a long, long argument about direction and acting; and what makes that particularly interesting is that today film writers who write about directors' work are impossible, they never mention actors' names. And they never tell you what's happening on the screen. A person who never saw a film, or never heard of a film, wouldn't know from these books that people came to see those pictures to see certain actors with certain personalities perform. It's amazing, because, as Sternberg shows in his book, the whole problem of a director is how to find out what an actor can do and how to get him or her to *do* it. And I can tell just from experience, because I was married to Eddie Sutherland and I remember he would come home every night after work, throw his feet down on the couch, grab a martini and start talking about Bill [W. C.] Fields: what he did at home, what he did in the scene, what he's going to do tomorrow. He wasn't occupied with the lighting or the camera or the costumes or the scenery, but *with his actors,* which is the whole essence of direction. And of course, in stating his case against Dietrich, Sternberg talks about this over and over, endlessly. Incidentally, his book is very well written. He wrote it himself, and it has wonderful cross-cutting, and movement back and forth in time. It's really an expert job of editing. But to go on—he does a marvelous portrait, of course, of Dietrich. And he does also a grand, illuminating portrait of [Emil] Jannings, because everything he writes about Jannings, his malice and his fights, his jealousy and how he tries to foul up the other actors so he could steal the scene, and his cattiness, you know it's true. You see all this on the screen when you see Jannings' pictures, you know it's true. But to go back to Dietrich, the most marvelous things about Sternberg's direction, whether he knew it or not, but in telling about Dietrich he solves the terrific mystery of her mystery! You know, most directors, or at least all directors whom I've worked for, give the choreography, the action and the words, and leave your inner thoughts alone because on the screen, like in life, a person is doing one thing and thinking another. Just as I'm talking to you now. You can also see that in Garbo, who I think is the greatest actress in the world, you can see that along with her actions is this wonderful mysterious thought line moving below, but it's harmonious, she's at one with her thoughts. But Dietrich always used to mystify me because I wondered what the hell she was thinking about with that long, gorgeous stare. And of course he tells you in one simple line of direction: he said to her, "Count six, and look at that lamp post as if you couldn't live without it." So, giving her these strange thoughts which she was able to concentrate on to fill her mind, he also gave her this strange air of mystery, which of course she never had with any other director. He says that she used to work with other people and say, "Oh, Joe, where are you?" And you can understand why.

He was the greatest director of women that ever, ever was. Most directors, you know, can direct certain women marvelously, and some can't direct them at all. But he could direct every woman he touched, he could make her lovely. He could take the most gauche, awkward, sexless dame and turn her into a dynamo of sex. There are three marvelous examples, and all are full of contrasts; they are Dietrich, Evelyn Brent and Betty Compson. First, you see, he's a very dispassionate man. I can't imagine he ever was very much in love, because most men look at women and they feel either a sexual urge or not, but they never analyze it . . . or they can't analyze it. And, you know, the direction, the terrible things that still go on, and it's gone on from Mary Pickford— when every director says "act like Mary Pickford," and then Lillian Gish, Clara Bow or Garbo . . . then Monroe and Bardot. That's the best most directors can do in trying to form an actress into an attractive shape. But he, that man, Sternberg, with his detachment, could look at a woman and say, this is beautiful about her and I'll leave it, not change it, and this is ugly about her, so I'll eliminate it. Take away the bad and leave what is beautiful so she's complete. As I say, with this Dietrich, if you ever saw her in those pre-Sternberg films, she was just a galloping cow, dynamic, so full of energy and awkward, oh, just dreadful, and the first time he saw her, he saw her leaning against the scenery, very bored, because she was working in a play, *Zwei Kravatten,* and didn't give a damn. And he saw that and it was lovely. But all of her movements were horrible. So he simply cut out the movements and painted her on the screen in beautiful, striking poses staring at a lamp post.

And in direct contrast was Evelyn Brent. I made a picture with her, and Evelyn's idea of acting was to march into a scene, spread her legs and stand flat-footed and read her lines with masculine defiance. Oh, I thought she was dreadful, and then I saw her in *Underworld,* and Sternberg softened her with all these feathers, and he never let her strike attitudes at all. He made her move. I remember the opening of *Underworld* . . . he makes her entrance the loveliest, most feminine thing, like bringing her from standing at the top of these stairs and reaching down, pulling up her dress, fixing her garter, I think.

Anyhow, it's lovely, it established her as lovely and feminine. And the other woman, who was so utterly feminine that she had no more impact than a powder puff, was Betty Compson in *The Docks of New York.* Well, you know, Betty was so soft, so frail, so delicate, so empty-headed that she was just meaningless on the screen, and he gave her emotional depth. He tells himself how he did it. For this one scene he had her sew the torn pocket back onto [George] Bancroft's coat. And of course every woman in the world knows that if she's in a tough situation with a man, that if she can prepare for his angry entrance by being found, you know, with a bit of sewing, stitching under the lamplight, that she's got everything going for her. And this is all I have to say about a really remarkable book.

The actors in this part can be divided into two categories: younger stars who emerged from silent film and more mature actors whose numbers began to grow with the coming of sound. All the writers represented here except Betty Compson and Greta Garbo were seasoned character actors on the stage by the time they entered motion pictures. All except Louise Closser Hale had acted in silent films before appearing in films with sound. This group, then (except for Hale), faced major adjustments when equipment and technicians associated with sound recording were added to cameras and camera operators.

By the 1910 or so, silent film had begun to breed its own stars, in proud and conscious independence from the stage. A number of these, like Betty Compson, came to film with only minimal experience before live audiences. Nonetheless, they helped to build a cult of glamor that quickly became distinctive to film, in which physical appearance outweighed more traditional acting skills. Launched with assistance from Hollywood's burgeoning journalistic establishment, silent film stars achieved a kind of fame without precedent among stage actors.

If the character actors who wrote the excerpts included here did not attract the same adoration accorded stars, they lent a cosmopolitan flavor to some of the most important films made in America from the late 1920s until World War Two. They were able to do this in part because their stage skills left them better adapted than rank beginners to meet the challenges posed by early sound. Once directors could no longer call out commands during filming, they were forced to rehearse their actors more extensively to achieve the results they desired. In this way among others, sound brought film acting into closer consonance with stage acting, and it lent veterans of the stage assurance in exploiting the latest film technology.

Measured against what has arisen since, though, "technology" is probably too flattering a word. The earliest sound equipment was crude enough to make it necessary for much filming to take place either indoors, in controlled conditions that only studios on the East Coast could offer, or, sometimes, in the wide open spaces of Southern California. In this connection, the advent of sound increased the importance of studios both as sites for production and as agencies for marketing and publicity. Until the mid-1930s, primitive sound recording also required actors to project their voices in much the same way they had needed to do before live audiences. This necessity made actors' work in films even more like what they had done in the theater and so placed a higher premium on stage experience than had been the case while silent films had enforced a more purely visual standard. Even after sound technology had improved, ways of acting and speaking derived from the theater continued to manifest themselves in films from Hollywood and Europe; these techniques had entrenched themselves on both sides of the Atlantic during the early years of sound.

Furthermore, actors with crisp delivery prompted more elaborate dialogue as time went on. Screenplays containing such dialogue, in turn, demanded subtler measures for their telling than the melodramatic and formulaic plots typical of silent films. Refinements in filmic narrative also had the effect of multiplying the number of character actors, who were generally charged with carrying the twists of plot characteristic of more complex dramatic material. This demand led to the reconstitution of the older theatrical "stock companies." These companies were enlarged in the 1920s and 1930s by American actors, of course, and by Europeans in search of higher salaries or refuge from political and economic ills in their native countries. Under the stewardship of the Hollywood studios, such companies of film actors grew more elaborate and cosmopolitan than any the legitimate theater had sponsored.

Character acting celebrates transformational capacities. The better the character actor, the more complete and diverse each transformation becomes. Among character actors, range and variety usually complement the physical attractiveness and stable characterization of the starring performers. Character acting over the last two centuries has, however, almost always depended on stars' work to set it off. Compson's and Garbo's accounts in this part suggest what kind of grounding character actors required to throw their efforts into high relief.

Louise Closser Hale evinces a patronizing attitude toward films, which was reinforced by her associations with both the literary establishment and the stage. But she does credit the necessity that sound in films imposed on actors "to appear natural in a new way," and she furnishes a brief synopsis of the advances in sound technology within the space of only a few years in the early 1930s. Besides giving an idea of the speed actors needed in order to adjust to changing conditions, her account suggests a cause for the precipitate decline of a number of stars who had prospered during the silent era.

Betty Compson was one who proved unable to extend her stardom from silents into sound, partly because of her age (she was in her thirties by then) and partly because of her lack of experience on the stage, her attempts to cultivate new vocal skills notwithstanding. Her interest in learning foreign languages suggests an attempt to maintain the appeal she had held for international markets during the silent period, when subtitles lent themselves to easy translation.

Garbo appeared in silent films in her native Sweden before arriving in the United States. In "What the Public Wants" she acknowledges the development of an enormous film audience since the early decades of the century, with a taste for escapism that was only heightened by the onset of the world-wide depression. Garbo's testimony indicates the growing aspiration of the film industry toward a Wagnerian ideal of "total art," realized in sound, animation, and increasingly sophisticated special effects. Taking up the theme that viewers see themselves in the characters that film stars portray, Garbo considers the collective nature of the film viewership but does not give the idea of a mass audience the usual pejorative connotations.

Unlike Betty Compson, Garbo easily sustained the fame she had built up during the silent period. She also reversed the experience of other foreign stars, who were often driven out of Hollywood once audiences heard them speaking with an accent. The durable nature of her celebrity was also evidence of the new capacity of studios to lengthen the performing lives of the leading players in whom so much had been invested, by rationing and controlling their access to the press and by supervising many aspects of their lives away from filming. Garbo and other stars of her generation may have lasted longer with such assistance, but they also found themselves increasingly confined and defined by the studios' paternalism.

George Arliss, Edward Arnold, and Lionel Barrymore all capped distinguished stage careers with successes in film. The British-born Arliss made an impression in Hollywood by directing films in which he also starred. He would assemble live audiences from among the studio personnel and then run through entire screenplays, in sequence, just before filming. Edward Arnold, who preferred spontaneity to the rehearsal Arliss favored, was one of the first actors to recommend restraint in film work—later to be called underplaying—as opposed to the enlargement and exaggeration associated with stage acting and silent films. Lionel Barrymore, like Arnold, saw that in film speech could be joined to an apparently spontaneous byplay, which actors could perfect by watching themselves in daily rushes. By such means, filmed performances could be regulated and controlled as those on the stage had never been. The sense of comfort Barrymore and others derived from the ability to control their performance before the camera lent a new kind of satisfaction to film acting. This in turn helped popularize such work among actors and audiences, too, who were impressed by noted stage actors' growing (though still far from universal) advocacy of film. Thus film was able to stake an early claim to legitimacy in America only a few years after it had succeeded in doing so in the postrevolutionary Soviet Union.

Lack of a vital, ingrained theatrical tradition helped film establish itself more quickly in the United States than in most of the European nations. West Europeans remained suspicious of film acting long after American (and Soviet) actors had recognized the advantage or at least the possibility that lay in acting before the camera, as is apparent in the accounts that follow. The lag is most conspicuous in the distinction between Arliss's passion for rehearsals (so clearly modeled on those of the theatre), and Arnold's and Barrymore's appreciation for the greater flexibility that film acting allowed. The two strands of opinion continue to reflect the divergence between Charlie Chaplin's view that film acting essentially derived from the stage and Edward Arnold and Lionel Barrymore's sense that it offered more novel and liberating capacities.

Louise Closser Hale The New Stage Fright: Talking Pictures

It was a very short part—my first one in talking pictures, in motion pictures of any kind. I said this to the Casting Director as I flipped the pages contemptuously. The director said it was quite a good-sized part. "The dialogue for a feature talking picture is about one-third as long as a play. That's a good part."

I mentally reviewed my several novels, now happily out of print. I envied the writers who fitted dialogue for this new device. A novel is generally three times as long as a play. So a movie writer spends but one-ninth of the energy a novelist must employ. Easy money. And easy money, I concluded (waving the short part) for the player. Still I was feeling a little nervous. I rather despised the thing, but I was feeling a little nervous.

In this first studio of my experience they were proud of the fact that they rehearsed the scenes even a day or two before they "shot" them. The principals went upstairs to a room with real windows and real sun coming through, and sat round in a semicircle. I was accustomed to these half arcs. I had been sitting in them for thirty-four years, but always it was on a dark stage with a single pilot-light on a standard down by the foots. The gleam continued mild until the director arrived, when a whole border was turned up. The dark stage always smelled like a cathedral to me. A lump came up in my throat as I sat down in the sunlight. What was I doing messing about with a highly technical apparatus? I was no scientist. I belonged to the theater. I grew a little more nervous.

We began on the scenes. They were so short that we could get little feeling into them ("get our teeth into them" as we say) before they were over. Besides, we didn't begin at the beginning of the picture. "We will run through the sequence that we will start to-morrow," said the director. That was as clear as mud to me. It was explained that a sequence is akin to an act. Not that it is anything like an act. It is a group of scenes in which the action is continuous. The director went on to say that they had built the sets of this sequence first. They would do the first sequence last.

"Why?" I ventured.

Excerpt from Louise Closser Hale, "The New Stage Fright: Talking Pictures," *Harper's Magazine* 161 (September 1930), 417–424. Copyright © 1930 by Harper's Magazine. All rights reserved. Reproduced from the September issue by special permission.

Louise Closser Hale (center) with Charles Farrell and Maureen O'Sullivan in *The Princess and the Plumber* (1930)

"It's the railroad wreck."

"Oh!" I inferred we might all be killed in the wreck, and it would be as well to have us safely through the less annihilating episodes.

"You have the first title," he said to me.

"I don't see any title."

"He means lines," whispered a nice girl who was both of the theater and this new dramatic medium.

I began an attack upon a police commissioner because he had done so little about finding the woman who had kidnapped my grandchild. I arose and strode about as I admonished him. A woman couldn't be that angry and stand still.

"Perhaps," said the director doubtfully. "We will see what the sound man says when we get on the set."

"I shall have to walk about," I said firmly. I was determined to be natural.

We went on reading our "titles." That is, all but one man. He had been a success in silent pictures—a rough comedian. He didn't understand that his cue was the line preceded by a lot of dots, and that the lines to be spoken by him were those beginning with capital letters, and when they were pointed out to him there were long periods of a thick mumbling from him. To our growing embarrassment we began to realize that the big, genial fellow who came originally from the prize ring, barely knew how to read—to read anything.

Finally he threw down the script and left the room. That was the last we ever saw of him. I wonder what his finish is! He was too old for the prize ring. "Othello's occupation's gone!"

I don't care to think what sort of a performance I gave in the theater that night. Through the flippancies of an aging Paris flapper I was mentally attacking a police commissioner. "Whoever the woman is she's got to give that baby up!" I kept repeating to myself. Someone said I looked wild. When I reached home I wrote out the speeches over and over. We give three weeks, anyway, to the rehearsing of a play. We know our lines so well that we need not be conscious of the words, but give all our attention to the thought that the words express. This over-night committing was something new.

I put a hot-water bag to my cold feet and nagged myself into an uneasy slumber. I must get up at six. For thirty-four years I had taken my ease after the night's work in the theater, leisurely supped, read when I got to bed, and slept as late as I pleased. "You go to sleep," I commanded my alert brain, "we get up at six." . . .

Before nine I went down on the stage. There were two stages in this studio, an upper and a lower one. And neither was a stage, but a huge floor space the size of a city lot. Our "set" was on the upper stage, and if I had yearned for cathedral darkness my yearns were realized. Scores of carpenters, under dim lights, were making sets for other pictures. They hammered leisurely and were perfectly willing to advise me as to the location of our set. I picked my way in and out of snow scenes, rubber plantations, and French ballrooms to a great circle of light about the police commissioner's office and anterooms. Some camp chairs were lined up in front of the scene. On the arm of one hung a megaphone, and that was the director's chair. An intelligent young woman known as the "script girl" sat in another and smiled a welcome. She also wrote down the details of my costume and my jewelry. If the scene held over to the next day I must wear the identical equipment. I remember seeing a big silent film in which the hero entered a lady's house in evening dress and came out in riding clothes. I suppose the script girl on that picture lost her job. But the actor was a careless fool—we must keep track of our regalia.

I made a discovery as I shifted from one icy foot to the other while waiting for the cast to foregather; and it holds good in every studio where I have worked: There is more courtesy shown in the Fifth Largest Industry in the World (*i.e.,* motion pictures) than in the theater. Yes, more courtesy—and fewer chairs! I think if anyone had been cross to me on that first dreadful day; if an electrician wheeling unwieldy lights had not said "beg pardon" when I got in his way; if the camera men had cried "clear out" as I unconsciously crossed their line of vision while they were focussing on an actor; if the sound man had really laughed as loud as he had a right to when I rehearsed my first scene in his hearing, I should never have survived those terrible nine hours. I, literally, should have died of fear.

For, as the day wore on and I was not put into action, a terror took possession of me that transcends De Maupassant's story of "La Peur." Who would have thought that a handful of pretend policemen who didn't have to say much beyond "yes, boss," who had been guardians of the peace in silent pictures for years, should have been so difficult to handle! Should have been so valuable to the picture! They were looked after like prima donnas. It seemed impossible to get the proper light on that bunch of cops. One would have thought them bathing beauties.

There was a stand with a mirror set up in the offing so that the actors might powder their faces the last moment before the "take." Each player carried from his dressing room a case with the powder suited to his skin and a puff. In the intense heat of the lamps during the light rehearsals the countenance would become shiny. The camera man would tell you this, if the make-up man in attendance wasn't on his job. I was a strong patron of the make-up stand, for as the morning waned each new discovery—a prelude to what I had before me—would oil my face like a machinist's waste rag.

I discovered a number of things happening to the police commissioner while he ran over his lines. The distance between his nose and the camera which was to take him was being measured with the beautiful kind of tape line which every housewife desires and never has; a microphone was being hung over his head, and when it was rigged up the principal sound man, who is known as the "mixer" went off and in some remote place listened to the police commissioner with fairly discouraging reports.

I listened to the commissioner also, and to my horror found he was saying other lines than those which were read the day before. When the light man cried "save 'em," and all the lights were turned off (for, of course, nothing was ready yet, as it was only eleven o'clock) I crept up to the actor and asked about these new lines. "They've changed them," he said, "they always do." I became greasy at once and raced off to powder.

I kept this up till lunch time, occasionally wandering off into the rubber plantation to go over my lines. "Lunch!" cried the director genially. Everyone seemed satisfied with the morning's accomplishment, which must have covered two minutes. But I had not yet "performed." I made my way to the studio restaurant. I shall never forget how nice that chicken salad looked and shall never know how it tasted. "I'm afraid I'll eat off my lips," I said, falsifying my nausea, to the assistant director who sat at table with me.

"You can put them on again. It will be some time before your scene," he said. I looked at him dumbly. Like everyone else, he was kind. "You go lie down in your dressing room. My assistant will call you." I moved out. The assistants have assistants and the assistants have assistants. . . .

Four o'clock! At four the elevator gates opened and did not clash. The assistant of the assistant intimated that I had better descend as I should be "shot" soon. I hoped so—and I preferred bullets. The director wanted me to run through the scene, as there were some changes.

"Changes—in lines?" I stammered. "But I've committed these."

"Just a few changes," he smiled.

I was given a slip of paper with the new scene typed out. I was still allowed the grand peroration about "whoever the woman is—" but I must efface some of the words that I had caused, in my agony, to be etched into my brain, and must substitute others.

I went over and powdered my caked face. When I returned a young man with an alert countenance was sitting on the edge of the golden-oak desk waving a leg nonchalantly. He was the sound man and he wanted to see how I intended to play the scene. I strode around, speaking the lines, new and old, and his leg became quieter and quieter. "You see," he explained, "you can't move around like that. The mike—the microphone—won't take it."

"Can't I rage?"

"You can rage"—he measured the width of the desk—"about that far." Two and a half feet of raging!

The camera man came up to me. "Where do you stand?" he asked. " I move from here to here," I answered.

"Get a chalk, Gus." Gus brought the chalk. The camera man's assistant made two big toes in white on the carpet. "You'd better step right into these marks and speak your titles, standing quiet," he advised. So that was the end of the raging up and down business.

Still there was left the indignation in the voice—the shrill note of the excited old grande dame. It didn't last long. "Better not pitch your voice too high," said the sound mentor, "and don't let your voice *range* too much." I looked wild-eyed, and the make-up man told me I was shiny. "Have I time to powder my nose?" And there was plenty of time.

Cameras encased in clumsy boxes, to keep the sound of the whirr from being picked up, were changing places like elephants dancing the old-fashioned lancers. To mix my metaphors, men were peering out of these bathing machines through the thick plate glass. All our noses were being measured. I was committing the lines. The sound man was telling me I couldn't speak while in the process of sitting down or getting up; and that I mustn't pound the table, for it would be enormously magnified. And to avoid sighs. The camera man was saying if I looked out and not *at* the police commissioner as I berated him the camera would get more of my face; and I had better not smile, as there was a tooth which would take black. I raced off and powdered my nose. Why *should* I smile?

It was after five when we had a full rehearsal of the scene with lights and sound. Word came that one of the cameras had "buckled," and that caused a delay. And this caused the letter I was to hurl at the police officer to become so dry from the heat of the lamps that it had to be wet by the property man again. If it was not damp it would rustle, and that rustle would be enlarged into a wind-swept forest. We actors were parched too and quite ready to rustle under the lights, so another property man brought us lily cups of water.

At a quarter to six they were ready for a "take." Voices shouted, "It's a take" as merrily as ever. The director, echoed by his assistant and his assistant's assistant, cried "Lock 'em up," and the camera operators, perfectly nice men, were locked into the bathing machines. Men ran to all of the doors leading from the offices to the stage and turned the keys. A great gong rang. A silence descended upon the huge space, the huge building. No one pounded, no one swept the floor, no one walked. The distant elevator stopped. Only my heart was beating noisily—great hammering beats. The director sat in his camp chair with a little machine by his side. A light showed in the machine (I am not sure of this) which indicated that the cameras and the sound process were synchronizing. In the midst of this eternal, infernal silence he dropped his handkerchief. It was my signal to speak. It was my zero hour.

I must walk into the toe marks without looking at them. I must speak distinctly but not too low—or too high. I must not project my tones, as we of the theater have learned to do for those in the farthest balcony. The microphone was not in the balcony, but directly over my head. I must not sit down or get up on my lines, or show my teeth. I must speak new words that had been given me a short time ago. I must forget the old committed words.

I must (I give it a paragraph) be spontaneous and natural.

I walked into the toe marks. I did not rustle the letter. I did not pound the table. I managed my new speeches. I reached my peroration. In velvet and chinchilla, a great lady of the old school, I delivered my ultimatum to the abashed officer of the law. And I said, "Whoever that *baby* is she's got to give the *woman* up."

The alienists call this reversal of words, born of panic, "substitutional aphasia."

The gong clanged three times that everyone might be unlocked and move about. The director announced cheerfully, "Retake on account of the baby." A smiling young man held before my face a square of black board with two white letters on it. They took a snapshot of the staring letters held before my burning face. They mustn't make a print of what we had taken of the scene. This warning snapshot would be on the roll of the film:

The letters were: "N.G."

After an endless delay, while the sound apparatus went through something called "relining," we did the scene again. My fagged brain, making a great spurt, raced far ahead of the lines I was speaking. I prepared for the baby. The accouchement was successful. The director called, "Nine on the set tomorrow." They had accomplished for the day four minutes and thirty seconds. Five minutes of absolute "takes" is a good day's work. Everyone was pleased!

My maid found me that night lying on the concrete floor of my small dressing room at the Music Box. But, as usual, the overture was rung in at 8:30 sharp—at the *hour* for overtures to be rung in. And by then I was off the floor and ready to "go on."

That was in December, 1928. Since then sound mechanism has become less exacting. Still the microphone hangs over our heads, and we huddle together as we speak, but the laboratory men who are continually improving this invention *know* that the day will come when one great disc will hang over the entire set, and we shall move about as on a theater stage and speak as freely.

In June of 1929, while making a picture out here, a clumsy fishing pole with the microphone on the end of it was employed for a pair of us walking and talking. As we moved a sound assistant, seated on a stepladder, followed us with his queer tackle. Now the fishing pole has given way to a steel trolley. We trot along under it, while a camera on wheels is pulled back as we advance. It is called a "dolly shot," and one never felt more like a mechanical doll than at such a moment. A brick wrapped in wadding is tied to the camera with a few feet of rope, and as it drags along our toes must keep directly back of it, yet not *touching* it, or we get out of focus and away from the radius of the microphone. Cold with terror we march along, dollies indeed except for the sawdust.

But the mixer of this summer of 1930 allows us great leeway with the voice. Indeed, I sometimes wonder if there is any use in having a voice at all. With a beautiful manipulation of little knobs on the mixing board, a small voice is brought up to a full tone, or a too strident one is subdued. On the day I was to do a lot of screaming in a recent picture, a "scream expert," with a different sound process, was introduced to me. I was advised by the expert to "scream high." That my expression of horror might naturally be manifested by a deep, hoarse tone had nothing to do with the case. We players during this period of sound development are still subservient to a marvellous discovery, the operators of which, electrical engineers of culture and intelligence, are making every effort to accommodate themselves to the human voice. But—not yet.

And this dissertation is not wandering from the subject of The New Stage Fright. In my effort to analyze the sources of the fear that all actors seem to suffer in talking pictures, surely a part of it comes from this strange contact of an emotional people with the exact demands of science. For years we have dealt with pliable flesh and blood. From the theater stage we have thrown the ball to men and women out in front—they have thrown it back to us. We are comic—they laugh. We are tragic—they cry. We stimulate the audience, the audience stimulates us. If we are not satisfied with our work we can do it better tomorrow night—or the next night. I have never driven back from the studio at evening, through these lovely hills, but I have cried, "I could do that scene better. I see it now."

But the scene is over forever. After a "take" we pick our way across the dim stage to a small room with hard benches. The director, the sound men, and the actors sit down in the dark. After some telephonic conversation little raps of warning are heard like spirits from out of the ether, and the "playback" of the scene is given. We listen in frozen silence. We long to have it "OK'd" by the powers that we may not go through the agony again, but never have I found that I have done as well as I could. Yet there is no "to-morrow night."

We learn much in these "play-backs." A girl whose voice has been artificially enlarged in volume must surely discover that her voice has lost its own tonal quality which differentiates it from other voices, which makes it recognizable as hers. I think that is the reason so many voices of the girls who have had no experience on the stage sound like the voices of men when we hear the picture. We learn, too, that the smallest hesitation in our speech (a perfectly natural grouping of words, pausing now and then, as we express our thoughts in real life) becomes so magnified that it would seem to the audience we had forgotten our lines. We must, among other terrifying lessons, learn to appear natural in a new way.

Betty Compson Acting in Talking Pictures

The task of the actress in talking motion pictures is one of the most difficult.

Before sound came to the screen, an actress had only to look well. Today she must look well, must be able to speak well, must be an actress and should be able to sing and play at least one musical instrument. She must be educated in order to do these things well. She must have had a severe training on the stage in order to learn how to act.

During the making of a talking picture, I make no social engagements. My early evenings are spent with my script, learning my dialogue for the following day. My lines learned. I spend the later part of my evenings in my room, acting out the things I must do and say before the camera next day. As a result, when I arrive on the set, I am familiar with what the day holds for me. I do things more naturally because I have practiced them the night before.

Those of us not fortunate enough to have natural voices must study and improve. Since it is daily becoming more important that players speak more languages, most of us are engaged in studying French, Spanish, German and other tongues. Dancing lessons and lessons in music occupy so many hours weekly on my time and the time of other actresses.

In addition, we must maintain freshness on the screen. Sleep is necessary to this end, which accounts for the fact that I make no social engagements when a picture is being filmed.

It is not possible to describe acting in front of a camera. When I step into a scene I try to as nearly as possible live the character or part I am playing. When I walk into a scene, what occurs *actually takes place* in my own mind. If it is a love scene I *really love the man* so completely do I throw myself into the part. In order to do this, I must concentrate so definitely on my character and

Excerpt from Betty Compson, "Acting in Talking Pictures," in Joe Bonica, ed., *How Talkies Are Made* (Hollywood: J. Bonica, 1930), n.p.

Betty Compson in *The Docks of New York* (1928)

action that I forget that I am really Betty Compson and become the person of the picture. Concentration, I have learned, is necessary to realism in acting.

Were I just starting on my career today I would enter talking pictures by way of the stage. So important is stage training now that few newcomers will be given film opportunities unless they are selected because of talent exhibited on the stage.

Greta Garbo What the Public Wants

The actresses of the legitimate stage have been sneered at for years by the satirists because after repeated curtain calls from an enthusiastic audience they have been moved to cry from the heart, "O my public, my public!" In later years the film actress has been called fanciful and affected for confessing a love for audiences which she never sees, but, after all, the film actress is privileged to gain the public confidence, and learns the qualities which the public admires and detests. My own view is that the admiration of the public is so genuine, and its detestations so rightly placed, that the film actor and actress who have to study these things cannot but feel

Excerpt from Greta Garbo, "What the Public Wants," *Saturday Review* (London) 151 (June 13, 1931), 857.

Greta Garbo in *The Saga of Gösta Berling* (1924)

the utmost affection for people whose likes and dislikes are so honest and simple. . . .

A noteworthy characteristic of the great mass of people is that they are on the side of the weak against the strong: they admire courage, and they loathe oppression. Look at the old, old fairy-stories—such as the story of Jack the Giant-killer. I must confess to a sneaking sympathy with the giants. They were good giants according to their lights, and loved and were loved by their own monstrous offspring. One of them, I remember, gave his seven daughters seven golden crowns, which Jack coveted for his own brothers and sisters. What right had he to cut off the giant's head? But there it is. The giant is large and strong: Jack is small and weak: all the chances are on the side of the giant: popular sympathy is on the side of Jack. No popular story could be written with the giant as the hero, unless Jack made up for his lack of inches by an unnatural amount of malevolence, cunning and villainy.

What does it all mean? Simply this, that popular sympathy the whole world over is on the side of the weak against the strong. For that reason a king unjustly deprived of his rights becomes a romantic and sympathetic character to a degree unattainable by the monarch in peaceful possession of his throne. Throughout history the characters dearest to popular memory are those of men and women who have been oppressed—Mary, Queen of Scots, William Tell, and countless others. The spectacle of the good man struggling with adversity has been said to be dear to the gods; it is certainly dear to men, with this one proviso, that the good man must emerge triumphant in the end.

Mind, I do not say that it is so in life, where perhaps good characters fail as often as they succeed, and knaves share good and ill fortune with the best and most honest of them—and where indeed it is not always too easy to differentiate between the knave and the honest man. But in romance, in popular fiction, on the stage, and on the screen, one lives in a world of ideals, in which the laws of poetic justice have to be observed. The villain must be very black so that his punishment is the most deserved, he must be very successful in the first part of the story so that his fall may be the greater. He must not be punished too severely, lest popular sympathy, always accorded to the victim of oppression, switches [sic] round to his side. It is necessary to paint villainy in very dark hues. There is more joy for one act of kindness and generosity performed by a bad or worthless character than for a hundred good deeds performed by the virtuous and sympathetic people in the piece. This is a well-known trick among novel and scenario-writers. There is no better way of stirring the emotion of kindliness and charity in an audience than by representing a character, who has appeared in an unfavourable light, as performing some act of sacrifice or generosity. We are reconciled to him at once when he appears eager to make amends for his evil-doing.

The great majority of popular stories must end happily. The very few which do not must produce adequate compensation of another sort. The members of the audience automatically put themselves in the place of the characters whose adventures they see being enacted. It is their own story which their imagination sees portrayed upon the screen. And who wants their own story to end unhappily?

The popular artiste who is loved and admired by a large section of the public must in his or her turn have a boundless kindliness and affection for the public. In getting to know what the public wants the interpreter of the silver screen learns to return the affection of that great majority whose taste is so manly and honourable, so kindly and sympathetic, so simple and unspoiled, whose instincts are on the side of weakness against strength, of justice against injustice, and whose justice is so often tempered with mercy.

George Arliss My Ten Years in the Studios

The silent pictures as I recall them had very little use for the "has-beens" of the stage. For the most part the early pictures were a primitive entertainment and enlisted the services of youth whenever possible. The selection of a cast for the silent pictures was on a very different basis from that of its immediate predecessor, the theatre. The most important person for the success of the picture was the director. He was a conjurer who could often make the most astonishing silk purses out of synthetic material. If I tell you later how he did it, my disclosure need not be regarded as secret and confidential, because, with the coming of the talkies, his bag of tricks, effective only in the silent pictures, became obsolete, and was relegated to the deeper silence of the attic. . . .

As soon as it became apparent that the audience who had once seen a talking picture was no longer satisfied with a silent one, there was a tremendous rush and scramble to produce talkies at lightning speed. It was then that there came to the producer an unhappy revelation. It was brought home to him (I think much to his surprise) that there is a great deal more in acting than meets the eye; that, in point of fact, a large percentage of the actors who were quite satisfactory in the silent films were, in reality, not actors at all. You may think it strange that this fact had been hidden from him until then, but the truth is that the producers (by which I mean the men who find the money to establish picture companies), although they are vitally interested in results, are frequently innocent of how those results are attained; those producers of silent pictures realized that the director was all-important, but they didn't know how often he could make a bad actor seem like a good one. Producers, however, are almost unbelievably active and intelligent in the face of difficulties. As soon as they were told (presumably by the long-suffering directors) that actors with theatrical experience were what was needed for the talkies, they started to snap up all the available good actors of the living theatre; sometimes they snapped up some bad ones, but a large army was needed at short notice, and almost any stage actor of experience was better for the talkies than the rank and file of the silent brigade. . . .

Excerpt from George Arliss, *My Ten Years in the Studios* (New York: Little, Brown, 1940), 5–10, 44–47, 122–125.

The snobbishness of my compatriots still clung to me. We were the actors who appeared before the Best People. It was for us to uphold the honor of our Profession. Once we stepped down into movies, we should lose prestige and the best people would never again accept us as superior actors. So we either boldly refused these Hollywood offers, or we hesitated. This reluctance of one class gave to another a tremendous opportunity. Small-part actors, whose "profession" was in the habit of neglecting them for periods of six to nine months at a stretch, came to the conclusion that honor was likely to get a trifle tarnished if it wasn't polished up with a little butcher's meat every now and then; so they rushed in where angels disdained to tread and many of them were actually sitting on the right hand when eventually the angels, with wings rather damaged, arrived at the gates. In the history of the stage there never was such a time for the aging actors and actresses, those who all their lives had had to fight for a living. They now found themselves actually in demand.

In a short time they were receiving salaries such as they could not have believed possible in their wildest flights of imagination. While the "superior" actor was holding back, these pioneers were going forward and many of them were able to dig themselves into assured positions which they could never have reached if the superior class had been a little closer at their heels. It has always given me a great deal of satisfaction to see these members of my own profession making a good substantial income and living in comfort. No one knows much better than I do the struggle they have had in the theatre, and how richly they deserve any good luck that comes their way. If they haven't made a success it is not because they haven't tried—and tried hard. And don't believe those stories about the improvident actor. If the average actor did not save during his good times he could not exist throughout those long, dreary disengaged periods that are always waiting round the corner. . . .

I am acutely conscious of the presence of an audience. I am conscious even of the quality of their varying degrees of silence: the silence that steals over them when they are approaching boredom and conveys itself to the actor and takes his very soul out of him; and again that breathless silence of acute interest which inspires him and lifts him to heights he never thought himself capable of reaching. There are many kinds of audiences: there are those that are with you from the start, and there are tantalizing ones that you can "never get hold of."

It is this variety of reception that teaches the actor his business; there are many Schools of Acting, but there is only one almighty teacher—and that is an audience that has paid to come in. It is for this reason that, when called upon, I feel it incumbent upon me to give fatherly and unwelcome advice to the young people who are eager to "go into pictures." They are very discouraged at the thought of wasting two or three years in stock and touring companies (which is what I advise), when they might be stars by that time if they went straight into the movies. I sometimes repeat to them a remark that W. S. Penley (of *Charley's Aunt* fame) made to me when I was a beginner. He said, "It may be easy, with luck, to get to the top of the tree, but the difficulty is, dear boy, to stay there." If the aspiring amateur goes at once to the screen he probably remains an amateur always. The luckier he is at the beginning, the worse it may be for him in the end. His early success leads to his being entrusted with important work for which he is unprepared; he disappoints his audience and his managers: and once he falls, he is going to find it very difficult to get up again.

It is because of the large part played by the audience that the really good actor is seldom if ever seen at his best on the screen. However good an actor may be the audience makes him better. There is hardly a night when the good actor does not learn something from his audience. I say "good actor" because there are cast-iron actors who are entirely unreceptive, who cannot be inspired either by their fellow actors or their director or their audience—who remain on a dead level of mediocrity. But it is the audience which tells the actor of imagination just how far to go in the expression of an emotion. It is his audience which causes to jump into his head effective bits of business and new and better readings. It is that magnetism which on occasion will lift an actor above himself and cause him to achieve a great moment which he may never be able to repeat. He is uplifted by his audience and inspired by his art. He may lose *himself*, but in my opinion he must never lose consciousness of the presence of his audience; and he must never forget his technique or he is in danger of becoming ineffective. It is good to hold the mirror up to nature, but you must be sure you get the right light on the mirror. I have said that the actor is seldom seen at his best on the screen, but perhaps on the whole there is some compensation, because he is seldom seen at his worst. When he is in front of the camera he is making an effort to uphold his reputation, and although he does not give an inspired performance, he may give a very good one. This performance is registered on the screen and remains at the same level, unchanged by temperament, repetition or fatigue.

I hope I have made it clear that the reason I am at the moment avoiding contact with an audience is not because I have not the utmost respect for audiences, not because they have ever failed to be exceedingly patient with me, but merely because I want a holiday. And the making of pictures after a great many years in the theatre is to me a holiday. I cannot imagine anything much pleasanter than what is called "location" work—that is, scenes that are shot in the open country. To be out all day in the pure air and sunshine of

California, and to be paid for it, is an aspect of work which seems too good to be true. . . .

My earnest desire for an audience, however, led me to evolve a plan that I have adopted in the production of every picture I have made since, a method that I have found most valuable. It starts with a series of intensive rehearsals. I never begin to rehearse until the script has reached its final state—that is, until it is finished. I fancy I hear some of my poor ignorant readers say, "Well, I should think no sane man would!"—but you'd be surprised!

Then I collect the entire cast and read the script to them. Then I rehearse the whole story with the whole company for two weeks. (This is precisely the same method as that used in the regular theatre before production, except that in the theatre we generally rehearse for a longer period.) The last rehearsal but one is known as my "dress rehearsal." It is not really a dress rehearsal, because we do not dress and we have no scenery. But we collect as many people as we can from about the studios—people from other units who know nothing about our picture. They are drawn in as an audience. We also invite all the executives who are likely to have any connection with the making of our picture—including the director, the cameraman, the cutter, and the higher and lower officials. Having got our audience, we go straight through the picture with as nearly as possible the same speed as the film will run when it is shown. There is no reading of parts; all the actors are letter-perfect. Maude Howell is there with a stop-watch and has men ready to put on quickly any necessary props and furniture; she rapidly explains where we are as the scenes change, and the actors act their parts just as they will appear (except for costume and make-up) when the film is actually being shown. We go through without pause from beginning to end, as though it were a play in the theatre.

This is the method I use as a means of finding out, to some extent, the effect of the story on the audience. It also has great value in discovering "holes" in the script. It is surprising how easy it is, even for the most careful and critical reader, to miss discrepancies when reading through a scenario. But when you see the whole story unfolded before you in the space of eighty minutes by the actors who have studied their parts, any inconsistency becomes clear and unmistakable. Of course a single audience made up of stray people in a studio cannot teach you all that you would learn by playing two weeks in regular theatres, but it is a great deal better than nothing.

This mode of preparation can only be accomplished with the co-operation of the management. It is very expensive, particularly in Hollywood where the system of engaging actors is on a different footing from that of England. In England the custom is to engage the actor by the day and pay him on that basis for each day that he is called for work. The leading actors insist on a guarantee of a minimum of so many days' work. This is reasonable, because during the shooting of the picture they have to be on call at overnight notice and so cannot engage themselves elsewhere until the part is finished. This means that they may be tied up with one picture for four or six or eight weeks. The "bit" actors, being easy to replace, are not able to get these guarantees, but their anxiety to stand well with the casting director gives sufficient security to the management that they will be there when called upon. I have found, however, that the directors are very reasonable, and will generally try to fit in the scenes for a small-part actor who has the chance of picking up a few days' work in another studio. So you see in England the actors have to be paid only for the days they rehearse and for the days they work before the camera. A standard contract is now under consideration which may change some of the conditions I have outlined.

In America the terms are far less easy for the producer. The actor there has to be paid from the first day he is called to the studio until his work on the picture is finished. That is why my system was a rather shocking innovation. The producer could nerve himself to withstand the shock of paying for rehearsals, but when the icy cold fact emerged that an actor, after rehearsals, might not be needed in the studio for three weeks, the effect on the budget was alarming. Supposing his salary to be a thousand dollars a week (the leading actors in America are generally engaged on a weekly basis) that makes (three times one is three) three thousand dollars for nothing! I think a certain amount of bargaining was resorted to, but only in the case of the large salaries.

So you see this preparedness plan of mine costs money. I am all the more grateful for the co-operation of my managers because I am not quite sure that they do not regard it as an unnecessary expense which they are willing to bear as a sort of compliment to my steadfast convictions. After nearly ten years in the studios, I am still of opinion that this system of rehearsals saves money in the end. Without rehearsals everyone concerned in the picture is handicapped. An actor is given a bit—perhaps overnight, perhaps on the day of the shooting—and he goes on and does it, having a very hazy idea of what it is all about, and what connection it has with the rest of the story. If there is a miraculously good director, the actor is told what it is about and gives an intelligent performance. If it is a worried director—one of those who claps his hands and says, "Come on, let's get on"—you have a combination of a worried director and a worried actor. The director thinks he tells the actor what it is about but in reality he doesn't. The director makes the actor feel stupid and eventually, inside the head of the actor, a condition of evaporation sets in and the newly acquired words which were just now under control begin to fight for air, and struggle to get out—not by way of natural delivery, through the mouth, but through the roots of the hair; so that when the director says "Shoot," the interior of the head of the actor has become a vacuum, and of course he dries up. Then follows the heartbreaking scene of an actor losing his nerve—I can imagine nothing more tragic—and becoming really stupid.

Edward Arnold Lorenzo Goes to Hollywood

When M-G-M began casting for *The White Sister,* starring Helen Hayes, there was considerable difficulty in getting an actor for the part of Father Saracinesca, the understanding priest. Whenever I was suggested for the part, practically everybody in the production department of the studio—writers, producers and directors—opposed the idea of my playing it. "How can an actor who plays crooks and gangsters possibly play such a character—a nice priest?" they said. I got this from every side until they almost convinced me that I couldn't do it. Finally, after prolonged discussion, I made a test and was given the part.

In the cast supporting Miss Hayes were Clark Gable, Lewis Stone, Louise Closser Hale, May Robson and myself, as Father Saracinesca.

It was rather an amusing coincidence as far as I was concerned, that when *The White Sister* was previewed in Hollywood, it followed the regular program picture—*Whistling in the Dark.* Because the last glimpse the audience had of me in the latter picture, I was handcuffed and being escorted out by two detectives who were shoving guns into Jake Dillon's back. Then a few minutes later in *The White Sister,* they saw me as Father Saracinesca, the gentle devoted priest, ascending the steps of a pulpit in a church in Italy. . . .

Now while we are on the subject of casting problems, I will cite another case.

Ben [Schulberg] had me signed to do two pictures for Twentieth Century. One with George Arliss in *Richelieu,* and a part in *The Call of the Wild.* This was before Twentieth Century merged with Fox. Arliss had asked Darryl

Edward Arnold (left) in *Diamond Jim* (1935)

Zanuck to have me play King Louis XIII. When they gave me the script to read I couldn't see myself in the part at all. I did a little research, to learn something about his appearance and characteristics. According to historians, he was not a large man, and rather weak and vacillating. One chronicler of his life and times told of his many idiosyncrasies. And the only thing I discovered that we had in common was an interest in the culinary arts! He was so fond of cooking that he concocted all the sweets he ate—jams, jellies and desserts.

But I decided I wasn't the type. Certainly from the viewpoint of physical appearance, a man weighing two hundred and ten pounds was not suited to an impersonation of this rather undersized monarch.

However, as you know, I did play the part. One reason why they selected a large man like myself was the fact that Richelieu is described by historians as being a very tall man, and if he had been played by anyone but Arliss, the king would have gotten all the sympathy in the picture, no matter how good the actor was who played the Cardinal.

In this picture Arliss had to have someone with a completely contrasting personality, so that his interpretation of the character would win sympathy.

With Arliss, we rehearsed the picture two or more weeks before starting to shoot. This may be a good system for some actors, but I don't like it, because when you come to shoot the picture, much spontaneity has been lost. It makes you sure of your lines, but that's all. There is an entirely different feeling when you rehearse a stage play for several weeks. After the opening you get a reaction from your audience, and that's the thing which inspires you to give a spontaneous performance. Whereas, if you rehearse a picture for any considerable time, all you've got is that glass eye, the lens of the camera, and if anyone can get a reaction out of that, he's a better man than I am.

While there is a difference between the technique of stage acting and motion pictures, I have never found it necessary to change my method. Because all through my life I have practised what I would call, for want of a better word, *naturalness.* I find so many actors I work with in pictures always want to know where the camera is. The majority have made a careful study of the camera and its relative position to the actor. They know just how long a step to take, for instance, and which side of the face photographs best. Also how much of the figure will show in certain angles of the camera.

These things never bother me. I go on and do my work as naturally as possible, and I feel that most of the results I have gotten with this method—if such it can be termed—are satisfactory.

In connection with this, it must be taken into consideration that when a picture is screened in a theater, the spectator, no matter where he is sitting, is really only a few feet away from the figures on the screen and, regardless of how many times they are magnified, they are seen in that size, and from that angle, by every person in the motion picture house. It is very easy to *overact* in pictures. You've got to restrain yourself because every move is picked up by that unrelenting and watchful "eye." It is always well to keep in mind that today we have cameras on wheels, instead of tripods. *The camera follows the actor. . . .*

Von Sternberg directed this picture [*Crime and Punishment*]. I consider the part of the Inspector General one of the best I have done in the talkies. It may be true that he is a destroyer of whatever egotism an actor possesses, and that he crushes the individuality of those he directs in pictures. Perhaps my own experience with him will be of some interest. At any rate, the first days we were on *Crime and Punishment,* I was quite unhappy working with Joe. I felt that he wanted to destroy my individuality. That he wanted to give the performance of the Inspector General as *he* would play it. So upon getting home the first night, I thought it all over and decided to retire from the cast.

When I came to work the next morning Joe noticed that something was wrong. He got me in a corner of the sound stage away from everybody and asked me what was the matter. I told him frankly that I didn't want to work in the picture, and gave my reason: that I had certain characteristics of my own I put into every performance, which I had capitalized on for many years, and I couldn't allow him to tear down in two weeks what had taken me many years to build up.

Well, we adjusted our differences, at least, temporarily. But two or three days later, I happened to be feeling very tired as I had been working on "retakes" at night in another studio, and I began to get drowsy. I yawned. Then yawned again. Joe looked like a thunder-cloud all through the scene. After it was over, I asked the script girl what had gone wrong, why von Sternberg scowled and acted so disagreeably.

She replied in an awed, sort of breathless tone: "Mr. von Sternberg was very angry. You yawned in his face!"

I laughed, and said, "Oh, tell him to go to ———" So I was on the war path once more.

Peter Lorre, who was playing the criminal I was tracking down, met me a few minutes afterwards, and inquired rather naïvely, it seemed to me, "Did you tell von Sternberg you were sorry?"

"No," I replied, " why should I? It was nothing personal. I am dead tired. I worked all last night at the Universal Studio."

"Well, if you don't do something about it," insisted Lorre, "he'll take it out on the rest of us."

Later this incident was also patched up. But I had a feeling all through the production of the picture that von Sternberg wanted to break me down.

Probably anyone working with von Sternberg over a long period would become used to his idiosyncrasies. Whatever his methods, I believe he got the best he could out of his actors. He is, without doubt, one of the finest photographers in the industry. His methods of lighting an actor are so simple that you never feel you are under the lights. That is to say, he *used less light* than any camera man I have worked with. Although he was peculiarly self-conscious and sensitive, as you will infer from the incident about my yawning, he also had a very genuine sense of humor, a quality rarely found in a person of his temperament.

There was one scene in *Crime and Punishment* where I (as the Inspector-General) had to enter Lorre's apartment, and discuss the crime with him. I picked up a poker while I was talking. Lorre had very few lines in this scene. It was a long one for me, and had to be timed in such a way that I grasped the poker on a certain word, took out a cigarette and lit it on another word or phrase, lifted a book from the table and opened it casually on still another sentence, all the while holding the poker under my arm. I kept moving about the room, and then as the scene ended, I had to put the poker back where I got it from—talking continuously, with only an occasional interruption from Lorre.

I rehearsed the scene several times and then told von Sternberg I was ready to "shoot." I hadn't spoken five words when I stopped and said, "I'm sorry, but I've missed the timing on this." Whereupon, von Sternberg, who was looking through the camera, inquired:

"Eddie, how many years did you say you were on the stage?"

"About thirty," I replied.

"Not long enough, not long enough," he repeated in a dolorous tone. Then we proceeded to shoot the fourth and last "take." The last close-up I had in the picture was a six-line speech. The afternoon we were going to shoot it, von Sternberg dismissed everybody from the stage except the camera man, the script girl, the property man and the electrician. He put a screen around the set, and then talked to me at some length about the importance of this last speech.

I had studied it thoroughly. We started to shoot. Whenever I began reading the speech, I would get just so far, and then he would correct the emphasis of a certain word—first one, then another. And that went on and on from one o'clock until half past four. He wouldn't allow me to speak the entire six lines the whole afternoon. Finally, toward the last, I began playing his game. I would start to read a line, and hesitate.

By actual count, there were thirty-seven "takes" of this six-line speech. And out of this number there were only three good enough to be printed—the first, the fifth, and the twenty-second. At exactly twenty-five minutes past four, Joe said, "I would like to get just one more 'take.'" "No," I replied firmly, "I'm very tired, and I'm going home. You've got enough here for fourteen endings." I said "Good night," and added, "I hope your picture is good."

When the picture was finished, I asked him to autograph a picture of himself.

"I never autograph my photographs," he said emphatically. Nevertheless, his portrait hangs on the wall of my study in our home, and across it is written:

"To Edward Arnold from Josef von Sternberg, with a reasonable amount of pleasure!"

Lionel Barrymore The Actor

For the actor who accepts the film as a separate medium of expression, the new technique is fascinating to learn and, when learned, a valuable and, I think, worthy equipment, developing the actor along new lines and enlarging the scope of his abilities.

There is a great deal he must unlearn first. If he thinks for a moment, he will realise that there exists in the theatre a whole series of artificial conventions. That may seem obvious, but many actors who accept the acting code of the stage as uncontrovertible gospel never see it at all. To take one small example, the stage actor has in his part some lines which, according to the sense of the play, are to be whispered. Now he cannot actually whisper, or the man in the back row of the gallery, who has paid for his seat and has a perfect right to be served, will not hear. So the actor speaks in the voice which the convention of the stage recognises as a whisper. (Think of the everyday expression, "stage-whisper.") But the film actor, whose whole eventual audience will be in the equivalent of the front row of the stalls or nearer, must *really* whisper. That small example illustrates a whole series of similar adjustments the stage actor has to make in films. Another thing, the stage actor has an audience trained to contribute a great deal to the dramatic illusion. The theatre-goer has, perforce, great power of imagination, a willingness to co-operate and accept the most obvious make-believe. Stage settings, happenings off-stage—these things the theatre-goer accepts naturally. That is his part of the game. The film audience is not so trained—and remember that a great percentage of the people who see a film have never been in a theatre in their lives—and has grown accustomed to be convinced by the actuality of everything. So the actor has to be actual too. A stage actor newly arrived in the film studio may be called upon to play a scene in which the only other object on the screen is a tree. And it *is* a tree—giving a completely natural, easy performance as a tree too! It is not something that the audience is just going to be accommodating enough to accept as a tree. So the actor has to compete with reality. And it takes a very "natural" performance to compete with a real tree! The overacting of the stage performance would provoke only mirth from the audience. . . .

Excerpt from Lionel Barrymore, "The Actor," in Stephen Watts, ed., *Behind the Screen: How Films Are Made* (London: Arthur Barker, 1938), 93–101.

Lionel Barrymore (right) in *The Bells* (1926)

. . . The actor from the theatre may go on missing certain things even after he has become a proficient and successful film actor. A common complaint is the absence of audience, the difficulty of acting in front of only a technical crew who are much more interested in their own jobs than in the performance being given, and probably extremely blasé about acting anyhow. I concede half of this difficulty. If what the actor misses is that strange, subtle contact which can be established over the footlights, then I see his point. Thought and feelings are almost tangible things, having a molecular existence just as electricity has. A personality can project itself and its emotions and make direct contact with the receptive brain of another human being just as definitely as if they were at the opposite ends of a telephone wire. That is the only way one can account for the almost hypnotic influence certain great actors and actresses have had on their audiences. If, when the actor complains of the absence of an audience, it is that direct contact he is missing (though he probably does not exactly know what it is), then I sympathise. But there is another complaint. That the actor misses the criticism of an audience, that only by "getting the feel" of an audience, and sensing their reactions during a performance, can he discover if he is doing right or wrong, and make the necessary adjustments. That has always seemed to me a singularly unconvincing objection to film acting. Surely the film actor has much more opportunity to exercise self-criticism, to discover the reactions of others, and to correct and perfect his work—*and all before his finished performance ever reaches an audience*. . . .

First of all, there is the director. . . . Surely it is better to have the criticism of the director before the scene is finally made than to be called to a rehearsal next morning—as would happen in the theatre—and be told that something done the previous night before several hundred people was wrong and must be corrected. Then there is the actor himself as his own critic. In films he can always see the "rushes" next day. He sits there in the projection theatre, detachedly watching himself as he performed the previous day. Now he *does* have to have a "feeling" about what is right or wrong in his performance, for he can see it there for himself and, if he is working in intelligent company, he can air his discontent and have an opportunity to put it right before the film ever reaches the public.

One of the things the actor must learn in films is that he is not always going to have a running jump at the scene. By that I mean that he may be called upon to act a scene out of its context, a scene from the end of a film right at the start, for instance. Well, he must just accept this as part of the technique of the different medium. If he can't have an emotional running jump he must just learn to get his results from a standing jump, and that's all there is to that. . . .

Films are collaborative because, in most cases, the output is too great for each to be the work of one man. That may be a bad thing, but that takes us far away into a new controversy—the wisdom or otherwise of the public in demanding such a steady stream of new films—and that is something upon which I do not propose to embark. But if the objection taken to a story's having several authors, and being created in conferences attended by writers, producer, and director, is that in the end there is a muddle and nobody quite knows what it is all about, then I can only deny from my experience that that is so. Never in the entertainment world have I seen such concentration on the subject in hand, such clarity about what is wanted, and swift efficiency in setting about getting it, as there is among the reputable film-makers of Hollywood. The costs are too high, the efficiency standards too high, for anybody entrusted with the making of a film to have any gaps in his mental picture of what he is trying to achieve, or any momentary doubts of how to go about it. . . .

I think that the coming of the talking picture which brought about a great traffic of players between theatre and film did good to both. A sufficient number of good stage actors and actresses grappled with, and mastered, the film technique, to give film acting a new and more cultured background, and the screen a dignity and dramatic scope it had not had before. The theatre benefited because these players, in learning the new technique, were forced to take stock of themselves anew, to look at themselves in the critical mirror of the screen, and, by adapting themselves to the new medium, they undoubtedly broadened and developed their all-round artistic and dramatic ability.

. . . To finish on a personal note about my job as a film actor, I must confess that I find it an infinitely easier life, in the sense of physical strain, than the theatre.

It suits me perfectly to do my job in the comparative privacy of the workshop with the knowledge that it can go to the public as an entity, and in the best shape into which I am capable of moulding it.

The term "European acting" may in some ways be misleading, for it suggests homogeneity. In the first place, strict distinctions between Europe and America often break down in the face of history and practice. Acting first became internationalized, and to some degree homogenized, with the advent of tours by rail and steamship in the nineteenth century. Silent films continued this process through their transcendence of language barriers and their ease of export. While actors continued to be trained quite differently from one nation to another, they have been traveling across the Atlantic both ways for the last two hundred years, and over the past century have traversed the Pacific as well to work on foreign stages and in foreign films.

In the second place, Europe is hardly homogeneous, any more than America or even Hollywood is. The Soviets, however, present the greatest anomaly in this section and, indeed, in the entire book. Working as they did in opposition to commercial imperatives—though quite in sympathy with an ideal of mass art—Soviet actors struck out in directions quite different from those taken by their counterparts in the rest of Europe and in America. They did this by recreating revolutionary episodes to glorify the regime that sponsored their films and by subordinating themselves to acting ensembles that achieve a collective celebrity for their film heroes, in contrast to the individual celebrity that stars have in capitalist countries.

The isolation of the Soviet Union from the capitalist mechanisms surrounding filmmaking elsewhere contributed to the even greater isolation of film communities located in the postwar Soviet client-states. These included the former Czechoslovakia and Poland, both possessed of distinguished film traditions in their own right, and Hungary, Romania, and Bulgaria as well. Moreover, lingering postcolonialist biases have worked to restrict films made in South America, Africa, and Asia from wide distribution in Europe and North America. Since the 1950s, Japanese and Indian films have offered the main exceptions to the longstanding domination of films from America and Europe. Because performance training and traditions in Japan and India differ rather widely from those in the West, however, only a handful of actors from these countries have found prominent places in films made outside their own countries.

British actors have often shared performance venues with their colleagues in America and, not surprisingly, have stood closest to American actors in their understandings of commercialism and stardom. This circumstance may help explain the contentiousness that has sprung up fairly often between two similar, if highly competitive groups. A certain professional rivalry has been sharpened further by the relative ease of British actors' access to work in America, where they have flourished since pre-Revolutionary times by speaking a kind of melodious English that has appealed to American audiences down to the present day.

Over time, however, British and European actors have shown a greater interest in history than their counterparts in America. This generalization holds true even of the Soviets, who reacted to history out of their shared conviction that it could be reinterpreted and reconstituted through revolutionary or, later, artistic intervention. Directors in Europe have also exercised greater influence over filmmaking than have American directors, as a general category. In fact, directors have often been treated as the virtual stars of European films. This status has followed from their frequent standing as intellectuals, critics, and theorists in their own right, and from the lesser emphasis in Europe on the use above all of starring actors to promote commercial ventures. Perhaps in consequence, European films have more consistently been associated with art and designated as cinema, rather than as movies.

In most cases, European actors have applauded high intellectual and artistic aims for film, and some have criticized the lack of such values in Hollywood. Consequently, actors from Europe, including a number from Great Britain, have often preferred the prestige attaching to an enterprise associated with high art in their native countries to the more lucrative offers they have received from Hollywood. At the same time, the sums they can earn in America will explain why some of Europe's most distinguished stage and film actors have chosen to ply their trade there, at least for a time.

In the final part of this book, "Hollywood Acting," several Americans speak similarly of the freedom or, contrariwise, of the confinement they have felt in working away from North America or with European directors. Taken in aggregate, actors' opinions, based on their firsthand experiences of filmmaking, identify some of the most important differences, and similarities, too, between the film acting practiced on one side of the Atlantic and that practiced on the other.

Stage and Screen: The British

Stage and screen do not always stand strictly opposed for British actors, who set them as often in dynamic tension as they do in polar opposition. Some of the actors whose excerpts appear in this section take it on themselves to defend tradition in recommending stage work over film acting, whereas others seek ways of extending a distinguished theatrical tradition into the future through the capacities of the newer and more readily accessible medium.

If some British actors defend the theater fiercely, others contend that film acting has wrought permanent and irreversible effects on stage acting while remaining subordinate to it. Still others assert that film acting has transcended its counterpart in the sophistication of its practice and the breadth of its exposure. All British actors, however, share a sense of commercial realities as a basis for filmmaking and in this sense stand closer than other Europeans do to sensibilities in America. Also like Americans, British actors tend to theorize and idealize filmmaking less than do actors from other European nations, although their frequent interest in the historical lineage of film acting aligns them more closely with Continental actors than with American ones.

George Arliss expressed attitudes toward film in Part Two that typified those of many British actors of his generation. He viewed film work as a respite from the stage, and he thought films needed much greater rigor to elevate them from what he saw as their low point during the silent era. Arliss's high-handed attitude toward films came in response partially to the degree to which commercial filmmaking had already caught on in his native country. British actors—especially those who like Arliss have worked in Hollywood— have often looked with disfavor on attempts to reconstitute the values and methods of Hollywood in their own nation.

Robert Donat presents a spirited defense of film in the light of improvements deriving from the introduction of sound and its refinements in the late 1930s. He contends that live audiences offer actors much less useful guidance in shaping their own performances than the camera can, and he considers in highly original ways the different emphases that film and stage can lend to identical dramatic material. Finally, Donat offers some practical advice about the shifting demands made on actors as the camera approaches them or moves farther away.

Eric Portman shares Donat's favorable view of film acting, though he does maintain that film actors are certain to benefit by beginning their careers on the stage. He also makes an unusual distinction between stars and more ordinary actors and attempts to define what constitutes star quality. Acting alone, he believes, can be shaped and controlled, whereas stardom cannot; and this warning of his prefigures Jeff Daniels' nearly a half century later: that actors should strive simply to become as skillful as they can, both before and after beginning their careers in film.

Like Portman, Michael Redgrave takes a generally balanced view of film acting. He regrets the ways in which it enforces a lack of collegiality, although he acknowledges film's subtle and distinctive challenges to actors. He refutes those who claim a greater inherent spontaneity for film work by arguing that good acting in any medium demands improvisation as an antidote to control. In Redgrave's mind, film and stage acting are nearly equivalent because both hinge on the primary ideas contained in scripts of quality. When actors lack such a framework, he feels, their efforts can never be as distinguished as when the script has provided them with material and impulses they can shape.

Albert Finney and Mary Ure are the first commentators in the book to take film acting for granted. Reasons for this may lie in their place among a generation of British actors determined to challenge tradition, or in their having grown up watching movies with sound. In any case, they regard the opportunities film offers them as career choices rather than as moral ones, and this attitude sets them apart from many of the British actors who preceded them.

Laurence Olivier, writing near the end of his life, considers the act of characterization in its artificial and constructed nature. In doing so, he resurrects Charles Chaplin's view that actors' virtuosity arises from the *range* of roles they can play. According to this addendum, or complement, as it may be, to the more Method-based interpretations of Konstantin Stanislavsky, actors' skill lies in their ability to create characterizations that stand at some distance from themselves, which they can shape and control in the way of artifacts, with a spirit of economy and restraint.

The term "classical" in reference to performances in this mold would apply to Chaplin's manner of film acting and by extension to Olivier and others schooled in a traditional classic repertoire. It is odd to consider Chaplin's legacy "classical," even if we concede its elements of frontality, emphasis on the presentational, and exacting control. The less classical aspects of that acting style are attributable to its refinement in popular venues such as music halls and vaudeville and then later to its purveyance in films made for the low end of the entertainment market. In this sense, "classical" film acting has its genesis at a considerable remove from traditions of aristocratic patronage and from the sort of high culture annexed over the last century by a newly elitist legitimate theater.

Writing as a partisan of that theater, Olivier distinguishes himself from Chaplin—and looks the future squarely in the face—by considering ways of adapting stage works for the screen and television. In this connection, he appears to have traveled a considerable distance—from his rejection of Hollywood following his success there as a matinee idol in the late 1930s to his later interest in employing cameras to revivify bold acting for television and the big screen, through works that had their inception on the stage.

Robert Donat Film Acting

There is a certain snobbery among stage actors where filming is concerned; they look upon it as a rather boring, well-paid joke. Their performances in front of the camera, if also rather boring, are not quite so much of a joke. They give rise to the oft-repeated cry: "Where *are* our actors?" Then, too late, they discover they have not gone quite the right way about it. Instead of just acting "a little less" they find out that they must try to act a little better. That is why actors who are successful both on stage and screen are few and far between. It is a very serious business, but increasingly fascinating and worth while. . . .

There is no such thing as Facial Expression, but there is such a thing as an expressive face. An expressive face helps to convey by natural means the messages of the artist's heart and mind; *helps*—but it cannot tell the whole story. Witness the celebrated wooden-faced comedian who, for some lamentable and apparently unaccountable reason, seldom makes pictures nowadays. Until he arrived, who would have believed that any one could have achieved screen fame by the deliberate avoidance of facial expression? It is the eyes and the voice that matter most.

"Facial" expression is only skin deep; it is superficial and therefore insincere. Your bad actor (invariably a lazy one) visualises surprise, for example, in terms of lifted eyebrows, quivering nostrils, parted lips and popping eyes. Your good actor goes to the very roots of the process and *imagines* (a) the mental state, and (b) the emotional state in which his character is involved at the time of the surprise, (c) the nature of the surprise, and therefore (d) the degree of mental and emotional shock likely to be produced. Also if he is wise (e) he thinks backwards and forwards in continuity to help "place" his acting in proper sequence and size and shape. All these processes are conscious (though very nearly instinctive in a good actor) but the rest of it, the actual putting-over of the message, should be unconscious. The face and eyes will light up, not with a "suitable" expression but with the *only* suitable expression—the real thing. It may be that in his early apprenticeship the good actor studied his own face and made stubborn muscles more pliable by exercise— but woe betide him if he made a habit of it. Your second-rater pulls a face,

Excerpt from Robert Donat, "Film Acting," in Charles Davy, ed., *Footnotes to the Film* (New York: Oxford University Press, 1937), 16–36.

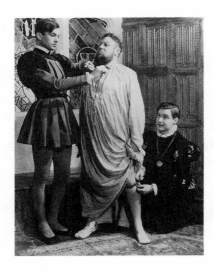

Robert Donat (right) with Charles Laughton (center) and John Loder in *The Private Life of Henry VIII* (1933)

your first-rater creates a face. Both methods are founded on pretence, the difference being in the use of the imagination.

In the early silent days they could get away with the face-pulling simply because it was new to us and we were fascinated by a novelty. . . .

Just as face-pulling twisted the silents, voice-pulling distorted the talkies—though not for long, for the very good reason that having been forced into the paths of sincerity nothing but sincerity of voice would match. Thus, by the time mechanical improvements had eliminated the tin fog-horn, the all-screeching, all-crooning, all-canoodling voice had disappeared. When Garbo took the plunge into talkies it was inevitable that she should succeed. If she had possessed the voice of a croaking raven it would have been accepted.

How much farther have we travelled since those days? Not so very far, really. It is true we have anchored the camera and put a faster and more delicate motor inside it and more sensitive film in the spools, and we have given the cameraman a host of novelties to play with and more suitable backgrounds to light; but fundamentally the Cinema has given us nothing more than the long-shot, the medium shot and the close-up, plus the variations that a mobile camera can play. . . .

Your stage producer rarely directs from the front row of the stalls; once the play reaches the stage and the curtain is up, you will find him either at the back of the stalls or in the dress circle. The farther rehearsals proceed, the farther away from his actors he tends to get. Filming employs almost the reverse methods. A scene is shot first in long-shot—then medium, then close-up. The film director tends to approach, the stage director to retreat from, the actors. But that is not the only difference. Having been manoeuvred practically under the skin of the actors, the camera takes the scene in miniature and later enlarges that miniature. (In this process certain changes occur, but they are not of great importance. For instance, the play of light, cunningly screened and filtered, may transform a made-up face so that film actors' mothers have been known to pay twice before recognising their own progeny. Since we are pursuing comparisons, the theatre has its illusions too, and many of them are shattered at the stage door.)

In the theatre it is the audience which receives; in the studio it is the camera, with this surprising difference—that whereas one can get away with flippancy, sloppiness and insincerity in the theatre, infinite care must be exercised in front of the camera. In the theatre the broad methods necessary to reach topmost galleryite and lowermost pittite sometimes cover a multitude of sins.

Much has been said about the theatre's living response in its audience, but little truth has been spoken. There is nothing to equal the electric give-and-take of a full house, but it is false to describe an audience reaction as "subtle." All mass reaction is collective; its emotions are simple, sometimes crude and often based on hysteria. It is an undeniable stimulus but no more potent than the creative stimulus of actual endeavour. I am certain that my best work has been given either in my own study or at rehearsals where there was no audience at all. The camera, if uncompromisingly critical, is at least unemotional and does not flatter.

With the searching eye of the camera so close upon one, how can one dare to be other than truthful? To say that the average film demands the minimum of veracity is simply a criticism of the average film and no indictment of film acting in itself. Because we are accustomed to seeing displays of pygmy emotion and magazine-story intellect, must we assume that cinematic art has nothing more to offer? Literature is not judged by the penny dreadful. . . .

It is one of the paradoxes of the Cinema that while it is supposed to succeed principally with mass effects it is actually at its best when it handles the little things, the seemingly unimportant. On the screen an apparent triviality can achieve as much pure drama as many a big effect which thrilled its way across the Lyceum footlights in its most theatrical days. Remember our limitations, dear reader. A flicker of doubt in the eyes on the stage is meaningless except to the first few rows of stalls. Contemptuous critics label the filmic process as "simply the real thing photographed." What a compliment—if a veiled one. Let us examine this reality for a moment, and if we bear in mind that technique is needed every bit as much for the overcoming of difficulties as for the actual exercise of the art itself, it may be amusing to recite a few of them.

On the screen, suppose we see a modern young man dangling a leg over a modern office desk with modern New York receding in the background. Suddenly we come closer to him. In other words, the camera moves into close-up. His eyes flash a look of doubt, and that is all. I have purposely chosen something elementary. The flicker of doubt is created in a blaze of light in a dreadful fug under the very nose of that terrifying taskmaster, the camera lens, with a "mike" on a boom hovering overhead, surrounded by the gang of electricians and props boys and faced by the unit staff headed by the director—who is expecting results. Behind him are the plaster walls and an unglazed window with an enlarged black-and-white picture-postcard of New York propped up behind it; above him and everywhere else, lights.

In actual fact, the young man's behind is probably propped up on a couple of cushions or books and the desk raised up on wood blocks to improve matters for the camera, so that his leg dangles at a very unnatural height from the ground, and he must gauge his movements so that at the moment of the close-up his head will be momentarily still and his eyes—almost imperceptibly—will flash their story; not into the lens itself (for the lens, though our most inquisitive neighbour, must be ignored completely if we would win it over completely), not precisely into the lens, then, but at a spot dangerously close. And an exact spot; remember, he is to convey a flicker of doubt—not a flicker of doubt as to where he should look, and so insidiously faithful is the lens that it will blurt out the whole story if given half a chance: "Damn! I'm looking into the lens." "Hell! I looked too low!"

But it is when one sits in the projection theatre at the studio the following day and sees one's previous day's efforts come to life, that the real strength of a mere moment becomes properly significant. Then, when one senses the value of detail and the unique opportunities afforded for perfection, the ultimate possibilities of film-making seem to gain a sort of sanctity. One leaves the stuffy little theatre mellowed and humbled but determined to aim high.

Imagine that I find myself faced with the problem of playing on the screen a part I have already played on the stage. Ideally, this could never exist—a stage play belonging emphatically to the theatre. . . .

For the sake of investigating the comparison, I will attempt it: James Bridie at last consents to the filming of *A Sleeping Clergyman*. Let me pause to warn you that if ever this does happen it will be neither "freely adapted from" nor "based on" the original; it will follow Bridie's scheme or perish in the attempt. The moment I will choose is the great one in the First Act where the pregnant sweetheart of Cameron the First deliberately smashes his culture tubes. For those so unfortunate as to miss this superb drama, I will explain that Cameron the First anticipated Pasteur's germ theory of disease, and these culture tubes meant so much to him that rather than be separated from them or in any way be hindered in his work he turned a deaf ear to the friends who offered him comparative luxury, sea air and the ravishing proximity of his mistress, and stuck to his combined discomforts in a Glasgow attic. Cameron, who is already half out of bed, seething with fury at the girl's taunts, cries out as she backs away from him into a collision with the table on which his experimental culture tubes repose in their rack. Seeing the mingled horror and love in his eyes—the love which she is denied—she deliberately turns and sweeps them to the floor.

Now so far I have played the purist, rendering unto the Cinema the things which are the Cinema's—and denying any co-operative truck with the Theatre. But I must confess it is a very fascinating comparison, because I have just discovered that the idea which dominated the scene in the reading, but did not dominate in the Theatre, could easily dominate on the screen—the decision being in the scenarist's hands. Which do you wish to predominate, Mr Bridie? The germ theory symbolised by the culture tubes, Cameron's inherent badness, or Cameron's inherent genius? (I haven't forgotten the girl, who, good as her chances are, really carried the baby in more senses than one.) In the reading, the germ theory won the day; in the theatre, Cameron's desperate race against death and his desperate ill-treatment of the girl.

Bridie, who knows the taste and smell of his theatrical onions about as well as any one writing in the Theatre to-day, realising that his little rack of test tubes would be an almost negligible part of the stage setting, built up an edifice of words. Many of these, Mr Bridie, will have to go from our scenario because they will be superfluous. Alternatively, Mr Donat, you will have to sacrifice some of your high-lights too, because those test tubes are going to be given a good deal of footage. Close-up after close-up will plant and re-plant them. Finally, a huge one, as the girl smashes them to the floor, then one of the table, and the awful emptiness where they had been. These things will intensify the drama culminating in Cameron's tragic eagerness to outlive his dream, his bitter hatred of the things that thwart him, his awful agony when he sees his dream destroyed, and his final uncontrollable suicidal rage; intensify it even more than Bridie's theatrical devices built them up for me on the stage. But the camera will now demand the greatest responsibility ever asked of an artist—absolute honesty and integrity. When that relentless eye goggles at us in close-up we may be sure of one thing—we must deliver up to it the finest work of which we are capable; nothing but the truth will do.

Eric Portman The Film Actor

A great many people dream of a star's success on the films. It's a good dream, for it answers the requirements of most of the wishes most of us want to have fulfilled. The screen star does get rewarded—money and fame are not small figures in the sum total of ambition. But I want to talk to those who are quite determined to turn the dream into reality, and who realise that such a transformation does require a terrific amount of determination.

Now most people might imagine that one of the greatest difficulties for the film actor is caused by the fact that a film is shot in a number of short scenes. . . .

. . . It is hard, but not so difficult if you remember that a good film actor studies in advance the entire script of the film as earnestly as he would study a play. The scenes in which the film actor has to appear may be isolated incidents; but, in his mind, the film actor carries the whole of the story. It's no harder for him to give his best in the isolated incident than it is for the stage actor to repeat, at rehearsals, a section of a play. For the good film actor knows the whole of his script as well as the stage actor knows his play.

I think that even the small-part actor—the man with but a tiny bit in the film—should study the whole script. The actor must know, must have experienced the sweep of the story in order to be able *to turn on his lamp.*

All right, if the division of acting into moments is not the film actor's greatest difficulty, what is? I would answer that it is the enormous amount of *concentration* which is needed to play a film scene. There is the necessity of remembering the action exactly. You must undo your coat at precisely one minute, pick up a brief-case at precisely another, etc. The scene is planned, with full consideration for the microphone and camera, to happen one way; and that is the way it must happen. On the stage, a good actor can get away with murder. If he forgets to pick up the brief-case on the right line, he can go back for it. A good stage actor can always catch up with himself again. But if the screen actor forgets the brief-case at the right moment, and if he attempts to go back for it, he will probably find that he is now cutting between another artiste and the lens, or interfering with some intricate camera movement.

Excerpt from Eric Portman, "The Film Actor," in Oswell Blakeston, ed., *Working for the Films* (London: Focal Press, 1947), 48–55.

Eric Portman (right) with Laurence Olivier in *Forty-ninth Parallel* (1941)

It has often struck me that women seem to be able to learn action-concentration for film work more easily than men. In studios the person who checks on and records the little details of routine is always a *continuity girl*. "No, Mr. X.," says the continuity writer without looking at her notes, "in the last scene you put the glass just here, and the siphon just there." But in films, whether it is a question of female star or male star, the function must be one hundred per cent concentration for the action—and the words.

On the stage an actor can be prompted, and the audience need never know that the actor has forgotten his lines. There can be no prompter during a film-take.

I would like you to think of a film scene as a sort of burning glass of concentration. I'm not exaggerating. You must remember that a film appears on the screen magnified to over life-size. In a close-up, the magnification may be forty times that of the living face. It is possible for a stage actor to think of other things while he says his lines. Especially if he is in the middle of a long run, a stage actor can plan in his mind his dinner at "The Ivy" while he talks to the heroine about the hunger of love. If he is a skilled actor, the audience need never lose conviction that the actor means what he is saying. But with the film actor, the merest flicker of inattention registers. All the actor's thoughts must be concentrated for the burning glass of the film scene.

Of course it is possible for a clever director to fake a bad screen actor into what seems to be a good performance. By expert cutting, by a very careful selection of exposed footage, it is possible, in certain limited cases, to make a woolly brained actor look as if he were getting down to business. But this is costly. I think we can agree that we want to talk about the good film actor, who can give the director what he wants without wasting time, and not the fake. For the fake, although he may have a short success, can never have a sustained one. His range is bound to be limited to what the cutter and the editor can do with him. After a few pictures, audiences tire of the illusion. Even a magician cannot build an evening's entertainment with one trick. Then, as soon as the box-office receipts fall, the fake is dropped. He is too expensive a trick. And there are plenty of genuine actors who can give audiences the variety they demand at a fraction of the production-cost of a puppet.

The fake probably got his chance because he was fantastically good looking. The novelty of his good looks was his fortune. When the novelty is spent, the missing qualities which do make a really successful film star become all too evident—I mean it isn't necessary to be good looking to be a film star. The thing you do need, if you want a career in lights and not just a meteor-flash, is the ability to arrest an audience.

It's hard to analyse this ability. It comes, I suppose, in part from sex motifs, and in part from the concentration, the professional touch of certainty, which the good actor gives to his performance. It isn't looks. It isn't the articulation of the voice, although the quality of the voice may have something to do with it. (And I would say, to those who wish to be film stars, that elocution classes are only useful if there is some defect to be corrected.) You can see a film in a foreign language, a language you do not understand, and yet be held by the performance of some of the actors. It isn't looks. It isn't the voice. It's *personality*.

I'm afraid that word has brought us back to where we started this attempt at analysis. Philosophers, biologists and psychoanalysts have all tried to define personality; but they haven't really been able to give us a workable formula of words. Perhaps the best definition is the old theatrical one of *audience-projection*. The actor with personality projects his inner force, he makes it leap across the footlights or from the screen. There is an actual psychic contact between the player and the spectator. It's a wonder, for those who have it, and a mystery.

In a rough way, I would say you can test your audience-projection in ordinary life. The next time you go into a crowded room, see if you can project your personality. See if people stop talking when you enter, look at you, rise quickly to give you a seat, a drink, a cigarette. But if we try to take the question of personality any further, we will land in mysticism. All I can say, in summing up, is that you should know if you've got personality from the reactions of your friends—and enemies.

So, personality can make you a film star. Whether you are a film actor or not, will depend on your histrionic talent. Obviously you must have some little talent for acting, if you are to avoid the fake class. Still, if you have only a little talent, and a lot of personality, you may succeed—as a type. This means you will always be cast for the same parts. Your film life will, then, not be a long one—longer than the fake's, for you will be able to give satisfaction to the production staff, but shorter than you might wish it to be. In fact the public will probably tire of you before the studio executives. The public has to be impressed by real acting before it will grant stars long life on the screen. Otherwise the favourite game is to make and break. . . .

My advice, then, to any young man or woman who wants to become a film star is—learn your business on the stage. Develop your acting talents. And the stage will also give you the self-assurance you need to face the camera and microphone. Believe me, it can be a terrifying encounter.

I know there are people who, because they are not interested in the stage as a career, think that their first move towards film stardom ought to be by way of crowd work in the film studios. Personally, I think this is a great mistake. Crowd work is an art of its own. You have to move in the crowd with the crowd. You have to learn to make yourself a background. The crowd artiste who is individual is a bad crowd artiste. The would-be star, who tries to get experience by way of the crowd, will be learning too many wrong lessons. He, or she, will be learning how to pass practically unnoticed by an audience. But the star—must arrest the audience's attention.

Without doubt, there have been exceptions: some crowd artistes have become stars. But I recommend stage training. Better to have a few weeks as a *stand-in* rather than years of extra work, if you want to get the feel of the studio and end up a top liner.

The stand-in is the man, or woman, who stands in the set in the position which will be occupied by the star, while the camera-man arranges his lights. But the stage trained actor will hardly need a stand-in experience. Part of his stage training will have been—self-assurance. . . .

. . . Film actors are very well treated in the studio. But, like all film workers, they have to work hard. The hours are generally from eight in the morning to seven at night. Six months of a film probably corresponds to about three years' run of a play in working hours. If I were a mathematician, I would try and give you that in terms of extra matinees.

So we come to the fact that cannot be shirked—the film star works. The gold is there, it glitters under the arc lights, but—the film star has to earn it.

Michael Redgrave Mask or Face

I held back from film-acting, for I could see that what one of them said was partly true: 'You only have to stand up straight and be able to talk the King's English for someone to *offer* you a film contract.' I remembered the advice from, oddly enough, a Hollywood director, George Cukor—a very shrewd observer: 'Don't go into films, kid, until they go on their knees to you.'

This advice and these persuasions I followed. I refused film tests—which only intrigued the producers more and caused my agent some embarrassment. I tried to explain to him that Edith Evans had done no film, Peggy Ashcroft only one or two, and Gielgud's attempts had not enhanced his great reputation. I told him that I couldn't learn to act by making films. . . .

. . . Having at last, in 1938, succumbed to the blandishments of Gainsborough Pictures (1928) Limited, I found from reading my papers that I was to be 'teamed' with a very popular actress who has since been described on occasions as 'the first lady of our screen.' This was somewhat alarming to both the lady and myself. We were first introduced at a Charity Film Ball in the Royal Albert Hall where we danced together and were photographed in a tight embrace which would suggest that, to say the least, we knew each other quite well. My first day's work consisted of a scene which was designed to show how boy meets girl and, as everybody who has ever seen films knows, boy must meet girl in a way that is unusual and, if possible, cute. The girl, a rich heiress stranded in a middle-European hotel, was arrogant enough to persuade the manager to turn the young man out of the room above because he, a student of folk music, and his companions were making far too much noise dancing in their room upstairs. The young man is evicted from his room and in revenge makes his way into that of the girl, announcing, with a degree of arrogance and bad taste which certainly caps

Excerpt from Michael Redgrave, *Mask or Face: Reflections in the Actor's Mirror* (New York: Theatre Arts Books, 1958), 124–142.

hers, that he is going to spend the night in her room. This beginning to my partnership with Margaret Lockwood, whom, as I've explained, I scarcely knew, may seem an amusing introduction. All the same it was not the ideal one for either of us. In the first place I immediately sensed the loss of that essential to good acting on the stage, the rapport between artists who have worked together for at least the rehearsal period. This is, from the actor's point of view, probably the gravest disadvantage of acting for the camera, for one is continually having to play important scenes with other actors with whom one has never played, possibly never even met. These scenes can sometimes be shot in a morning after a hurried introduction and there they are, inexorably, in the printed film. Often the other actor has not been given the advantage of reading the full script.

The next thing I found I had to learn in my first film was rather surprising to me, for I would have expected the very opposite. It is generally supposed that acting for the stage involves a number of artificial gestures and movements which the actors would not conceivably use in ordinary life. That is not quite so. In the theatre it is not only possible but essential for the actor to find a sequence of physical movements which—allowing for certain conventions such as raising the voice when playing up-stage—seems completely natural to him. Indeed, a break in the flow of his physical movements can disturb or even destroy the stage actor's sense of inner reality. A good director and good actors can so arrange the movement that the characters do not mask each other or make disturbing movements during each other's lines, and yet individually feel that each is in his right place. It is not all the same in front of the camera, where one is frequently obliged to stand much closer to one's partner than one would ever do in ordinary life, or balance one's voice to a more even level because the microphone cannot 'take' extreme changes of volume.

I was prepared, to some extent, for the rigid pattern imposed by the camera movement. What I was not prepared for was to find that I had to 'cheat' my movements and that the camera by being able to point in any direction does to some extent upset the audience's judgment of where things are when seen from a different angle, so that at each 'cut,' actors, furniture and even the set are subject to a series of 'cheats.'

Indeed the elaborate realism of a big film set is for the actor only persuasive at the first rehearsal of the first shot on that set, when it is unlit but, after all, complete. From that moment on, the set disintegrates until finally it is, probably, a mere corner, brightly lit in a forest of lamps and lighting apparatus. It is often difficult to get onto what remains of the set at all. It is hard for the actor, when he begins making films, to understand that whereas in one shot he, say, entered a room and could see another character waiting for him in a certain spot, he may be required to look somewhere else when the two characters come face to face in another shot.

I understand all that now, of course, and have adapted myself to it. But to this day I find on occasion the inflexibility of the cinema, which demands, for example, that if you have sat down on a certain word of a sentence you should sit down on precisely the same word in another take or from another angle, can produce a wooden effect. It will inhibit the actor until such time as, when he has done enough films, he has developed a technique of doing all those tricky little things such as hitting chalk marks, adjusting his gaze to just right or left of the lens and all the rest of the complicated artifice of film-making to the point where they become second nature. For, contrary to what you might expect one who is primarily a stage actor to say, I believe that in good acting there is a continual flow of improvisation, a little tributary stream to freshen, as it were, the main current in its set course.

In the early rehearsals of a stage play or a film the actor is to a large extent improvising, however carefully he may have studied the words and meaning of his part. These improvisations then have to be swiftly selected and notated until they are no longer strictly speaking improvised. But within this notated framework there must be a quality of the moment, an imaginative freshness each time the scene is played so that the actor feels that he is saying those very words or doing those very things for the very first time, every time. If I say that even the finest actors and actresses of the stage will admit that it is only from time to time that they satisfy themselves in this matter throughout a long stage rôle, how much more easy is it to understand that the film actor, conceiving and developing and constructing a long part over many months, usually out of continuity, jig-saw fashion, very seldom satisfies himself throughout even one morning—there is always some line, some move, some look, some little hesitation he feels he might have done better. Here he is often wrong. Occasionally perhaps, when we see a scene as finally 'cut,' we realise that extra emphasis here, or a lesser emphasis there, would have made it neater and clearer. But it is a common fault of film acting that we tend to suppose we must be expressing something or other through every foot of film. The actor can never be wholly unconscious of the effects he is making, but frequently his most telling moments are those when, as in life, he does nothing very much or reacts in exactly the opposite way to what we might expect.

Frequently certain moments of early 'takes' are altogether more plausible and effective than when, after repeated 'takes,' the actor has begun to 'set' his performance. As he begins to do this, consciously to polish little moments which grew out of improvisation, he tends to lose that first impetus which gave life to the scene. He sometimes begins to forget the situation, or to anticipate a climax. This anticipation of a climax is one of the commonest traps of the actor, either on the stage or screen. It is easier to avoid this pitfall on the screen, for the actor is not conscious of how the climax of the scene will shape—whereas on the stage the actor has heard it all through rehearsals and night after night.

This is all to do with that creative mood which must be found before real acting can begin. When it is found nothing seems an effort. Unless it is found everything is. Fortunately for actors who love acting with all their heart and soul and who do not secretly despise their craft this mood is at hand more or less at will.

I have learned nearly all of the little I know about film through my directors. From Hitchcock who directed my first film I learned to do as I was told and not to worry too much. Hitchcock, being the brilliant master of the technical side of his script that he is, knew that he could get a performance out of me by his own skill in cutting. He knew that mine was a very good part, that I was more or less the right type for it, that I was sufficiently trained to be able to rattle off my lines and that mercifully, since I was aware that not even the cleverest cameraman in the world could make me look like Robert Taylor, I was never particularly camera-conscious. But he also sensed that I thought the whole atmosphere of filming was, to say the least, uncongenial compared to that obtaining in the theatre where every night I was playing in a Chekhov play with John Gielgud, Peggy Ashcroft, Gwen Ffrăngçon-Davies, Alec Guinness and a completely remarkable cast. One of Hitchcock's tricks which he works on the psychology of the public is to cast actors against their type, a trick he has managed often with great success; he also uses shock tactics on actors and besides his famous practical jokes he likes to 'rib' his actors, believing, sometimes but not always correctly, that actors, who have an infinite capacity for taking praise, are jogged into a more awake state if humorously insulted. I well remember him saying 'Actors are cattle!' I can see now that he was trying to jolt me out of my unrealistic dislike of working conditions in the studios and what he thought was a romantic reverence for the theatre. *The Lady Vanishes* is considered by many people as vintage Hitchcock. I could never bring myself to see it until fifteen years later, in New York, where it is still frequently shown.

The method of my second director, Paul Czinner, was in most ways the complete reverse. He overwhelmed me with subtle praise in order to make me feel that I was a good enough actor to play opposite my adored Elisabeth Bergner. He further explained to me that whereas there was never time for what stage actors would call proper rehearsals, the camera was often able to catch the artist's emotions or reactions when these were still in their early, improvisatory stages. He printed all the takes, and there were usually a great many, of all the shots. 'Rushes' each day frequently ran for three quarters of an hour or more. He explained that by frequent close cutting and the selection of a look from one take, a line from another and a particular though perhaps quite irrelevant expression from the third, a performance was often very much richer than the actor felt it to be even in his 'best' take. He personally directed the editing of the film over many months, and no editing was begun until the shooting of the film was completed.

This of course is a very expensive method and has gone completely out of fashion. The tendency now is to use less 'cross-cutting' and a great number of tracking shots, and much work is done from 'dollies' and cranes. In a way this would seem to be preferable from the actor's point of view for it allows him to build up a scene, to know how he is going to make his effects more or less on his own. But some of these moving shots are extremely tricky for the technicians as well as for the actor and it is very galling for the actor to find that the take which he has felt to be unquestionably the best from the acting point of view has to be scrapped because someone fancies he could see a mike shadow. After a time the actor learns to be philosophical about this and to realise that it puts a further onus on him to be as good as he can be all the time. Nevertheless only very few actors can afford half way through a take which they know is not to their liking deliberately to 'dry' and compel the scene to be started again. Filming is, after all, an enormously expensive business and there are always too many film actors out of work. However, if it is permitted for the cameraman or the sound department to reject takes or whole scenes because they were not personally satisfied with the technical result, it should also be permitted to the actor to veto certain takes. The usual objection to this is that actors only look at themselves in the rushes anyway, and are quite incapable of judging the scene as a whole. There is some truth in that but in my opinion each department of the film industry does exactly the same thing and only concentrates on its own work. A mike shadow or a camera wobble seldom really disturb the public in a good scene.

It is perhaps from Carol Reed, with whom I made my third film and with whom I was to make two more, that I learned for the first time how intimate the relationship between actor and film director can be. Reed understands the actor's temperament perhaps as well as any director alive. The theatre and acting are in his blood and he is able, with infinite pains and care, to give the actor the feeling that everything is up to him and that all the director is doing is to make sure that he is being seen to his best advantage. A very warm and friendly feeling prevails, not only on the set, and the actor is encouraged to feel that he has also assisted in the preparation of the film. Indeed Reed frequently did ask my opinions and I think on several occasions adopted suggestions of mine. Such as when we were shooting *The Stars Look Down* in a narrow street of miners' cottages in Cumberland and I noticed a child sweeping up a puddle in the road with a determination in its face and a sensuous pleasure in every sweep of the broom. I do not remember now whether this decorative incident is in the finished film, for by the time the camera had to turn the child's mother had dressed her in her Sunday frock and put her hair in ribbons. I do remember Reed being infinitely tactful about this. He is enormously considerate of other people's feelings but underneath this gentle velvet glove is an iron will which eleven times out of ten will have its own way in the end. I find this entirely admirable.

Reed is one of those dedicated beings, the artist who is completely absorbed by his dream. He eats, drinks and sleeps cinema. You might hear him carrying on an eager conversation with a farmer, a chemist or a nuclear physicist but that would not mean he is even for a moment interested in farming, chemistry or nuclear physics. It would be more likely that he was studying the farmer's way of scratching his head to punctuate his conversation, the chemist's tone of voice or the particular physicist's calm way of letting drop horrendous statistics. He would not be purposely observing these. It is his habit. If he had nothing else to observe he would watch a flea. He has a very friendly and charming way of asking a lot of gentle questions and watching you as you give the answers with his big blue eyes as wide as a child's when listening to a story. The wide ingenuousness is almost too good to be true and his repeated exclamations of surprise or incredulity: 'Do you really?' 'That's fascinating!' 'How true!' would strike one as naïve to the point of absurdity if after a short time one did not become aware that these simple, direct questions are not so simple nor so direct as they seem. Unwittingly you have supplied him with an answer or clue to some quite different question. He would, I think, disclaim this and he seldom, I am sure, consciously lays traps. He is not an intellectual man and like most intuitive artists he mistrusts analysis. He is not startlingly original, nor particularly daring. Being schooled in the hard school of commercial cinema under such experts as the late Ted Black, and of success by his early master, Edgar Wallace, one of his big blue eyes always has at least an oblique squint in the direction of the box office. This, I would have you understand, is not intended as criticism of Reed's achievement. Some of the greatest and most daringly original artists are often considerable showmen. One has only to think of Picasso. And sometimes the best originality is the originality that conceals itself. Our commercial cinema which, to do it justice, is not so slow to take up and use bright new talents as some may think, either destroys them, swiftly rejects them or forces them to conform. An original cinema artist would prefer after all to conform to some extent and make films rather than cease to make films at all, though there are exceptions, such as von Stroheim. The tyranny of the 'boys in the front office' so brilliantly reported by Lillian Ross in her book *Picture* about the making and massacre of John Huston's *Red Badge of Courage* should be compulsory reading for armchair critics who do not realise that 'Art Cinema' is to some degree even in such countries as France and Italy, and to a much greater degree in the English-speaking countries, ineluctably geared to the statistics of the box-office and the distributing circuits.

This is the inherent and inevitable trap of dealing in a medium which is economically expensive. Korda once said to me: 'No actor is worth all the money your agent is asking.' My reply was that for that matter no film is intrinsically worth its cost. The cost and the ever increasing cost of film-making touches every member of the film industry. It has driven writers and directors to the streets and the open air where most of the true poetry of the cinema has been found. That has been good. But the cost of the box-office and the exhibitors' fondness for a 'predigested' diet have banished a brilliant, original mind like that of Cavalcanti back to his native Brazil, and they have hung round the neck of Orson Welles his own wanderlust till it has become a millstone.

Cavalcanti I miss most bitterly not only for the little we did together but for the much we planned to do.* In the 'Ventriloquist' sequence in *Dead of Night* we both felt that it was impossible to tell where direction or acting ended or began. This is, I must stress, ideal not only from the actor's point of view, but from every point of view. Ideally, there should be no line of demarcation between writer, actor and director, and the cameraman should be as sensitive to this phenomenon as his negative is to light and shadow. It is worth noting, in passing, that nearly all the best cameramen have this gentle, hypersensitive but co-operative and dependable nature.

This creative collaboration I have in varying degrees experienced a number of times and when it happens film-making becomes every bit as absorbing and exciting for the actor as the creation of a great rôle on the stage. There have been occasions, as when working with Orson Welles, even till 3:30 in the morning, when I have not wanted to stop. I had it also with Asquith, several times, especially in *The Browning Version*. With Reed again in *Kipps,* when we worked at Shepherds Bush throughout the 1940 blitz, when we were both living in flats in the same building, so that we could meet in the evenings and

*Cavalcanti is now working again in Europe.

talk; a time I remember above all because of its utter divorce from any reality except that of imaginative work. For to face the cameras each morning as a younger man than myself I was obliged to take heavy sleeping pills each night in order to sleep through the noise of the bombardment. No question then of retiring to a shelter. And there in the morning on the set would be Diana Wynyard, who often had to drive through the tail-end of the raid to have her hair washed and set and be made up and ready to appear by 8 o'clock, ravishingly gowned by Cecil Beaton and only a degree less beautiful then than she is now, several years later. In the evenings we left the studio ten minutes before blackout and as we drove home in the dusk the sirens would start. If they did not, I remember, we were faintly worried. No wonder that my memory of the blitz is largely a picture of a fictitious Folkestone in Edwardian dress.

I could ramble on at length about working with different types of director. I could tell you of working with Fritz Lang—one of the great names of the cinema, surely—who taught me what it is like to be caught up in the Holly-wood machine, working in a studio where your personal telephone calls are liable to be tapped. Lang would often ask me about working in England. It seemed to be the dream of most of the lively creative talents in Hollywood and New York in 1947. I urged him to come and direct Dylan Thomas' *The Doctor and the Devils,* which I had persuaded the Rank Organisation to buy for me—for Lang had shown by his first film for M.G.M., *Fury,* that he, like Renoir in his *Swamp Water* and *The Southerner,* could triumphantly absorb material which was not native to him. *The Doctor and the Devils,* which Dylan Thomas later published in script form, was one of many subjects I tried hard to get made about that time. I was told it was impossible because a 'B' picture with, I think, Boris Karloff, on the subject of the body-snatchers, had been made a year or two before.

The film I made in Hollywood with Lang—and which, by the way, I have never seen—had a silly story, pseudo-psychological and pretentious, but as Lang had just made two very successful and exciting pictures out of stories which seemed to me equally preposterous, I accepted it. I wanted to work with Lang. I thought I could learn something from him. I certainly learnt one thing, even if I did not know it already: that in ninety-nine cases out of a hundred, the creative germ of a picture is in its idea. With a good germinating idea and with the help of a good script, you have the best chance of making a good picture. I have often found, when people have asked me what my new picture is about, that if I can give them an answer in one or two sentences: 'It's about a ventriloquist who is obsessed by the idea that his dummy controls him'; 'It's about an elderly, embittered schoolmaster whose defences break down because someone is kind to him'; 'It's about an unsuccessful barrister who is given an almost impossible case, which nobody else will touch, and who wins it,' etc., their swift reaction of interest is a fair indication, if not a final one, of the film's popular appeal. Not all good pictures are subject to this reduction but if you have a germinating idea, the idea that may not only catch the imagination of the public, but which fires the minds of the writer, the director, the actors and everyone working on the picture, you are half-way there. Best of all, as I have heard Welles say, is to believe that each film you make will be a *great* picture. 'If you don't believe it will be *great* there's little chance of it being anything but just another picture.' He is right. And it is something one must believe, not just something one says.

Joseph L. Mankiewicz is a man who believes that. Here is one of the most talented men I have ever worked with. In common with all the finest directors he has, of course, the prerequisite: the gift of being able to tell his story through the lens. To this one may add scholarship and a wide erudition, a piercing judgment of character, and an intelligence which takes him swiftly to the heart of the matter. He has the curiosity of Reed, the culture of Asquith, the apparently inexhaustible vitality of Gene Kelly—with whom I worked in Paris on *The Happy Road* and was seldom happier. Mankiewicz also has the on the whole enviable, American quality of making life seem as if it were happening as he has ordered it to happen. When it does not, even his considerable patience has a hint of thunder in it. As a script-writer I would say he has few equals, as a producer the drive of a large locomotive, as a director he gets what he wants. Since he sometimes combines all three of these functions, as he did in *The Quiet American,* it is a good thing that he does not wish to be an actor as well.

Not only is he not an actor but he never could have been, for anyone with such positive beliefs and forceful opinions must be the least suggestible of men. An actor is nothing if not suggestible.

Mankiewicz never praises, except inadvertently or by implication. When an actor would occasionally ask, after a final take, if it was 'really all right' he would answer: 'I wouldn't print it if it wasn't.' I liked this myself, having formed a very high opinion of his critical faculties, but I noticed that he seldom tried to get more out of some actors than could be seen to be there and I wonder, knowing how insecure most actors can feel, whether an occasional pat on the back might not have produced something which would have surprised him. But there is no knowing whether he may not have done this by another method which is the most stimulating of all: to receive praise through a third person.

What is certain on this matter is that no praise at all can be as harmful as extravagant or faint praise if the actor thinks the director doesn't really care.

The trouble is, of course, that there are never enough germinating ideas around every week of the year to supply films that will fill all those thousands of cinemas, let alone the ravening maw of television. The director or the actor will be forced to accept ideas which do not immediately hit the jackpot of his imagination. There are many good ideas which seem intractable at first.

There are dozens of films which have been lifted out of the ordinary by men of talent. There is that script lying there on my table; why should that not be just such another? There are good germinating ideas which tumble into the wrong heads; a *trouvaille* of Henry James, who should have written *The Spanish Gardener*. There is also the rent to pay, or the children's school bills.

Albert Finney and Mary Ure
Talking About Acting

MARCORELLES. You've both acted for all three mediums—stage, screen and television. Which do you like best?

URE. Oh, the cinema! There's so much less in the way of outside distraction than there is in the theatre, and I find I get much more satisfaction out of cinema acting than from any kind of theatrical acting.

FINNEY. I really hate TV; I find that all distractions. But it's too early yet to say which of the others I prefer. My bit in *The Entertainer* only amounted to one night, and it was like a bad dream, really. I enjoyed doing *Saturday Night and Sunday Morning* very much, the whole process of working in the cinema. But I also like the breadth and the dimensional aspect of the theatre, the sense of space and time . . . What I don't enjoy is re-creating the same thing eight times a week during a long run. Then the problem becomes one of keeping it fresh rather than acting: one's just concerned with looking spontaneous. You can see yourself putting the same glass down in the same place at the same time four months from now. That's ridiculous! Actors should be able to play more than one part in a week.

*Excerpt from Louis Marcorelles, "Albert Finney and Mary Ure Talking About Acting," *Sight and Sound* 30, no. 2 (Spring 1961), 56–61, 102. Reprinted by permission.

Albert Finney (right) and Shirley Anne Field in *Saturday Night and Sunday Morning*
(1960)

MARCORELLES. Do you mind, when you're playing a screen part, having as it were to splice your acting together?

URE. Not at all. In fact it can be a good deal more difficult in the theatre. The cinema takes much more out of you because more concentration is put into one single thing. Say you're doing a very difficult scene—your husband has been shot, for instance, and you have to walk into the room and find him— then everything about you, from your brain and emotions to the way you speak, has to be tremendously concentrated. But I find that exciting.

MARCORELLES. Do you think film directors pay enough attention to the actor? Do they give you time to prepare your part and achieve the kind of concentration you want?

URE. I don't really think so. I've only done five films so far, and of course I don't know how they work in Europe. But I think the best thing would be to have a group of actors improvise round scenes, get to know each other, and then work the film through. That could be exciting.

FINNEY. Preparation's essential. Making a film involves such a long period of creation, and in theory at least the first day's shooting is intended to be part of

Mary Ure (center) with Dean Stockwell in *Sons and Lovers* (1960)

the finished film. So it's important, even on the first day, that you should all know what you're aiming at. Of course you're bound to find out more about the subject as you work, but the more preparation you can do beforehand the better it is for everyone.

URE. But you ought not to work on the scenes themselves. I'd like to work round them, to get to know how the other actors and the director work, to get a feeling of everybody's attitude to the film. If you work too hard on a scene, though, I find the vitality just goes—at least it does for me.

FINNEY. Well, it doesn't for me because I like to know just what I want to achieve with a scene. I want the dress rehearsal, if you like, of a shot in a film to be as perfect as possible technically, and then when we're actually shooting it I like to be able to forget that side altogether. But in filming they never seem to rehearse enough: they're not that interested, so they treat it as a sort of joke.

URE. But you can over-rehearse.

FINNEY. Well, of course. It's a question of balance: all art is, in any case. At the moment—I like to say at the moment, because I never know when my ideas may change—I believe very strongly in form. Improvisation can be dangerous, and I felt that about *Shadows*. After all, if you want to make a film about a certain subject you must also want certain things to emerge; and you can't just leave it to chance that those things are going to emerge in the right balance.

MARCORELLES. You get a good deal of improvisation in a film like Truffaut's *Tirez sur le Pianiste*. He wants his actors to show their characters through their nerves and their physical reactions as much as their dialogue, and he's not particularly strict about his text. What do you feel about this?

URE. I think it works. I felt *Tirez sur le Pianiste* was a remarkable personal statement, which every great film has to be; and it gave me the feeling of a progression in the cinema, some kind of advance.

FINNEY. I agree that Truffaut's feeling about his subject emerges very strongly, and of course this is what should happen. You ought to feel that the director is cajoling you, or bullying you, or seducing you into his attitude. At the same time, the conception of some of the performances seemed a bit untidy: they didn't communicate to me, and I felt that perhaps because of this freedom and improvisation they weren't always certain about just what they *meant* to communicate.

URE. But it was such a relief to find a film that didn't give you everything on a plate, all neatly worked out with a beginning and a middle and an end, and all technically perfect . . . You don't sense that Truffaut has a cameraman saying "You can't do *that;* it's too difficult," and a producer saying "You can't shoot *that;* it'll be too expensive." You feel he does exactly what he wants; and if we had more directors in England who were in love with their subjects, and who felt that they had this kind of personal freedom, I think our cinema would be a very different thing.

MARCORELLES. In fact Truffaut's film was shot entirely outside the studio, on a small budget and with complete freedom. I was there, for instance, when he did one of the scenes between Aznavour and Nicole Berger, and he was alone with just the two actors and the cameraman.

URE. Well, of course, that's wonderful. And it's an enormous help to be in a real location. When we were doing the last scene in *Look Back in Anger*—the scene at the railway station where I meet Jimmy Porter again—we shot it at four o'clock in the morning and we did it in a single take. We couldn't possibly have managed that in a studio, without the help we got from the atmosphere, the smoke and the rain and the way the station felt.

FINNEY. In *Saturday Night and Sunday Morning* I felt like that about the scenes where I was working at the lathe. I felt almost like a sculptor—working a real lathe, with real metal, and working it myself. It's wonderful for an actor to be able to pour his concentration into an actual object like this, until in a way it becomes part of him. I found that one of the most exciting things about filming.

MARCORELLES. I'd like here to bring in Brecht and the so-called Brechtian attitude, which means that you are very conscious about what you are doing and why you're doing it and also involves a certain sense of distance—the opposite, in a way, from Truffaut's method. Do you think this is just a matter of theory, or does it mean something for you in practical terms?

FINNEY. Well, I'm very consciously trying, as an actor, to keep myself free from theories. I'm very much concerned with the particular way I'm growing, with the way I think one thing one week and another thing next week. Of course I'm interested to read about theories, but I'm not too anxious to adopt them or become too engrossed in them . . . The process of the emotional and mental growth of a part ought to combine very closely with the technical growth, and if one wants to communicate a certain effect or feeling, one has got in rehearsals to try to find the clearest way to achieve that cleanly. If you can manage that sort of perfection in rehearsal, then when you actually get in front of an audience, or when the cameras are rolling, you can give it the breath of life in the actual performing of it.

URE. I agree that it's essential for an actor to have read widely about all kinds of theories, but it's just as important for him to be adaptable. He ought at a moment's notice to be able to work in a completely different way because that's what an exciting director wants him to do. Perhaps a Brechtian director doesn't believe there *is* any other way.

MARCORELLES. You believe more in the kind of chance happening which may come up during the actual shooting.

URE. Of course it's important to rehearse properly, to know what you're doing in a scene. But in the cinema—and this is one of the reasons why I find such excitement in films—there is always the chance that something in a shot may go slightly wrong; and in that case you need this little bit of freedom just to give something truly creative. Surely this chance thing is terribly important: some of the best things in the cinema have come about by chance.

FINNEY. But if something goes wrong and you have to cope, for want of a better word, you can cope in a way which is good for the film or one which is bad for the film. Even if I'd only dropped a cup and saucer, for instance, I'd like to feel that the way I pick it up would be influenced by the fact that I was in the right rhythm of the scene.

URE. All the same, we're tending rather to generalise. There are certain scenes about which a director can say "This is exactly how I want it done," and you can't do it any other way. On the other hand, he might say to you: "All right. You've got a glass of water; you are feeling ill; it's night and you are going into this room . . . and now do what you want." I find this exciting.

MARCORELLES. You seem to have a lot of faith in improvisation. Yet when I watched you play *Antigone* on the stage, for instance, I felt you were giving a very highly concentrated performance and that every night you must be acting at virtually the same pitch.

URE. Certainly, because everything was completely fixed as it had to be. But that didn't stop us from improvising in some of the early scenes; and the improvisation uncovered certain feelings and attitudes in the characters for us.

FINNEY. Well, that's the advantage of improvisation. There may be certain scenes which are so written that points don't emerge clearly during rehearsal and improvisation can help to release them. Then you can appreciate whatever it was that was missing, and you carry that in your head into the text.

MARCORELLES. You seem to want to be secure, to leave nothing to chance, and I notice that you talk about acting mainly in terms of rehearsal, while Mary believes more in details that may arise during shooting. It that right?

FINNEY. I think my job as an actor is to produce the effect, if you like, of improvisation in the final result. If improvisation seems more real than acting, it may be because people have been seeing such a lot of bad acting. And if actors look more spontaneous while they're improvising, perhaps it's because they are not very good actors . . . Acting is the craft of knowing exactly what you want to communicate and then making it spontaneous, making it seem just to happen. And you have to know exactly what second, I feel, is the best moment in a scene to put that cigarette out. But don't do it as though you were beating time, so that the audience can say "Oh yes, he's putting it out so that we'll realise he doesn't like her . . . " When you put life into it, everything should flow. That's our craft, and that is also why I insist on the danger of improvisation. I don't like to feel that what the audience might respond to is something I haven't really intended.

URE. But you do intend it, you see . . .

FINNEY. When you improvise? But you can't intend an accident.

URE. It's not an accident. I'm not talking about making a completely improvised film, and in any case I don't believe that is possible, and I wouldn't want to act in it. But sometimes a thing may happen when you do a scene for the first time which couldn't happen the third or fourth time.

FINNEY. That's our job: to be able in some way, on the fourth take or for that matter the eleventh take, to keep the life in it.

MARCORELLES. Do you feel there is any basic difference in attitudes to the cinema between actors of your generation and stage actors of an older generation—people like Sir John Gielgud, for instance, and Peggy Ashcroft?

FINNEY. I've always felt strongly about the fact that the cinema in England has been regarded as a kind of hobby. An old actor who came to see *Billy Liar* asked me if I'd enjoyed doing *Saturday Night.* I said, "Yes, very much," and he said, "Well, they're all right for the money . . . " Of course acting in the cinema and in the theatre amount to completely different crafts, although the process of acting is to a certain extent within oneself the same. And I find that I simply enjoy acting, whether it's in a room on my own, or on a stage or in a studio: I enjoy assuming an emotion, acting with other people. So I can't feel about the cinema that it's just a sort of hobby which pays a little extra on the side, while the theatre is the place where I do my real prestige work. I want to do my prestige work in the cinema as well; and I think this feeling is growing. But the cinema has always been a kind of club . . . a special place where the people are very nice, all the films are very nice, and nobody does any real work.

URE. I don't believe the cinema has ever been taken really seriously in England, as it has been in America or in Europe. And of course this affects the acting profession itself. There are too many people who are only interested in making some kind of product which will sell.

MARCORELLES. Do you think films might be made more cheaply? Can you imagine, for instance, working on some sort of co-operative basis yourselves?

FINNEY. Yes, but it would be difficult. *Saturday Night* was quite a cheap film, for instance, but it still cost about £120,000. You can't make films as cheaply as they do in France. The unions come in here, though perhaps it might do them more good if they could relax their regulations now and again. Some remarkable films might get made which would give the whole cinema a boost, and would then give their own jobs a boost. But this seems part of a whole attitude towards the cinema . . . You know, you're going to do a little picture which will take four months, and perhaps you get £5,000 for that. Now that one's gone: well, I'll take a month's holiday, then I'll do another picture for four months. And that's got rid of another nine months of my life without any trouble.

URE. All the same, it's difficult to make good films cheaply: I think *Saturday Night and Sunday Morning* was made about as cheaply as any good film could be in this country.

MARCORELLES. What is your feeling about the star system? After all, some of the best actors in Hollywood are British, and some of them only became stars after they went to America.

FINNEY. I don't give a damn whether I'm a star or not. It's splendid to have money because then you needn't think about it, and that's a great advantage. But I just want to have a go . . . to act, and to mean what I say, whether it's said jokingly or seriously. If I should incidentally become a star—well, all right, I'll be a star as well.

URE. There are very few real stars anyhow: you can almost count them on one hand. But it's very difficult for a young actor in this country to organise his career properly, and it's becoming even more so. When I was twenty-one I signed a film contract with Alexander Korda and he had complete script approval. Last year, in Hollywood, I was offered a film contract—one film a year, for an enormous amount of money—but it wouldn't have given me script approval. It makes it very difficult—what can you be put into?

MARCORELLES. Previously you seem to have had leading English stage actors who once in a while did a character part on the screen, and film actors who were prepared to become involved in the star-building machinery. Do you think there is a new attitude, that actors want a greater measure of responsibility?

URE. I don't think so. You may say that Albert feels more responsible, but you can't say this about all actors: you can't really generalise at all.

FINNEY. I don't think it has much to do with feeling responsible. But I am concerned to learn about acting in both mediums, while I'm not particularly aiming at becoming a star. For instance, although I don't yet know what my next film will be, I do know that I want the character I play to be someone very different from Arthur Seaton in *Saturday Night*. I don't want to cash in on what Arthur's done for me, whether audiences have hated him or loved him . . . I hate that kind of idolising of a performance because it seems to stand for certain things, so I want those people who are going to idolise me for the wrong reasons to get a surprise.

URE. But you're going to find it very difficult. The strange thing, when someone has a really great success in a role here, is the amount of time the public takes to come round. Unless the actor comes along with something completely different, and as soon as possible, they go on identifying him with that character.

FINNEY. I suppose, in a way, I could go on playing Arthur Seatons for ten years—I'd go mad!

MARCORELLES. What do you feel about the importance of a classical train-ing, particularly in relation to your screen acting?

URE. It's important for an actor to have had a very varied background—

classics, modern plays, verse, everything. All experience is a help in the cinema.

FINNEY. A classical training is terribly important. I was at Stratford for nine months in 1959, doing Shakespeare, and I was very uncomfortable, I found that for the first time I didn't really enjoy acting. But the whole way one responds to a Shakespearean text, to the costumes and the size and conception, is quite different from the way one responds to a modern or a Restoration play.

. . .

MARCORELLES. What are your feelings about the actor's relationship with the audience? Do you find it a satisfactory one?

FINNEY. . . . One difference between the theatre and the cinema, I feel, is that in the theatre our job must be direct, instantaneous communication: the audience must feel that we *want* them to sit there, that we *want* to say this to them and we *want* to be sure they understand it. They've got to feel that it's all happening for them now, this minute, with a real sense of sharing.

. . .

URE. Maybe I'm not really a theatre actress, because I don't have this feeling of wanting tremendously to communicate with an audience . . . The actor I'm working with is more important, and it's what I say to *him* and what I have to do with *him* that really counts as far as I'm concerned. In fact, I find that the most irritating thing in the theatre can be interruptions from the audience— somebody coughs, someone drops a tea-tray—which completely destroy the rhythm of a scene. And what I find marvellous about the cinema is that you get this intense concentration. All the technicians, everyone around, is interested, you have just those few minutes to bring the scene off, and everything is concentrated right down on to the minute.

. . .

MARCORELLES. You seem in any case, Albert, to be more interested in the theatre.

FINNEY. No, I was talking basically about the actor's communication with his audience in the theatre. His communication in the cinema is quite a different thing. There it's channeled through the director: the way the director looks at the actor is the way the audience is going to look at him.

URE. Well, I'm, afraid that I like a wonderfully creative director and I like to play the scene to him . . . If you are going to be serious in the cinema, I think it's essential at the beginning that you should have classical training and theatre experience. But if tomorrow someone told me that I'd never work on the stage again, but that I was going to make fascinating, exciting films, each part different, then I'd say *that* is what I want to do. It would never happen, though, because this isn't something that happens in England.

. . .

MARCORELLES. When you're acting in certain plays, you speak a kind of theatre English. In the cinema you use different intonations, and you are bound in a way to be more realistic. Can you switch easily from one to another?

URE. I can't separate the two, because basically one wants to be realistic in the theatre as well. It's the degree of intensity.

FINNEY. Realism and truth can be two inches in diameter, but they can also be a foot . . . It's fascinating, anyhow, this business of accents—working on a different accent. It's really a great advantage, though it's usually treated as a disadvantage.

MARCORELLES. You agree, I think, on one final point: that actors must play a creative part in the making of a film.

FINNEY. After all, the people whose faces are on the screen or the stage when the audience is there *are* the actors. And if, during the time he's rehearsing, the actor doesn't feel that what he's doing is right, somehow that is going to affect the moment when the audience sees him. He mustn't be pampered, and of course he must be directed. But he should be able to act from the strength of saying "Well, they're going to be seeing me, so . . . "

MARCORELLES. Some film-makers—Bresson, for instance, or Antonioni—take the view that actors should be used. They want to play on their nerves and emotions, but they don't want the actor to have any real say in the creative process.

FINNEY. Well, quite a lot of actors don't think! And as long as they employ them and not me, that's fine.

Laurence Olivier On Acting

I have always been an actor who moulds characteristics to hide my personality. I take parts of
the character *into* myself—not on to, otherwise
they'd fall off. I do not search the character for
parts that are already in me, but go out and find
the real personality I feel the author created. I
work all this out before I begin to rehearse the part and build the role up from
within, knowing that the camera will expose me if I am not true, if my
imagination is askew or only at half power; if I am doing anything unreal. I
make use of my natural talents and make sure that I do not waste other
people's time on the set. . . .

I went to one of Lee Strasberg's New York classes once and saw him
bullying a boy who I saw had a good feel for character. 'He's got so many
faults,' Lee said, and went off into a lot of hot air, sprinkled with clichés. 'The
only fault he's got is the confidence you are draining from him,' I said, or
words, I hope, to that effect. Probably more pompous because I was angry.
No doubt Strasberg thought English actors knew nothing of Stanislavsky,
but we had all read him avidly when his books came out. Some of us—
misunderstanding him—even used to come in an hour earlier and smell the
furniture on the set. He was no high-falutin' phoney, he was an intensely
practical man in the Wyler mould. By all means have Stanislavsky with you in
your study or in your limousine or wherever you are three hours before the
scene, but don't bring him on to the film set, where the schedule is tight and
the time is ripe for fizzing action to carry along the story. . . .

Film acting taught me to have sincere eyes on stage. There's no point in
exaggerating your eyes in the theatre because they only reach the first five
rows of the stalls anyway, and there's a danger they'll become detached and
flash to and fro across the footlights like coiled china eyes worn by clowns at
children's parties. Archie Rice had to have flashing music-hall eyes, which
were dead underneath, and we achieved that much better on film. (Full circle
from the passion I finally achieved in Heathcliff's eyes by ridding myself of the
habits of the stage.) As with Richard III, the camera relished the intimate parts
of Archie—and John Osborne wrote some more scenes to give the film of *The
Entertainer* what it wanted, craved: more emotion. I think the film allowed

Excerpt from Laurence Olivier, *On Acting* (London: Weidenfeld and Nicolson, 1986),
214–220. Used by permission.

John to show more of Archie Rice. I tuned up my stage performance, often changed it. I looked to the subtlety, the expressiveness, the reality of his mannerisms and accent (based on music-hall chums I'd lived with in theatrical digs, and artistes I'd seen in my youth), rehearsed the cheap music-hall flickers and flutters for the surfaces of the eyes, and made him dance expressively (at almost full theatrical throttle) and badly—which I achieved by dancing as well as I could! And the camera caught the deadness behind the eyes. Archie Rice was a hollow man. We are the hollow men. I felt Archie's hollow mood because that's what the camera wanted. Or was I feeling middle-age disillusion at the time? I am not a hollow man, but I know what it feels like to be one! . . .

. . . For the first and last time I was able to cry tears on the screen, in the scene when Archie hears that his son's all right as his mistress is washing after fornication. I don't quite know how it happened. Relief at the news of the son. Maybe the challenge that a cheap music-hall artist would have the versatility to cry to order. . . .

Several theatre productions of mine were made into films, including *Uncle Vanya,* a play with which I had great success at the Chichester Festival Theatre; and *The Three Sisters,* based on a beautiful production from the National with a marvellous cast. It was a celebration of the acting rather than a thoroughly conceived filmic version of the play. That would have been a mammoth task for which we had neither time nor money.

I had a couple of 'visual' sequences, such as Irina's dream of a better future in Moscow, and the camera seemed to like Chekhov's dialogue and his shifts of mood. I had little to do with the screenplay, which made it not-a-director's film in my book. All encouragement to the film man who will tackle Chekhov wholeheartedly. He could have much reward. Too wordy, maybe, but I've a feeling that as we go further into high tech, cassettes and private entertainment, people will have a yearning for more words. Especially if conversation dies. . . .

Fundamentally, I think, television is a more 'hearing' and 'listening to' medium than the cinema, where the picture is bigger and the eyes can wander only to darkness. So you can use more words, more details in characterization, you can give a more intimate performance. Startling effects are permissible if you've got the audience in the mood for them. You can sustain emotional effects for long periods, with relatively bare settings. . . . I found that the medium can take any play, any performance, provided—yes, back to it!—the feeling is right. I can do anything if I am prepared. I can look the littlest man in the world if I am *ready.* I could play so little, you wouldn't recognize me. But it takes time. Get your integrity together and you'll integrate with the medium.

Acting and Ideology: The Soviets

An acute awareness of their own place in history marks the accounts of actors who lived through the Russian Revolution and the Stalinist period. It may seem striking that actors from both the former Soviet Union and Great Britain should have shown interest in putting film into historical context, yet it is hardly surprising that such interest produced very different results in the two nations. Almost from the moment V. I. Lenin nationalized the film industry in 1919, Soviet actors set about imagining the qualities of a mass culture that might be realized through film. Soviet actors also showed themselves more willing than those in other nations to celebrate the mechanical effects of filmmaking on their work, and to idealize the social and professional leveling that might attend their labor in a mechanized medium. Accordingly, discussions centering on the mechanization of films figure everywhere in this section.

Among nations that have spawned their own filmic traditions, the Soviet Union may have been influenced perhaps more heavily than any other by contemporaneous political events. Mechanization often took pride of place because it upheld the aim of the Soviet regime to industrialize a relatively backward nation. Part of the appeal that machines and their capabilities held for Soviet artists came from the conviction they shared that a new art, conceived in precise, scientific terms, could redeem the suffering of the tsarist past. Many believed that mechanization would lend art a utility it had lacked and exposed much larger numbers of people to it. In this connection, because film was duplicable, it lent itself to utopian visions of the possibilities for the broader dissemination and more egalitarian consumption of art.

The noted Soviet director Sergei M. Eisenstein formulated a theory of filmic montage that stressed the power of the director to create meaning by composing and juxtaposing disparate images. When he did this, he was responding in part to conditions of scarcity in the Soviet Union and the simple necessity to use every scrap of raw film. Eisenstein contended that mechanical means could enhance the power of film not only through the workings of the camera but also in the ways images were manipulated once they had been recorded on film. He derived these notions from the work of his own teacher, Vsevolod Meyerhold, whose theory of biomechanics treated the human body as raw material for visual composition on the stage. Actors' bodies, Meyerhold believed, could be isolated, molded, and then joined with other visual elements onstage in modular and machinelike ways. This element of Meyerhold's practice anticipated and helped bring about the theories of filmic montage hatched only a few years later by Eisenstein.

Konstantin Stanislavsky, though he had been Meyerhold's early teacher and later collaborator, was relatively little interested in mechanical models. His notions of acting drew heavily on individual identity and organic metaphors, and so they stood in tension with the ideology of the Soviet state in its earliest stages—although they fell more easily in line with Stalin's imposition of socialist realism as time went on. Unlike their American successors in the 1950s, early Soviet film actors believed Stanislavsky's teachings needed to be either updated or amended.

A revolutionary attitude toward acting manifests itself in the account of Nikolai K. Cherkasov, who commenced his film career during the heady years just before Stalin came to power. Cherkasov was fascinated by the logistical complexity inherent in film work, and he argues that any distractions actors might feel on film sets or locations must be overcome in the interest of serving collective goals. He believed that watching daily rushes enabled him to criticize and alter his own performance as it unfolded and so helped him to direct himself. In this he restates the view of his contemporary (if far from ideological fellow or compatriot) Lionel Barrymore, though Cherkasov worked in contexts far removed from the rampant commercialism of Hollywood, where Barrymore lived and worked for many years.

Cherkasov's emphasis on film actors' critical capacities implies his willingness to challenge Stanislavsky's notion of the largely subjective identification between actors and the characters they play best. At the same time, Cherkasov struggles to reconcile the sort of actorly inspiration Stanislavsky idealized with the mechanical workings of the camera, and indeed with the entire process of editing and production. Cherkasov views the tension between the imaginative and material demands of filmmaking as constructive, and his writing suggests the pervasive influence of dialectical models in theories of art that originated in the Soviet Union.

Vsevolod Pudovkin's experience of acting accords more with reactions against artistic formalism, including filmic montage and mechanized images of the body, that prevailed during the Stalinist period. As Stalin and his minions enforced socialist realism, Soviet esthetics shifted away from the previous interest in the transformational qualities implicit in actors' images subjected to montage. Reacting to such pressures, Eisenstein largely abandoned practical filmmaking and retreated into academic life, as Stanislavsky's theories proportionately gained influence.

In line with this reactionary tendency, Pudovkin attempted to apply Stanislavsky's theories directly to film. He viewed montage not as tension, but as synthesis and reconciliation. As a result, the acting he describes seems more relaxed than that suggested by Cherkasov and more consistent with Stanislavsky's interest in eliminating tension from the actor's work, or at least calibrating it in relation to the character's state of mind from moment to moment. Tension for Pudovkin does not inhere in the processes of filmmaking, as it did for Cherkasov, but in the emotional life of the character: Stanislavsky's theory of a "through-line of action" is thus rendered more necessary by virtue of the actor's having to adjust to continual narrative lapses from the shooting sequence.

Michael Chekhov left the Soviet Union in the late 1920s, driven into exile by the growing climate of repression. Years later, then, shortly after viewing Eisenstein's long-delayed *Ivan the Terrible,* Chekhov derogated the effects of montage on actors, especially when it worked to subordinate the spoken word. Whereas Stanislavsky and Pudovkin advocated actorly restraint, Chekhov postulates size, boldness, and clarity of characterization as worthy goals for actors in any medium. As an acting coach in Hollywood, Chekhov had the chance to witness the sort of restraint invoked in accounts as early as Mae Marsh's in 1921; but he showed little interest in this model and suggested that film acting could be as energetic and extravagant as anything conceived for the stage.

Like many other Europeans, Chekhov was interested in playing characters drawn from remote historical periods, and he dwells on the capacity of "atmosphere" to help actors transpose themselves into another place and time. Like Cherkasov, Chekhov celebrates acting in its transformational capacities, for which historical material offers only one means of expression. And like the writers on acting who remained in the Soviet Union, Chekhov exhorts actors to consider whatever social world their character may inhabit as central to the process of characterization. In this way, he believes, actors can best uphold their professional responsibility not only to the screenplay, but to the audience that will watch them on the screen. Chekhov's advice runs counter to the spirit of artistic individualism that has often characterized Stanislavsky's adherents in the United States; instead, it places actors' efforts at the very heart of filmmaking as a communal endeavor.

Nikolai K. Cherkasov Notes of a Soviet Actor

The Screen Actor's Technique

Film work makes it possible for the actor to watch himself on the screen and note the places that are flat. When the director tells the actor that he has made a mess of something, he needn't take the director's word for it but should see for himself when the scene is run off for him.

Working in films also enables the actor to get a very complete picture of his looks: neither photographs nor the closest scrutiny in the mirror can compare with the screen in this respect.

But the actor's first meeting with himself on the screen is generally very disappointing. He is surprised to find that his figure and face at certain angles are far from attractive. Most discouraging of all is that he often does not recognize his own voice.

When I first saw myself on the screen I was horrified to find how tall and thin I looked. Nor had I previously suspected that my physical assets ran so low. This feeling of keen disappointment lingered for a long time until I finally grew accustomed to seeing myself as I really was. To this day every time I see my films run off I can't help virtually ogling myself, eager not to miss any let-downs, actual and imaginary, so that I may avoid them the next time.

On the lot the director often asks the actor, "How are you going to do this bit, how are you going to walk up to the camera, how will you make your exit?" In the theatre, on the other hand, the question is always, "What are you going to do?" In film-making the question "What are you going to do?" arises at the very first rehearsals at which the script, the picture as a whole, and the movement and action of certain scenes are discussed. At these early rehearsals the actor already should have a clear idea of "what he must do." When scenes are run through before the camera the actor gives all his attention to the question "How am I going to do this bit?"

Thus when he steps in front of the camera the actor must be ready to do exactly what is required of him and what has been decided upon at the rehearsals. The success of a scene depends on many elements apart from the acting—lighting effects, compositional arrangement, etc. The actor must keep this in mind, get his bearings, avoid the slightest movement or gesture that has

Excerpt from Nikolai K. Cherkasov, *Notes of a Soviet Actor* (Moscow: Foreign Languages Publishing House, 1957), 162–178. Trans. G. Ivanov-Mumjiev and S. Rosenberg.

Nikolai K. Cherkasov (left) in *Ivan the Terrible,* part 2 (1946)

not been rehearsed, otherwise he runs the risk of going beyond the camera lines, getting part of his head or hand out of the picture and spoiling the whole scene. Of course minor digressions from what had been decided at previous rehearsals may be quite legitimate from the actor's point of view, may even lend greater emotional value to the scene, but they must not be indulged in to the detriment of the technical plan of the scene worked out jointly by the director and cameraman.

Stanislavsky teaches that muscular tension must correspond to the emotional state of the actor. In films the actor cannot always keep to this golden rule, particularly in sequences where close-ups are intermingled with long shots, and where compositional elements must be given much attention. Here the emotional mood of the moment must be sacrificed to the general emotional reality of the whole scene which the audiences will see when the film has been edited and cut.

Long shots, particularly when they are intermingled with close-ups, require special training. When approaching the camera for a close-up from a distance, the actor must time his movements so as to know exactly where to pause. A mistake of ten inches one way or the other may put the whole scene out of focus and wreck it.

Certain scenes can be "pointed up" in the film medium so that a single movement, a single word may reveal depths of meaning. This reminds me of a scene I did in *Peter I* in which Tsarevich Alexei, learning that his father is seriously ill, weighs with the nobles the possibilities of the tsar's recovery. Suddenly the door is flung open, and Menshikov appears. Alexei rises from his seat, approaches him and anxiously asks: "Dead?"

When we were shooting this scene the camera was stationed at the door through which Menshikov enters, filming first what he saw in the room. As Tsarevich Alexei I walked up to the camera, stopped short at a fixed distance away and, looking a little to the right, had to convey to the audience that I had caught sight of Menshikov. And in the one word "dead" I had to express my innermost thoughts which actually ran something like this: "I believe you come with happy tidings. You come to tell me that my father, that monster of cruelty, is dead, and that at long last I shall ascend the throne! That is what you come to tell me, isn't it?"

After countless rehearsals I succeeded in doing what was expected of me more or less well. The scene was shot three times, then a fourth time with new hints and suggestions from the director and cameraman. At the fourth retake, when I finally came to the word "dead," I felt so fagged out I lost my bearings, stumbled over the word and spoiled the scene.

Hence, too many rehearsals and too many retakes of highly emotional scenes so overtax the actor that he loses control over himself and even forgets his lines. I remember one well-known actor stumbling twice over his lines because of the strain of too many rehearsals.

I have cited these examples to show how important it is for the actor to keep absolutely cool and controlled on the lot no matter how many times he may be asked to redo the scene and repeat his lines. It is very seldom that a scene does not require several retakes. . . .

It is wrong to think that an actor *lives* the emotions he portrays. If he did he would probably land in a lunatic asylum after the first few performances. As Ivan the Terrible I grieved through ten or twelve takes (not counting the rehearsals) over the illness and death of the tsarina. Playing the part of Tsar Ivan on the stage in *The Great Tsar,* I kill Tsarevich Ivan, my beloved son by my marriage to Tsarina Anastasya, no less than three hundred times (again minus the rehearsals). It is not difficult to imagine what would have happened if I had *lived* these scenes. Actually the actor does not live the emotions he portrays, whether it be great grief, despair, happiness or ecstasy. He only *seems* to live them. We are in a creative state when we act. This state plus our talent and professional knowledge make it possible for us to *create* emotions and to make our audiences really believe that we *live* them. Hence, the actor's emotions are *created* and do not affect his nervous system.

On the other hand, the very process of creating or re-creating feelings on the stage or in films requires great emotional strain and over-taxes the nervous system. For this reason, perhaps, over-sensitiveness is common among the acting profession. Sometimes in following the script the actor is called upon to do things injurious to his health and nerves, and to repeat them many times. There may be scenes and retakes of scenes in which the actor gets water poured over him or in which he must eat, drink and smoke to excess. A scene requiring of the actor to smoke may seem harmless enough. But when there are many retakes he gets an overdose of nicotine that almost knocks him out, and, of course, neither his physical state nor his nerves are any the better for it. . . .

There is a popular belief that actors pose off stage or screen. This is an accusation for which there are no grounds. In pre-revolutionary times the actor who played the "irresistible lover" may have tried to look and act the part in real life, dressing and behaving in a fashion that would attract attention. I believe that such exhibitionism is beneath an actor's calling and intellectual pursuits. Besides, indulging in one's histrionic gifts off stage or screen means unnecessarily spending oneself. The actor should preserve every surge of artistic talent and inspiration for the moment when the curtain rises or when he must step in front of the camera.

Versatility in the human character is limitless. There are all kinds of people, good and bad, brave and cowardly, clever and stupid, handsome and plain, healthy and ill, cheerful and morose, old and young, frank and reserved, open-hearted and treacherous. The formative factors in human character are many. They are background, environment, education, labour habits, social conditions, trade or profession.

I have played people from all walks of life on the stage and screen—factory workers, peasants, soldiers, sailors, army and navy officers, eminent scientists, writers, statesmen and royal personages. A man's station in life, calling or profession certainly leave[s] a stamp on his personality. This the actor must bear well in mind. And the actor should study carefully just how his character's profession affects his personality, habits, his views and his outlook on the future.

It is not necessary, however, to go to extremes. When we were making *Alexander Popov,* one of the assistant directors suggested that I would be more convincing if I learned the Morse code and knew how to assemble a radio set.

Then one might as well have recommended to Konstantin Skorobogatov who played Pirogov, the father of Russian surgery, to dissect rabbits and cats so that he would look more convincing as a surgeon. Of course, for the actor to occupy himself in any such manner is entirely superfluous. Yet the actor who plays a surgeon must know how to hold the scalpel if the action calls for its use. More often than not the actor must study the professional habits of the man he plays. . . .

In silent pictures much store was set on scouting for types, on photogenic qualities and on the cutting process. Shrewd handling of this process helped the director out of many difficulties, particularly when the acting of non-professionals fell short of expectations.

But in talking pictures it is the gifted professional actor who holds undisputed sway. Non-professionals are now taken on only when strongly marked types are needed for minor episodes. But this is a practice which is becoming less and less common because film directors often have difficulty in teaching non-professional extras to act. . . .

In silent films the actor was a far less important figure than he is today. Abundant cutting and editing minimized his role. Close-ups as a rule were left to the end. For these the actor changed his attire, make-up and even the expression of his face. When an actress had to be shown with tears rolling down her cheeks, an onion would be brought close to her eyes or she would smell spirits of ammonia or drops of glycerine would be squeezed out of a tube on her face. Sad music also helped. In sound films, where the importance of the actor has grown immensely, the problem of realistic portrayal has acquired greater significance. Screen acting now requires of the players to be so deeply emotional as to be able to shed real tears. Of course, "genuine" though the players' tears may be, they are not the same as those in real life. A player's tears are merely the result of the ability to capture an emotional state. . . .

Screen art—an art with its own rules and principles which must be thoroughly understood and assimilated by the actor—offers immense opportunities. The spectator sees on the screen what he may never see in real life— Nature's innermost secrets, the latest scientific discoveries, life in all parts of the globe. But the prime mission of film art is to show ordinary people and what they live and struggle for, to portray their feelings and aspirations, their thirst for happiness.

The Actor and the Cameraman

A close creative bond exists between the cameraman and the cast. Actors know full well how much they depend for their success on the cameraman's work. The actor begins to cooperate with the cameraman at the very first tests. The latter is able to tell at once from what angle the actor can be photographed to the best advantage. And it is on the basis of the cameraman's test shots that the question is decided whether or not the actor fits the part.

I have had the good fortune to work with some of our best cameramen who have contributed much to the advancement of their art. And they have helped me greatly in my characterizations.

When the actor performs in a scene at such a distance from the camera which enables him to come into personal contact with his partner he feels quite at ease. It is then very much like being on the stage, and the problems set before him by the director and the cameraman present no difficulty whatever.

A shift to medium shots makes it necessary for the actor to come much closer to the camera. Sometimes the cameraman wishes to rearrange the scene and tells the actor to turn his face to the left or right. The actor then does not see his partner, and carrying on a dialogue with an invisible partner is no easy matter.

Most difficult for the actor are close-ups with dialogues. Here, too, he does not see his partner. He is told to look at a certain point in the camera or off it and imagine that point to be the eyes of the person he is speaking to. It is a great strain for the actor to imagine how the partner he does not see reacts to his words. The cues are generally given by the director who, for technical reasons, cannot always take up the position from which the actor's partner is supposed to speak. And it confuses the actor to get cues from a position he least expects. On the screen, after the cutting process, the scene is so presented that the impression of a perfect dialogue, a give-and-take in thought and movement, is unmarred.

In close-ups the actor often has to take up a very uncomfortable position and remain in it for some time. This happened when we were shooting the scene from *Ivan the Terrible* showing the tsar at the coffin of his dead wife. Eisenstein and cameraman Andrei Moskvin suggested that I get behind the coffin in which the tsarina lay, look at her and speak the line, "Am I right?" Getting no answer I was to lower my head and touch the edge of the oak coffin with my forehead. I thought their suggestion of how the scene should be played interesting and began working on it at once. But we were so cramped for space after I had changed my position to the back of the coffin that the settings were in my way. To move or reconstruct them would have meant spending extra time and money which we could not afford. And so I had to rehearse the scene over and over again and act before the camera with my body in a most uncomfortable position. This, of course, interfered with my acting and made it difficult for me to keep in the emotional state of my character. . . .

It is the cameraman who gets the first look at the scenes when they are run off. And when he reappears on the set from the projection room a silence falls, with all eyes expectantly turned towards him. As a rule he does not break the silence but goes up to the director, takes him by the arm, and the two walk off into the next room. When they return, they share their impressions with the cast, after which the whole company troops to the projection room to see the scenes. The director and cameraman make their selection of what they think is the best take. Preference should be given to the first, in which acting is always more natural. In retakes, on the other hand, the actor is liable to concentrate too much on the technical directions given to him. And what the scene gains in technical effect it may lose in creative inspiration. . . .

The actor should never judge by the first few scenes whether or not the film will be a success. Nor do a few brilliantly photographed shots in any way indicate what the final result on the screen is likely to be. Separate scenes may call forth admiration but the whole picture after the cutting process may prove to be dull and fall sadly short of artistic expectations. Often it happens that the first flashes seem flat and uninteresting but clever editing and direction may result in a splendid picture.

When the silent pictures gave way to sound films, another important figure appeared on the lot—the sound engineer. Like the cameraman, he is a creative artist. He blends and mixes the sounds that make up the tonal quality of the picture. He helps the actor to "point up" what is best in the volume and quality of his voice. And the factor of tone is a very important one in pictures.

It is the work of the sound engineer to bring to the screen not only the dialogue of the story but the most complicated sounds—from nature's faintest whisperings to the stirring bars of a symphony orchestra. . . .

Soviet films have an important message to carry to the public. The cameraman and the sound engineer have penetrated into all the technical mysteries of film production in close cooperation with the director and the cast. The acting of the cast, the arrangement of mass scenes, the settings, the fine outdoor scenes and even small "props" breathing "period" and "atmosphere"—all these the cameraman and sound engineer weave into the emotional pattern of the picture.

Vsevolod Pudovkin Stanislavsky's System in the Cinema

Stanislavsky's aim was to create a realistic theatre. All his artistic conceptions, the whole of his
intuition, were applied to breaking away from
the hackneyed theatrical technique and to finding such lines for the actor's work as would
always make the theatre a vivid reflection of real life. To attain this, Stanislavsky began by applying the full power of his creative analysis to a careful
study of the basic principles for an artist's work on his part, and on himself, in
the process of creating a stage character.

Though before Stanislavsky's time others had tackled similar problems,
the majority had been content either to depict personal emotions or to formu-
late general principles of a poetic rather than scientific character. Stanislavsky
never rejected what had been done before his time, but he succeeded in
showing that the achievements of exceptionally gifted individuals were merely
isolated victories of outstanding talent, and not the result of a proper training
of the artists. Stanislavsky's great merit lies in the fact that the results of his
theatrical analysis, scrupulously verified by experiment, have produced a
number of objective principles which can serve every actor and every producer as a basis for methodical and fruitful work, irrespective of their individual temperament or talent. By collecting and analysing examples of outstanding acting, Stanislavsky sought to reveal the essence and the causes of
individual success, and thus discover objective rules suitable for a systematic
training of actors in general.

The cinema, which is closely linked both with theatrical art and with
literature and the graphic arts, has naturally adopted the basic principles of
Stanislavsky's school and continues to develop them successfully.

Although Stanislavsky did not directly concern himself with the cinema, in
his theatrical work he had to face a number of problems to which the art of the
cinema alone could offer a complete solution. In his book *My Life in Art*,
Stanislavsky gives the story of the premiere of the play *The Loss of the Hope* in
Studio I of the Arts Theatre. The play was staged and acted in a hall so small
that the audience was close up to the actors. Owing to this closeness of the
public and cast, all exaggeration of gesture and intonation had to go and every

Excerpt from V. Pudovkin, "Stanislavsky's System in the Cinema," *Sight and Sound* 22,
no. 3 (January–March 1953), 115–118, 147–148. Trans. T. Shebunina.

half-tone and subtle nuance acquired extreme importance. The unusually intimate association between actor and spectator produced a feeling of particular sincerity as in real life. The lifelike quality of this performance impressed Stanislavsky; it revealed to him new possibilities of altering existing theatrical forms and transforming the stage performance into a more direct reflection of real life.

He wanted to carry this Studio I experience on to the big stage of the Arts Theatre, but this proved unexpectedly impossible, for the studio performance, created in a small hall, literally could be neither seen nor heard in one built to hold hundreds of spectators, and the charm of the intimate association between cast and audience vanished in a hall that demanded emphasis of voice and gesture. This experience showed Stanislavsky the limits beyond which reproduction of real life in a mass theatrical spectacle could not go. He decided to seek ways of completely fusing the actor's realistic behaviour on the stage with the emphasis inevitable in theatrical expression. He did not know, of course, that everything that had been discovered during the intimate performance at Studio I, though impracticable on a large stage, was perfectly possible to the new cinematic art, which both brings the actor close to the spectator and yet broadens out the hall to the ends of the earth.

Stanislavsky's endeavour to bring the actor's art as close as possible to a truthful and delicate rendering of human experience was more than once brought up short by the limitations of the stage. He tells how once he tried to introduce a long pause full of complex inner life. He sat for a long time on a bench set close to the footlights and went through a series of thoughts and emotions, but it was all lost on the audience because of the distance between. In close-up, however, the public would have been able to follow on the screen all the fine plays of eyes and features and thus take in everything Stanislavsky wished to impart.

Stanislavsky's attempts to create scenery and surroundings as close as possible to reality were often criticised as an unnecessary introduction of superfluous realism onto the stage. This reproach is quite ill-founded. Great artist that he was, Stanislavsky sought to give a consistent unity to the life of the characters by means of the reality surrounding them, though he realised the limits set by the technical possibilities of the stage. In his reminiscences he tells how, when he was in the Crimea with his company, one day in a park he came upon a spot very similar to the setting of a scene in *Month in the Country*. He and Olga Knipper were moved to try out their scene in this natural setting, but after the first few sentences they gave it up. The conventional acting elaborated on the stage was in too great contradiction to the natural surroundings for these sensitive artists to go on with their scene. The acting of a screen actor, however, approximating as closely as possible to normal human behaviour, can merge completely with a natural landscape faithfully reproduced on the screen.

The cinema provided the realistic actor with many new opportunities of giving a direct reflection of life, and it became the highway to the development of his art. Stanislavsky's work over a period of many years laid the foundations of this development. The immediate contact between the art of the cinema and that of the stage came naturally through the actor. So it was with me in the very beginning of my independent work as a producer. Among the large number of actors of various theatrical schools I found those trained by Stanislavsky the most congenial.

On starting independent work I was already convinced that the art of the cinema came nearer to giving a true reflection of real life than any other art, and that it could perfectly well do without the theatrical conventions that trammelled the stage. Stanislavsky's system became my school, and my first experiments in cinematography aimed at shaking off every convention of stage technique unnecessary to the screen-actor. From the first I took a dislike to artificial scenery, realising all the cinema's capacity to absorb creatively the natural surroundings in which living people—the actors—can move.

Having acquainted myself with Stanislavsky's method of training actors I realised that while the essence of this realist method was indispensable to cinematic art, much of its technique—created in the special conditions of the stage—was foreign to the very nature of the cinema.

The basis of the Stanislavsky method is first of all how to form a link between the character and the actor's natural personality. Stanislavsky's profound analysis of the process that he called the "transmutation" of the actor— once supposed to be accessible only to men of genius—coupled with incessant experimentation, enabled the producer and actor, by means of consistent and concentrated work, to come closer to the great truthfulness in acting that always conquers the audience, which had previously been regarded as accidental or even of divine inspiration.

The first precept of Stanislavsky's that I studied was that of "living the part". By this Stanislavsky understood the process taking place in the actor's inner self. He knew what a deep gulf lies between the theoretical concept of the inner life of a character formed by the producer and the actor when thinking out the part, and the actual acting on the stage, between even the clearest realisation of what should be done and the acting itself. Every actor and every producer knows how difficult is the first step in this transition from the imagined to the real. The genius of Stanislavsky blazed the trail for this transition. He insisted that every actor should live his part as he would in real life if he were the character he is creating. Naturally, the actor's first steps in this direction must be connected with the world of his personal experience, with memories of how he has behaved in similar moments. When the actor lives some part of his role fully, be it only for a brief moment, he immediately experiences the joy of success so necessary to every artist. In order to progress, a creative artist must not only understand success but feel it. Such direct personal memories, introduced into the life of the character he is creating, give the actor an example of how he should feel throughout his part, though he has to bridge many gaps between his own consciousness and that of the character.

When I first met Stanislavsky's pupils and followers, during the production of the film *Mother,* we found it hard going. How was I to find a way to the hearts and minds of the people I was to direct, who were to create characters which as yet existed only in my imagination? That was my difficulty. Theirs was of a different kind; for they were artists, masters of a technique elaborated in close contact with the conventions of the stage. As a producer I found much of their technique unacceptable. Not that their acting had anything artificial about it (as was quite unjustifiably suggested at the time), but there were external peculiarities of acting unwanted on the screen, a theatrical emphasis of speech and gesture needed on the stage in order to be visible and audible to an audience separated from the actors by considerable distances.

Feeling as I did that the screen demanded from acting the nearest possible approach to human behaviour in ordinary life, the first task I set myself and the artists was the search for the greatest possible spontaneity and simplicity. I knew, of course, that a superficially natural reproduction of life was not sufficient, and that the screen, like the stage, needed somewhat heightened expressiveness, but even then I realised the special capacities that distinguished the cinema from the theatre. Clearly, with an actor taken in close-up, what was needed first and foremost was complete truthfulness of acting.

My first experiences in producing met with a sincere and creative response and I felt that the foundations of complete mutual confidence had been laid. One of the first scenes which I took with the actress playing the part of the mother was the following: under the floor the mother finds weapons hidden by her son. This unexpected discovery reveals the terrible danger that threatens him—prison, Siberia, death. She is kneeling on the floor holding the weapons in her hands. There is a knock at the door. She raises her head. The door opens and the first thing she sees are the soles of the feet of a man who is being carried in. Without yet understanding what has happened, she guesses that the man is her husband. Here the task of the actress and of the young and inexperienced producer was an exceptionally difficult one. To begin with I left the actress to act this scene in her own way, and she naturally tried to do this as she would have done on the stage. She sought to arouse in herself a strong emotion expressed only by gestures: she stepped back, put her hands to her head, made various movements—each of which horrified me by its exaggeration. I felt all this to be unnecessary, but what was needed I did not yet know. First I removed all that seemed to me superfluous and exaggerated, and then I decided on a step that even today, as I recall it, amazes me by its temerity, for I was much younger than the actress and far less experienced. This was to suggest that she should act this scene without making a single movement or gesture, while retaining the inner emotional state she had found. The actress did this, and I saw how the complete immobility of one who could arouse in herself a strong and sincere emotion gave her an almost physical sense of suffering. Then I decided on a further step and allowed the actress to make a single gesture which I had noticed among the many she had made in the beginning. It was a movement of the hand as of someone naively fending off some terrible threat. I was so deeply persuaded that the inner truth of the emotion would find its best expression in this chosen gesture that I took the risk of filming this scene without any previous rehearsal so as not to lose its freshness.

Thus I began to discover the value of the actor's art through Stanislavsky's training. . . .

Stanislavsky created a whole system of work intended to develop the power of imagination in the actor. And it is up to the producer, when helping the artist in his search for truthful acting, to do all he can to remove obstacles to the free play of imagination; further, he must help him by creating a series of impulses that support and develop it, for the less imagination the artist has to expend on picturing the external surroundings, the more easily will he concentrate on his emotions.

Temporarily and conventionally I shall separate two fields of work on creative imagination which in reality are closely linked together: the one connected with the external expression of the actor's thoughts and feelings, his behaviour, and the other connected with his emotional state. When speaking of the behaviour of the actor we must turn to that part of the work on the role which Stanislavsky and his pupils called "physical action". In his search for complete unity in the actor's living of his part Stanislavsky was impelled in the later stages of his work to pay particular attention to this field. The actor is expressive, he vividly and clearly impresses the spectator, when he is active, when he solves not only the inner problems arising in his mind, but also the external physical problems confronting his will and impulses. The solving of the physical problem, as Stanislavsky rightly understands it, is as it were the culmination of the inner process and must be organically integrated with the whole of the actor's experience of living his part. The "physical action" can be best described as the directed action of one moved by thought and feeling.

The spectacular nature of stage and screen give particular interest to such human actions as are of a vivid visible character. The art of the actor in silent films developed first of all in the field of physical action, where both he and the producer had to seek the greatest possible truthfulness of expression. Here Stanislavsky's ideas proved exceptionally fruitful, while the practical experience of the silent cinema was in its turn useful and important for experimental work on a scale impossible for the theatre. The sub-titles were a sort of summing-up of the deep and subtle unspoken acting which gave full expression to the actor's emotional state.

It is important to note at this point that the cinema did not follow the road of pantomime, that is to say an art which had elaborated conventional signs to replace speech. The fact that the actor was brought close to the spectator, who could thus perceive the most subtle expressions of human emotion—a glance, a hidden smile, a barely perceptible gesture of the hand—freed the cinema from the need to invent artificial conventional signs.

The first claim made on the actor, on which Stanislavsky always insisted, is "transmutation", the ability to transform, by the power of his imagination, his whole self with all his individual traits and qualities, into something different, which belongs no longer to him but to the character he impersonates. In this process of transition it is vital for him to preserve even in imaginary conditions a live personality, thinking and behaving with the same singleness of purpose as does a real man in real life, and neither break nor lose the links indispensable to this singleness of human behaviour. That is why the basis of the actor's art must be the faculty of finding, preserving and strengthening the inner links which make every moment of his acting an indissoluble part of the whole. It is the indispensable co-operation between actor and producer, directed at the main goal—that of giving life to the created character—that produces the capacity to feel when these links are broken and to restore them. The producer who remains an objective observer can immediately realise any such break in the natural unity in any fragment of the part being acted, and he can stop the actor the moment the false note is struck as an inevitable result of this break.

Many know the difficulties experienced by the actor searching for the right intonation, when he tries to utter a word or a phrase first in one way, then in another. Even if as a result of such blind attempts he does find an intonation which he or the producer regards as successful, he may well be unable to remember or to repeat it. The true intonation should be sought, not by hit-or-miss methods, but purposefully in the natural sequence of feeling, gesture and speech. This complex whole, indivisible in real life, should not be formally memorised by the actor but mastered as a real complete activity. This is the path towards realist art.

If these precepts of Stanislavsky's are applied to the cinema it will appear that the entire period of the silent film was in essence a development and elaboration of the school of acting linked with the search for the truth of physical action. In this sense the period of the silent film provided all that was basic and necessary for the later stages, when sound and speech came in. All my work with the speaking actor, our common search for realism in his acting, have proved that it is in the field of gesture, meaning the primary physical movement born of emotion, that the actor must particularly seek to perfect his technique.

I knew what it was that frightened me in the acting of artists who did not belong to the Stanislavsky school. It was that their theatrical gesture was stronger than their feeling, and in some particularly bad cases the gesture had become fixed and conventional and quite unconnected with feeling. The Stanislavsky school does not in any circumstances admit such misconceived theatrical effects.

The screen offers the actor a special opportunity for reducing gesture to the minimum, which in itself makes it all the more expressive. The screen actor has the advantage over the stage actor that he can behave towards the spectator just as he would towards someone standing at his side: but these special opportunities demand from him the closest possible attention to complete truthfulness in the subtlest of external expressions of his state of mind.

Behind the drama or scenario there always lies some phenomenon of life disclosed in the form of conflict. This conflict is always shown in the most expressive spectacular forms. The character's every thought and feeling must lead him to physical action, and speech expressing the content of the thought must be organically fused with physical action. Such is the law of any stage or screen production. Thus physical action may and should be considered as the most important, and in most cases the decisive, element with which the actor and the producer must concern themselves from the outset. That is why Stanislavsky concentrated so much on physical action as the starting-point in the actor's assimilation of his part. . . .

It is not only in separate fragments or scenes that unity and continuity of action are necessary. The actions of the actors carry the characters created by them through the whole play and bring their destinies to fulfilment, to the final aim of the general development of the play or picture and the final formulation of its ideas. Attaining purposefulness and continuity in this general movement means making the play realistic. In the general purposeful movement of the action every actor must have his personal basic aim, which he achieves at the moment of the play's ending. The directed impulse of his will, in opposition to the surrounding circumstances which help or hinder the attainment of the final aim, ensures what Stanislavsky called the "follow-through" of the actor in the play.

It is easier for the stage actor to achieve this "follow through" than for the screen actor. During rehearsals the stage play is, as a rule, run through in its entirety. Besides, on the stage the actor can continue his search for continuity in his living of the part as it passes through the whole play. In the cinema the purely technical conditions of camera work seldom afford this opportunity. In the great majority of cases it is quite impossible to rehearse the scenario as a whole.

Nevertheless, thorough and concentrated work on obtaining this follow-through of Stanislavsky's is as necessary to the screen actor as it is to the stage actor. The problem of preserving the unity and continuity of an acted part lies mainly with the producer. This demands first of all intensive imaginative work, the faculty of being always able to see the future picture in its entirety, in the form not of abstract situations and aims but of animated, visible and audible scenes; it demands secondly an unfailing visual memory which can retain vivid impressions of everything already acted by the artist. Only when he possesses and constantly develops these faculties can the producer help the actor in the complicated conditions of filmmaking, which force the actor to play disjointed parts of his role without an immediate perception of the natural sequence. I remember how when making the film *Mother* I purposely began with the last part of the picture, which demanded the maximum effort from the actress: the mother, tearing herself from the body of her dead son, lifts up the red banner and walks towards the onrushing cossacks. This is the supreme moment of the part. Both in the beginning and the middle of the film there were scenes demanding strong emotional expression, but I realised that none of them should be allowed to equal the power of that final scene. . . .

The idea-content of the picture must be the moving force in every scene; it must live in every detail. This can be attained only when each part, and the whole picture, are perceived by producer and cast as one continuous movement in which there are no gaps between the feelings and gestures of any one of the actors, between gesture and speech, between the text and the translation into physical action of the idea it contains, between physical action and its direct physical object, and finally between this particular aim and the general aim towards which the action as a whole is directed.

Work on a stage or a screen play may present two possibilities: either the producer and the actor discover the truth of life hidden but actually existing in the scene, or else they introduce it as a necessary correction suggested by their perception of truth trained by practical realist experience. In both cases a clear and definite method of work is imperative. This is the method Stanislavsky discovered for theatrical art, which has found tremendous new possibilities of fruitful development in cinematic art.

Stanislavsky, the great realist artist, scholar and teacher, cleared the true path on which the great realist tendencies of Russian art become the living practice of the art of socialist realism.

Michael Chekhov Actor's Feeling and Director's Form

An Open Letter to Soviet Film Workers
Concerning Eisenstein's *Ivan the Terrible*
May 31, 1945
Beverly Hills, Calif.

Dear Friends:

In his book *The Film Sense* (I have access only to the English translation of this book), Eisenstein in speaking of montage expresses the idea that "our films are faced with problems of narration that would be not only logically connected but also emotionally *exciting to the maximum.*"

And it is this "maximum of emotions," this living, stimulating maximum of feeling, that I do not get enough of in the acting. My impression is that the actors know all too well that they are acting, know it to the detriment of their feeling. They know that here they are angry, there they are jealous, here they're afraid, there they're in love—but they don't feel it. They think they feel it, and deceive themselves with this illusion.

Excerpt from Michael Chekhov, "An Open Letter to Soviet Film Workers Concerning Eisenstein's *Ivan the Terrible*," originally published in *Iskusstvo Kino* no. 1 (1968), 117–124. Trans. Steven P. Hill.

Michael Chekhov (right) with Gregory Peck and Rhonda Fleming in *Spellbound* (1945)

Feeling in stage art is more valuable than thinking, and when there is a distinct form, as in *Ivan*, feeling gains primary significance. The form of *Ivan* obligates the actors: they should rise to it with their feelings, not just with understanding alone and not just with thinking. (I do not say that actors shouldn't think, no; but they should not overthink their roles to the point of dryness. An actor's thinking is *imagination* and not *cerebration*.)

Actors' feeling not only fills in the form but also justifies it. Eisenstein's concept has much fire and power, which far surpasses the psychology of everyday life. He has created a tragedy of Shakespearian sweep. And that is how it comes across to us visually. The form is given by the director; it enchants us but leaves us cold. A question arises: Can it be that Russian actors lack those Shakespearian-Eisensteinian feelings, fire, and passions?

Of course they don't. I'll say it again: no actors in the world have such strong, fiery, emotional, and exciting feelings as the Russians do. But they need to be dug out, it's necessary to learn to summon them up within oneself when one wishes, it's necessary to practice great feelings, in order to become a tragic actor. How to do that? In the first place, remove the obstacles blocking their manifestation, and in the second place, apply correct methods for arousing the feelings necessary for tragedy. Let us speak of these two things.

What blocks your feelings in *Ivan?* First of all, *speech.* You speak a thought, stressing the main word, and draw out the sentence, making unjustified pauses between words. This manner of speaking is, to a greater or lesser extent, an affliction of all of you. The entire sentence you pronounce in a cold (I would even say dead) way, putting your hopes on the main word. Feeling cannot break through this manner of speaking, which is unnatural to man. A stress on the important word or sentence is necessary, but the question is how and in what way to produce that stress. You, for the most part, do it by means of your voice, making a mental effort in the process. *But the emphasis can also be produced by means of feeling, and that is the most valuable kind of emphasis.*

In your acting, though, it is encountered all too seldom. From constant deliberate-voice stresses, your speech very soon begins to create a monotonous impression. It becomes difficult to follow your speech. Separating the words in the sentence and using the voice to stress the main one among them, you do not give feeling any "room" where, after flaring up, it could fill in your speech with nuances and make it varied and emotional. Feeling in speech holds the audience's attention and forces it to wonder, with excitement: "What next?" Speech that is only willed (so to say, metric speech) weakens the audience's interest. And finally, mental effort and voice, if they are not colored with feeling, inevitably create a mechanical impression—and that, I'm sure, cannot enter into your artistic concepts.

It is only the entire sentence (not fragmented with artificial stops between words) that you will be able to fill in with feelings, to convey them to the audience. The sentence is a living organism. It cannot be dissected with impunity. And not only a single sentence—but a whole series of sentences, linked by feelings, form a living organism. But if the words of one sentence break apart and lose their life, how can the living connection between many sentences survive intact? . . .

Not only the actors are harmed by such speech but also the director: it deprives him of one of the most powerful means of expression—the pause. The audience no longer perceives it, exhausted by dozens, eventually even hundreds of little "pauses" in speech.

And finally, your heavy metric speech excludes the possibility of changing tempo. Your acting becomes slow and monotonous. In *Ivan* there are not a few spontaneous moments for tempo devised by the director, but this spontaneity is often shattered against the slow tempo of the actors' speech. Without changes of tempo, the theme begins to seem overextended and insignificant, individual moments become repetitions, the details move into the foreground, and the audience loses contact with the main thing. Without changes of tempo, the actor, too, cannot come alive with the elevated feelings necessary for tragedy.

Tempo in our days is a thorny and exciting problem. Over here I recently met a film worker who had come from Moscow. He told me that Russian actors want to learn the American film tempo. I replied that American "tempo" should not be learned by Russian actors. American films do not have tempo, they have rush. With the latter, for the most part, directors and actors attempt to cover over the emptiness and lack of content in what is happening on the screen. (I am not referring, of course, to a few films of great significance.) Actors here are afraid to be silent even for a half-second—they might reveal a total void. You have to talk, talk, talk. And as fast as possible. That is not tempo. Many things can be learned from American films, but just not tempo. Real tempo depends on two conditions: first, the removal of unnecessary slow spots (in speech, acting, directing), and second, the living, mobile feeling of the actor. . . .

. . . We feel, think, and walk faster than ten or fifteen years ago. Our audience also watches and understands what is happening on the screen "sooner." It's very possible that people of Ivan the Terrible's epoch did think, and speak, and move, heavily and slowly. Perhaps that was indeed, so to say, their lifestyle. But we, in our days, are no longer capable of tolerating that "historical truth." In the interests of the artistic impression, we must reject it. It is possible to depict heavy and slow people on the screen, but that surely can be done better through the means of artistic expression (hints and character traits), but not by copying imagined "historical truth." The tempo of our epoch has to be taken into account by the actor as well as (and mainly) by the director. The director also makes a misstep, in my opinion, when he drags out the tempo of scenes whose meaning is clear and quickly taken in by the audience. . . .

Now some words about how an actor can summon up in himself the great feelings he needs for tragedy. I do not know what method you use now, but if you should choose to ask me, I could give you the following advice.

Look in your imagination at the character played by you so long and so intensively, until his feelings—which you "see" in your own imagination, too—awaken inside you the same feelings, until his feelings become your feelings. Again, may I be permitted to say, at the risk of being mistaken: you underrate the inner life of the character depicted by you. Those feelings you show on the screen are too superficial, too general, abstract, and not individualized. In creative imagination, no such feelings exist. There they are more profound, complex, and interesting. You start too early to depict that which perhaps has only flashed for an instant in your imagination. Allow your feeling to ripen under the impact of the image observed by you. Look at it (into it!) every day, several times a day. Then you will not be depicting fright in general, love in general, malice in general. The image created by your creative imagination will not allow you to do that.

Make an experiment: imagine that you are Shakespeare, Michelangelo, or an ancient Greek sculptor, and begin to create anew either Lear in the wilderness, Moses, or Laocoön. Let these creations become the images of your imaginations. Achieve a state where you actually have experienced that spontaneous power of feelings which was experienced by the makers of those great creations. And then with the same power of imagination, work on your roles, and you will soon notice: the further and more persistently you peer into the external and—especially—into the internal shape of your character, the more he grows and develops under your persistent, questioning gaze. He unfailingly will show you every feeling in an aspect that is more complex and interesting for you and the audience. . . .

Another method of strengthening and developing the experiences you need, which I can recommend to you, is the following. Almost every scene in *Ivan,* according to Eisenstein's concept, is filled with atmosphere; but it doesn't always get across to the audience. You ought to have worked on strengthening these directorial atmospheres, in order to utilize them later for awakening in yourself the feelings you need. The impact of atmosphere on an actor's individual feelings can be very great, if he chooses to give himself up to its effect. Take a close look at everyday life, and you will be convinced of the power of atmosphere. Every landscape, every street, house, or room has its own atmosphere. You will enter a library, a hospital, or a cathedral differently; and you will enter a noisy hotel or a museum differently, if you "tune in" to the surrounding atmosphere, as to music. The same familiar landscape will "sound" different for you in the atmosphere of a spring morning or in a lightning and rain storm. You'll learn much that is new through this "resonance," enriching your creative soul. . . .

It is necessary, before acting, to spend a certain time in it, together with your partners. It is necessary to create it around you. You need only *imagine* that the air around you is filled with that atmosphere which the director demands of you, and it almost instantaneously will appear of its own accord. Imagining an atmosphere is just as easy as imagining, for instance, an aroma or light which fills a space. Even short practice will teach you to master the atmosphere and to put it to use as a means for *awakening your feelings.* If you like, I can recommend a simple exercise to you, which you can modify as you wish.

Imagine a scene known to you from literature or history. Let it be, for instance, the taking of the Bastille. Imagine the moment when the mob bursts into one of the cells and frees a prisoner. They hug, kiss, dance with him, sing around him, shout, and finally rush with threats to a new cell, together with their freed comrade. Peer closely at the characters and types of men and women. Let this scene, created by your imagination, appear before you with all possible clarity and vividness. Then say to yourself: the mob is acting under the impact of *an atmosphere of extreme arousal and intoxication with power and force.* All taken together and each in isolation are enveloped by this atmosphere. Stare at the faces, movements, groupings of figures, at the tempo of what is happening, listen attentively to the shouts and timbres of the voices, stare at the details of the scene; and you will see how all that is happening bears an imprint of the atmosphere, and how it will dictate the mob's actions.

Change the atmosphere somewhat and watch your "show" once again. Let the former aroused atmosphere take on a *malicious,* vengeful flavor, and you will see how it is reflected in the movements, actions, facial expressions, and shouts of the mob. Again change it. Let the *pride, dignity,* and *solemnity* of the moment envelop the participants of the scene, and again you will see how the figures, poses, groupings, voices, and faces of the mob will change by themselves. What you have performed thus in your imagination you may, if you have the time and the desire, perform in reality. Construct yourself a number of group exercise-studies in atmosphere. Ask your director what atmosphere he recommends to you in order that you may "live in" it especially painstakingly, keeping in mind the further work on *Ivan.* There will be no shortage of subjects.

By working in this way, you will be convinced also of the fact that atmosphere has the power to unite the actors with the audience. Thanks to atmosphere, the audience not only objectively perceives what is happening before it on the stage or on the screen but also endeavors itself to participate in the performance together with the actors. And that is more than half the battle. Finally, the audience, too, being enveloped by the atmosphere of the scene, understands its content better. Neither the text nor the most colorful acting can convey to the audience everything that a scene includes, if it is not permeated with atmosphere. Atmosphere is the soul of a scene and of the stage. Without it the audience is watching a sort of "psychologically empty space." . . .

It seems to me that there is one more respect in which you can raise the quality of your acting, and of the entire production along with it. In the way that you depict various emotions and feelings, you often begin to resemble each other: you become angry, outraged, joyous, and so forth, using always one and the same stage technique ("device," in Stanislavsky's terminology). In real life you would not find two people who would rejoice or love in the same way. But on the stage that often happens. This mistake has crept into your acting, too.

This occurs partly because you underestimate the distinctive features which are characteristic of your personages. In order that the acting of each of you would acquire an *individual* flavor, you would do well to construct a correct profile [composition] for the characters. If you ask yourself what predominates in a particular character—willpower, feeling, or thought—and then what is the specific nature of this predominant trait, you'll be able to construct your acting so that it will be differentiated from the acting of your partners. Those who act in the same play should not duplicate each other in anything. In this case, the director's concern, in the interests of the whole, should boil down to

1. emphasizing the specific features of each character,
2. nuancing their differences, and
3. constructing a profile of the character of each personage so that [the characters] would complement and not duplicate each other.

In *King Lear,* for example, you will find a whole group of *evil* characters. So that the actors would not fall into the temptation of playing *evil in general* (that is, playing identically), they should find specific traits of each of the evil characters. Let us see how this can be done.

Lacking the ability to feel, Edmund displays before the audience a number of psychological states: his sharp intellect, entering into various combinations with willpower, engenders lies, trickery, sarcasm, contempt, and also courage, firmness, and fearlessness. All these patterns are woven from intellect in combination with willpower. The absence of heart makes this character a virtuoso of amorality. You see that he is handsome inwardly, but in a cold way, without an appealing quality. He talks and acts like a man who is "free" of moral doubts. Goneril is the opposite and complement of Edmund. All her being is woven of feeling. All her feelings are passions, and all the passions are sensuality.

Regan, in terms of profile, is placed between Edmund and Goneril. She has neither a brilliant intellect nor ardent feeling. But she reflects another's thinking as well as another's feeling, when she comes into contact with them. She is necessary in the play as a personification of *weakness,* which becomes a tool of those who are stronger. Cornwall, on the contrary, represents willpower that is not illuminated by intellect. He and Regan, on the one hand, and he and Edmund, on the other, complement each other. In love with himself, Oswald introduces an element of humor into the theme of evil. His profile is significant among the other characters also in that he shows a narrowness in all three areas of spiritual life—thinking, feeling, and willpower. . . .

Now a few words about the external side of the production. The extraordinary beauty and sculptured quality of the sets, costumes, and mise-en-scènes are stunning to the audience, who admire them for a long time. They are caught up in the original composition of almost every shot. With delight they follow your gestures and movements of your bodies. But then comes a moment when the audience begins to feel dissatisfaction and an inner coldness amid all the wealth and beauty. Just why does such a change occur in the audience? Is it not because the external aspect of the production, with a multitude of diverse and rich details, eclipses and crushes the actors? Is the reason not that the actors, in moving and gesticulating in the midst of this luxury, themselves become something like a part of their surroundings, which may be fine but still are not living? Perhaps this is the very reason for which the actors lack inner strength to conquer their external surroundings.

The tragic style, conceived by the author, is too strongly accentuated by him in the external side of the production. (Was it necessary to show, for instance, the lower hem of the Mongolian envoy's rich garment, or the play of shadows on the wall—a device repeatedly used in film and on the stage and which distracts the audience's attention?) Style begins to turn to stylization— that is, it becomes externally artificial. This danger can be removed in two ways: either the external side must be shown more modestly, to make room for the actors with their experiences; or else the actors must find in themselves enough strength to rise up to the level of the external side of the production, which is crushing them. The ideal solution, of course, would be the latter. . . .

Sincerely grateful to you,
Your admirer,
Michael Chekhov

Continental Alternatives

Matters of collaboration figure as prominently for this group of Continental actors as they did for the Soviet actors in the last section. For the West Europeans, however, collaboration does not usually imply work within an artistic collective so much as it does work under the inspirational and unifying capacity of a single director. More than any other in this book, this set of actors acknowledges the capability of directors to shape film acting in the service of a highly personal vision, sometimes, though not always, while taking a clearly defined political stance.

Given their own pronounced and often politicized interests, it is surprising how many of these actors have starred in Hollywood films. Considered in another light, though, either Hollywood or Europe (leaving the Soviets aside) may present an alternative that grows more attractive to film actors who find great success first on the opposite side of the Atlantic. If acting has to do in some fundamental way with making choices, then choosing which country to work in or which language to speak may come as a natural extension of actors' common desires for expressiveness, variety, and exposure.

Part of the prestige surrounding film acting derives from the potential a film has to be viewed all over the world. Internationalist visions of art may circulate more widely in Europe, where proximity and ease of travel regularly throw citizens from various countries into more frequent contact with one another than is the case in the Americas, Asia, or Africa. The power that the English language has come to enjoy as a medium for commercial and cultural exchange has enlarged the appeal of acting in that language, before audiences much larger than the ones that see most films made in French, Italian, German, Swedish, or Norwegian (the native languages of the actors in this section). Still, the choices that present themselves to the most noted film actors in Europe depend on more than their ability to speak English. The following accounts show that the film traditions of European nations vary substantially, from the relative obscurity of Norwegian and Austrian films to the more familiar and widely distributed pictures produced in Italy and France.

Eminent film actors from all over the world face career choices that touch on issues of nationalism and, in a fundamental way, on the actors' very identity as artists. Conditions on film sets are often so hermetic that they obliterate, at least momentarily, the world outside. Films launched from conditions of such isolation can, however, expose actors and their personal lives to flocks of eager consumers far from the source of production. To the degree that acting originates in something personal and local, there may be risk in removing a film from its native context and presenting it to audiences who may regard it as merely quaint or exotic.

Of all the actors in this book, Mai Zetterling offers perhaps the most concise comparison between stage and film acting. She sees the director as a surrogate, above all, for the audience that will eventually see the film, but she also envisions actors as potential film editors; this aligns her with the Soviets working under Eisenstein. Zetterling's account, together with Liv Ullmann's, recapitulates the synthetic and mediatory qualities of Scandinavian social democracy as a set of compromises between capitalism and socialism, especially during the time the Cold War raged.

Jean-Louis Trintignant has little but praise for film acting, and he discusses how he came to regard acting on the stage as outdated. He places great faith in improvisation before the camera and regards characterization as something perpetually in process. Trintignant asks many small questions about his characters as he moves through filming, and he admits that there are some things about those characters he may never know, or decide. Such views reflect post-structuralist theory in France, of which Trintignant seems at least to be aware and which may even have been anticipated by his views of personality as shifting and unstable. He is the only dramatic actor in this collection to stress the importance of humor in serious characterizations, as a practical way of realizing Bertolt Brecht's injunction to objectify dramatic characters so that the audience can judge them dispassionately.

Marcello Mastroianni claims to want to demystify himself in relation to the unusually wide range of roles he played. Like most attempts to relate acting narrowly to personal experience, though, he succeeds only in turning the interview into a kind of game in which he speculates, in teasing and elliptical terms, on the sources of his own creative impulses. Whatever definition he appeared to lack in his own life, Mastroianni was usually able to supply to his own satisfaction in his work for the screen. His interest in playing antiheroes abundantly endowed with weaknesses distinguishes him from stars in the Hollywood mold, and he mentions John Wayne several times as a counterexample to himself.

Liv Ullmann offers some of the most telling distinctions between filmmaking in Europe and in Hollywood, as well as indictments of American Method acting and of the cosmetic concerns that seem to her often to drive filmmaking in the United States. Her comments also offer insight into the idiosyncratic working methods of her frequent director, Ingmar Bergman. In fact, her recollections of Bergman's dealings with his actors echo eerily the testimonies of the American silent film actresses Lillian Gish and Mae Marsh about D. W.

Griffith, and of Louise Brooks about Josef von Sternberg. Ullmann's sense of Bergman at work evokes the curcial dramatic importance of silence, not only in Bergman's films but also in Ullmann's own expressive acting range.

Klaus Maria Brandauer came to Hollywood in the 1980s through the same channels as other European stars who brought with them substantial reputations in film, on the stage, or like Brandauer, both. Just as the Norwegian Ullmann gained her reputation as a film actress in Sweden, Brandauer, who is Austrian by origin, began his career at some remove from the major film capitals. He seems always to have regarded his stay in Hollywood as an aberration, though, regretting the ascendance of "transnational" films over those addressed to smaller, more culturally specific audiences. Brandauer's decisions in conducting his career reveal a professional orientation that more closely resembles the Soviets' than those of any other nationality among this rather disparate group of Continental actors—and make his fleeting associations with Hollywood more surprising still.

Mai Zetterling Some Notes on Acting

I shall write not so much about acting, as the difference between stage and film acting. There are people who believe that film actors are not real actors, and it must be admitted that some of the people who believe this are actors themselves. But before going any further, ought we not to decide what we mean by an actor? *An actor is a person who tries to imitate humanity.* He spends his life learning the symbols of human behaviour, to reproduce them at will. In the theatre, there are four points to be made about the actor:

1. *Rehearsal and preparation* before showing the finished article.
2. For the stage player, continuity is unbroken.
3. The stage actor is in complete control of his performance.
4. The audience contributes towards the performance and is for the actor a source of inspiration.

These four conditions are inseparable from acting as a creative art. One must prepare exhaustively; one must maintain a sequence of ideas and emotions. The theatre helps the actor by its method of rehearsal. In the cinema we must find means of following the same path. The system of rehearsal is the most important factor of theatre work. Of the actor's struggle to incarnate his role, Pudovkin writes: "It might indeed be said that realism, the lifeline unity of the image, is a problem more pertinent and urgent to the film actor than even to the actor in the theatre".

Film acting offers none of these conditions. Firstly, rehearsal and performance are nearly always identical. Secondly, the script is a set of fragments which can be shot in any order, according to the will of the director and the technical necessities involved. Thirdly, in films, effects of pausing, of timing, tension and relaxation, are created in the cutting room by people who may never have seen the actors except on celluloid, and of whom many don't like actors either in the flesh or on celluloid. They are essentially technicians.

There is no reason, it should be pointed out here, why the work of the real actor should terminate before the editing process. I believe the actor should

Excerpt from Mai Zetterling, "Some Notes on Acting," *Sight and Sound* 21, no. 2 (October–December 1951), 83, 96. Reprinted by permission.

Mai Zetterling (right) and Alf Kjellin in *Torment* (1944)

take a creative part in editing, as the finer polishing of his performance, and should be as close to it as to the director.

Fourthly, of course, the film actor has no audience. He creates his fragments of acting time after time without love, laughter or applause. He goes through it until the director is satisfied that he has got one good shot and one or two good covering shots in the can. Under present working conditions the amount of rehearsal possible in a film studio is very short when compared to the time that a stage actor can devote to his work. In any case, it is not altogether true that a film actor need come to his work unrehearsed. In most cases he receives the script at least a week before the film goes on the floor, and has got enough time to read and re-read the script and work out his approach to the part. The trouble is that, under the present factory system (that is to say, the more quickly a film is made, the cheaper will be its cost of production), the actor is bound to look upon film acting as the kind of acting which can be pushed through with the minimum of thought and preparation, provided he is slick in a purely surface way.

But under *ideal* conditions it is just as possible and just as necessary, I believe, to rehearse every shot of the film as minutely as every scene of a play, to sustain those breaks of continuity which for the actor are the most difficult to overcome. It is true that film acting is fragmentary, but it is quite wrong to pretend that any stage play (except for an occasional one-act play in which the characters never leave the stage) really preserves continuity for the actor. The play is divided into acts—two or three—and these acts divided sometimes into many scenes. The total can be as many as fifteen or twenty scenes. Also, the characters go on and off the stage. All these interruptions constitute the very acting in fragments which is complained of in film acting. The fragmentary nature of stage work is, in fact, overcome by systematic rehearsal over a long period, whereby the actor gets an idea of his part as a whole, and its relation to the play.

How much more, then, does the film actor, whose part is much more fragmentary, need rehearsal over a long period to overcome these breaks in continuity. In the early days, of course, scenes could be shot as they were played in the theatre. This was film theatre. No one thought of shooting a scene in any other way. The camera framed the scene at a fixed distance, and the actors went through it in stretches of 500 or 1,000 feet of film, and then another length of film was loaded into the camera. This went on until D. W. Griffith's development of the close-up, and his discovery of the great power of the camera to select. The second development was that of putting the camera on wheels—that is, tracking down a street, mounted on a car or a boat; and then came the discovery by the great Russian directors of the 1920's that new forms of tension, rhythm and excitement could be achieved by splitting up images, by putting one against the other in a particular order, which they called montage. These are reasons for the lack of continuity in film acting, and they are in fact the essence of film-making. To a film actor deeply interested in his job they will cease to be irritations and obstacles, and will be appreciated as a new means of expression.

It is true that in the film studio we are surrounded only by the camera, the camera crew, the electricians, the director sitting in front of the camera. The director is the only witness of the acting during the shooting of a film. He should try to help the actor by being a responsive and friendly, if sole, audience, by expressing admiration or disappointment. There must be an inner contact between director and actor, and trust and respect between them.

The stage and the film actor must know equally how to imitate humanity, must speak with conviction and know how to master his body. This is another thing very important for the actor; how he works with his body and his muscles, to get the utmost from every part of his body. When he acts, even the little toe on his right foot should belong to the character that he is trying to portray. It is vitally important, therefore, for an actor to have some kind of dance training—not necessarily ballet—to know what relaxation really means, what tension means, to heighten his portrayal of character with his body. The stage actor may insist on having certain conditions fulfilled before he can create. The film actor has discovered new ways, in fact new qualities, and a new craftsmanship. His new discoveries are a part of a very new and very young medium.

Jean-Louis Trintignant The Actor, a Witness of His Time

For Truth, Against Realism

. . .

In a theater, the audience is there, in front of you, to witness your work directly. They [the members of the audience] live, they breathe with you. They demand everything from the actor, and their demands increase your potentialities tenfold. The dancer Jean Babilée, a friend of mine, told me that he sometimes manages to perform extremely difficult leaps in front of an audience, whereas he is incapable of performing them in rehearsal before an empty theater.

Sarah Bernhardt use to say that acting in front of a thousand people was like making love to those thousand people.

I don't have Sarah Bernhardt's temperament, but I have felt that thrill in front of a theater audience, which is both anonymous and formidably present.

In the cinema, the relationship with the audience is completely different. It is difficult to imagine behind that small machine [the camera], which is often noisy, the thousands, the millions of eyes that are watching you.

In that respect, the cinema is far less thrilling for an actor than the theater. And yet I prefer the cinema. . . .

Excerpt from Jean-Louis Trintignant, "The Actor, a Witness of His Time," *Cinéma* 163 (February 1972), 104–111. Trans. Alain Piette.

I don't agree with the idea that an actor can be good in a bad movie. For my part, I want to sink with the movie if the latter is a flop. I consider myself as the collaborator of the filmmaker, and I think I would be a dishonest collaborator if I came out of a failed movie successfully. I am extremely demanding before I accept a role, but once I have accepted it, I collaborate with the director, honestly, for better or for worse.

Any way you look at it, however, the actor is only an interpreter. He is not a true creator. He is only a secondhand creator. It is only natural that he should feel a little cramped and should feel the need to express himself by assuming more responsibilities.

. . . The last time I was in a theater play, it was a failure. I'm afraid I have lost touch with the theater.

These last few years, I had made great progress as a film actor. As I look at it now in retrospect, when I went back to the theater, I wanted to adapt to the stage the technique I had developed for the cinema. I wanted to focus my acting on myself, without "showing" anything. I thought that if I was fully "charged" deep down inside, I wouldn't have to externalize anything in order to make the feelings of my character carry over into the audience. It seems that I was wrong.

I wanted to break away from all the conventions of the theater, which seem to me rather dusty; I wanted to break away from the theater gestures, the theater intonations. . . .

Perhaps film is also more suitable to my modest temperament. In the movies, you simply have to exist: the camera comes to get you inside of you. In the theater, you must project toward the back of the hall.

This is how I prepare a movie. I know for example that I am to play the role of the judge in Z. I think about the character and I try to become this character in the smallest details of my everyday life. In the morning when I brush my teeth, I wonder how the judge would brush his. At lunch, when I'm sitting at the table, I wonder how the judge would eat an apple. I try to find the character in a multitude of physical details, which will be of no use in the film. I don't prepare the definite situations that I will have to play during the shooting at all. I want to be totally open to the filmmaker's directions when I arrive on the set. I don't want to have any preconceived ideas.

I don't learn my lines. I have read and reread the script about ten times. I know the lines without actually having learned them. When the director shouts, "Roll'm" or "Action" or "Eighty," I don't know what I'm going to do or say. I feel as if I were improvising, even if I say the exact lines of the script and if I make the exact movements [blocking] foreseen in the screenplay.

If we shoot the same scene several times, I must be careful not to imitate what I have already done before, even if it was successful. Before each take, I must start from scratch, empty myself, and be open to the inspiration of the moment.

. . .

Acting is undoubtedly changing. We are evolving toward more restraint, more truth in the actor's performance.

The film negative itself has become more and more sensitive. Consequently, less light is required. That is why films are shot less and less in the studio. They are shot more and more on location. Films are now shot in the street in the midst of people. In order not to be out of place amid the street people, the actor has had to remove his makeup (so much the better) and give up his actor's intonation (and it's a good thing, too).

I like the truth in an actor's performance, but I reject realism. Truth is a personal commitment, realism is an imitation of the truth.

An actor must never imitate. He must make the lines that the director wants him to say his own. He must invent them as he speaks. This holds true for the gestures, the silences, everything that pertains to the character's life.

Something else has changed in the actor's performance: humor. It's probably what Bertolt Brecht called distanciation. The modern actor must have a sense of humor and have a taste for it. Even in the most tragic situation, he must always look for a humorous counterpoint. We live in a derisory age, and humor is the most perfect expression of this derisiveness.

I believe, even if it sounds a little naïve, that the actor, like all creative persons, must be a witness of his time.

Marcello Mastroianni The Game of Truth

The important thing is to know what season of your life you are living, and not to try and be something on the screen which is ridiculous. To be conscious of the time, of your image . . . but that doesn't mean that you have to calculate ahead and steer your life and career like an accountant. . . .

I didn't plan my progress. Having had a background in theater before coming to the cinema—ten years with Visconti and his theater troupe—I felt a need for diversity, to play ever new types of characters, even in the cinema. I wanted to be like a chameleon, always changing my color, to enter into new skins, new faces. And that, in the cinema, is not easy, because your physical characteristics are seen so clearly by the camera, and the audience begins to recognise you under the skin of the new *personage*. You can only change your hair color so often, or have a mustache or a beard so many times, in the end the character is in something that is not physical, the change has to occur *inside* you.

For example, I could never have played parts like John Wayne or Gary Cooper or Clark Gable . . . I would look ridiculous on a horse! In the end I found that people liked me not because I was this or that character, but because it had a certain part of me. John Waynes are loved because they represent a certain type of hero, never changing costume or horse—that wasn't my type of acting. Nevertheless, I wanted to be loved by the public, that's in the veins of an actor, and of course it's an economic necessity.

Maybe that is the only planning I ever did: not to take on parts that were outside of my ability, both physical and psychological. I was always aware of the fact that my appearance on a screen would not, in itself, nail the spectator to his seat like the appearance of a Clark Gable. So I decided I had to find other ways of holding his attention. What those actors achieved by always being the same kind of hero, I did by always changing. As it happens, that fits my nature: I love to change, to be different from moment to moment. Changing helped me overcome the problem of not having a strong personality. In the end, the public liked my many faces, although often they pretend (and the producers support them in this view) that they would like to see the same thing again and

Excerpt from *Film Quarterly* 46, no. 2 (Winter 1992–1993), 2–7. Trans. Gideon Bachmann. © 1992 by the Regents of the University of California. Reprinted by permission.

Marcello Mastroianni in *The Organizer* (1963)

again. In a way, I won my battle. I've played everything: a pregnant man, a homosexual, a whole series of impotent characters, a man who could get excited in love only under conditions of extreme danger, all roles diametrically opposed to this label that has been affixed to me, this "Latin Lover" nonsense—a part, by the way, which I have never played. . . .

And in all this time I've never played a hero in the traditional sense, rather parts in which the complications of life, its drudgery, its pitfalls, are accepted with compassion and simplicity. I don't want to sound pretentious, but I actually prefer characters with certain limits, with weaknesses, not winners. That corresponds more to my own character, I'm not a winner in real life. Heroes actually put me off. I feel, somehow, that they are irresponsible. Even the saints put me off. I mean, how can a human being be so exceptional? Does that mean that I, in comparison, am a shit? Or maybe I'm just envious. . . .

Anyway, real people are much more ambiguous, much more complicated than the saints and the John Waynes of this world. I wish we could straighten everything out with a sharpshooter or a fist . . . ridiculous. But these are elements of cinema language. Except that I couldn't use them. On me you'd soon see how ridiculous those postures are. . . .

. . . As the years pass, I find that my choices become more precise. I have continually refused to participate in those major films, these American monster projects, these international blockbusters, which are occasionally offered to me. All my friends told me I was mad, refusing big films and accepting small, intimate films—films which were clearly destined to make little or no money at the box office. Sometimes dangerous films, but somehow I feel proud about them. The film I made in Greece with Theo Angelopoulos clearly wasn't made for a large public.

The only really "big" films I've agreed to make were the ones with Fellini, but these big films have a lot more content, more weight. But I like the ones with small casts, small crews, made with a few friends, an enterprise like an adventure, not counting the outcome, made for the fun of making them. . . .

There are many philosophies, religions, and social and psychological theories that all state that man has to find himself before he can be of use to others. I feel just the other way around: I must be of use to others before I can be myself. And by "being of use" I don't mean to do a lot of theorizing or analyzing. Even when I was in school we had a saying among the boys—I can't repeat it here in its original Neapolitan because it isn't exactly a polite expression—which stated that the best way to get out of a jam was to stop thinking about it. . . .

When I make a film, I never go to see the rushes, for example, because I don't want to risk not liking what I have done. It's simpler to put your head in the sand, like an ostrich, and that may be what I do in my real life as well. This tendency I have, not to look at myself in the mirror, may just be a bit of cowardice. A bit of dishonesty. Not to want to know, really, who I am and what I am. I tend to say to myself, I'll go and look at myself tomorrow, tomorrow. . . . Domani . . . domani . . .

Liv Ullmann Conversation with the Actress

QUESTION. . . . How does Ingmar Bergman work with and direct his actors?

LIV ULLMANN. He is very different from what most people seem to believe. He has a reputation of a demon, which is totally untrue. He depends very much on his actors. He knows whom he has hired. He listens to them and he watches them. He tries to get out of them what they have to give, not what he would want to do in a similar situation. He is a fantastic listener and he has a fantastic manner of looking. He

Excerpt from "Dialogue on Film: Liv Ullmann," American Film Institute Publications 2, no. 5 (March 1973), 1–23. Copyright © The American Film Institute. Reprinted by permission.

sees what you are trying to express and he builds on that. He helps get it out of you. He also makes very good scenery. Do you call it scenery? I mean the movements of the scene are always telling in itself very much of the scene. He doesn't explain very much.

QUESTION. Do you mean his blocking of the scene?

ULLMANN. Yes, his blocking of the scene, in that blocking actually is what he wants the scene to be like and then it is up to the actor to film it.

QUESTION. Where does he actually sit?

ULLMANN. He sits very close to the camera. You feel him very much and if he is not close to the camera, you tend to act towards him. He always is very, very close to the camera and he is terribly inspiring. I don't know what he is doing, but it is something that makes you want to give everything you have. You feel that there is somebody who is really there.

QUESTION. Does he tell you that or is it something you have to feel out?

ULLMANN. He hates to discuss and analyze. He feels that if you have chosen your profession as an actor, then you know a little how to act. He feels that you are fairly intelligent. He sort of feels that an analysis would take away the fantasy. He knows that is the way an actor creates. The actor has to use his own fantasy and imagination.

QUESTION. How many takes does Bergman usually shoot of a scene?

ULLMANN. It depends. Sometimes he uses the first take. Sometimes we go on for 20, 30, or 40 takes until you are completely exhausted.

QUESTION. Does he allow rehearsals?

ULLMANN. Yes, he allows technical rehearsals. As I said before, the blocking is very important. But then he likes to take on the first emotional rehearsal because sometimes that is the best take. . . .

QUESTION. How much improvisation is there in a Bergman film?

ULLMANN. More and more. In my experience it started in *The Shame*. If you remember they are sitting by a table and they are drinking wine and eating. Then they fall down on the grass. That was improvised. We knew what he wanted to say. But the way that we wanted to do it was more or less left up to us.

QUESTION. That was a change from the way he had directed you before?

ULLMANN. Yes. He has always been very strict in wanting us to keep to his sentences. There was the dinner party in *The Passion of Anna* where the four tell their own story. That was our own complete freedom. But we had to stick to the character. One day a lady came and she made a beautiful dinner. First it may have been Max von Sydow's turn. He drank red wine and all of us could ask him questions. He had to answer as the character and the camera was on him all the time. He did the same thing with all four of us. Then he cut it together.

QUESTION. There are scenes in *The Passion of Anna* where he interviews each one of the actors. Did he write those interviews?

ULLMANN. No. As it was before, in the script he had written what the characters themselves spoke as characters. Then he had written a text. Do you understand what I mean? He broke the picture in four places. The characters sort of came out and spoke as the character.

RESPONSE. Yes, but you speak as an actor.

ULLMANN. Yes, because then he didn't really feel that it was good. He took it away, and after the picture was finished he asked us to come to the studio and to speak as the actor. Bibi Andersson used the text which her character had when she was the character.

QUESTION. You have played different women's roles in Bergman's films. How accurate do you think his interpretations of the different women have been?

ULLMANN. They are accurate for that sort of woman. I think he has a great understanding for women, maybe even more than for men. I think his women characters, especially in the last years, have been more interesting.

QUESTION. Does he allow you to tell him more about what you would feel if you were that woman?

ULLMANN. First of all, he knows which actor is going to play which part when he writes the script. So he knows something of what he is going to get. He is also very open for suggestions. He hates it if you start to analyze, but he is very open to your own kind of interpretation of the kind of woman that he has written.

. . .

QUESTION. Why do you think he prefers women?

ULLMANN. He finds them more interesting than men. They're more emotionally open. Also I think he finds actresses easier to work with than actors. Many men actors are really ashamed of their profession. And they really take care of their image. Look on the screen: they are all so virile. What Jack Lemmon did in *Save the Tiger* was very unusual, or Erland Josephson in *Scenes from a Marriage*. Mostly they are all bigger than life. And that's not only because they're men but also because they're men actors.

QUESTION. Since you began your career on the stage, did you run into a problem adjusting your technique for film roles?

ULLMANN. I'm more comfortable in film now. With the close-ups I've been able to find an intimate technique that works very well for me: you think right and it will show in your eyes. Of course, you can't do this on the stage. So I have more trouble every time I go back to the stage. Movements and everything else have to be bigger than life, and I feel myself false because I want so much to be real when I act.

QUESTION. When you mention make-up, it makes me think of the Bergman films in which you don't seem to wear any.

ULLMANN. No. Never in his films, nor in the theater do I use make-up. There are so many benefits, because so much can come through that can't come through with make-up. And this is true on the stage too. You can be red in the face or you can be pale, and these things actually happen to you when you go through these emotions, on stage and in life.

Bergman actually denies make-up. Oh, we have tried to cheat. In *Passion of Anna* we sneaked off and curled up our lashes, and I know Bibi tried some false things. But no, he came and took them off. And it's a little unfair, because we all look a little more ugly than we are sometimes, and older. And he's the first one to admire a woman with lovely plucked eyebrows. He says, "Look at her; she's not made up." He can't see that she's made up. But he knows our faces so well that when we try to do it, he knows.

QUESTION. How do you prepare for a scene?

ULLMANN. Well, I'm always very well prepared when I come to the set. I know my lines. I don't come with hangovers. When I'm working, I go to bed early so I'm prepared in the morning.

Emotionally, I don't prepare. I think about what I would like to show, but I don't prepare, because I feel that most of the emotions I have to show I know about. By drawing on real experience, I can show them.

QUESTION. What do you think of the American style of method acting?

ULLMANN. I think it's bullshit. I don't believe in it. I've worked with some method actors, and they're very difficult to work with because you never know who's coming in on the stage. Every day somebody new comes in. They have been behind stage concentrating so much that they're spaced out when they come in. Or else they've suddenly got themselves into "It was such a cold day outside," so instead of doing what should happen between the two people, they are doing a big thing about a person who is getting warm after having been out during a cold day. And that's very interesting, you know, but it's not what the play is about.

But most good actors actually do the same. The fantasy thing they do is just about the same. Sam Waterston, for example, could just as well be acting in Norway. And Marlon Brando is a method actor, but he is also a great actor. I don't think any method will ruin a good actor, because a good actor will always use what he needs. It's for the bad actors that the method can be dangerous, because they don't know what to take and what to leave.

QUESTION. Your own British training, then, didn't attempt to teach you how to conjure up emotions?

ULLMANN. No. I don't think that can be taught. That's something you have to learn through the years: how to concentrate, how it works best for you to be clean and real for the moment when the action takes place. And that is a kind of concentration and not getting uptight. I really think it's a kind of relaxation.
. . .

QUESTION. We know you are here to do a film with Ross Hunter, the remake of *Lost Horizon* as a musical. Why have you chosen to pick that as a project?

ULLMANN. I will be very honest. I came here to promote *The Emigrants*. I just finished *Cries and Whispers* with Ingmar. It is very sad. It's about someone who is dying of cancer. I've always done terribly sad women, mostly farmers. I know that producers when they hear about me must think, "Oh, no. She's not right for the part." I knew Charles Jarrott and he wanted me in this picture. Ross Hunter said, "No, she's sad." Then they said, "Oh, we would like you to do it. You could be happy. It's a musical." They also pay much more. He said, "Do you sing?" I said, "No." He said, "It doesn't matter." I thought it sounded fun. I am living in Beverly Hills. I always wanted to know how that would be. I have my family here. We have a swimming pool. That is the first part of the deal. The second part is that I wouldn't have done it if it had been *The Godfather* or something which I would really be against. I believe in the naive way of telling a story which I think many people need today. Maybe we all, deep down, dream of a place that is Shangri-La where people live in peace and in love. It is artistic in its way. It has Burt Bacharach. It has a very good cast: Charles Boyer, Sir John Gielgud, and many other people. I am very proud to be among them. I don't think that there is anything shameful about saying to people, in a naive way, that we can still hope for a Shangri-La. That's my excuse.

QUESTION. How often do you get out here to do films in Hollywood?

ULLMANN. I've already told you my problem with the producers. I've gotten several offers from directors and some of them I didn't want to do. Others stranded on the producer. In a way it is very good to be with Ingmar Bergman but you also get a reputation of being neurotic and bad looking and all of that. I have worked some, but I am not overwhelmed.

QUESTION. As an actress, what do you look for when a project is presented to you?

ULLMANN. The director.

QUESTION. The director more than the script?

ULLMANN. Well, if he's a good director, he wouldn't accept a bad script. Of course, I do look at the script. I don't want to be naked and I don't want to be in any violent pictures. I've done that once. But if it is a good director whom you respect, he usually offers you the kind of script that you would like to do.
. . .

QUESTION. On pictures like *Persona,* how many weeks before shooting started did you get the script? Also how long did you rehearse before the shooting started?

ULLMANN. We did not rehearse at all. We got the script, actually, because he had been very sick. They did not know if they were going to make the picture at all. They just asked Bibi Andersson and me to be free for the summer, and they would pay us something if the picture didn't come off. Then he finished the script and it was decided very shortly before, three weeks before, that they would make the picture. Then we had one meeting at Bibi Andersson's house where he told us some of his visions about the script. That was all done before we started. To me it was very difficult because I didn't know him before. I was terribly shy and frightened because he was sort of a god to me.

QUESTION. So, in fact, you rehearsed with the technical crew before the shooting started. Was it just before he shot?

ULLMANN. Just before each shot. He never has rehearsals before the actual shooting starts.

QUESTION. That scene in which you created a great mood where you were humming when you went out in the country in that particular picture, was that the first take? You were peeling mushrooms and humming.

ULLMANN. He got the idea of that actual situation when we were sitting in between takes with our big hats. We were humming. He said, "This is wonderful. It looks relaxed. I want this in the picture." So that was perhaps the only time when he used a personal relationship.
. . .

QUESTION. How did you prepare for the role in *Persona* where you didn't have dialogue to either play with or against?

ULLMANN. That was a script that I had to read many times. It was very difficult for me because I was 24 at the time. I had experienced a lot which I didn't know about then. The way that I prepared was to read the script many times, to try to block it into sections. I would try to think, "This is the section where this is happening to her, and now he goes a little further with this section." That is the way that I very often work. I divide the manuscript into sections which always makes you know where you are at the shooting.

. . .

QUESTION. Which do you enjoy more, acting on the stage or acting in film?

ULLMANN. I used to say acting on the stage, because that is where I belong. But I think I have been fortunate to work with very good directors in pictures. The directors in theater in Norway are not very good. So in a way working in film has been more fun.

QUESTION. Do you find that you employ different techniques acting in film than acting for stage?

ULLMANN. Yes. That is also something that I now like about pictures. What I feel I want to express is something human, something natural. On the stage when you play the classics, sometimes you feel that there is a big gap between you and the audience. Everything has to be so much bigger, so much farther from life. This is even true if what you say is for people today.

. . .

QUESTION. Are you tempted to do anything else besides acting? Do you think that acting will meet all of your challenges and expectations?

ULLMANN. I would like to write. When I write I feel that I am . . .

QUESTION. More at ease?

ULLMANN. No, not more at ease. I feel I give it more time. I give it every time of my life. With acting I want to be proud of it and I like the day to end. But when I write I feel that I can go on.

QUESTION. What do you write when you write?

ULLMANN. I write what I feel about different things. When I am here I write about Hollywood and my approach to life. I have written to some newspapers, and I am trying to write a book about what I feel like being a human being today. I am not a good writer. I am not saying that. I just feel that it is a fun way of expressing myself.

QUESTION. Have you ever written any short stories or scripts?

ULLMANN. No, I've only written essays.

QUESTION. Do you feel that there is a difference between acting and writing, in the sense that with acting you are forced to act at the moment that the camera rolls? When you write, you are free to write when the inspiration comes to you. Do you feel that freedom?

ULLMANN. Yes, I feel it is a wonderful freedom. At the same time it is more difficult. There is nobody there to really push you to do it. If you are lazy, then you may not do it as much as you should.

. . .

QUESTION. Moving from the close ensemble filmmaking of Bergman to Ross Hunter and Columbia Pictures, the last bastions of Hollywood production must have been quite a change for you. How have you reacted to the scale of the production?

ULLMANN. It is bigger. I have never seen a producer like Ross Hunter. Mostly the producers don't appear in Sweden, and he is there all the time. He is very happy. He is like a boy. He is childishly in love with this project. That is very inspiring. I think we are most organized in a way. If it's to start at a certain time, then it starts. If you have to be there at a certain time, then everyone is there on time. Here, the people come too late, and sometimes they don't even come at all.

QUESTION. When you say "we" are you talking about Sweden? In Sweden, is it more organized than it is here?

ULLMANN. Yes. I feel that it is more organized. So many people here are really doing the same thing and they don't really communicate.

QUESTION. Have you found it harder or easier to act in that setting? Of course, this is a very different picture than what you have done before.

ULLMANN. I'm not sure that I know how to answer that. If it was something very serious dramatically, then I would find it harder. But since it is this kind of picture, I find it to be easier. They serve you all the time.

QUESTION. When you say "they serve you," are you talking about the crew and the director?

ULLMANN. Yes. It's different.

QUESTION. Do you feel like a star?

ULLMANN. Well, yes. You get some strange serving which you are not used to. If you are dressed in beautiful clothes and look beautiful, it's much easier. But in a way you feel a little homeless. I am more happy at home. But then most of the crew here is European so it really shouldn't be that different.

. . .

QUESTION. How big is the film industry in Norway? Are there films made in Norway for Norwegians or do they mostly watch American and Swedish films?

ULLMANN. We make movies. We have also started to co-produce with Americans. Charlton Heston is there making a picture right now. They have very good technical equipment, very good. What they really lack is great talent. I think that by co-producing maybe they can establish themselves as a film country. They can learn from the people who come because they can make it so much cheaper there.

Klaus Maria Brandauer Human Masks Are Dangerous

C.C. Theater came first. Let's say stage experience had a decisive impact on your career.

K.M.B. That's right. From the very beginning it was an enthralling experience, and I don't think I could ever live without it. I studied acting and stage directing in West Germany and performed in Düsseldorf, Vienna, Munich, Hamburg, Berlin, Zürich. I am a theater man who had the wonderful opportunity to become a film actor. But then I always have to go back to the stage; I feel I need that to build up my energy again.

C.C. Your experience in the two media may very well improve the quality of your work in both fields. Why do you say you need to go back to the stage after making a film?

K.M.B. In each film, the actor faces the danger of being affected by the requirements of the director and of being manipulated by film producers. The stage is a fleeting event which "is written on the wind," as Peter Brook would say, but its autonomy and greatness stem precisely from this immediate truth, from the tremendous and momentary strength which, day after day, the actor must produce to move different audiences; from the fantastic communion of feeling with the audience, which is the very essence of theatrical magic.

Excerpt from Wilfredo Cancio Isla, "Brandauer: Human Masks Are Dangerous," *Cine Cubano* 88 (1988), 31–39. Trans. Isabelle Boutriau and Alain Piette.

c.c. Do you mean that it is impossible to be a convincing film actor if you are not a theater man?

k.m.b. I am only speaking about my personal experience. I am not setting up a general rule. There are excellent theater actors who are bad film actors, others are brilliant on the screen but not credible onstage. These are different skills.

. . .

c.c. Your crowning glory as a movie star is linked to the theater, with a role inspired by the sinister Gustav Gründgens. He went from his provincial theater to the Berlin State Theater. Between 1944 and 1955, he directed the Düsseldorf Theater, and finally, he was at the helm of the Hamburg Theater when he died in 1963. You followed exactly in his footsteps: you went to the same places and played on the same boards. Don't you think that these "coincidences" helped *Mephisto?*

k.m.b. Yes, I do. My theatrical experience helped me a lot to define the character. Besides, when I was working on the set, I was told that I had been awarded the prize for Best Actor in the German-Speaking Countries. But when Szabó suggested that I should play in *Mephisto,* he insisted that the important thing was to stress the psychological complexity of a changing personality and to avoid any concrete identification with Gründgens. From the beginning, we wanted to make a topical film, and not a historical one, and that is exactly what we did.

c.c. Would you then say that the strength of the character you play in *Mephisto* lies in its topicality?

k.m.b. That's right. Gründgens represents the irresponsibility of the artist playing the roles he is assigned. He is the classical opportunist who developed an impressive ability to adapt, who would do anything to succeed. *Mephisto* was an illumination for me, as I had had a constant worry since the beginning of my career: What is truly transcendent in an actor's life? Great though it might be, and whatever perfection it might reach, your life is nonsense if you can't sustain a personal viewpoint on society and the world.

c.c. István Szabó sees human life as a succession of commitments.

k.m.b. A man who doesn't commit himself can't live in society. Even Robinson Crusoe, who escaped into loneliness, found he needed the company of Friday and had to commit himself to get his services. Human beings assert themselves as human beings through their commitments. To commit oneself is a wonderful thing, but the essential question is to know where you stand.

c.c. Szabó also says that an actor should be more responsible than anyone else. What do you think?

k.m.b. I don't agree with Szabó. Everybody wants to fulfill their dreams, whatever their position or skill. Friendship, the commitment par excellence, implies the same investment from all of us who want to make friends, whether we are artists or not. But in reality, I don't think we artists are that important. We influence other people through our actions, sometimes we manage to make them think, but social changes, people's satisfactions or frustrations, the course of their lives, all depend on more important forces. Ministers, businessmen, and presidents have larger responsibilities because of the tremendous consequences of their decisions, declarations, or mistakes. If I make a mistake, the only thing that can happen is a bad film.

. . .

c.c. Opportunism, disguise, the conflict between truth and falsehood seem to be recurring themes on the screen . . .

k.m.b. I am fascinated by the subtleties of the human being, and I try to reject any sort of disguise that denies people's real identity, any circumstance that favors atrocities against mankind. The reason we investigated Europe's past in these three films is that we wanted to understand what made fascism possible and to avoid the repetition of such barbarities in today's world. I think my entire work is no more than an intense conversation with the audience, with my colleagues and myself, about themes and stories that inspire me and that I want society to reflect on. Nowadays the artist must seek a constant dialogue with the audience.

. . .

c.c. Some of your roles are not well known: the film *The Streets of Gold* by Joe Roth, with Spanish actress Angela Molina . . .

k.m.b. It's the story of a Soviet boxing champion of Jewish origin, who emigrates to the United States, thinking the streets are paved with gold and it's going to be like paradise. The confrontation with reality leads him to irremediable frustration.

c.c. With *Out of Africa,* you started at the top in Hollywood. What attracted you most? Was it one of your goals?

k.m.b. I'm rather curious by nature. I am attracted to any kind of professional experience, and once the script was revised, I thought it was a good opportunity to work with two wonderful actors like Robert Redford and Meryl Streep, and a director like Sidney Pollack. Everything worked as planned. The international market was just one step further. In Hollywood, as anywhere else, there are some good and some bad films, some good actors or directors and some bad ones. If you have the opportunity to make a film with artistic value and to show it worldwide, you seize it. It's stupid to make a quality film if you don't promote it.

c.c. Now that you mention the controversial issue of distribution and promotion by transnational film companies, could you tell me what you think of the dangers facing national film industries? How do you see the future?

k.m.b. We live in a period of high inflation, of important economic contrasts. That's the reason we must fight together to preserve what there is in each country: national film industries, movie theaters, and their audiences. That is the intelligent way. The cinema is there to unite, not to divide people. There is no reason we should get rid of each country's specific film style, its own identity, its indigenous quality, but there should always be a universal preoccupation. The modern artist should try to find a way to preserve tradition and to make it universally attractive. That is the challenge. Hollywood's power lies not only in its market and stars but also in its capacity to promote a film worldwide.

c.c. Let's talk about your working methods. What methods do you use when working on a character?

k.m.b. Actors can't afford ignorance. They must know all the different methods and schools: Stanislavsky, Brecht, Grotowski, the Actors' Studio's requirements, Peter Brook . . . , before choosing their own way. Acting is some sort of schizophrenic state, because you have to live the lives of various characters: you have a good time, you dream, you laugh, but you also suffer and break down with the character. Speaking for myself, I can't explain about fifty percent of my capacities as an actor, which are a mixture of feelings and intuition.

c.c. Jack Nicholson says that an experienced actor must cultivate his naïveté.

k.m.b. Of course. But in a mature way, not in a childish way. The actor can never come onstage and let somebody else decide for him. He must be very well prepared and confident in order to defend his own status in the work. Otherwise he becomes a mere puppet.

c.c. If we examine your theater and film career, tragedies are clearly in the majority: *Mephisto, Colonel Redl, Out of Africa, Hamlet, Leonce and Lena* [*sic*] . . . Why is that?

k.m.b. Life is a mosaic of events and behaviors, but in reality "devils" outdo "angels"; evil and pain always lie in wait for kindness and laughter. I think that is why I like talking about serious matters, but I don't underestimate the possibilities of humor and entertainment. Tragic statements are important, but sometimes we should make people laugh and combine both meditation and entertainment. We should always bear in mind that we are dealing with human beings and that they need entertaining films of one kind or another. It's no use having a terrific theme with a transcendent message and meaning if your film is boring.

c.c. Next to film and stage acting, you also tried your hand at other artistic media. What are your objectives as a mature artist?

k.m.b. I am a twentieth-century artist living in Austria, where only five films are produced each year. I was very young when I started directing plays. I work for television, radio; I make records. I get some professional fulfillment each time I work with artistic dignity.

Part IV Hollywood Acting

In purely geographical terms, Hollywood is a much smaller place than Europe. Since the early part of the century, however, its place at the center of filmmaking in the United States has endowed Hollywood with a more striking mythic profile than those of the film capitals of London, Paris, or Rome. The part "European Acting" furnished glimpses of Hollywood through the sometimes skeptical eyes of foreign actors; this part provides perspectives at closer range.

Hollywood has long been in the business of manufacturing images calculated to reflect, to flatter, and less often to change life in America. The films made and promoted there have often captured Hollywood itself in what some might say are obsessively self-referential treatments of life behind the cameras. Meanwhile, the landscape of Southern California, together with its architecture and plant life, have become familiar around the world. American fashion has drawn inspiration from, and assumed much greater visibility through, the agency of Hollywood. In recent times, the filmic images produced there have been reinforced and reconstituted by television, which has come to contest film's place in the economy of what has become the most populous and wealthiest state in the United States.

Economic issues figure more centrally in the accounts grouped under this heading than they did in those of the European actors. This does not mean, though, that art and matters of conscience disappear entirely in Hollywood. If anything, mainstream American filmmaking has aroused more spirited debate around how money can be used in the service of art or reconciled, at least, to demands distinct from those of the marketplace. Films from Hollywood have furnished a testing ground for ways that business and art can coexist and for the forms a highly commercial entertainment can assume while serving shifting and politically sensitive notions of the public good.

If American actors can be said to lack the interest in tradition of their counterparts in Europe, they frequently show themselves to be more heavily invested in the future. In each of the three sections in this part, the sense emerges that because film acting has been invented over time, it can also be reinvented. In this regard, the synthetic qualities of American culture have served the vitality of film acting from Hollywood. Hollywood film actors have borrowed from other traditions to ensure that their efforts will continue to appeal to a broad popular audience all over the world. American film actors have proved as adaptable in this way as they have to changing demands for their services: first in the transition from silents to sound films, later in the face of competition from television, and over the last generation as the number of films has shrunk and shooting schedules have lengthened.

Facing such pressures, actors in Hollywood, together with American filmmakers, have sometimes claimed imported tradition as their own or modified it in drastic ways to appropriate it for themselves. *Auteur* theory originated in France in the early 1950s; in fairly short order, it was applied retroactively to the films of major Hollywood studio directors whose work had been little recognized. Part of the impulse for this interpretation arose from the decline of the studios. People felt a need to resurrect them as they had existed in their glory days, to memorialize their achievements even as they acknowledged their passing. As we shall see, film actors were centrally involved in both these projects.

In a more original way, perhaps, acting teachers in America reinterpreted some of Stanislavsky's intermediate theories and relabeled them the Method. Consistent with Pudovkin's notion that film demanded a more controlled emotional authenticity than the stage did and that Stanislavsky offered the key to such control, the approach Americans began to pursue to acting was influenced by the particular demands of film rather than of the stage. The techniques generated have been proclaimed different from acting in the theater and have found exposure before an extremely wide audience. Many American film actors regret the commercialism that drives their industry, yet they would like to believe that their best films, by appealing to viewers the world over, represent a cultural extension of American democracy and free enterprise. Even when such ideals are pursued in a spirit of self-examination, they reflect the coupling of commercialism with the ethos of individual expression that Hollywood has recommended as its own version of the American dream.

The Golden Age of the Studios

Hollywood has long been interested in identifying responses to its wares. At times it has claimed that it does so as a democratic exercise; at others it has done so under political pressure, as with its enforcement of the Hays Code in the 1920s and 1930s or its blacklisting of suspected Communists in the late 1940s and early 1950s. Given studio employees' immersion in commercial values, it is hardly surprising that film actors should have grown skilled at anticipating responses to their work. Any native or acquired instincts about the reception of their acting could counteract their very limited mobility under their long-term studio contracts and uphold their ability to choose roles for themselves, intermittent though it was.

At the same time, though, life at the studios demanded concessions to collegiality from stars and supporting players as well. As Hollywood studios grew to surpass even the largest nineteenth-century theatrical stock companies, not to mention the European film sites, which specialized generally in smaller-scale and director-driven productions, a company mentality replaced the narrow professionalism that had characterized stage acting. This development had the effect of enlarging film actors' circle of daily collaborators to include businesspeople and technicians, many of whom, like the actors themselves, were unionized.

Accordingly, matters of collaboration figure in broad terms in many of the accounts that follow. If few Hollywood actors have spoken about their directors with the reverence common among their counterparts in Europe, it may be owing to sharp disparities in salary between stars and directors at the studios. Or then again, the lack of reverence may be due to the pervasiveness of antiauthoritarian sentiment in America. As you will see, stars often consider themselves as having sprung from the people, and this belief supports their common view of filmmaking as a populist endeavor and of themselves as stand-ins for those who watch them on the screen.

Accounts written before 1950 differ strikingly from those written after the studios' decline had become pronounced. Before midcentury, most actors took studios for granted, seeing no other model for making films. Far from merely feeling disempowered by the studio moguls, though, several actors writing after 1950 praise these men for occasionally producing highly complex and ambitious films. When actors criticize the studios, they are likely to base their reservations on the worth of particular scripts. Actors seldom criticize the working conditions that prevailed during the late 1930s and

1940s, and it is easy to hear the notes of nostalgia sounded by some of the later writers.

Bette Davis offers a detailed view of her life first as a studio player and then as a studio star in the late 1930s. Still a relative newcomer when she wrote this excerpt, she sees her "part" to be working dutifully within the routines and resources specified by her employers. Her own routines, like those of other stars of her day, included lavish attention to makeup and costumes, along with various activities to publicize her films. Although the concerns for appearance that Davis expresses surface frequently among Hollywood actresses, her remarks regarding studio publicity are more candid than is customary. Davis's opinion that "Actors and actresses are notoriously bad judges of story material" may seem surprising on the surface. But her own exceptional judgment—and her willingness to decline parts the studio offered her—go a long way toward explaining her record of success despite her lack of conventional good looks, of which she was well aware.

Both Joan Crawford and Mary Astor give retrospective descriptions of their time at the studios. In showing herself to be an actress of tenacity and discipline, Crawford belies her largely posthumous reputation for megalomania and one-dimensional acting. Like Bette Davis, she speaks of the importance of choosing the best roles available at any given time and identifies her personal and professional interests as sometimes lying close to the studio's, but sometimes not. Mary Astor, who considers herself much more a collaborator than an independent agent, examines the intrinsically collective aspects of filmmaking. Her remarks provide some idea of how exacting film acting can be, and she makes sensible suggestions about ways actors can tap the experience and skills of the people working just beyond the camera's range, as an aid to their own efforts.

Hume Cronyn came to films as a character actor seasoned in the values of the stage. His recurrent success in character parts and comic material was owing in part to his slight stature, and quizzical features. Elaborate planning may have been especially necessary at the beginning of his film career, when he played a succession of small supporting roles demanding that he achieve his effects quickly and efficiently. One of his key questions for film actors is, "What is the action?" His approach derives from Stanislavsky's and allies him with the American Method acting that was coming into its own at the time he wrote. That approach runs counter in some ways to the acting traditions of the British stage, with which he was clearly affiliated. Cronyn's suggestions, synthesized from several ordinarily distinct traditions and theories of acting, are relatively easy to follow.

James Stewart touches on something approaching Hume Cronyn's care with details by contending that "pieces of time" are crucial both to actors' characterizations on film and to the ways film audiences receive those characterizations. But whereas Cronyn applied his meticulous approach to character roles, Stewart employed a similar technique for leading parts. The nuance and precision he brings to comic acting, in particular, resemble Cronyn's. Stewart also credits the Metro-Goldwyn-Mayer studio for having provided him with valuable experience while he was a beginner in films in the 1930s, and he praises several directors he worked with then and afterward.

Henry Fonda's career was similar to Stewart's in many respects. Both actors were known for conveying the goodness and simplicity at the heart of American life, in contrast with actresses like Bette Davis and Joan Crawford, who matched them in fame and longevity, but who were often called on to play less sympathetic roles, especially as they aged. Fonda identifies the ear for dialogue as essential to his technique. He also shows a disposition more critical than Stewart's, when elaborating on the qualities of his directors that made it difficult in certain cases, or easy in others, for him to work with them.

As the 1950s wore on and the studios' influence waned, Fonda felt a growing need to produce his own films. His remarks on the difficulty of financing and marketing ventures of uncertain commercial appeal anticipate concerns expressed by actors in the next section in this part, "The Business of Acting." Although studio actors may have been highly attuned to the commercial nature of their work, Fonda was unusual in his willingness to take production matters into his own hands. Such impulses were needed more frequently once commercial television began to sap the vitality of the studios and weaken their monopoly.

Bette Davis The Actress Plays Her Part

An invitation to present the motion-picture industry from the viewpoint of its actresses is a
great honor—and a difficult assignment. Never
for a moment think I am going to be able to do
justice to the problems of all my famous con-
frères. It is impossible to generalize about the
picture business, particularly our branch of it; I can only tell you what I have
found out for myself. However, I do believe I have seen it in most of its
moods—when it has completely ignored me, and when it has been more than
generous in its belief in me. There is much to be learned from both of these
attitudes and the variable temperatures in between.

If the studio weather department will hold back the artificial fog of glamour
for a while, I want to show you what it's really like to be a star, and to convince
you of two things: First, we are just plain workers here, and second, we are
more anxious to do work for which you will commend us than we are credited
with being. That ought to be obvious. You will continue to make us and break
us as long as pictures are shown. In other words, we are your humble servants.
Oh, yes, we are!

The most important consideration in a star's career is choice of story.
Without the proper vehicles very few of us would ever have arrived where we
are. A kindly disposed critic may take the trouble to note a good performance
in an otherwise inferior picture; but the average theatergoer is interested in
entertainment, and the entertainment value of a screen play never rests with
the star alone. Studios employ many talented people for the sole purpose of
finding suitable material for their top players, and only in rare cases is the star
permitted to make her own selection. Her opinion may be asked, but the final
decision rests with the studio officials. Usually Joe Doaks on Main Street
knows what her next assignment will be as soon as she does—it all depends on
who reads the morning papers first.

I personally believe this is not as unfair as it seems, for I am of the opinion
that actors and actresses are notoriously bad judges of story material. Principally interested in the part intended for us and the number of good meaty
scenes there are for us to play, we are apt to lose sight completely of weak and

Bette Davis and George Arliss in *The Man Who Played God* (1932)

insignificant plot construction or the development of the rest of the characters in the story. It would be extremely bad taste for me to name the stars who, in the past and in the present, have measurably damaged their careers by insisting on contracts which permitted them to choose their own stories.

Neither does it follow that the studios are always right. Often a studio has a script ready to go into production with an inferior and uninteresting leading role for either the actor or the actress, but the picture must be made immediately to meet a release date. Since players are put under contract in order to retain their exclusive services, they must be paid whether they are working or not; and when they are not working they are a worrisome item of expense. If the studio has scheduled nothing suitable for the star at such a time, she may be requested to go into this production even though they know it is unjust, and there is nothing for her to do but play the part, knowing the public will think less of her for it—or refuse to do it, which usually results in suspension without salary for as long as it takes to make the picture in question. In short, she gets spanked either way.

When the public reads in the newspapers that a star has "walked out on" her studio, their natural reaction is to say, "Tsk! Tsk!—Temper—Temper

. . . !" Actually the reason for it is more likely to be her refusal to disappoint her audiences by letting them see her in a role wholly unsuited to her talents and below the standard that she has consistently fought to maintain.

The number of pictures a star makes annually is almost as important as the selection of her stories. It is easy for an audience to tire of an actress it sees too often—and it appears to get just as weary of her if it doesn't see her often enough. In my present contract there is no limit to the number of pictures I make in a year, but I believe that a contract limiting an actress to four is neither detrimental to her career nor unfair to her studio. If I were free-lancing, three would be my limit; first, because screen acting is such exhausting work that I think we need long vacations between pictures; and second, because it is almost impossible to find more than three stories in a year's time which are both well-suited to me and worth your money at the box office.

Nothing is more staggering to me than to be asked how I create a character. There just isn't any one answer to that question. It depends entirely on what the assignment happens to be.

If I am to play the leading lady in a modern picture, my worries as an actress are concerned with wardrobe, hairdress, learning the script, and interpreting it to make the most of whatever opportunities it offers me. I make a practice of discussing all these things with the director as soon as possible, to make sure that our conceptions of the character are enough alike to avoid misunder-standings and costly waste of time on the set while the film is in production.

I should like to add, here, that I have never played a part which I did not feel was a person very different from myself. The character I am playing stays behind in my dressing-room at the end of the day and is waiting for me there the following morning. I do not intend this to sound as if I were "arty" about my work. On the contrary, I am extremely workman-like. Perhaps it is ex-plained by the fact that I have never—except when I am actually working—been able to realize that I am known as an actress. You have no idea how grateful I am for this frame of mind in Hollywood, where it is not easy to keep a normal outlook on oneself as a person. While I am acting I am living in an imaginary world, bringing imaginary people to life, just as I used to "live" the fairy stories I read when I was a little girl. And I think it's the grandest game in the world. Whether or not I am always successful at it, I am constantly trying to make my audience know these "phantom" friends of mine as well as I do.

When the director and I have agreed on the appearance of the character, the head costume designer (Mr. Orry Kelly) and I confer for hours. He makes many sketches which we discuss as to their suitability for both her and me, and when we have finally decided what she is going to wear, the pins, shears and needles start flying in the workroom.

Fitting and sewing costumes year in and year out, the skillful women in the workroom are faithful and loyal to their stars. Though they receive no credit for the final product, they are as interested as we are in seeing that gowns are perfect in every detail. Often they are more patient than we during the long hours we must stand for fittings. They know how the camera will emphasize the slightest wrinkle or bad line, and avoiding these defects is a matter of pride with them.

The completed gowns must be tested before the camera. This is very important, for even though our costume designers are trained to know what colors, materials and body lines are photographically "right," they sometimes make mistakes. A costume which is charming to the eye often proves most unattractive photographically, and must be replaced or changed. Preliminary tests of wardrobe may save the studio large sums of money which might otherwise have to be spent on retakes during production.

"Hair tests" are necessary for the same reason. If the camera doesn't happen to like our hairdress, it can do disastrous things to us. And unless the cameraman is accustomed to working with us, he usually wants to make photographic tests to discover our best "angles" and the most effective lighting for our features.

By the time all of these tests have been made and approved by the director and the production head, we are ready to start on the actual work of making the picture.

All of this, as I said, is the customary preparation for a simple, modern leading role. If, however, I am assigned to portray a famous character from history or a well-known fictional character, or a person with an accent unfamiliar to me, the little duties really start piling up. Endless hours must be spent in reading about them, studying their lives and habits, until I feel I know them so well I couldn't possibly do anything inconsistent with their characterization. Imagine how much of such preparation Paul Muni must have spent on Pasteur and Zola. I also collect pictures of these people at all stages of their lives if they are historical, so as to be able to resemble them as closely as possible physically. Make-up must be minutely tested to get the nearest facial similarity we can, and the costumes of the period must be studied thoroughly to avoid anachronisms and errors in detail.

For a fictional character such as Mildred in *Of Human Bondage,* the novel is used as a textbook—read and reread until I am thoroughly acquainted with her every thought. Scattered descriptions are carefully checked for indications of dress and mannerism. With Mildred I had the added problem of the cockney accent—a frightening one for an American actress. My solution of it was to invite an Englishwoman with a knowledge of cockney to live at my house with me. For six weeks before the picture began we spoke nothing but cockney, with the result that the accent became so natural to me that a great part of the time during the shooting of *Of Human Bondage* I did not even realize I was using it. I sometimes think that people who see us on the screen demand much less of us in this respect than we do of ourselves. But I have a passion for authenticity.

Every actor has a different method of memorizing lines. Though I spend a great deal of time on the script before the picture starts, absorbing the story as a whole and developing my characterization, I seldom actually learn my lines until the night before the shooting of each scene. Then they are fresh in my mind for the day's work. But, if I have a difficult scene with many long speeches, I start learning it weeks ahead, as I find I am usually too tired at the end of the day to memorize a scene of this kind thoroughly in one evening.

When the shooting begins, the studio does everything in its power to help the star concentrate on her performance. She has her own hairdresser, her own wardrobe woman to see that her clothes are at all times pressed and clean, and a make-up man to watch for any flaws in her make-up. And she has her own dressing-room on the set, where she may study or rest during the long waits which are part of the daily routine.

Once we start working on a production, that is *all* we are able to do until it is finished. After hours, an actress who is conscientious about her work is too tired mentally and physically to think of anything but a nice, long, beautiful rest. Fortunately or unfortunately, I am one of those. If the material in the picture is worthless, one has to work twice as hard to make something of it; but I have a sincere desire always to be able to say when the picture is finished that I have done the very best I could with the part.

You smiled when I said we get dog-tired. The surest way I know to convince you of this is to show you just how we work, by describing an average *shooting day.*

I get the gentle but compelling touch on the shoulder between six and six-thirty in the morning—depending on how far I am living from the studio and how elaborate my make-up is for the picture I am doing. After I have arrived at the studio, it takes at least two hours to have my hair dressed and dried and my make-up applied. There is usually just time to get to the set by nine o'clock and put on my costume. I am then ready to rehearse for the first scene of the day.

The amount of rehearsing we do is entirely dependent on the director. Some directors believe that lots of it insures a better performance when the cameras start grinding. I agree with them. As far as I'm concerned, there can never be too much rehearsal, for during this time the cast learns to work

together and often discovers bits of business that give the screen play naturalness and smoothness. The director of a "B" picture, with a small budget and a
two or three weeks' shooting schedule, obviously cannot spend much time
trying scenes out, and the picture usually suffers from imperfect performances. But on an "A" picture, with an ample budget and six to eight weeks'
shooting time, it is possible to have plenty of rehearsal and still conform to
schedule.

When we have finished rehearsing, the cameraman is given free reign to
light the set. Stand-ins, resembling the actors in height, weight and general
coloring, go through the action to be shot, while the cameraman arranges the
lights. This gives the cast a chance to cool off, refresh their make-up, see that
all the curls are where they belong, and to discuss the scene with the director if
necessary. Then one final rehearsal for the actors, the camera and the sound
department—and the scene is ready to be taken.

If a scene is shot only once, the incident is recorded as a major miracle.
More commonly it has to be repeated from three to as many as fifteen times.
Before a take is O.K.'d it has to be right for the director as far as performances
are concerned, for the cameraman, and for the sound department. The last
is a particularly exacting master. The sound man must hear every word distinctly, unimpaired by outside noises such as airplane motors, passing trucks,
coughs, footfalls, or any of a million and one other incidental sounds. All of
the things which may spoil the take for any of the departments are utterly
unpredictable. Since the members of the crew know how difficult it is to keep
a scene alive beyond the third take, they do everything in their power to keep
things going smoothly. You never saw such a display of mass patience and
precaution! Often, of course, the actors themselves are responsible for spoiling the shot. We just can't get that "something" the director is looking for—
and we *have* been known to muff lines. The success of a day on the set is
determined by the degree of co-operation between director, crew and players.
No one of us can work alone. We need each other.

An hour for lunch, then back to freshen make-up and hairdress and begin
again. The day is usually over at six, after which most of us spend half an hour
in a projection room seeing the rushes of the previous day's shooting. Now we
go to our dressing-rooms, remove make-up, put on street clothes—and go
home, arriving there between seven and eight o'clock, slightly the worse for a
working day of from twelve to fourteen hours.

But that is not the end of it. Dinner, then off to a quiet corner with the
script, to batten down enough dialogue to carry us through tomorrow. For us,
ten-thirty is bed-time; there's very little a make-up man can do with circles
under our eyes.

A day's work, and work it is—every minute of it. I don't think you can name any other profession that requires so many actual working hours spent in producing something to be seen and judged by millions of people the world over. It is largely our awareness of responsibility to all those people that makes the actual shooting of a picture so nerve-racking. Every take must be approached as if it were the one which you will see in your theater. Everything we've got must go into everything we do.

Fortunately, inside most of us is the love to create, and we are more than willing to devote the best years of our lives to it. Hollywood pays us well, but the applause we receive from our audiences stimulates us to go on and do finer things. We want you to let us know you like us. Call it childlike if you will; but since our profession is dedicated to bringing you moments of pleasure, the measure of our success is your response to what we do. You, the audience, are literally the fuel that keeps the fire going. Never for a minute think we are bored by your praise. It is what we live for.

Another problem peculiar to the life of a motion-picture star is publicity. It is a tremendous consumer of time apart from our other studio duties, and because it plays such a vital part in the development of a star's career it necessitates a great deal of understanding.

Thousands of men and women are employed by the studios and by the stars themselves to take care of publicity. Their job is to discover the type of exploitation best suited to one's personality, then use it as frequently and as tastefully as possible. These are the people who give you your ideas as to what we are like apart from our roles, and it is to our advantage to co-operate with them.

Everywhere we go, it seems, someone is waiting to take a shot of us with a still camera. We pose for portraits, for fashion pictures, sports photos of every description, and for those so-called "intimate" shots in our homes.

Personally, I have never believed in the sort of exploitation you see in commercial advertising, although early in my career—due to circumstances beyond my control—my name was used in connection with certain products. Nor do I like publicity pictures taken in bathing suits or semi-undress. I consider both of these forms of publicity disrespectful to the public's taste. And I get rabid and foamy over what we call *gag* or *stunt* pictures. I refuse to believe that they fool anybody. If an actress who doesn't know a putter from a pogo-stick has her picture taken swinging a golf club, the rankest amateur of the sport has every right to a good laugh at her expense.

It is quite possible that I am worrying about something that is not particularly important, but I feel the same way about acting. If I am playing a scene in which I am supposed to be soaking wet, I believe in looking wet even if the general effect is perfectly horrible. Or if I am beaten up by a gang, as I was in *Marked Woman,* I don't want to come out of it looking as if I had just been released from a convent. Audiences are too smart for that sort of thing, and it makes me a little ashamed to try to fool them. It all goes back, I suppose, to those puritan ancestors of mine—they left me with a frightening conscience.

Aside from the time it takes to pose for stills, we spend many hours with members of the press, both on and off the set. Many of them come from all over the world to meet us. There are also a large number of writers for fan magazines who want to know our ideas on millions of subjects. Though I can't imagine why my ideas on any of these matters should be worth anything to anybody else, I must admit that by the time the clever writers have their stories ready to print, the words they put into my mouth impress even me. They are more than generous in their descriptions of us. For all this we are truly grateful, but I will never cease to feel inadequate with them during interviews. I am always wishing there were some great, dark, hidden thing in my life for me to tell them so that they would go away thinking, "What a fascinating life Bette has had!" But my life for the last ten years has been mainly hard work.

One of the greatest dangers of publicity is its tendency to be forced. Excessive amounts of unwarranted publicity are far more dangerous than none at all. I am often reminded of a remark made to me by George Arliss very early in my career. It is far more important, he said, for young people starting in pictures to worry about the actual value of their work in front of the camera than to rely on undeserved exploitation. There are countless sorry examples in Hollywood of newcomers overpublicized before they ever appear before the cameras. It would be impossible for them to live up to the public's expectation of them based on their advance notices. Almost invariably they die an early professional death, really through no fault of their own. I sincerely believe that all young players breaking into Hollywood should carefully guard themselves against such exploitation.

On the other hand, a well-established player, to whom publicity comes naturally, should not scorn any interest shown by the press, for this is just as essential to the length of her life in pictures as the actual work she does in front of the camera.

Success in any profession is an interesting subject for speculation. I don't believe that it is ever completely unwarranted. There must be reasons for it. Success in my profession is, of course, the most difficult to understand. One minute an actress may be down and out and unwanted. Then something happens, and in the next minute—figuratively speaking—the whole course of her life may be changed and she may find herself the idol of millions.

There is much talk in Hollywood about the well-known "lucky break," but that is seldom a satisfactory explanation. The successful actress has probably spent years of her life working and hoping. She has had sufficient courage and self-confidence to stick to the profession she loves in spite of what looked like insurmountable obstacles. She has earned at last the right to be an important person in her field. No one in this world *ever* gets anything for nothing. Luck helps a lot in getting to the top, but it won't keep you there for long. Any actress who credits the fickle lady for her entire career is being either very modest or very apologetic about her accomplishments.

It's hard work becoming a first-rater in the picture business, but once we've arrived the going seems to be subtly rougher. We are open to criticism and jealousy from friend and foe alike, and we must constantly struggle to maintain whatever standards of excellence we have set for ourselves.

In our contracts there is an amusing clause stating that the producer considers our services "of a unique and extraordinary nature." Flattering, but still no key to the secret of success in Hollywood.

Hard work does it, health, and the determination to let nothing stop you.

If you are ambitious to be a leader in the acting profession, make your belief in your talents strong enough to brook any discouragement that may come to you, work every inch of the way—and the chances are that some day you may become a new star in the theatrical firmament. See if you won't!

Mary Astor A Life on Film

Resent it or not, what I was doing—and didn't realize it—was learning a craft. If one is *basically* an artist, maybe he doesn't need experience and practice, practice, practice. Maybe it's a little easier for him. It all comes to him in a glory flash and he knows exactly what to do to be a great artist. Even the word talent seems to denote a special gift, an X quality. But I don't think any talented artist ever created a work of art without the constant use of the material of his particular medium. . . .

So, sullenly, dissatisfied and unhappy, I was learning a craft. The materials began to have a familiar feel. I could, figuratively, walk in the dark and not

Excerpt from Mary Astor, *A Life on Film* (New York: Delacorte, 1971), 114–118.

Mary Astor (right) and John Barrymore in *Don Juan* (1926)

bump into anything, find articles without thinking or fumbling, know where there were openings to go through, barriers to stop at.

With a few words to a camera operator, "How low you cutting?" answered by a hand signal, I could form my boundaries in the air, my proscenium, the limits wherein I could move—and they were *felt* as though I could reach out and touch them. From then on (until the next setup) I needed to give it no more thought than you give to the edges of a street when you are driving a car normally.

A multitude of varying physical instructions: "Give a little when he comes in." "Move down, rather than up, we need a matching shot from the reverse." "On your move, be sure to clear that inky." "Your look's gotta be camera right." There are literally hundreds of these little sentences between an actor and his cameraman—just little information pieces, little necessities. (What's surgical procedure without the word "scalpel"!)

This kind of thing is my answer to the pseudo-artist who throws a palm to his overheated forehead and exclaims, "I *hate* these limitations!" I got furious at an actor who said that at least once during every setup, and I finally said, "Well, the hell with them, then. Go play your scene down on Times Square."

There are limitations everywhere; be aware of them and work within them. Freedom has its limitations. We're not free to walk on water—not yet.

I learned how to modify my own limitations. To a cameraman: "I need more room, Joey." "You got it," pulling the camera back a foot or switching a lens and saying, "Harry, watch that overhead, spread it a little." From the sound man: "When you gonna move, Mary?" "Why? you need a word cue?" "Please." "Well—uh—lemme see. Gee I'm not sure, Hank." "I don't want to conk your head when you get up, is all." "Okay, move as I put out the cigarette. I'll get it all in before then."

All the time, all around you is a babble of these little instructions, from crew to crew from director to cameraman. When you come onto a sound stage it sounds like bedlam, but it can be sorted out easily—if you know.

It all quits in a minute and then you're on your own. And in the meantime, inside of you, you've been keeping a little pot simmering on the back burner—the character, the relationships: break up the little fat chunks of emotion, and let them mix and spread. You keep up your often wordless communication with the director, you touch and exchange words with other actors. You say, "Can I help?" If he feels crowded, if the pace is wrong; we talk and answer with few words. There is often a very high level of communication between actors, and when there is, something of excellence happens.

And what's the director doing? If you're a pro, you save him time by working with the crew. He shouldn't have the menial task of relaying technical information to his people. He shouldn't have to go through something like the following:

"Now honey, we want you to—ah—see that light there right beside you? No, not that one, the one on your *right, that's* it! Now, when you turn, don't back out of it. You see that funny gizmo in front of it? It's called a cucaloris—I'll tell you why someday, not just now, dear. Well that's throwing some nice shadows on your shoulders and we don't want to lose that—it's a nice effect and—uh—you won't forget, will you dear?"

Or: "Dear, when you're over there against the wall and you're crying—and that's all marvelous, dear, but we can't hear you unless you turn a *leetle* bit toward us. No, I don't *want* you to turn clear around, just kind of drop your head and say the words over your shoulder. We can't put a mike in the wall, you understand."

During rehearsals and between takes you must come to an agreement with the director as to what the scene's about, and what you're going to do to play that scene and project these particular emotions or thoughts or actions. In the studio he is your only audience; he has to look with fresh eyes and be millions of people and decide, "That's what they'll think or feel when this moment is shown on the screen." If you know what you're doing, it is up to you to help him preserve this freshness.

It took me years and years to find out that the highest satisfaction I could get out of my work was this achievement of communication between myself and the director, first of all, then with other actors, and then, the crew. And not least of all the crew. The prop man, for instance. I've found him at my side in times of little troubles. Like maybe in a scene where I have to use a cup and saucer, picking it up, putting it back on to a table. Worrying because it's going to clatter during the scene. (Always, the anxiety tremors.) And I've looked up to see him with a roll of adhesive tape to make a few strips of padding inside the saucer. Thousands of little aids from these most resourceful men.

But at the highest level—the director—I have felt moments of knowing, of feeling, that are like moments when you're in love. You do love, in a way. You don't have to like him, but you have to respect his judgment or you're in trouble. A good director isn't "out there" *telling* you what to do—although I had to learn that too! You may even disagree with him, violently, and you chew it out and try to understand each other. You negotiate and compromise, you talk it out, but finally you *dig!* . . .

So it's no trick, really. It just takes energy, lots of it, to concentrate deeply and at the right moment and keep the inner images going the way *you want them to go.* Then there is the problem of repetition. In movies it's "over and over" sometimes. And in the theater it's eight times a week. But the mind is such a wondrous, flexible instrument that it will present the same image, on command or stimulus, and it will be slightly different each time. That makes the repetition not only endurable but fascinating.

Of course, fatigue is the enemy, and the mind will balk completely. Then, if you have to do it again, or you've got a night performance after a matinee, you have to resort to the externals completely—remembering what you did, and doing it mechanically. And it's never as good. It is bound to be superficial and slick and the audience knows it. Oh, does it ever!

Joan Crawford The Player: A Profile of an Art

On New Year's Day, 1925, I left for Hollywood to begin working for M-G-M, at seventy-five dollars a week. When I signed my contract, I thought that M-G-M wanted me because I could dance. Now I know that right from the start I was considered promising as an actress. I hardly had a chance to know what I was doing. My first role was as a chorus girl covered with imitation snow in *Pretty Ladies,* in 1925. Dancing roles in movies were easy for me, even though I had never made the front line of the chorus on the stage. At that time, movies were still silents. We would work late at night, and on Sundays, if necessary, and it would take us all of four weeks to make a movie. I danced in almost every role. From the very first, it was important to me to become known as a movie star, to show the people back home in Kansas City what I really was. They had never believed in my talent. In *Sally, Irene, and Mary,* which was made in 1925, I played the role of Irene, a dancer, and it was then that the studio changed my name to Joan Crawford. Among my other early films were *Old Clothes,* with Jackie Coogan, and *The Only Thing,* with Eleanor Boardman, and in 1926 I was Harry Langdon's leading lady in *Tramp, Tramp, Tramp,* and then played in *Paris,* with Charles Ray. I was still a teen-ager, and even though I still wanted to be a star, I was really dancing to please my leading man and my director and my producer. I would do any kind of part they asked me to. I was working so hard I didn't have time for anything else. I played ingénue roles in *The Unknown,* with Lon Chaney; *Twelve Miles Out,* with John Gilbert; *West Point,* with William Haines; and *Across to Singapore,* with Ramon Novarro. It was work I thrived on and loved. In 1928, I was still thinking that dancing was my inborn talent. When I played in *Our Dancing Daughters* that year, and appeared dancing on a table, after coming out of a huge cake, I became known as a movie star, and my salary was raised to five hundred dollars a week.

The next year, 1929, I danced in *Our Modern Maidens,* with Douglas Fairbanks, Jr., and I also danced in *Hollywood Revue of '29.* It was between these assignments that I first had a chance to look around me and see what acting was. I admired Eleanor Boardman, and I watched Greta Garbo on her

Excerpt from Lillian Ross and Helen Ross, "Joan Crawford," in Ross and Ross, *The Player: A Profile of an Art* (New York: Simon & Schuster, 1962), 66–72. Copyright © 1961 by Lillian Ross. Copyright © 1962 by Lillian Ross and Helen Ross. Used by permission of Lillian Ross.

Joan Crawford in *The Taxi
Dancer* (1927)

sets every chance I could get. I grew determined to become a dramatic actress.
I started nagging Louis B. Mayer and Irving Thalberg to cast me in more and
more dramatic roles. I would hang around the studio and get my hands on the
new scripts, then take them home with me to read, and decide on the role I
wanted. I relied on my instinct in choosing what was right for me, and my
instinct rarely let me down. After deciding that I wanted a certain role, I got up
and went after it. The written words weren't too important. I knew that if
certain words or phrases stuck in my throat, I could call a little conference
right on the set and have them changed to suit me better. I would go off in a
corner with the director and the leading man, and together we would decide
what we wanted the writer to change. I knew that the writer would be grateful
to me. His words were dead words. They were brought to life by me.

I was at M-G-M for seventeen years. In the thirties, I was considered one of
the ten biggest money-making stars for six straight years. Once I'd started on a
role, it became like a horse race. I couldn't wait to go on. I worked hard on my
preparations. If the script had been based on a book, I'd go back and read the
book. I have almost total recall and a vivid imagination. I usually chose my
own writers, producer, and director—I still do—and I'd enter them in the
race. Once in a role, I eliminated myself completely. I became the character I
played. I portrayed so many girls and women who went from rags to riches
that L. B. Mayer thought I represented Cinderella to the public. My audience
was composed mostly of women. I began to beg to play bitches, so I got that

kind of part, and liked it. I've known so many bitches, who never cared about the feelings of other people as long as they could get their own way. They just never gave a hoot how many people they rode over and hurt. Then I'd play another kind of role, and it was exciting to become the queen bee again. I've made about seventy-five pictures, and I remember every one of my important roles the way I remember a part of my life, because at the time I did them I *was* the role and it *was* my life, for twenty-four hours a day. When I was a teen-ager, comedy was the most difficult thing for me to do, and it still is. But dramatic roles are easy for me. In 1946, I won an Oscar for my role in *Mildred Pierce,* and it was the easiest thing I've ever done. I've always drawn on myself only. That's one of the reasons nobody has ever been able to imitate me. And nobody can duplicate anything I've done. You always see impersonations of Katharine Hepburn and Marilyn Monroe, but no one can imitate me.

The pictures I loved more than any others I've ever made were the films with Clark Gable—*Possessed* and *Chained,* among others—and *Mildred Pierce* and *Humoresque.* The picture—and especially the opening—that I keep trying to forget is *Rain,* in which I played Sadie Thompson. I did it in 1932, and I didn't understand that role then. If I were to do it now, I would understand it much better. Today, I would start my characterization from the inside. For the most part, though, the roles I've played have been right for me, even if not all my pictures have been successful. In the old days, we seldom had a single rehearsal. Our dream was to have two whole weeks just for a rehearsal period. Before going into a picture, I'd have a talk with Adrian, my costume designer, and then I'd have a talk with the director and the leading man. I'd work on getting the clothes fitted, and my wardrobe tested and just right, and the dialogue changed to suit me. When I make a picture today, it's still the same; there are so many people involved that I have to please—the co-star, the cameraman, the director. And I love to please them. Sometimes, in a difficult scene, when I have words I simply can't say, I call in the director or the dialogue director and I suggest just walking through the scene—not really doing anything, just indicating what I can do. That helps in getting the dialogue set.

When we actually start to shoot, I ask for one minute by myself. Then I go off into a corner and bring up the exact feeling I want to show. It can be tears, hysteria, laughter—anything. I need just one minute, and I can do it as high as the director wants it. If it feels true, and if techniques don't get in your way, it's right. Techniques grow with experience. Developing techniques is not like getting a whole new wardrobe; it's not planned. . . .

My instinct in choosing the right part has failed me very seldom. In something called *Great Day,* I was supposed to be a little Southern girl, digging her toe in the sand. Well, I'm a big gal. I'm only five feet four and a half, but I have very wide shoulders, and they give people the impression that I'm big. We had been shooting for ten or eleven days, and each day I began to feel more wrong for the part. I sought out L. B. Mayer and pleaded with him to look at the rushes with Thalberg and to take me out of the movie. I cried, and told him that I was a big dame and I couldn't, for the life of me, dig my bare toe in the sand. After ten or eleven days of rushes, they called the whole thing off, with $280,000 still sitting on the shelf. They told me to stay home, and I've never been sorry. I was just too big for the part. I'm so broad I would look dumpy if I put on a little weight. My measurements have changed very little since I started acting. I learned to stand tall right at the start, and I've always exercised to look tall. Dancing did a lot for me, giving me more freedom of body movement and more grace. If an actress has no talent, she may just as well quit before she begins. Every actress must have inborn talent.

In June of 1929, I was married to Douglas Fairbanks, Jr., and we worked with each other to improve our acting. We were divorced in 1933, and two years later I married Franchot Tone, and began to think seriously about going on the stage. I began to learn about things like the Moscow Art Theatre. We built a theatre in back of our house, in Brentwood, where we rehearsed and co-starred in radio performances of several adaptations of movies. We studied singing, too. I started to study opera, and continued with it after our divorce, in 1939. In July, 1942, I was married to Phillip Terry while I was making my last M-G-M picture under contract, *Above Suspicion,* and we were divorced after two years. I am a contralto, and for seven years I thought I might become an opera singer. In opera, the whole body moves and has a rhythm to it. It can contribute to acting a role. Every actress should take some singing and dancing lessons. The opera lessons gave me better control over my voice. Many beautiful actresses are spoiled because they have no control over their voices. I've always been terrified of the stage and of live audiences, and I still am. Sometimes when I go backstage to pick up Ethel Merman or Mary Martin for supper and have to wait for her to dress, I go out on the stage and, remembering her lines, I begin to imagine myself in her role and start speaking her lines. Then, suddenly, I see all the empty seats and imagine how it would be to see that many faces instead, and I just get sick. When my fourth husband, the late Alfred N. Steele, who was chairman of the board of the Pepsi-Cola Company, started taking me with him on business trips for Pepsi-Cola to make promotional appearances, I was terrified. Once, in Chicago, I was asked to appear before the food editors of every publication in the city and answer hundreds of questions. The only way I could answer in front of them all was to have the questions submitted on cards first. Acting in front of movie crews is different. You know they are friends, part of the family, and are watching out for your best interests. Now, after working for Pepsi-Cola for several years, making appearances on my own, it feels like a family, too. I prepare for each appearance the way I do for a movie role. It's all part of acting. Acting is the greatest of all the arts. I wish I had five hundred years to study it.

Hume Cronyn Notes on Film Acting

Good actors usually act and don't talk. Whenever they may be prodded into discussing their approach to work, they're inclined to disagree on ways and means. Coquelin and Irving are an excellent example. Here the disagreement in approach was so fundamental as to result in a celebrated debate between the two actors. It is nonsense to expect, or to try to impose, a standard attack in the work of any category of creative artist—and an actor can be such. We may pick up a little here, a little there from the example or advice of other actors; but like everyone else, we learn chiefly from our own experience.

I went to Hollywood in 1942 to play a part in *Shadow of a Doubt,* a picture directed by Alfred Hitchcock. Life was full of surprises. Nothing was as I thought it would be. Most of my preconceptions were to be confounded and I was to find little basis for the anti-Hollywood prejudice which is so carefully nurtured along Broadway.

A great part of *Shadow of a Doubt* was shot on location in Santa Rosa, California, a small town north of San Francisco in the heart of the vineyard country. I was required to report there. For the first few days I wandered around disconsolate on the edge of the crowd, watching the shooting. It was obvious that in theatre terms there was to be practically no rehearsal. My first scene was quite a long and important one, establishing the character. I grew nervous and depressed in anticipation of the moment when, like that figure in an actor's nightmare, someone would say to me "You're on!" and I would be totally unprepared. My script became grey with anxious fingering, and the

Excerpt from Hume Cronyn, "Notes on Film Acting," *Theatre Arts* 33, no. 5 (June 1949), 45–48.

Lana Turner and Hume Cronyn
in *The Postman Always Rings
Twice* (1946)

wallpaper of my room at the Hotel Occidental took on a crazy pattern of
dialogue à la Reginald Gardiner.

With the director's permission, I was allowed to choose from a secondhand store the clothes which I felt were right for the part. These and my hand
props helped a little, giving me something to hide behind.

I now had words, wardrobe and as a result of study, a theoretical sense of
"my" relationship to the other characters in the screenplay, as well as some
detailed ideas on my own character's background and his action throughout
the story. A feeling of complete inadequacy persisted. I remained outside the
material without any sense of personal identification whatever. I tried an
extension of the theatre's prop and dress-rehearsal routine—that time when
you familiarize yourself with doors, drawers, steps, the furniture and light
switches. I chose "my" house in the district in which we were shooting, "my"
place of work and walked the routes between, absorbing whatever I could use.
These locations were neither seen nor referred to in the picture. Nobody gave
a damn about them except me, and had I discussed what I was attempting at
the time, anyone bothering to listen would have justifiably thought me crazy.
An actor's search for security is his own private affair, in which a successful
end justifies almost any means that does not impose on the other players or
waste the director's time. . . .

An actor's security cannot be achieved merely through familiarity with
externals. What goes on within the character you play? What makes him tick?
What motivates his actions and reactions? What are his values, his strengths,
fears, obsessions? What does he want? What has he had? *What has been his*

experience? I must have at least a nodding acquaintance with such a history. In the course of theatre rehearsals, under a good director I might reasonably expect to discover or create appropriate answers to all these questions. But without rehearsals, I needed a substitute activity. I began to keep a notebook. A notebook has certain practical and psychological uses. To start with, it provides a record of first impressions. Picasso, again, has expressed the principle with admirable insight: "It would be very interesting to preserve photographically, not the stages, but the metamorphoses of a picture. Possibly one might then discover the path followed by the brain in materializing a dream. But there is one very odd thing—to notice that basically a picture doesn't change, that the first 'vision' remains almost intact, in spite of appearances. I often ponder on a light and a dark when I have put them into a picture; I try hard to break them up by interpolating a color that will create a different effect. When the work is photographed, I note that what I put in to correct my first vision has disappeared and that, after all, the photographic image corresponds with my first vision before the transformation I insisted on."

Secondly, a notebook gives the actor a point of reference if it becomes necessary to return to, and recheck, character fundamentals (weird things can happen in the logical development of a performance when the schedule requires you to shoot the middle of the picture first, the first scene last, and that big emotional scene out of relation to anything that comes either before or after it). Thirdly, it requires that you be specific in your study. Those blank sheets of paper must be filled with exact words, words that make sense when strung together and bear on a particular problem. No airy generalities are acceptable. No muddy thinking to the accompaniment of the bedroom radio will let you off the hook of a notebook's demand. Alternately, once done, once the digging is over, you have material proof that part of your book is accomplished. You have the security of knowing you know something about the character and the job in hand.

The camera, the old saw notwithstanding, lies like hell and the actor must be prepared to aid in this deception. A move which would be utterly false on stage, which goes directly against every reasonable impulse, may be camerawise effective and necessary. In *Shadow of a Doubt,* I had a scene in which I sat down to gossip with a neighbor while he and his family had dinner. During the meal, I said something upsetting to the character played by Teresa Wright. She turned on me with unexpected violence. I stood up in embarrassment and surprise and automatically took a step backward. However, at the point of the rise, the camera moved in to hold us in a close two-shot, and to accommodate it—that is, to stay in the frame—it became necessary for me to change the instinctive move so that when I got up from my chair, *I took a step toward the person from whom I was retreating.* Because of my inexperience and the falseness of the move, this made a hazard for me in the middle of an otherwise simple scene. I was convinced the action would look idiotic on the screen, but I was wrong. When I saw the rushes, I had to admit that the occasion passed almost unnoticed even by me.

You have to learn to adjust to such requirements easily and with a minimum of rehearsal. The problems of lighting, camera movement and sound are liable to get considerably more attention than the actors. This is unfortunate and indefensible, but it is not likely that you will be able to change the situation. So again, you must learn to adjust and to be so well prepared that you are secure in spite of it.

The difference between acting for the screen and acting for the stage is negligible and the latter is, despite the exceptions, the best possible training for the former. The screen brings the actor into front row range for an entire audience throughout most of the picture and occasionally it puts him into their laps. It is obviously unnecessary and irritating to speak or move as you would for the benefit of people in the back of a gallery. It may take a little time and some guidance for the stage actor to become accustomed to the degree of projection which will be most effective on the screen, but the technique of film acting is no unique or mystic formula.

Almost everything in picture-making stresses the importance of mechanical perfection. I think the actor does well to trust in the people who are experts in this field and paid to insure it. His business, as in the theatre, remains with the character he is to play and this will require his full powers of concentration.

In "closeup" very little becomes very much; a whole new range of expression is opened to the actor. He can register with a whisper, a glance, a contraction of a muscle, in a manner that would be lost on the stage. The camera will often reflect what a man thinks, without the degree of demonstration required in the theatre. . . .

There is little time for analytical discussion on the set, and none for doing what you should have done in your study. If you can *step before the camera with a clear and logical plan* of what you would like to do and how you would like to do it, the chances are that you will be far better off than if you had just learned the lines.

There are many scenes which an actor cannot study or conceive of playing without considering the character's movement in detail, so intermeshed are words and activity. What can you do when the director is not available for discussion of such a scene beforehand, when it's not even possible to familiarize yourself with the set because it won't be up, let alone dressed, until the day it's to be used? (This is an extreme situation, but it does occur.) I find it best to plan your own set at home, indicate the furniture, plant your own simulated props, imagine your fellow actors and *rehearse!* Walk through whatever pattern of activity seems logical to you, explore the possibilities, decide on a course, and turn up for work with an idea. It may have to be changed. Your timing will depend on the *actual* action and reaction of the other players, not on what you imagined; the set may turn out to be the reverse of the one you indicated for yourself; the whole thing may have to be altered, but the chances are that much of the work you have done will help you, and that your conception can be adapted to the director's to achieve a more successful result than if you offer him nothing other than memorized lines and sublime negativity in regard to the scene's execution. . . .

There's a line of Tennyson's in *Locksley Hall* about "a little hoard of maxims" being preached to someone's daughter. I think of it now because I am going to list a little hoard of maxims. They are offered without apology despite the fact that they're quite obvious—so obvious that it's surprising how often they're forgotten. I didn't make them up, although the way in which they're worded may be my own. They've been culled from various sources: The American Academy of Dramatic Art, Benno Schneider, Lee Strasberg, from some of the authorities I've read, or from an occasional director under whom I've worked. I've been asked repeatedly by students at either the Academy or the Actor's Lab in Hollywood about "rules" for acting. There may be none; at any rate, they are never precisely the same for any two actors. However, I've often been rescued on a set by returning to what I consider are first principles. All actors find themselves involved in difficult scenes where they can't see the woods for the trees and on such frightening occasions anything—maxim, platitude, rule, call it whatever you like—that will return you to security and the right path is worth remembering.

Establish the facts. It's surprising how much information is contained in the text, how many questions are answered by careful re-reading. Don't insist on doing work that has been done for you. Your own creative work should be based on the fact and suggestion supplied by the author, rather than on independent fancy.

Establish the relationships. Nobody, other than a bad actor, behaves in an identical manner toward all other persons—with the possible exception of behavior toward strangers of the same sex, size, age, appearance, manner, and so forth. A proper appreciation and understanding of all the other characters in the play is essential to understanding and performance of your own part.

Establish the surroundings. I hate actors who bump into the furniture, or stand where they seem to be goosed by a chair arm, or are frightened by tables, beds, lamps, doors and the surroundings in general. You can make an obvious liar of yourself and the character you play by pretending familiarity with props you've never bothered to consider. My references to "things" comes under this heading.

If. That word seems to be the key to the complexities of an actor's imaginative and creative processes. "If" provides an answer to innumerable questions, it's the equivalent of the algebraic X. *If* I were in this situation, what would *I* do? *If* I were *this kind of person* in this situation, what would I do? How would I feel, think, behave, react, etc.? "If" will often do for you what an author may have failed to do.

What is the action? (Purpose, intention) Neither you nor your character are ever without one. You may have to consult an analyst to understand your own, but if there is any mystery concerning the "action" of your character during any moment of his life on stage or before the camera—look out. The vacuum will be filled with either an actor's uncertainty or an actor's cliché.

What is the activity? (Physical business) You carry on some activity as long as you remain alive, even in absolute repose. "Activity" often contradicts action. For instance, the activity of sleep does not necessarily reflect the action "to rest." There are many examples. King Richard says quite accurately: "I can smile and murder whilst I smile."

The actor has great range and opportunity in the field of "activity" for, except in its broadest sense, it is rarely dictated by the author, being left, wisely, to the collaborative effort of actor and director. A good director will control "activity" but try to refrain from imposing it.

Correct "activity" on the part of a sensitive actor may provide a perfect reflection of, or delicate counterpoint to, the all important "action".

The character's problem—never the actor's! Actor's problems are always intruding on the concentration which the actor should lend to the *character's* problems (that sounds like double talk, but I'm afraid I can't express it more simply). This is a constant difficulty in motion pictures and television, where much emphasis is laid on mechanical operation. Having attacked the actor's problem in study and rehearsal—sometimes only immediately prior to the "take"—awareness of it in performance must be sublimated by concentration on the character's problem (his action and activity).

In discomfort, look to the object. There is an object toward which every action or activity is directed. Have you ever watched a jeweler, glass in eye, probe the internals of a watch or a confectioner dipping chocolates or a cook flipping pancakes? (In each such case, the action and activity happen to complement rather than contradict one another.) There is a certain fascination in the simple concentration on the object involved.

An actor, playing the part of a man who wishes to please and impress another character to whom he is introduced, may not have such a theatrical activity in the business of a handshake as he would in flipping pancakes, but his concentration on the character, the "object" of "to impress," will carry some of the same fascination.

When consistent with the text, create a mood opposite to the one you're going into. Clumsily expressed, but worth remembering. "Change" is the essence of "color," and in acting terms almost synonymous with "variety" and "development." *You must not manipulate the changes, but be aware of them.* Too many motion picture performances remain in one key. To risk a broad generalization, I would say that tears are usually more effective following laughter than as the logical result of lugubriousness. It's dangerous to talk about "effect" because of the temptation to substitute effect, a trick, for simple honest development. On the other hand, it is stupid not to recognize what is effective and not to try to come to it honestly.

An emotion always outlives its usefulness. That is, it will color an attitude long after the climax has passed and the incident provoking the emotion has been neutralized. This, too, is often overlooked in motion picture performances. Sometimes the reason for the oversight is understandable. If a scene is left uncompleted, in a state of emotional suspension, for a day or a week because the schedule or weather dictates that the company shoot something else, it may be difficult for the actor to recapture the exact emotional pitch when he returns to it. It is easier to match lighting or props than performance. The director's responsibility?—Yes, but also the actor's. However, this maxim is not meant to apply only in such emergencies. Emotional scenes, big scenes, which are not fully rehearsed are inclined to be contrived, with the result that the characters seem to run hot and cold at the same time. The leading lady suffers exquisitely in one moment and is picking her teeth in the next. This is "change" all right, but the wrong kind.

Sometimes both actor and director will prefer to shoot a big scene, usually a highly emotional one, with a minimum of any sort of rehearsal. They hope to capitalize on the spontaneity of the First Time. They are frightened that, with familiarity, the scene will go stale. They gamble on an *actual* first time rather than work toward a more complete *illusion* of the first time. The danger in this method is that the emotion evoked in the actor will be general rather than specific—belly emotion—having no object and being created out of equal parts of acting excitement and nervousness. Good readings are often based on this false stimulation which occurs in the initial run-through of playable material.

I can't list any more, although there are many. As I intimated in the beginning, the thing to do about acting is to act rather than read about it—or write about it.

James Stewart The Many-Splendored Actor

Mr. Stewart, when you first came to Hollywood, you began to work for the large studios, MGM in particular. Could you say a word about your experience there? We would also like to know about your experiences with directors: over your long career you have worked with Lubitsch, DeMille, Capra, Hitchcock, Ford, Wellman, Wilder, and King Vidor.

I came to Hollywood in 1935 as a contract player; MGM probably had the biggest list of such players in town. The contract players did the many small roles in the dozens of pictures that were shot constantly. The directors, the writers, and the producers were also under contract. This is the way the studios operated at that time.

About the contrasting styles of directors at the studios, I wasn't particularly conscious of them. You see, acting is a craft in so many ways. I just felt that the more work I got and the more discipline I had, the better it would be for me in the days ahead. One of the differences as compared to making pictures today is that one worked a great deal. I can't figure out many who are acting in films nowadays—those who are absolutely dedicated to themselves, feel they owe nothing to anybody, and only want to work on what they approve of. Well, I'm getting off the subject.

That's all right. It helps to understand acting and directing in the earlier days of Hollywood. So the criticism of the big studios in the 1930s overlooks certain advantages.

Well, yes. The big studios had a different theory of operating. I know that people call them "impersonal factories." I completely disagree with that. Frank [Capra] would probably *not* completely disagree with that. He would fight with Harry Cohn, the big boss, as if they were two mad dogs. Nevertheless, he had great respect for the idea of the big studio. You hear talk of these

Excerpt from Neil P. Hurley, "The Many-Splendored Actor: An Interview with Jimmy Stewart," *New Orleans Review* 10, nos. 2–3 (Summer–Fall 1983), 5–14.

James Stewart (left) in *The Last Gangster* (1937)

terrible people—L. B. Mayer, the Warner brothers, Harry Cohn, Darryl Zanuck—all of these awful people had this wonderful love for the picture business. It was complete love and devotion. Strangely enough, they had judgment as to the type of material which would be acceptable to audiences, and, strangely enough, they also had good taste. They were disciplined enough to know that what went up there on the screen didn't have to be dirty to be good.

That change came about after World War II, I believe.

Well, yes. I worked up until the war for MGM. I did little parts in big pictures, and big parts in little pictures. I made, I think, 23 pictures for 1935 until I went into the service. A lot of them are hard to remember, and several were not made at MGM—like those I did with Frank [Capra]. They traded us to other studios like ball players—on loan. Sometimes they traded us, not for another actor, but for the use of a back lot. I remember someone told me that I was traded to Universal Studios to do a picture so that MGM could use a street Universal had built on its back lot for shooting certain types of pictures. This type of thing.

You're saying that the studios provided work and that that element of dependable employment is gone today.

Well, yes. Frank [Capra] is a good example of the importance of discipline and experience which can't come from any other thing than work. There's no other way I know of to build a successful career.

Speaking of Capra, they say he had a "happy set," that his relaxed manner of directing led to an improvisation which reminded one of the stage.

Well, this was the feeling Frank created, and by the way, this was also the feeling on a Hitchcock set. The complete opposite was true of John Ford's set. Everything was completely tense. No one knew what was going to happen on any given day. You didn't know if you were going to be the fall guy of the day, whether Ford was going to have his gun pointed at you. But it was very effective—all of it completely planned by Ford—and, as I said, very effective. It got up there on the screen the way he wanted it and the way the audience liked it. Of course, that's the only thing that matters.

Ford told a story visually and created "believability" through using the screen to tell a visual story. Of course, Hitch did that also. He said that if you're not able to tell a story visually you're not using the motion picture medium correctly. For example, the scriptgirl would come up to Hitch after a scene and say, "Mr. Hitchcock, they're not saying their lines correctly. Mr. Stewart changed that and he didn't say this." Hitch would say, "It looked fine and that's a print." Ford would do that also. Both thought in pictures.

They thought photographically—in images.

That's correct. I'd say of all the directors I worked for, Hitch was the best prepared—to my way of thinking, at least, He worked for months on the script. If you even saw his script, which every once in a while he would look at, on the blank page you'd see the scene. The lamppost or dinner table or the trees in the forest would be sketched there. It would all be visually suggested. Hitch didn't worry about the words; he wanted to forget about the words. He was a very good artist, and he put the script into picture language. You know, Hitch never looked through the camera. They say that he was too big to get near the camera, but, of course, that wasn't true. He never looked through the camera because he had very good cameramen. They knew their jobs. He'd call over, say, Bob Burks, who'd stand behind Hitch, and he'd frame the shot by holding up his hands. [Mr. Stewart held up both hands about a foot apart with each index finger and thumb perpendicular to one another.] If he wanted a moving shot, Hitch would say, "I want that," and then he would move his upheld hands to show the scene which followed the first shot. Then he would go and sit in his director's chair and watch the shooting of the scene when the cameraman got ready.

Actors felt that they were "under-directed" by Hitchcock; not so much veteran actors such as you, for you were a seasoned actor when you first worked on Rope *in 1948, but newcomers such as John Dall or Farley Granger who also worked in* Rope. *Perhaps they may have been made nervous by Hitch's seeming indifference and silence.*

Well, *Rope* was an entirely different kettle of fish. Only Hitchcock would try to do a picture that looked like it had no cuts, doing it without stopping.

Yes, using only one-reel takes, ten minutes at a time.

Well, Hitch tried it. Of course, what he was doing was forfeiting one of the most valuable things in the picture business, and that was the cut. I always thought that on the set of *Rope* that if we had had bleachers around that one set and charged admission to the public so they could see how the technicians moved around, then the film probably would have earned more money than it did in the theater. It was fascinating. The camera moved all over the place. Even the walls moved, but they moved on rubber rollers so as not to make noise. But there were so many rubber rollers they made some noise. Hitch would take us through each scene. For instance, I would go in and get a book. The camera would follow me. Then the walls would move on the rubber rollers. I'd then take the book and put it down on a table, but there was no table there—only the camera. There would be a man there hunching below the range of the camera to take the book from my hand. Then I'd move somewhere else. The walls would move and the camera would follow my movements.

A different way of making a movie, isn't it? It was really a photoplay, in a way.

Well, yes. They even had a man who would point to, oh, about thirty circles on the ground which represented where the camera would shoot takes. Well, on cue this man had a pointer and would point to circles so that we, the actors, would be ready when the camera would appear behind a disappearing wall right above the indicated circle. The union didn't know what to call this man. The job was invented just for this film. As I say, only Hitchcock would have tried it.

Recently, I was talking with a few of Hitch's old crew, and they felt he created problems and challenges as if he wanted to push back the known limits of filmmaking.

Yes, in a sense, that's right; he was convinced all his life of the visual power of the medium, and that was his goal.

Do you know why he chose you to appear in Rope? *Capra had seen you in* Navy Blue and Gold *and chose you on the basis of your innocent manner and charm. Had Hitch seen you in a particular film?*

No, I really don't know why he picked me.

Have you ever thought that Hitchcock cast you in his films contrary to the stereotype of the "man-child" idealist which was the image of you in such Capra films as Mr. Smith Goes to Washington *and* It's a Wonderful Life? *You had a star image which he seemed to change.*

I don't think Hitch paid much attention to a "star image." I never heard Hitch discuss a scene with an actor. He never did with me. I heard him say that he hired actors—you know, the "cattle" as he referred to them—because they were supposed to know what they were doing. When he said, "Action," he expected them to do what he had hired them to do. This was pretty much his feeling about it. He never tried to talk to the person and mold him into a certain type of character or try to change him.

They say he was very conscious of directing the audience—through the editing process.

Well, he was so prepared that he knew how a particular scene would join up with the scenes he would shoot later to give the effect he wanted. Yes, in this sense he directed the audience rather than the actors. The way his mind worked and the way he fit things together was unique. Only he knew—and maybe Bob Burks, his cameraman—what the final effect was intended to be. This was a very disciplined and masterful man at work.

Is the transition difficult from the live stage performance to motion pictures where the process is fragmented and merely a sequence of bits of celluloid, or, as you would call it, "pieces of time"?

The big difference—and the big danger—is that you have to change your projection. On the stage you have to reach the persons way up there in the last row of the second balcony as well as those sitting there ten feet away from you. On the stage an actor does more things—you have to project more. In the movies there's more work with the eyes and small movements. Everybody thinks that in making movies you have a microphone over your head so all you have to do is whisper. Well, that's nonsense. That is not the type of cutting down on the projection I mean. No, I didn't find that change very hard. If you talk with Hank Fonda, I think he would agree.

You did Harvey *on the stage and then did the movie. Do you feel that the transition was challenging?*

No, not really. It was different, but not that different.

The thing I've always felt was that movies were made up of tiny "bits of time." People remember not the film but certain scenes, certain "bits of time." I know that Hitchcock and yes, Ford, too, believed in that principle. Capra never said it, but he understood it and practiced it. I remember how often someone would come up to me—maybe from Philadelphia—and say I remember seeing you in a picture. He doesn't remember the name of the film, who was in it, who was with him when he saw it, where he saw it, but he'll say something like this, "You were in this room [now this is a lot of information I'm getting] and you said something [now he doesn't even remember what I said in the picture], but you turned and the look you gave this other person, I'll never forget that." Now, nine times out of ten, I'll remember the picture, the title, the scene, who the fellow actor was—everything about it. Then I'll say, "Was it this picture?" And the answer will be, "yes, that's the picture I meant."

I can see how true that is of audiences. They remember "pieces of time," not the entire sequence.

Yes, it's strange, but a fact. I knew Hitch and Ford mentioned this explicitly. The motion picture is made up of these little "pieces of time" and influence the audience and crate the "believability" for which we in this business are working all the time. The "believability" in motion pictures comes in bits, in small pieces. In the theater, when the curtain goes down after the first act, you have a feel for the plot and what has happened and the characters who have come at you during that time. In pictures it's different—it happens in little bits of time.

Like building a mosaic floor or putting together a stained glass window. Mr. Stewart, did you feel that your role as the young senator in Capra's Mr. Smith Goes to Washington *extended your range of acting?*

Well, it certainly was the most difficult thing I had tackled—probably as difficult a thing as I've ever had, I suppose. I remember that we worked on the filibuster scene for three weeks. I had been talking at the top of my voice trying to sound hoarse. I remember Frank [Capra] coming to me and saying. "I don't have the feeling that you're losing your voice. You're trying to force an imitation and you don't convince me." Well, that got me. That night I stopped at the office of an ear, nose and throat doctor and asked him, "Could you give me a sore throat?" He smiled and said, "Well, I heard about you Hollywood people and knew you were all crazy, but this takes the cake. I've been working for the last eighteen years to keep people from getting sore throats and other illnesses, and you want me to give you a sore throat. I'll give you the sorest throat you've ever had." He dropped some bichloride of mercury down my throat. It made me hoarse. The doctor asked, "When is it? Tomorrow?" I said, "Yeah, the big scene is tomorrow." He said, "I'll be there. What time?" I said, "8:30 in the morning." Well, he came and stayed there the whole day. I don't know what happened to his practice. Every once in a while, I'd come to him and say, "I'm better. Make me hoarse again." He'd drop more bichloride of mercury down my throat. When people found out, they said, "This is acting? It's cheating, if I ever heard of it."

I heard that It's a Wonderful Life *was your favorite film and Capra's as well.*

Yes, it is. For both Frank and me it's a sentimental and emotional favorite. We were both in the war for four and a half years. Frank had made some pictures, but I did no acting whatsoever. The story was completely original; it didn't come from a book, a biography, or an actual happening. I remember that Frank called me up and said, "I've got this idea. You're in a small town and you're going to commit suicide and an angel named Clarence comes down. You're on the bridge and you're going to jump in. You jump in and Clarence jumps in, but he has no wings. He has to earn his wings and you have to save him." Well, when I heard the story, I said, "Frank, if you want to do a picture about an angel named Clarence who hasn't won his wings yet and I'm going to commit suicide, then I'm your man."

. . .

Regarding the "Stewartisms,"—the slow take, the slight drawl, and the hesitating speech mannerisms—did they emerge full bloom in one particular film, say, Navy Blue and Gold, *or was it rather the result of a slower, ongoing process?*

I think they slowly worked themselves, mainly through the many parts I played in the early years. I know the critics helped me a lot in those days— keeping those mannerisms in control—you know, the pauses, the slow takes, and the ear-scratching. It's the type of thing with which you shouldn't get tagged too much. The critics would help me by saying, "Well, maybe he does not have to be that bashful. The character was all right without exaggerating its modesty."

After the war you seemed to change, to get away from the more simple and innocent attitudes with which critics and the public identified you.

Well, I was becoming more mature. By that time I was thirty-seven or thirty-eight years old. I'd been away from the business. Although I found myself back acting, I suddenly realized that no one was going to see the two pictures I had made when I returned to civilian life.

You mean It's a Wonderful Life *and* Magic Town?

Yes. The thing that helped me to develop into other kinds of roles was the good advice I had. Frank helped; so did Hitchcock and Henry Hathaway. I needed help and luckily I got it. The audience wouldn't accept this kind of story we did prior to World War II. *It's a Wonderful Life* and *Magic Town* were like *The Shop Around the Corner* and *You Can't Take it With You.*

You adapted to the changes in feelings and expectations in postwar American society, but Frank Capra apparently could not. He went on to do remakes of some of his earlier films and musicals with Crosby and Sinatra. It's harder perhaps for a director to change than an actor.

Yes, it is. In my case it was just a maturity which snuck up on me. There had been that uncertainty since I kept relying on what I had learned before the war in that wonderful training I had had at MGM in the craft of acting; but there was more to it than that. There were changes demanded by the new roles offered to me.

Such as Hitchcock's Rope *and Hathaway's* Calling Northside 777?

Yes, by those types of pictures.

Many critics and a large part of the public were confused by Vertigo. *It dealt with a man obviously in psychological conflict, but the plot meandered and Kim Novak played a dual role which was not always immediately intelligible. How did you personally feel at the time? And, were you conscious at the time that you were making an art classic?*

It was a fascinating film. I think it was the first time the zoom lens was used, and I am not sure it was worth all the trouble. They use it so much today. Well, anyway, in one scene Hitch wanted to get a shot up the building. It cost $4,000 to rent the crane for a day in addition to paying to have it driven up to San Francisco. The whole thing cost $10,000. When they set up the shot, a man showed Hitch this lens he had. When it came to using the crane, the zoom was attached to it by adhesive tape and rubber bands. The shot turned out fine.

Talking recently with some of Hitchcock's old crew, I discovered that he accepted "input," that he was willing to listen. The image is of a director with his mind all made up who dictated all the terms. Did you find that he listened to actors who had suggestions?

Oh, yes, he was willing to listen. He was not too keen on long discussions between an actor and a director. He felt that not a great deal came out of it. I remember in *Vertigo* when Kim Novak—bless her heart—I thought she was, well, just wonderful in the picture—well, she came up to Hitchcock. I think it was the second or third day of the shooting and said to Hitch, "I didn't feel right in this scene with Mr. Stewart. It's not the right emotion. I should be extending myself more to him." Hitch leaned over and said, "Kim, it's *only* a movie." And she never said another word. She gave a beautiful, wonderful performance.

. . .

There were some directors who did not want actors to see the rushes because it might influence the continuity of the acting. Did you see the rushes and try to learn from them?

Oh, I never went to the rushes. Frank [Capra] had a projection room in the basement of his home. I lived in Brentwood and he wanted me to stop and see the rushes at the end of each day since he lived between Brentwood and the studio. Well, I went with him and in a short time he fell sound asleep. Well, if Frank as director was going to sleep through the dailies, I found a way to excuse myself. That was the last of rushes for me. Oh, I might go the first few days to see how I look, if the chemistry is working. I don't think they do much good. Whether you admit it or not, you only look at yourself. That's no way to see the rushes.

Didn't they do a number of prints from a take so the star could choose?

Oh, yes. Some stars especially insisted on that. Norma Shearer is one example. I forget what director it was—Norma was coming downstairs and turned. It didn't come out right, so they had to keep doing it over and over again. The director gave orders to make five identical prints of the same take. Norma didn't know they were the same. She thought they were different, and she said she liked number two the best of the five. Since then, they don't do many extra takes for the rushes.

Did you get better as you rehearsed or was "one take" sufficient?

It depends. You have to be flexible. Sometimes it works and sometimes it doesn't. Remember what I said about films made up of "pieces of time"? Well, sometimes you get that moment you want on a first take; sometimes you need several takes. You have to experiment with it. Ford did that. People say that for him the "first take" was it, but that's not absolutely the case. He could go up to "twenty takes," and would, if he needed it.

Since Hitchcock was so well prepared, would you say that actors got off the set pretty fast with him as compared with other directors?

Well, Hitch believed you were hired to do your job. You were expected to know your lines and carry your part. In Marrakesh in Morocco I could see Hitch in the square amid complete confusion with all those extras in 110° heat, and over there was Hitchcock in a blue suit and tie, sitting in a chair, waiting for the cameraman to get ready. Everything quieted down, and people did what they had to do. He then said, "Let's move over here now." You know, I really don't think he cared much for the spoken word. He was interested in getting those "pieces of time" and he just used the words as little as possible. For example, in *The Man Who Knew Too Much*, the scene in Albert Hall. You remember that last part with the cymbal. The assassin was going to kill this man while the London Symphony is playing. During all this I'm charging up the stairs trying to tell Doris Day what's happened to our kidnapped child. It was a long speech, and I had done it a couple of times. I had memorized about three pages of dialogue. Well, Hitch came up to me and said, "You're talking so much, I'm unable to enjoy the London Symphony. Why don't you just not say anything? Try to hold Doris and whisper some-thing." Well, the audience was way ahead of the people we were playing in the film anyway. Hitch didn't want words to get in the way. Words have their place, but you have to know when to use them.

Anything you want to say by way of conclusion and summary.

There was an excitement about it all. As I said, everything was very quiet with Hitch and everything was very tense with Ford—but they got results. They got what they wanted.

I remember the first day I was ever on a set with Ford. I was the sheriff in an old Western town and I'm in front of the bar that I own. Ford said, "Put your feet up on the bar and put your hat down. You're sort of snoozing." And he didn't say anything else. He went back and said, "Are you ready?" And this is all there was. I didn't have anything else to do so I yawned, but I did an immense yawn. My hat almost fell off. Then he said, "Cut!" And I waited for something, and I looked; but he was gone. The cameraman was gone. They went somewhere else to shoot something else. Three days later we were in a different location—I was on a horse or something—Ford came up and said, "I like the yawn," and went away. All I ever heard.

Henry Fonda Reflections on Forty Years
of Make-Believe

HANSON. *As a member of the audience, I think it
is the absence of any visible method in your work
that distinguishes you as an actor.*

FONDA. That is one of the goals I have set for
myself—to disguise acting. Not to let acting show. I arrived at that basic rule
for myself *watching* actors. Watching anyplace where there was a performance, a stock company, a movie, a local playhouse, or Broadway. I learned
that no matter how fine an actor is, no matter how hard he works, if you are
aware of the wheels going around, that robs it of the illusion, the illusion I
wanted to create. If you can see what the actor is trying to do, and his method
shows, then that's not good for me. I don't care how good he is. So I, for as far
back as I can remember, said to myself, "Don't let them see you working.
Don't let it show." And that, in a nutshell, is what my credo is.

HANSON. *Could you tell me how you go about not letting it show?*

FONDA. Not really. Somebody could write a book about it maybe. I couldn't,
because I am not that articulate. I think it's largely instinctive. I think maybe
it's . . . I am now going to use words and talk about myself in a way that I don't
like to because it sounds like I am giving myself a medal or an award or
something. But I *do* think I have an ear. And a lot of it has to do with having a
good ear. You hear a line or read a line and your ear tells you if it is true.
Would the character say it? There are writers who have ears. John O'Hara has
one of the great ears for dialogue. It's one of the difficult things for actors
because our medium is of the spoken word and it has to come out like it is
coming from inside. Made up at the moment. It must be said for the first time,
every time. When I have a bad time with a line I don't say "My ear doesn't like
that." It's just an instinctive thing. "That doesn't *sound* right." And I try to
either make it sound right by working on the reading or, if necessary and with
the director's permission, sometimes the author's permission too, juggling the
words. Say the same thing, but say it in a way that doesn't offend my ear.

HANSON. *When working on a script, after the lines do seem correct, how do you
go abut making them sound correct. In other words, how do you get into
character?*

Excerpt from "An Interview by Curtis Lee Hanson: 'Henry Fonda: Reflections on
40 Years of Make-Believe,'" *Cinema* (Calif.) 3, no. 4 (December 1966), 11–17.

FONDA. I suppose you are talking about film acting. There is a great difference between film and the theatre.

HANSON. *I'd like to talk about the difference also.*

FONDA. There is a great difference in many ways. An actor generally starts rehearsing a play sitting around a table with the director, stage managers, and the rest of the cast. They read the play, depending upon the director, one or more times for one or more days. Sometimes the director likes to read it once, and then you are on your feet. Sometimes he likes to read it three or four times the first day, and then you are on your feet. *Two for the Seesaw* we read for seven days without even standing up, just around the table, the two of us with the director. With that opportunity to *know* that you have four weeks before anybody is going to be judging you, that is, audiences and critics, you don't have to indicate anything right away. I feel that too early an indication could be false, because an actor is trying too hard to impress somebody, too soon. How do you know that *that's* right? So when I'm allowed to, as you are in the theatre, I "baby up" on a part. I don't try to do too much at first, and I let it come gradually. I can tentatively try something, in readings, in expressions, in emotions, whatever they are, and discard them or build them as they seem to fit and feel right. As opposed to film acting where, because of the nature of the industry, and it is an industry, you don't get the chance to rehearse as intensively. Most of the time, you don't get a chance to rehearse more than the few times—minutes, or hours at the most—before you actually shoot the scene in the camera. The assistant director will call you the day before you work and say "We are going to start tomorrow morning at nine o'clock and do scenes 104 and 105." It is not only not the beginning of the story, but you only have that night to prepare for the scene. You learn the lines. You come to the studio ready at 9:00 prepared as far as knowing your lines is concerned, and with your own idea what you would like to do with them. You get on the set, and with the cameraman and the director, and the other actors, you rehearse for business and position. You do this until the director is satisfied with the way he wants it to play, and the cameraman is satisfied that he can anticipate *your* moves so that he can do his technical things—moving the camera, dollying, panning—and know what positions he has to light. Then you sit down and the stand-ins come in for the lighting. When you are sitting down, the most you can do is just run lines with the other actors. Sometimes you don't even do that. It depends upon how tough the lines are. And usually within an hour, depending upon how difficult the scene is to light, you are back again doing the scene. When it is to the director's satisfaction, it goes to the laboratory, and that is your performance. And all *I* can think of is, "I wish I had another chance." Whether *they* are satisfied or not. So there is just not as much gratification for me because I never feel I am really as good as I want to be. I haven't had a chance to become. I haven't had a chance to try, to discard, or try and build a little bit more.

HANSON. *You haven't had the chance to, as you say, "baby up" on the part.*

FONDA. That's right. In the theatre I really "baby up." That's an expression that I remember as a kid. Playing marbles. I don't know whether you are too young to have played marbles, but you draw a ring on the ground with the marbles in the center, and you outside. A real hot shot would try to knock one out from there. I wasn't that good, so I'd baby up, which means hit it once easily and then shoot again. It was an expression, and I use it about the way I work in the theatre. You learn your lines gradually as you rehearse the first several days. You are still carrying the script as you walk around. You are not really indicating at all. You are reading it with one eye on the director. Gradually you can do it more and more without looking and eventually you put the script away. You begin to look into the other actor's eyes, and that's when you begin to put the blood and the breath and life into the character, gradually. And when something is right, I can feel it sort of tingle in me, just the excitement of knowing "That's right, that's on the right track, stay with that, and build from that." You can do it for four weeks in rehearsal, and you can do it for the rest of the run. In *Mister Roberts,* the last performance after four years was better than the first, only because we took the graph up instead of down. When you play a part over and over again, the danger is in becoming automatic, to stop listening. And it is noticeable. Just like that, the audience can tell. So to stay on your feet and not let it become automatic, to keep the graph up, you find little subtleties in the part. The graph should be up always. It *has* to be an improvement. Every time you do it, it should be that much, and maybe only that much, better. That to me is the joy of acting. To be able to go and do it and then to know, "I have another chance tomorrow."

HANSON. *What are your relations with a film director, as opposed to a theatrical director?*

FONDA. I'm not conscious of any difference in the relationship. There are fewer directors in cinema who have real communication with an actor, who can help an actor build a performance. And I don't mean, again, to put down movie directors. It is another technique. A movie director needs to know how he is going to tell his story with the camera. But there are some who can communicate. Some of them are from the theatre, are former actors. Sidney Lumet, who was an actor years ago, has *great communication.* He knows how to talk with an actor. There are others like him. But they are in the minority.

Most cinema directors are cinema. Meaning they know their camera and know how to use it, and they hire the best actors they can get and expect a performance from them. Burt Kennedy has had no theatre experience, but he, instinctively, seems to know what words to say to give a new approach to a scene. This is one of the excitements—to be doing a scene as well as you know how, and then have the director come up, and just, in a very few words, say "Why don't we try . . . if you were to do *this*." And it is something that makes you think "Oh, my God, why didn't I think of that?" Or "I know what you mean! I'll show you!" He has given you another dimension or subtlety. It's exciting to get a director who is like that. You don't get many of them any more.

HANSON. *What is the difference between acting for a camera and acting for a live audience?*

FONDA. There isn't a great deal. The main difference is projection. In film, your camera—that lens—is your audience and you don't have to do anything that you wouldn't do naturally. That was my first big lesson in the cinema. I was in the theatre for ten or more years before I came out for my first film. My director was Victor Fleming. A dear man, and I was in love with him before we started the picture. The first day at work we were shooting a scene, and I was playing it the way I played in the theatre. I didn't know any better, nobody had told *me* about this camera. And Victor . . . I could see that he was sort of wondering what he was going to say. He finally took me aside, and with his arm around my shoulder, said, "Hank, you're mugging a little." Mugging to me is a dirty word. It's a terrible insult. So when he said that I was mugging a little bit, I just stopped dead. And I realized what he meant and what I was doing. You don't need that projection in film. So I pulled way back and learned my first big lesson.

HANSON. *How was working with John Ford?*

FONDA. John Ford. One of the great experiences I have had. I had the opportunity to work with Ford in his heyday, the great years. I had him from 1937 to 1953. I had known his work, and I had been a fan of his for years, never having met him.

HANSON. Young Mr. Lincoln *was your first for Ford, wasn't it?*

FONDA. Yes. When I was first asked to do it I was afraid of the part. I thought, "I can't play Lincoln, It's like playing Jesus." But I did a test. Without committing myself, I sat and had them put makeup on me for three hours. I went to the test stage and they photographed me, and I went back the next day and saw it on the screen. I remember sitting there and seeing this tall character with a big nose and the wart and everything, and I thought, "My God, it is!"

Then I started to talk. And my voice came out. I said, "No, I'm sorry fellows." I wouldn't have any part of it. Months later they assigned Ford to the picture. He ran the tests. Sent for me. And, using all the four letter words, he shamed me into it. He said, "What's all this shit about you thinking you're playing the Great Emancipator? For Christ's sake! It's just a young jackleg lawyer from Springfield." He shamed me into it, and I am awfully glad that he did. It was the first of many happy experiences with him. He is and was certainly one of the greats. He always worked with the writer closely on the script and yet, the scripts were always very spare and economical. He would put things in as you were shooting. Whether they had been in his mind from the beginning and he just didn't put them in the script, I don't know but I don't think so. I think they are things that occurred to him driving to the studio, or driving out to the location.

HANSON. *Lines and bits of action?*

FONDA. Sometimes lines, pieces of business. Just the other day somebody on the set here came up and said, "You know what I always remember when I see you? I remember that scene in *Darling Clementine* where . . ." I stopped him and said "When I put my feet up on the post and did the little thing." He said, "That's right." Well, that was Ford. On the set I was supposed to be lounging in this chair on the porch, in Tombstone. And there was a post holding up the roof of the porch. Ford said, "Back up so that you can put your feet up there." It was a narrow post so I could only put one foot here and one foot above it. He said "Change your feet." And then, "Do it again. Keep doing it. It became sort of a ballet. Sitting there, enjoying doing this, until somebody comes along. It didn't really mean anything, and yet *everybody* remembers that. Another bit from *Clementine* I remember, Ford put in on the set: I had just come from the barber shop. I had had my hair cut and it was slicked down. Ward Bond came up and stood beside me and said, "Smell those desert flowers." I said, "It's me." That's all. That's one of Ford's bits that made the part memorable.

HANSON. *What about working with Ford on* Grapes of Wrath?

FONDA. Like the other ones, it was one of the great experiences, and one of the *great* pictures. There is one thing I remember most about *Grapes of Wrath,* and it will give you another facet to Ford. One of his incredible instincts. I say incredible, because he is not *of* the theatre. He had not had acting experience. He is the first one to say that he is lace-curtain-Irishman from Maine. He came out to do stunts and double his brother who was a Western action star. He became a director when he was about 19 years old. The studio wanted to spite Harry Carey or something and made him a director. He had these instincts that were so fantastic, sensitive in every way. In *Grapes of Wrath* I had the good-bye scene with Ma—Tom and Ma Joad. Tom had realized that he had to get out. They were after him, and he has to leave. He wakes up his mother. They are in one of those Oakie camps, in a tent. There had been a dance the night before and there is a raised platform in back of the tent. The shot started, a continuous shot, inside the tent, when I come in, in the darkness, and shake her, and whisper that I want to talk to her. The camera pulls back, and I come out, and wait for her a moment while she pulls on a robe or something. She comes out, and together we walk around and down the side of the tent, and sit on the bench that is just below this dance floor. This, in a continuous shot, and *then* we go into the dialogue, as we are sitting on the bench. It was an emotional scene. It was one of the best scenes in the picture for actors loving to work, because it was *all there.* We were aware of what there was in the scene. But Ford *knew* it too. I can say this from the viewpoint of twenty years later looking back, but I wasn't aware of it at the time. Ford knew, and he never *let* us rehearse. He never let us go into the scene. He knew, as he well should, that both Jane and I knew our dialogue. He wasn't worried about that. He also somehow instinctively knew that he should get the first take, the first emotion. Technically the scene was difficult. The cameraman had to light the interior of the tent. I think I just struck a match in there. Then come outside, pan the camera and dolly up to where we were sitting down. So there were two or three hours of technical rehearsal. But every time we would get to the bench and sit down, he would say "Cut." Not make a point of it, just cut. So we never did do the lines, just the technical things. Eventually, everybody was technically ready. Now we, Jane Darwell and myself, by this time were like race horses at the wire. We *were ready.* We hadn't been allowed. Both of us, without even saying it to each other, wanted to say "Shit boys, let us show you. This is a hell of a scene." Finally we were allowed to. We began that scene, and it *went.* We both went with the emotion. The emotion was there in the face, in the eyes, and in everything else. That was it. And Ford never . . . he just walked away from it. He didn't even say "Wonderful." He just got up and walked away from it and everybody knew that meant that we could print that take. He didn't cut it into two shots or close-ups or anything else. He just *did* it. And that's typical of Ford—he knows how.

HANSON. *How was working with Fritz Lang on* You Only Live Once?

FONDA. I hated that. I couldn't get along with him at all. I didn't know what to expect with my first picture because I hadn't worked with him before. I'd seen *M* and *Metropolis,* and liked his work. He is an artist certainly. A creative artist. But he has no regard for his actors. He doesn't think about it as having no regard . . . it just doesn't occur to him that actors are human beings with hearts and instincts and other things. He is the master puppeteer, and he is happiest only when he can manipulate the blank puppets. He would actually manipulate you with his hands. If you were cutting that close, he would manipulate your hand, while you were sitting there looking at the camera. That in itself isn't too bad, but if you are trying to work from here, from inside, it's disconcerting to have somebody else doing something that has become automatic for you. Anyway, it was not a happy experience for me, although the picture, the first one we did, was good.

HANSON. *Fritz Lang used to do many takes on each scene, did he not?*

FONDA. He took *forever,* 16 weeks or longer. He would do 30 or 40 or 50 takes because he would think of a little different way to do it. If you were eating dessert at a dinner, for instance, he would squish the dessert up a little bit and put the spoon on the saucer, and do it. Then we would put the saucer in the ice cream dish, and do it. This had nothing to do with us, you know. Or he would sit there blowing cigarette smoke in from the side of the camera and do it. He'd set the prop this way and do it. It was a lot of shit as far as I'm concerned. The second picture, which was some years later, was the *Return of Frank James.* He knew how I felt and he came to me with tears in his eyes, great big crocodile tears, and said he had learned his lesson, and so forth. I finally went along and said, "Okay." But, not only was it a wrong picture for him to have done, a Western, but he hadn't learned any lessons at all. He killed three or four horses on location. He was riding them too hard, making the wranglers ride them too hard up hills and at an altitude. Anyway, that was Fritz Lang.

HANSON. *How was working with Alfred Hitchcock on* The Wrong Man?

FONDA. Very good experience. It was not one of his more successful pictures, possibly because it was unlike the typical Hitchcock. It was documentary. He bought this story, from a *Life* magazine. He filmed it where it actually happened, in the Stork Club, in the subway, in East Brooklyn. We shot in the courtroom where the actual trial was.

It was a good experience for me, working with him. He is very well organized, and all of his assistants—his production manager, his assistant director, the script girl, and so on—they know, because they have been working with him in preparation, exactly what he wants and how he expects to get it. To such an extent that he could be absent and they could set up the shot. Blueprinted practically. He knows exactly what he wants. His direction is very sparse. He hires the actors and he knows what he can get from them.

He puts them in the positions that he wants them in with his camera and that's it.

HANSON. *Does Sidney Lumet work the same way as most film directors in that there is no rehearsal to speak of?*

FONDA. On the contrary. We rehearsed two weeks for *Twelve Angry Men.* I have done two other pictures with him since, and in each case, we rehearsed two weeks.

HANSON. *Is that rehearsing with the camera movements?*

FONDA. Well, not with the camera itself, but with the cameraman. Take *Twelve Angry Men* as an example. From the first day, the cameraman and script girl were right beside Sidney every moment. He was working with the actors, up to the point where they started to have run throughs, as in the theatre. Then he was right at the camera, with the cameraman, and with the script girl taking all the notes in shorthand. By the time we went on the sound stage, every shot was plotted.

HANSON. *Is that technique of rehearsing successful when the action doesn't all take place in one room?*

FONDA. Well, of course it is. It's not as completely beneficial, because it's not possible to have that same kind of run through. We could have opened in the theatre with *Twelve Angry Men. Fail-Safe,* which was the most recent one I did with Sidney, had many scenes. I was primarily involved in that subterranean bomb shelter Office of the President. But there was the scene in the War Room in the Pentagon. There was the scene in Omaha, at the Strategic Air Command. Scenes in cars in Rock Creek Park in Washington. A cocktail party in a hotel. There were lots of scenes. We rehearsed in a great, big rehearsal hall. In that big hall, which was one large room, there were, marked off on the floor and with pieces of furniture, all of the sets in the picture. When we were ready for run through, we had them. It was really the run through for Sidney and the cameraman and the script girl. They might be 300 feet away at somebody's cottage set, and the next scene in the picture would be back to the President. They had a stop watch and everything, so I would—even if I couldn't hear them, somebody would wave his hands—and I would start my scene even before they got there. They would be running to compare notes about camera angles and everything, and then run to the next set up. But it was still a run through performance for the actors. It's not quite the same as rehearsing in one room, of course, but . . .

HANSON. *I'm wondering why other directors don't rehearse in that manner.*

FONDA. I think they are becoming more and more aware that it pays off. Producers discover that, contrary to its costing a lot of money, it saves money in the other end. For *The Best Man* we had, at Columbia, all the sets set up and dressed, and we rehearsed for two weeks. This was for Stu Millar and Larry Turman, with Franklin Schnaffner directing. It must have been Columbia's money and nobody objected. Somebody had finally been persuaded that it was worthwhile, and it sure was. It paid off in performance. It paid off in that it went much faster once you were in production. I think Willy Wyler rehearses today. He didn't when I worked for him, 27 or 30 years ago. But on *The Detective* he rehearsed for a week or more.

HANSON. *How was it working with him on* Jezebel?

FONDA. Great. Just great. I had been warned that it was going to be terrible, I resisted it, as a matter of fact. But he seemed to want me and he was willing to make several compromises in order to get me. My daughter, Jane, was going to be born in December. We knew the date because she had to be Caesarean. Willy had never in his history made a picture in 16 weeks, so I said that I wasn't going to get started and not be there for the birth of my first child. This was in October so I turned it down, and he said, "But I'll finish shooting in time." It wasn't a direct communication; it was through agents. Finally he gave us a contract that had a stop date, guaranteed to finish me on the 20th of December. And he did. He went on and did eight more weeks on the picture, shooting and picking up scenes after my exit. It was a good experience. He is certainly one of our all-time top directors. And he is unlike a lot of other directors who have the reputation of doing a take and a take and a take, fifty or sixty takes until it gets monotonous. He often *does* do many takes, but there is always a reason, a reason that makes you look forward to doing it again. It is a little bit different. He may be rehearsing with film, but that's all right, because it is the same as rehearsing in the theatre as far as I'm concerned. It's getting a chance to do it again. He may say, "Why not this time reach up and swat a mosquito." There will be something each time, a reason for doing it that made it worth trying again for other effects. I was crazy about Willy, still am.

HANSON. *Just out of curiosity, that scene in* Jezebel *where you* do *swat the mosquito on your hand as you walk down into the garden, was that in the script or was that . . . ?*

FONDA. No. That was one of the things that occurred to him at the time.

HANSON. *You produced* Twelve Angry Men. *Do you plan to produce any other films in the future?*

FONDA. I am inclined to doubt it. The kind of pictures that I would be interested in producing are not box office. *Twelve Angry Men,* for all the awards it won around the world, was not a box office picture. Nor was Bill Wellman's *Ox-Bow Incident. Ox-Bow* is typical of the kind of pictures that I am proud of; that I would like to make again.

HANSON. *You don't foresee any change in the market then, whereby these pictures possibly could become more successful?*

FONDA. No. I'm afraid I can't. I *hope.* I can only hope that there will be one day more of an audience for that kind of picture than there is today. Today I am persuaded, and I know they're right, by my agents, that if I want to do a *Twelve Angry Men* or an *Ox-Bow Incident* or a *Welcome to Hard Times,* I have to do a certain number of *Sex and the Single Girl*'s, and *Battle of the Bulge*'s, to be able to *afford* to indulge myself. Because if you just did *Twelve Angry Men* and *Ox-Bow Incident* and *Welcome to Hard Times,* you wouldn't be doing them very long. After two or three that didn't make any money, nobody is going to hire you.

HANSON. *This picture then, you would place in that category?*

FONDA. This one that I am doing? Oh, yes. When the novel *Welcome to Hard Times* came out, it was likened to *Ox-Bow Incident.* Not because the subjects are at all similar, but because it was such an off-beat, non-commercial kind of Western. It is probably very wrong before a picture has been finished to call it non-commercial. It may be putting the kiss of death on it. But I think everybody involved is aware of it. The studio knows. They have already earmarked it to be one of their films that they are doing for ABC Television, with the right to release it to theatres if they think they could realize even a small profit on it. I don't put that down as a deal because I think they are right. They can probably get their money back with one big showing on television. Which is fine. Then it can be released theatrically around the world and pick up a little profit. I don't think anybody should be in the business of making movies, hoping to open in art houses, and not make five cents. There is no reason for it.

The Business of Film Acting

The actors in this section do not consider economic matters alone. In ways that differ from the studio cohort in the previous section, however, they see business as central to their careers and in some ways as formative. How film actors get their roles, who hires them, and under what terms—these are factors bound up intextricably with what actors do when they finally come before cameras.

The paternalistic nature of Hollywood film studios at their height dictated whom actors needed to bargain with to carve out the kind of careers they wanted. Actors are still subject to commodification, but they have more options now with regard to how they want to be commodified. At the same time, the disparity between the salaries of stars and supporting actors has become even greater. The result is that the vast majority of film actors have to scramble for their living in ways they might not have if they had remained in the protective embrace of the studios.

One change over the last two generations has come in the variety of work actors pursue. Television, of course, has furnished a set of opportunities into which film actors can move with relative ease, at least in theory. Whatever else can be said about it, the demands television makes on actors are much closer to those of film than to those of the stage. Some of the most celebrated film stars now make commercials, which provide another outlet and in a sense a hedge against the often capricious nature of the movie business. In an age that values celebrity at least as highly as during the silent or studio eras, film actors may become spokespersons for various organizations, sell their faces or voices for commercial work or animated cartoons, or resort to the more traditional stand-by of stage acting. In addition, since the decline of the studios, films in America have also been funded and produced in more diverse ways. Actors have generally welcomed the disappearance of assembly-line techniques and the greater measure of creative freedom they have gained as a result.

Even as opportunities have proliferated, however, so have the number of actors competing for them. Willingness to work on television does not, of course, guarantee that a film actor, except at the very highest levels of the profession, can do so. Even then, celebrity actors are not guaranteed success, much less longevity, on television. Some actors have suffered from having their images translated from a larger screen to a smaller one—and vice versa— in ways reminiscent of the difficulties actors experienced in moving from silents to films with sound. Acting for television has also proved susceptible to changes more rapid and fashions even more transitory than those in films, by virtue of shifting demographics, trend- and rating-sensitive programming, and ever-restless network and, more lately, cable channel policies. Through all this, and in some measure *because* of it, film acting has maintained the prestige within the acting profession in America that it first established in the 1930s.

As collegial as it has been, at least in some respects, film acting also can breed professional jealousy. Over time, the fondness for dramatic close-ups in films has fed the notion that actors can or do or *should* work by themselves. Oddly enough, those actors most willing to credit their crew members as collaborators do not always acknowledge their fellow actors in the same way. This tendency testifies not only to the economic realities of filmmaking, which usually remove actors from their colleagues as soon as their own roles have been completed, but to the rivalries among performers, a consequence of the enormous financial rewards that accompany international stardom.

Such rewards were manifest in the career of Gloria Swanson, who in her role as an aging silent-film star in the movie *Sunset Boulevard* presents a caricature of celebrity quite at odds with her own hardheaded views of fame. Her most memorable film role hardly reflects her own life, for her career bridged silents and talking pictures. With her style she was able easily to achieve the larger effects that marked silents, as well as the lighter and less obvious ones that typify films with sound. As an actress, Swanson possessed a versatility she has not often been credited with, which helped explain her durability as a film attraction and a box-office commodity.

Katharine Hepburn's breezy account of the demands of studio publicity probably masks the depth of her own ambition. On the other hand, her tastes in acting, even in her first film, suggest that she focused more on artistic issues than commercial ones. Whether authentic or not, Hepburn's supposed indifference to the concerns of the marketplace may have served her well during an unusually long and varied career as a film actress; and her willingness to return to the stage also enhanced and at times revived her appeal in Hollywood. Like Swanson, she regrets the passing of the more "romantic" sensibility that marked the films she remembers most fondly, and she attributes this development to the degrading effect of commerce. It is the business which has changed, she feels, and not the audiences.

Sidney Poitier offers a considered view of how the shifting tides of the marketplace have affected and been affected by the issue of race. His own fame has followed a cyclical pattern, and he sees the same commercial forces that brought him into vogue contributing to the climate that later dictated his obsolescence. Poitier is that rare actor who can discuss criticism of his work—

and of his person—and respond to such criticism in a graceful way. His notion of "beating the system" lies in his own willingness, which he seeks to inspire in others, to solicit financial backing for films on the local level, from smaller communities and ethnic minorities.

Issues of gender figure for Meryl Streep in something of the same way that race does for Poitier. A classic backlash is illustrated by the dearth of roles that she contends women found in the late 1980s, in spite of the inroads that feminist consciousness had made on other, less heavily commercialized areas of American life. As she views matters, action films and superheroes have taken a toll: directors, writers, and actors have defined film audiences too narrowly. In accord with Gloria Swanson and Katharine Hepburn, Streep suggests that new audiences can be created and older ones recovered if more films are made that appeal to people who have chosen recently to stay at home rather than go to the movies.

Jeff Daniels reflects on life as a film actor away from the commercial nexus of Hollywood. In this connection, he is part of a trend toward making smaller, independent films in places that once would have qualified only as "locations." For Daniels, as for most of the other actors in this section, personal choices affect professional ones. A simpler life may be necessary if an actor is to survive in a business that has always been tough and demanding. Daniels' dictum that "'commercial' isn't a dirty word" provides a guideline to the balance that actors need to find between their own work and its mode of consumption. In this connection, the performances film actors give radiate outward, continually, from the film world itself into the broader arenas of finance, commerce, and trade.

Gloria Swanson Interview with the Actress

J.K. Let me ask you . . . Lillian Gish told me, "When sound came in, imagination went out." Do you think this is true?

G.S. I don't quite know what she means, and maybe taking it out of context like that . . . What was that apropos of? Did she say they showed more emotion in their faces when they were silent? . . .

I agree that the silent-picture actor really had to believe and feel a lot more than the stage actor. The stage actor can be convincing in a love scene or a tragedy by the intonation of his voice, because if you were in the tenth row you could not see his eyes, and you cannot see a muscle quivering from there. But in a picture everybody is in the first row of a motion-picture house. Because when they want to see what's really going on in the mind of that person, or emotionally, they come to a close-up. They don't give you a long shot, do they? I mean, you cannot be thinking about your income tax or if you'll be late for dinner when the scene is over. Yet on stage, out of the mouth of the person who can be thinking all kinds of things there are coming lines he has said a thousand times before.

Back then I'd often wonder why careers came and went, why the light that had shone so brightly for a person at one time should suddenly have turned off. Of course there were the obvious reasons; tastes change, new faces supplant old ones, people become smug, stale, too secure to be of any great interest; and sound came in and amplified a lot of these problems. . . .

J.K. You were one of the few big stars of that era who made the transition into sound without the difficulties others had, like John Gilbert, who I've heard did not have a high voice at all, but Mayer wanted to eliminate him.

G.S. Well, we'll never know the truth about that one. Neither will he, because he couldn't see what was going on! You know, *they* [the masterminds] wouldn't have Jean Arthur because they said her voice wasn't good . . . so she came back to New York and made a tremendous success on the stage, and then of course they couldn't wait to get her back to Hollywood. You see, one thing is often forgotten, and shouldn't be: this is business. And how anybody gets a job in business we'll never know. Sometimes it's influence, sometimes

Excerpt from a 1964 interview with Gloria Swanson in John Kobal, *People Will Talk* (New York: Aurum Press/A. Knopf, 1986), 2–21. Copyright © 1986 by The Kobal Collection, Ltd. Reprinted by permission of Alfred A. Knopf., Inc.

Gloria Swanson in *The Affairs of Anatol* (1921)

it's working hard from the bottom up, various ways . . . maybe it's a pattern of life, or fate. I don't know. Maybe because . . . But I *did* make the bridge from silent pictures to talking pictures, and some of them didn't. But, as you say, it's a possibility that the studios didn't want to pay the big-star prices and maybe I, who happened to be my own producer, went from one to the other in good pictures. Sound in those days . . . everybody's voice was much higher, everybody's voice was not quite normal, I don't believe. Even the singing voice—some of us had our own.

I sang in a picture and I can hardly believe I hit those high notes! I sang in a lot of my pictures, in *Indiscreet,* with music by De Sylva, Brown and Henderson. That was made by Mr. Sam Goldwyn, on the same lot at the same time I was producing, I did that one for him. And *Music in the Air** was later, in 1934, and that's more normal, but even then I couldn't believe I had that kind

*The first of several publicized projects to actually get off the ground, it was her last Hollywood film (except for a 1941 RKO programmer) till *Sunset Boulevard.*

of operatic voice.* John Boles and I sang that together again just a year and a half ago [1963]. But that was how I made the transition, you see. Audiences make stars, either they like you or they don't like you. And if you are liked equally by men and women, you have a longer life than if you are just going to be liked by men. A woman will go out of curiosity once, but won't want Harry to go again because it's too sexy or something. Women who have enjoyed longer careers, female stars, were stars who were adored by men *and* women, where audiences could hold hands together and enjoy it. The realism that came into pictures after the war, the last war—hopefully the last war—was so realistic that I think it drove a lot of women away from the theaters. Then you got into the sordid things that children adore because they don't have the problems of living life or responsibility, so they get a vicarious kind of kick out of seeing somebody else suffer. But the young married couple, after they have had a day with the children screaming or knocking their second tooth out, or measles, or a mortgage on the house having to be paid, they want to be entertained, they want comedy, they want to laugh. And then you get the next category, the women who helped make the motion-picture business, who used to go into darkened auditoriums and dream dreams because there was no harm in wanting to be a millionaire then [Gloria had made and lost millions several times over and was shrewd enough not to end up poor]. Now it's just foolishness because you can't . . . but we didn't have taxes then. . . . So now they want romance.

The first real romance that came along in years was *Summertime* with Katie Hepburn and Rossano Brazzi. I was his escort to the premiere of the film in Venice, we went in a gondola to the theater and he was a wreck because he was sure it wasn't going to be any good, and I kept saying, "Now you see, this is wonderful," and he said when it was over, "Do you really think it is going to be an enormous success in America?" and I said, "I'll tell you two things. One is that you have brought back romance to the mature woman and you are going to become a star. And the other thing is that Venice is going to be ruined—tourism. You're going to find that for every one man there will be twenty-five women looking for you, or your equal." And years later we met and laughed about this, because it's exactly what did happen. But we don't have stories for the people who made this business, the women. I say women more than men, because most of the men died before the women, and it was the women who would say, "John, take me to see so-and-so," and he, being a nice gentleman, would take his lady to where she wanted to go rather than say,

*Why didn't anybody think of Swanson for *Hello, Dolly!?*

"Now you come to where I want to go, to see Bronco Billy"* or something. But it's also a difference of the times, as we said before, you see; it's the '20s versus today. Then everybody tried to do a better job than the next person because there was tremendous competition. Today we are talking about paying people who have less than $4000 a year and making up the difference. Work is one of the greatest joys in the world in life. I always say that I don't think I could stand Paradise for more than eleven months of the year, I would have to go to Hell for the other month.

J.K. Fame has its own rewards and its own troubles. It's something I want to ask you: you have been famous for just about all of your life. Ten thousand kids scream for your autograph and just want to look at you. People stand in line for hours just to look at you on screen.

G.S. Well, you see, it all happened . . .

I am just very grateful to Mr. Edison and Mr. De Forest, and all the people who had anything to do with an invention. It made it possible to put us all in tin cans, like sardines. We could have been bad actors, it didn't matter. It was the fact of volume . . . you were just shipped everywhere and people got accustomed to that face, like they would get accustomed to the emblem of a Rolls-Royce, that little statue of the lady on the hood. . . . I'm *not minimizing anything!* [She says the latter in a burst of irritation at my suggestion she might be making too little of the cost of thousands, the work of millions, the fortune she earned et al.] I don't say that I didn't grow up in the business, that I didn't learn and grow. I hope to goodness I did, because of my insatiable curiosity. I was hungry for knowledge. So I started, at the age of seventeen, just getting my hands on books. If I take you to my bedroom now, it's not so much that a storm hit it, we don't know what to do with all the books! I love books, books, books. I'd rather read a good book than go to any ball, or these invitations that come in for this and that. It's because I had no real teenage life. I was never an ingenue, I went from being a little girl, starry-eyed, in awe not of fame or of a career, but in sheer awe of life. I also wanted to have my cake and eat it too. I was the only child, so I wanted to have children, and I wanted to be married. As you know, I made several attempts, many attempts, but this wasn't in my nature.

There's a price to pay for fame, as you can well imagine. When a woman works and she wants children too, you cannot have your cake and eat it . . . so you get a lot of heartaches over this. If you have to turn your children over during the day to someone else, and then when you're home and they run towards you and they trip and fall, they turn around and run back to their

*"Bronco Billy" Anderson was the screen's first Western star.

nanny or whoever is looking after them, rather than to you. Those are the things you have to give up. About the only thing you do have of another individual or child is their babyhood and childhood . . . you can't claim anything else. I have been blessed with having three fascinating people for children, seven grandchildren, and no delinquents yet or beatniks, knock on wood.

Katharine Hepburn Dialogue on Screen Acting

J.K. Did you enjoy working at the studios?

K.H. Well, then, of course, the enjoyment, the jokes, the fun of being on the set from 9:00 in the morning until 6:00 at night, it has to have a lot of get-up-and-go and a lot of joy. Because it's a longer day than in a factory for actresses, most of whom get there at 6:30 in the morning for makeup. Well, I don't get there at 6:30 anymore, I get there at 8:30. I put on my makeup in five minutes, wash my hair the night before, curl it. . . . I no longer go in for any of that nonsense. I did ninety years ago, but no more. I caught on!

J.K. As with all stars, glamour and the publicity surrounding it were part of your work. You certainly did a lot of portraiture work. Did you take much interest in which stills went out?

K.H. I'd kill certain ones, but I was lucky. I was very easy photographically, so I suppose that made me confident and made me more amiable than some people. I wouldn't be so amiable now. Time has laid its ugly hand . . . [She laughs.] I'd be much more critical now. I think one probably likes to see oneself in a certain light, but then I was obviously fascinated by myself, for there I am posing away!

J.K. How long did those sessions take, since I suppose you had to . . .

K.H. I didn't have to do anything. No. But I worked mainly with Ernie Bachrach, and I did it for him just because I liked to do it for him. We usually took two or three hours. I think he had an assistant or someone to light the

Excerpt from a 1979 interview with Katharine Hepburn in John Kobal, *People Will Talk* (New York: Aurum Press/A. Knopf, 1986), 324–338. Copyright © 1986 by The Kobal Collection, Ltd. Reprinted by permission of Alfred A. Knopf., Inc.

background, though I can't be accurate now, but I think he did most of the work himself. And I'd arrive with a lot of clothes that I thought were amusing-looking, and then we'd go. He didn't have to do much to get me into a mood. I changed my clothes fast, did my makeup fast, did everything fast. I've always used the same pancake makeup all my life, and that's all I used for portraits. In *Bill of Divorcement* you'll see a girl with a *lot* of makeup on; they were trying to cover up my freckles. Then, when I'd do a sad scene and tears would roll down my cheeks, they'd make a big track down my face, and it would take about an hour and a half to change my makeup. Then, your eyes get red. If you have my coloring, your eyes get red very easily. So then I said, "Why don't I wear what I used to wear on the stage?" Which was a wash makeup which Max Factor made, makeup that you could apply with water and a sponge, and that's what I used. He created it for me. Other than that, there's a certain amount of eye stuff, eyelashes, lipstick, but very little pancake. Very little makeup. The lipstick back then was intense, though I use nothing now.

J.K. You mentioned *Bill of Divorcement,* which was your first film.

K.H. Yes, I remember that when we finally started on it, I remember very accurately the first scene I ever did. Jack Barrymore came in with a hat and raincoat on, and he was fiddling around with some pipes on the mantelpiece, and then he turned around and looked at me. I was standing off-camera, watching him, as George Cukor had told me to do, acting away, full of sincerity. I was watching him do this. And I looked at Jack with the cold eye of youth and thought he was overdoing it. I did. I thought he was overdoing it a bit. I thought, "That's not very good." But while I was thinking all these unkind things, I was acting away, tears streaming down my face, doing a little too much myself, you see, and the take was over. And Jack came over, and he took my chin in his hands and looked at me and said to George, "I'd like to do it again." And he did it again and it was entirely different, he was entirely different to me. Maybe it still looks overdone now, I don't know. But his mental attitude was certainly entirely different. And I think he just saw a kid to whom it meant a tremendous amount, and he felt, "Well, the poor thing, I'd better do a little better here." It shows what a sensitive actor he was. Spencer always said, "Young actors must show respect." And I would say, "Well, I never showed the *dimmest* respect." When I did *Lion in Winter,* we re-hearsed it for three weeks. They said, "This is so unique. We're going to rehearse the picture." And I laughed. "It ain't unique to me," I said. "I rehearsed the *Bill of Divorcement* with Mr. George Cukor for one week, with Jack Barrymore, before we shot, in the restaurant at RKO. And that was the first picture I ever did." Not so unique. They think they've stumbled on something new. I think it's all part of the same thing. The books are too long. Why? Because the people won't cut them, and they won't work over them. The people are all falling apart because they won't bother to have any character, and they won't try that hard. Everybody wants it to come easily. We live in a terribly easygoing society.

You see, I think the people who survive are the people who are not such insane egomaniacs that they have to put their mark on everything. Now, George is a very generous man. He is a very generous director because he lets the actor put his mark on what he's doing, and he doesn't have to put a big sign on my back saying "George Cukor." Never did have. He was very happy to have somebody else get the credit for it. He was interested in character. Now, character doesn't change. Material changes. He didn't get wedded to material, he got wedded to people. People were his interest. He was totally an artist. He would resent this . . . he thinks he's very practical. I don't think he was terribly practical. I'm much more practical than he is. But I think he was a real, a *real* artist. He was dealing in values of . . . love . . . and hate . . . and sex . . . uhh, villainy, which don't change. He could do that for a thousand years and would never date. The form of the thing might date, and everything else, but he's not easily shocked. He has very high standards. He didn't in the least even notice nudity, any more than I do. I don't give a rap; but I give an enormous rap when people are disillusioned. Now, sex . . . everybody . . . it's the style now to show everybody doing everything. This is a bore. Privacy and the magic of life, and the possible romantic magic between two people, which is what sex should represent, is nonexistent. I don't look at him, and he doesn't look at me, and we've known each other for fifty years, but we don't look at each other with any sense of reality. If he looked at me the way I really am, and I don't spark him, he would never have hired me. And if I didn't feel what he was, and respond to what he had to offer, we would just have been two old things. This is what matters in life.

Now we are living in a totally realistic age. They think sex is what they're showing. I don't think they know what they're talking about. Because I see a woman sacrifice herself totally for a man, I see a man sacrifice himself entirely for a woman; this has nothing to do with reality. It hasn't even to do with character. This has to do with magic. Because character is a bore if you're only doing it because you're worthy or something. But if you love someone, as a woman and some men love a child or a dog, and the dog is run over and you pick up and try to help it or something, *that* is love. That is blind . . . affection. Now, *that* quality goes on forever. Because you can't describe it to me and I can't describe it to you; it's the magic of life. It's the come-on. It's the hope! And that magic can make anything survive.

I was brought up in a hospital, and I talked endlessly to my father, and he would operate on people who were very old, and he would say it was marvelous the way people with an upbeat spirit and a determination, people who couldn't die because they'd be leaving people who couldn't get on without them, and they lived! They *lived!* It's the spark of life, and without it, it's hopeless. You can take this regard for life too far, to the point of eccentricity where some won't even kill a mosquito or a moth without feeling guilty; but apply that to people, but most people are too goddamned lazy to apply that to people if the people become any trouble.

Now, people in our business go just up and down in their careers, up and down, up and down. Sometimes you've got to help them, and sometimes they've got to help you. And it has nothing to do with any sense. I'm in an up period. Nothing to do with any sense at all. Doesn't mean the snap of your fingers. And I'm smart enough [she laughs] because I've been up and down a number of times, so that it makes no impression at all. But there are a number of people who are your great friends and think you're fascinating and marvelous when you're up and they don't when you're down. But I do think that people who stick, regardless of whether you're up or down—now, that is a rare quality and a wonderful quality.

J.K. Did you study lighting or anything like that on the sets of your films?

K.H. No. I thought it was too dangerous. I didn't pay any attention to that. I thought it was too dangerous for actresses to know how they were lit, I thought it was a poor idea. I mean, the main thing you have is not how you look, but how you do it, how you come across. And if you're thinking of how you look, you'll be in a bad way. . . .

J.K. *Little Women* was one of those movies that really quite successfully incorporated innocence without being totally innocuous. . . .

K.H. *Little Women* had that extraordinary quality of lost innocence and also of character. It was a child's book, it was always considered like a child's book, but it was like *my* childhood, you see. We were in New England, we had a big family, and everything was always rather exaggerated and I was a *very* dramatic sort, you know, "Chri*s*topher Col*u*mbus! What *rich*ness" type. And all that sort. It rather suited my exaggerated sense of things. And they [the *Little Women* family] were a good sort. All of them. They had character and they were funny.

Oh, I remember there was a sound strike in the studios at the time we were shooting, it was during the scene where Beth was dying for the nth time, and although I admired the book enormously, I was getting a little bit unable to play it because I had wept day after day after day, and I had sixteen and twenty takes on these weeping scenes, and they wouldn't get them correctly. We had all of these amateur sound men. Finally, she did die, and I threw up. I cried so many times, I just threw up.

Then we switched and did the scene where I went to New York to seek my fortune and I went to the opera with Professor Bhaer. And I came back home, you know, in the movie, and I said, "Ohhhhhhhh, Ih donh't whahnt to be ah hwritah. Ih whahnt to be ahn ohperah singhah." [Hepburn does an astoundingly good takeoff of Hepburn.] And I came into this room, in this *ex*quisite dress, and I rather fancied myself, full of too much energy, terribly young, all of ten, and I twirled around in this beautiful dress which had been copied from one of my grandmother's dresses and sank to the ground in a curtsy and said, "I want to be an opera singer," and down from the ceiling, on a rope, came a large ham. That was George's idea of a joke. It was terribly funny. And nothing like that ever happened to me until one day when I got stuck on the Milford Turnpike, and a cop came up to me and said, "Well, if it isn't the little girl who sold us those sandwiches all these years." And I asked, "What kind of sandwich?" and he said, "Ham." Isn't that divine? [She burst into laughter.]

J.K. But you had an enormous appeal . . . your hair comes down and you are transformed. Or, as in *Alice Adams,* at the moment that Alice is at her gauchest, as the man turns from her, you/Alice are as beautiful as can be . . . Your appeal was in the ability to transform yourself from duckling to swan.

K.H. But I was not in any way pretty. I was not pretty. And a lot of the people around then were extremely pretty. But all of them, every one, they were maintaining the illusion. It was a romantic business. The stories were romantic. It was a fascinating never-never land. I mean, look, the theaters were covered with gilt and cupids. I always wanted to be a movie actress. I thought it was very romantic. And it was. It still can be. Granted, there was a dearth of material and I made the great mistake of saying yes to some of it, but there were others.

In a way, the whole business has come full circle, people today are as romantic about the movies we made then as we were making them at the time. They created . . . Louis B. Mayer was romantic about the industry. Today it's all money. Today they have turned that never-never land into . . . They have to offer people something they can't get at home, all these sorts of sexual perversions and weird happenings. That's what they go for now. And that's what they're selling.

I've run into a lot of people who are miserable, and the world is passing [them] by, and I've lived long enough to know why, and that is because a lot of them have just been pigs. They were wildly selfish. They were wildly self-centered, and they don't take anything in. They are giving out, they are not taking in. And the minute you stop taking in, you're dead. I think everybody has about twenty to thirty years' impetus from their childhood, and then look out! Writers especially. Writers go dead. And I've seen directors go dead, and actors go dead. You've got to fill up the well, and the only way to fill up the well is to fill it up with deeds that are generous enough that your imprint isn't on them. Otherwise you're just drinking your own water. It's a terrible state to be in. It's very common today.

Sidney Poitier Walking the Hollywood Color Line

About ten years ago I came to realize that the kinds of films which had made me so successful during the sixties had fallen from favor with the critics and were no longer viable at the box office. In 1969 Universal Pictures released *The Lost Man,* a remake of *Odd Man Out* in which I played the doomed fugitive. It was not a successful picture by a long shot. But I came out of that experience richer because I had the occasion to meet and work with one of its producers, a man named Mel Tucker. I was impressed with his integrity. Although I made a picture for him that didn't make any money, it didn't affect our relationship. He was as caring, as concerned, and as interested as anyone you might find who has your best interests at heart.

Some two years after *The Lost Man,* after many, many years of being a part of the hierarchy at Universal Pictures, he was let go in one of their reshuffles and was about to go into independent production when I thought of him as the kind of guy I would like to have produce for me. He joined my company, Verdon Productions, about the time I was looking for a decent piece of material to honor my first commitment to First Artists. We commissioned a rather touching script called *A Warm December,* which accomplished what I wanted it to. Hollywood had produced no love stories for blacks; *A Warm*

Excerpt from Sidney Poitier, "Walking the Hollywood Color Line," *American Film* 5, no. 6 (April 1980), 24–29. Adapted from *This Life,* by Sidney Poitier (New York: Alfred Knopf, 1980). Copyright © 1980 by Sidney Poitier. Reprinted by permission of Alfred A. Knopf., Inc.

Sidney Poitier (left) with Canada
Lee (center) and Charles Carson
in *Cry, the Beloved Country* (1951)

December was made with that in mind. It is the story of a successful black
American doctor whose wife has died and left him with an eleven-year-old
daughter; he goes to London on a vacation with his child and meets an African
princess with whom he falls in love.

But the picture didn't do any business. It was released in 1973, a time when
black exploitation films were in full swing in the United States—a particularly
distressing time for me because I was going through a period of being persona
non grata among certain militant elements, especially in New York. That
period started after my most successful movies—*To Sir, With Love, In the
Heat of the Night, Guess Who's Coming to Dinner.* There had been no other
black actor anywhere near my level of success, and in the community of black
actors resentment was developing. I was earning hundreds of thousands of
dollars while a discouragingly small number of my black colleagues were
lucky if they connected with a $300-a-week gig.

I was a perfect target, but there wasn't anything I could do. I could have
ended my career, but what would that have accomplished? It wouldn't have
got them hired. To tell them of the countless times I had confronted studio
people and extracted promises from them to do something about hiring black
actors would be of little comfort, since they had seen no tangible results.
Worst of all, with the sharp instincts of hungry outsiders, they knew a naked
truth about Hollywood. The motion picture industry was not yet ready to
entertain more than one minority person at that level. I knew it, too, and
couldn't fight that.

The first shot at me came after I had enjoyed a dozen years of press that was
more often than not favorable and fair. Even for my pictures that didn't work, I

generally received very good personal notices. Then a writer named Larry Neal saw *The Lost Man* and said to me, "You're heading for big trouble. Black people aren't going to like that picture." He was right.

At about that time a man named Clifford Mason got an assignment from the *New York Times* to write an article on me. It was called "Why do White Folks Love Sidney Poitier So?" It was the most devastating and unfair piece of journalism I had ever read. And on the Sunday morning I read it, I said to myself, This definitely signals a bad period for me. On that Sunday morning I was convinced that the brick-by-brick growth of my career was complete—it had peaked, and there was no place to go but down.

In that article Clifford Mason ripped to shreds everything I had ever done. He ripped up *In the Heat of the Night,* and in particular the character I played, to show why white people thought I was so terrific. He went on to destroy *To Sir, With Love* and *Guess Who's Coming to Dinner,* and then he went further back into my career and proceeded to skin me alive retroactively. I was "an Uncle Tom," "a lackey," "a house nigger"—terms then current for highly visible blacks who were perceived as not doing whatever they could to win the applause of all their fellow blacks.

I didn't know who that Clifford Mason was. But he scalded me awfully. I got on the phone that very day and began asking around about him, but I couldn't assemble more than a sketchy portrait from the fragments of information I was able to obtain.

The following week—which, needless to say, was a tough one for me—I received an invitation from a young man at the American Negro Theater to see a play he had directed at a high school auditorium in Harlem. I'm sitting there in the first row of the packed room waiting for the curtain to go up, when the man sitting next to me leans over and says, "Hello, you don't know who I am, do you?" I look at him a moment, then say politely, "No, I'm sorry, I don't." He says, "My name is Clifford Mason." Well, instantly a bell rings, but I'm cool. I say, "Oh, I see," and that's all I say. I turn my attention to the program to see who's in the cast. Mind you, that isn't really what I'm doing. I'm trying to collect myself. He says, "Did you read my article?" And I say, "Oh, yes, I did." Period.

The play begins, and it's quite an interesting show. Whenever he gets an opportunity, he leans over to make some kind of comment. My response is cold. Intermission comes, and I decide I'd better get up and move away from that man because there's something not quite right about him. Whenever I'm at the theater, it's my habit to go outside during the intermission to get away from the autograph seekers. That night I don't make it; I'm intercepted by lots of women who crowd around. I settle into signing, and suddenly a voice over my shoulder says, "Don't push, ladies, just take your time. He's going to sign them all for you, so don't get excited. He's going to sign them all." I look around, and there's Clifford Mason. He's taking the papers or programs from the women, passing them to me for signing, then taking them back for redistribution. The bastard is orchestrating my autograph signing! At the end of the play, having no desire for further conversation with this strange man, I go over to the guy who invited me, tell him I enjoyed the play, and split.

The next Sunday afternoon, the Nigerian musical artist Michael Olatunji was giving a concert at Town Hall to raise funds for a civil rights organization. I go, and there's Clifford Mason again, and again he makes himself known to me. By this time I know a little more about who Mr. Mason is. He's a playwright—of sorts. He's worked in radio as a kind of announcer on a small station. By this time I've realized that the article in the *Times,* aside from being an expression of his own feelings, is a career opportunity for an up-and-coming writer of sorts.

What I resented most about Clifford Mason by the time of our second encounter was his laying all the film industry's transgressions at my feet. I respected the rage and hostility of my fellow actors against the unfairness that, first, kept them out so long, and second, when the door did begin to open, showered so many opportunities on one person. With only a handful of jobs to be scrambled for, they had to watch that one guy getting all the real opportunities over a twelve-year period. They were right in being angry, and they had to have a place to dump their anger.

It was no secret that Hollywood wasn't interested in supplying blacks with a variety of positive images. But thanks to a handful of committed souls, the perennial image of the black man was changing. A black man was put in a suit, given a briefcase; he could become a doctor, a lawyer, or a police detective. And that was a plus for us, to be sure; but it certainly was not enough to satisfy the yearnings of an entire people.

A people are a community, and a community consists of bus drivers and laborers and street sweepers and dentists and schoolteachers and hustlers and prostitutes and students and ordinary workers. Where was that kind of representation on the motion picture screen for blacks? It didn't exist. The closest Hollywood came over a twelve-year period was the one-dimensional, middle-class imagery I embodied most of the time.

My unique relationship with each side of the problem trapped me in one hell of a dilemma. There was nothing I could do in quick relief for the guy who works in a factory, who's married to a good wife, who doesn't look like Denise Nicholas or Dorothy Dandridge but who loves him and has given him a couple of fine kids with whom they have a very good black family home life, the likes of which he wants to see reflected on the motion picture screen when he plunks down his $3. I couldn't do that for him because I was not in control of the film business. Until the early seventies I was not even in control of my career in the film business, beyond making a decision to play or not to play in a given piece of material. Furthermore, nothing in the material from which I had to choose had anything to do with the kind of family life thousands of such guys lived. More than a few of the selections I made were merely the best of a bad lot.

Clifford Mason's article started a kind of deluge. The *New York Times* published several more articles in which I was dumped on. I was aware that the *Times* Sunday entertainment section would often get somebody to write an article on a director or an actor that might be controversial and uncomplimentary. After they printed such an article, they would allow the subject to respond. And so they would get space filled for free, at the expense of that particular artist. As a faithful reader of the *New York Times,* I watched these exchanges, and for five or six weeks that poor director or actor would really be throttled. Probably no clear-cut verdict can be given on whether this practice constitutes a cheap shot habit or a good journalist ploy to fill space. But given a choice, those of us who have been stung by the Sunday theatrical section will opt for cheap shot habit, even while we prize our home delivery subscriptions to the good old *New York Times.*

I was sought after to respond, and I thought about it. But as much as I wanted to reply to Clifford Mason, I decided not to. In no way was I going to let them sucker me in to that. The fact that I didn't respond seemed to trigger further attempts to provoke me. In any case, the negative mentions kept coming, but I kept myself firm against drawing myself into an exchange.

At about the same time, the black exploitation films began to take hold in America. Finally some elements in the industry were beginning to view the black community as a viable audience in itself, one hungry for entertainment in its own image. The realization that there was money "across town" waiting to be made set in motion a flurry of activity for black actors and actresses unprecedented in an industry that long ago had built racial exclusion in to the rules of its game. They gave us *Shaft* with Richard Roundtree, *Slaughter* with Jim Brown, *Super Fly, Cotton Comes to Harlem,* and *Three the Hard Way.* Fred Williamson began doing his numbers, and between him and Jim Brown, a new kind of hero was born. Their "macho" films were quite unlike mine. Generally these black heroes were seen beating up on white Mafia guys; it was a "get whitey" time—which certainly added immeasurably to the popularity of their films.

I know because I was there at the box office putting down my $3 to see Jim

Brown and Fred Williamson do their stuff. I, too, enjoyed seeing the black guys beating up on the white guys for a change. It was delicious. Not only did I like watching the revenge syndrome at work, I also liked watching my fellow actors at work. Suddenly, after too many years of little more than Sidney Poitier films, came a profusion of movies with black stars, male and female.

My own career went into a decline at that point, and I recognized that there would be no reviving it for a while. So I went into a kind of retirement for a year. I didn't announce it formally, but I went on down to the Caribbean and just cooled it. I bought a boat, a lot of books, and I sat around enjoying my family, my house, my boat—and my Sunday *New York Times,* which kept me abreast of the wildfire spread of the black exploitation film, that yardstick against which I was clearly able to measure my own decline.

Having slipped into a kind of twilight zone, I chose to stay away from my fellow actors unless and until I received an invitation. It's long been common practice for "at liberty" actors to visit the sets of friends who are lucky enough to be working, but there had been such a chasm between my career and those of most of my black colleagues that I would never go visiting them at work unless invited. When Ossie Davis was directing *Cotton Comes to Harlem* in New York, I stayed away from his set even though it was populated with actors I started out with, and with whom I was more than casually acquainted. I stayed away because I didn't want any of my colleagues to feel apprehensive about my raining on their parade.

One day I happened to be on a plane with Jim Brown heading for California from Atlanta, where we had been participating in something concerning Martin Luther King, when he came over and sat down next to me. At that time he was at the height of his career. Sitting there next to me on that plane, he said something that made him a guy I would like forever. He said, "A lot of things are happening now, and a lot of us are working. I just thought I'd stroll up here and say thank you for the contributions you've made to us all having a little piece. I just want you to know that it's appreciated." He got up, shook my hand, and went back to his seat. That made my day. A man of few words who never bit his tongue, that was big Jim, a prince of many colors. That was the way he was and that's the way he is.

But that was not the way it was with most of my other actor friends. Somehow I got the impression that the threat of Sidney Poitier could only be allayed properly if it could be fixed so that he never worked again. I got those vibes from a lot of quarters.

I went to see each exploitation film as it came out. In the course of my four years in the Bahamas, they were the most popular movies being shown in the islands. You ain't heard nothing yet until you hear a theater filled with a

Saturday night audience of blacks talking back to the screen, telling Jim Brown and Fred Williamson what to do with the Mafia heavies.

After a year or two, it began coming to me that the producers of such films were making a mistake—a mistake which, in the final analysis, will be borne by the black actors and actresses who at that time were jubilantly approaching the light of day after languishing so long in the shadows. My understanding of the film business told me that the producers who were making black exploitation films were not interested in much beyond the buck; there wasn't a genuine interest in the black audience as such. A healthy interest in the black community would have required a noticeable shifting of emphasis in the content and intent of such films, yet I noticed a dangerous disregard of the hopes and aspirations of black people.

I reluctantly concluded that the black exploitation filmmaker, seeing the overwhelming response to the revenge syndrome, elected to use that one-dimensional theme as the dramatic frame for almost all the films they would make for black consumption. They seemed to feel that as long as Fred, Jim, and Richard went on beating up and subduing white crooks, that would continue to serve as the strongest ingredient in a successful film; if, in addition, the women were good with a gun and terrific in bed, they had an unbeatable combination that black people would never weary of. Not one among these producers, to my knowledge, cared to think otherwise. After all, one of the principal rules of the Hollywood game is to never, never, monkey with success.

Had they taken time to look beneath the surface, they might have discovered that the appetite they were banking on would be satiated quicker than their greed, that the "get whitey" formula would be enjoyed only for a short time. That was not what black people were all about. The pleasure they derived from seeing their actors function on that level was only a momentary satisfaction. They knew their actors had a bigger responsibility and anticipated their going on to represent the community on levels more important to its existence. They saw the other thing as a nice introduction, a wonderful way for their actors to open up their involvement in film—but not as something to go on repeating forever. Neither the exploitation films nor my films were sufficiently about them, sufficiently representative of what in fact they were. Hollywood was still wide of the mark in relation to their dreams, their aspirations, their frustrations, the things they lived with every day.

The exploitation film began to show unmistakable signs of wear at the box office, a condition that prompted more than a few producers to prepare to jump ship, with remarks like, "Well, the black audiences are no longer interested in seeing black films" or "Hey, there's no money to be made in the black community any more; they're not coming out to see movies that have been tailor-made for them."

And at the same time, those black actors who were aware of the state of things were themselves making a mistake. They weren't coming to grips with the fact that the man—the white producer—wasn't really servicing the needs of the community they represented. There were those black actors with the requisite talent who should have moved quickly to learn the tools of the producers' trade, so that they could begin to produce their own films that would be closer to the needs of their constituency.

Now anyone with even a layman's knowledge of the business would recognize that for black actors to become producers was easier said than done. But when the stark alternative is just standing around helpless while a meaningful start fritters away to nothing, then the stakes involved warrant—no, demand—that one hell of an effort be made to move the mountain.

Most of my colleagues expected the exploitation trend to last at least five or ten years, and that out of it would eventually grow the kind of black filmmakers who could take things to the next level. It didn't last that long, and when it disappeared, there disappeared with it the fledgling job opportunities it had brought.

As the black exploitation filmmakers began dropping out, the black performing personalities were left without an "initiator," a head, a source capable of "putting a package together." All those displaced performers were reduced to sitting at home and waiting for the phone to ring. Those performers who didn't anticipate these conditions are to be excused. But those who had the requirements for learning the skills of putting the package together—raising the money, producing the picture, and ultimately walking away with the profits—they should be held responsible in part for missing what might have proved to be a pivotal opportunity. After all, isn't it likely that things would be appreciably better today if we had five or six functioning black producers among our hundreds of unemployed performers?

In the meantime, we are in a state of limbo. I'm surviving because most of my black colleagues are also not going to receive many calls. The number of jobs available to us all is woefully few. . . .

Fortunately for me, I was not at the mercy of the marketplace, having formed my own production company with guaranteed financing as a result of my deals with First Artists and Columbia. This allowed me to create my own employment; in the absence of those agreements, I might have found myself twiddling my thumbs through most of the last seven years. Which is not to say that I didn't receive offers during that period; but the eight or ten scripts that did come my way were without exception the kind of material I preferred not to work with.

So how does one get to develop one's own company, and through it make one's own films? First of all, you have to be damn lucky; foresight is not necessarily the chief factor, but the stroke of good fortune that positions you in the right place at the right time is essential.

An excellent example of luck at work occurred after *A Warm December,* the first picture I made for First Artists. When it was clear that the picture would make no money, I went to the company and said, "For my next picture I'm going to need approximately two million dollars." They had no alternative but to give me the money, because of our contractual agreement. Needless to say, the management of the company tried to talk me out of it. They were afraid that after *A Warm December* didn't do so well, maybe the second one would also go down the drain. They said to me, "Why do you want to make this new picture? This *Uptown Saturday Night?* We frankly don't think it stands a chance." They spent hours trying to talk me out of it.

Somewhere late in the second hour of this discussion, as I realized how they would relish any tiny legal loophole that would allow them to write me off, I suddenly knew I was at the crossroads. I knew that with *Buck and the Preacher* (a Western I had directed and starred in, with Harry Belafonte) struggling to break even and *A Warm December* making no money, if I didn't make that new picture—if I didn't continue to generate my own employment—I could segue into oblivion in a couple of years. And that would be the end of a career. Recognizing that my survival as a movie actor rested exclusively on my own initiative, I said to the First Artists people, "Look, whether you like it or not, my contract calls for you to give me up to three million dollars to make a movie. I intend to do this picture, so let's not create a problem for each other."

I had them on paper and they knew it. That document, free of tiny loopholes, could be traced back to the day when my good fortune thrust me at the right time (the most successful point of my career) to the right place (in the commissary at Universal Studios), where I received the invitation to join as a full partner in the formation of First Artists.

The management people wished me well after OK'ing the money, and I went off and made *Uptown Saturday Night.* When it was done, I invited them to come and see it. They in turn invited the Warner Bros. people, who were our distributors. Ten minutes into the picture the head of First Artists fell asleep. My picture had been running barely ten minutes, it was nine o'clock in the morning, and he started snoring. But I was cool, even though he slept through the whole picture. At the end of the screening the lights went up and an awkward silence prevailed. They didn't know whether they liked it or didn't like it—maybe because it was about black people and, moreover, about the kind of black people they hadn't seen much of.

To the credit of Ted Ashley, the head honcho at Warner Bros., he looked at me and just asked, "What are your plans for the picture in terms of underscoring and source music?" I gave him an outline of what the music would be and touched on other postproduction work that had to be done. After a short pause, he said, "Well, I don't understand all of it—I'm not as familiar as I'd like to be with the milieu—but I wish you luck with it, and thanks for letting us see it." Now there is a man I have subsequently grown to respect highly, a straightforward, to-the-point guy.

The rest of the crew didn't say a word. About a minute after they'd cleared the room, Leo Greenfield, then a wheel in the Warner Bros. distribution department, came back in, looked me straight in the eye, and said, "I'll tell you what I think about your picture. It's going to be a hit. It will do at least nine or ten million dollars. That's what your picture is going to do. With the exception of Ashley, those guys are too scared to pass a comment, because they don't know—" He then walked out of the screening room.

Well, he was dead right. And that should give the black filmmaker an indication of what he's up against. When he starts making films for the black community, he'll have to go to the white banks or white distribution companies or white studios to get his financing, all of them principally interested in making money. Of course they want to do it with a certain kind of distinction, but the bottom line is money. If they don't understand where you're comin' from artistically or don't see obvious signs of commercial vitality in your material, it will be damn near impossible to get money from those areas. And since in most cases the black filmmaker and his constituency remain unfamiliar, even discordant, oddities, the filmmaker must husband his strength and deepen his resolve to be ready and prepared for that day when a stroke of good fortune comes his way. Until then, he should remember that learning the rules of the game will crack a nut, and when a nut has been cracked, you can beat the system.

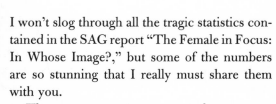

Meryl Streep When Women Were in the Movies

I won't slog through all the tragic statistics contained in the SAG report "The Female in Focus: In Whose Image?," but some of the numbers are so stunning that I really must share them with you.

Three years ago, women were down to performing only one-third of all the roles in feature films. In 1989, that number slipped to 29 percent. Of course, that was before the figures for this year were tabulated. Just wait till they factor in our contributions to *Total Recall, Robocop II, Days of Thunder, Die Hard 2, The Hunt for Red October, The Abyss, Young Guns II, Miami Blues, Last Exit to Brooklyn, Dick Tracy* and *The Adventures of Ford Fairlane.* We snagged a good six or seven major roles in those movies. If the trend continues, by the year 2000 women will represent 13 percent of all roles. And in 20 years, we will have been eliminated from movies entirely.

But that's not going to happen, is it ladies?!

There is some good news in these statistics. The average earnings by age and sex show that "after the age of 10, men earn consistently higher average annual earnings under SAG contracts than women do." That doesn't immediately sound like good news. However, it does mean that from birth through age nine, a girl can make a pretty fair living. In fact, we may have located one of the few areas in American enterprise where there *is* equal pay for equal work. My advice is: little girls, hold out for the big money, invest wisely and investigate other careers, because after fourth grade, it's all down hill.

By the way, as the mother of a 10-year old boy, I would like to know precisely *when* they begin to demonstrate their superior earning potential. I'm always looking for the light at the end of the Nintendo tunnel.

What is the problem? We all know what the problem is. One, there's very little work for women. And two, when we do work we get paid much less than our male counterparts—about 40 cents to 60 cents on the male dollar.

And what work there is lately is odd. Somebody at The *New Yorker* said recently that if the Martians landed and did nothing but go to movies this year, they'd come to the fair conclusion that the chief occupation of women on Earth is hooking. And I don't mean rugs.

"What has happened to women in the movies?" asked Janet Maslin, a critic for the *New York Times*. Peter Rainer of the *Los Angeles Times* recently wrote, "an entire generation of female performers is being squelched by an industry that finds no percentage in accommodating their talents."

Why is this happening? The three monkeys volunteer their answers:

"I don't see any good scripts being written for women," say the producers, covering their eyes.

"I can't continue to write screenplays that won't sell," say the writers, covering their mouths.

"We'd *love* to make that picture, but nobody would go to see it—nobody wants to hear from women," say the studios, covering their ears and their bases, their wallets and their faces all at the same time.

Bottom line: the real reason for the disappearance of women from films has a lot to do with the way movies are financed today. Many films are currently financed by foreign pre-sales. Production costs are significantly offset by fees paid to secure a certain film for foreign markets. So the big scramble is now on for international money.

Revenues from overseas can represent half or more of a picture's total haul. Action-adventure films traditionally pre-sell best. You don't have to understand what little English is contained in a film to know that something is exploding and enjoy the spectacle. This also means that sometimes the movies *we* get to see at home are pre-determined by what deal makers believe will eventually go big in the Far East or Southeast Asia.

The trouble is, when the bottom line drives the dream machine, some things get paved over and flattened (they don't call it the bottom line for nothing). Anyone wondering nostalgically where the crackling wit and stylish verbal surprise of classic films has gone can look under the wheels of the blockbuster. They do make money—sometimes. And sometimes they just *cost* money.

For whatever reason, the targeted worldwide audience—the audience that studios *most* want to reach—seems to be 16 to 25 year old males. In a recent article in *Los Angeles* magazine, 20th Century Fox production executive Melissa Bachrach stated, "Most moviegoers are men. You can't make movies just for the women's audience anymore. There has to be broad appeal. Men have the power, and women respond to that power."

In that same article, screenwriter Michael Mahern says, "Women got pushed aside. Movies today must appeal to both men and women. Relatively few women go to the movies alone. It's easier for men to be appealing to both men and women."

So people will tell you it's all about sex appeal. "Women's careers don't last as long as men's," says Interscope production exec David Madden. "There's a romanticism about the older male, not the female."

Well, certainly in a season where most of the female leads are prostitutes there's not going to be a lot of work for women over 40. Like hookers, actresses seem to lose their market appeal around that age. At the age of 40, however, most male actors are just approaching their peak earning potential. This boon continues into their 50s and 60s. According to the 1989 SAG statistics, men aged 60 to 69 years of age earned on average almost twice the annual salary of women 30 to 39 years old. Does this really reflect what the market demands?

It's interesting that everybody knows who goes to the movies now, but there's not a lot of data on who is deliberately staying home. If I were in the business end of this business, I would certainly be looking worldwide for markets, especially as the known one shrinks, for whatever reason.

There is, for instance, a generation (or two) of people out there who represent a huge (and with the greying of America, growing) market. These people grew up going to the movies not twice a month, but two and three times a week. They had the *habit* of going out to the movies. They have the money to go, and they don't need a sitter because the kids are grown. They have a VCR but they don't know how to program it, and they can't be bothered to sit down for an hour to plod through the Satellite/Cable Guide (which is now as big as a phone book) in order to find the two or three things they'd like to tape. And the novelty of cassette rentals has worn off as the overwhelming supermarket effect of video stores sends them slouching back to the car empty-handed.

These people are grouchy, but with reason. They are being ignored by the movie industry. We should find market strategies that court this audience which has forcibly weaned itself from its moviegoing habit. They have the time, the money *and* the inclination to go out to the movies—and not just on weekends.

Who else is staying home?

I always wonder about the people who came out to see the story of a little known (in this country) Danish woman writer who tried to make a go of coffee farming in East Africa. I have little doubt that if Sydney Pollack went seeking financing for *Out of Africa* in the current marketplace he'd be told "nobody wants to see that—it's a woman's story."

Janet Maslin, in her recent *New York Times* article "Bimbos Embody Retro

Rage" (great title), tells of an agent who informed her client, a writer, that if he wanted to get his script financed he'd better change the female protagonist to a male. Centering a story on a woman makes it harder to sell.

Anne Thompson, in her *LA Weekly* article entitled "Battling the Big Boys: The Decline of the Woman Star," says, "Actresses are as unclear about their screen roles as American men and women seem to be about their roles in real life."

I'm not sure that's true. I do know what roles are around, and I'm not confused about which ones realistically I'm able to portray. But the *range* of roles simply doesn't exist. All through my career, I've been barely able to contain a guffaw when an interviewer asked, "What drew you to this specific character? Why, out of everything available, did you choose *this* role?" As if there always existed a veritable rainbow of well-written roles for women! "The blue, the orange, the red, the green, the yellow, the puce, the vermilion—and you chose the olive green. Why this odd Australian film? Are you drawn to accents?" They happily pounce upon the obvious.

No. It's because I'm drawn to good writing and ideas and controversy and drama and feeling and emotion all packed into the character of the protagonist—the *person* who drives the action, not his girlfriend. Now in the prime of my life, I want to play the lead. Why? Because I grew up and was nourished on the legacy of the great female stars: the grand and glorious work of Bette Davis and Barbara Stanwyck, Carole Lombard and Lucille Ball, Katharine Hepburn and Greta Garbo, and on stage, Geraldine Page, Irene Worth, Maggie Smith, Colleen Dewhurst, Ethel Merman, Kim Stanley, Jessica Tandy and many, many others.

These women inspired me. The derivation of that word is from the Latin *in-spirare:* to breathe life into, to fill with life, to breathe in—and I did. I gasped when I saw these women. It made me want to be something, to achieve something, to express my humanity, my aliveness, my connection to that radiant, important creation which was woman.

I was inspired by actors, too. In fact, the first time I was aware that there was such a thing as the craft of acting was when in high school I saw Marlon Brando in the film of *Julius Caesar.* What he was doing was so in essence different from everyone else that it pulled me out of the theatrical reality and made me aware of his choices as an actor. Elements of his technique, his timing (which was odd), his movements, his use of an unlovely voice which became nevertheless unforgettable, excited and intrigued me and inspired me as an actor.

But when I saw those actresses, I was inspired *as a woman.* When I saw them on the 4:30 movie or on screen or on stage, what sent me out of the theater buzzing like a hovercraft was the idea that if *she* counted, if that woman was significant in the shimmering landscape that was a movie, then *I* counted, *girls* counted, we *mattered*. Evidence to that effect is not always manifest in this culture. If we don't have these images of women we feel for, admire, recognize and esteem, then we stifle the dreams of our daughters; we put our hands over the mouth of their inspiration. If we erase our dreams, we disappear.

If most of the women we've seen in films this year are slapped, kicked, raped, murdered, bruised, begging for help or duplicitous and just asking for it, this is *not* an indication that *actresses* are confused about their roles. It is rather an indication of the kinds of images the industry has confidence in, green lights and feels will sell.

One thing is clear: the two questions, "Why are there so few roles for women?," and "Why are we paid, relatively, so little?," are linked. My dad said it to me, "Supply and demand, Meryl, supply and demand." As long as there are a lot of us to fill only a few parts, the economics are very pleasant for the people who pay us. Why *should* the studios create more jobs for us so that we no longer undercut each other's salary demands? (If we can't get her cheap, we'll get her, or her, or her.) Imagine what these stupendously-budgeted movies would cost if we were working in equal numbers and paid commensurately with our brothers, the male actors.

If it's not in the financial interest of the studios to change the status quo, then I don't have much hope it will change. But the market *will* dictate what is on the screen. That's up to you and me and millions of moviegoers to demonstrate. This summer's disappointing performance of some of the expensive self-styled blockbusters may be evidence that our voices are being heard.

Michael Brenson, who is a fine arts critic in New York, recently wrote an article entitled, "Is Quality an Idea Whose Time Has Gone?" In it, he talks about that feeling that overtakes you in confronting certain masterful works of art. I've extrapolated a bit of it to refer to an experience that you and I and anyone who works in the movies has had once or twice in a darkened theater, in the face of a certain performance or some such cinematic wonder. He calls that feeling "aesthetic emotion," and it's part of what I would hope is the legacy of our generation of filmmakers to our children, because we really are at a turning point now.

"Aesthetic emotion," he says, "is an experience at once personal and impersonal, specific and general. It is rooted in the object, but it also suggests something beyond the object. It suggests the depth of feeling and knowledge of which human beings are capable. It brings an intensified awareness of life and death. It is related to the experience of revelation and love, and is ultimately just as resistant to theory and language. Indeed, it suggests that what is most profound can never be analyzed or held in words."

This past weekend we celebrated my mother's 75th birthday (she'll be thrilled I told everyone which birthday). As I agonized to her about what in hell I was going to say in this speech, she said, "Why don't you just tell them that when there were more women in the movies, the movies were better?"

Jeff Daniels "Commercial" Isn't a Dirty Word, Any More Than "Comedy"

L.W. How much of what you learned as a stage actor were you able to apply when you began to act in films?

J.D. I was lucky because Marshall Mason's approach to acting, as he taught it at the Circle Rep, was cinematic. The acting style there is so moment-to-moment. It's very honest and truthful. And the theater there also seats only 160 people. It wasn't as though I was going into a 500- or 1000-seat theatre and doing a Broadway musical. So I didn't have to worry that much about making it smaller for the lens, where the "audience" is only about three feet away. At Circle Rep, the audience always felt like it was that close. Marshall directed and taught acting in a way that I still draw on a lot now: "Be honest, be truthful, play Ping-Pong with the other actor." That way, you let people watch you from up close, almost as voyeurs. And the camera catches you, then, just talking to another person. The result should be that when they say, "Cut," you look up and say "What happened?" because you're so involved with the scene.

L.W. Had you gotten any of this approach before you arrived in New York?

J.D. Not at all. Central Michigan University was a good place, in that it gave me a lot of experience and a fundamental introduction to acting. I'd come out of Chelsea having done only a lot of musicals, and just figuring things out as I went along. I'd had no classes, and I hadn't studied acting in any systematic way. But it was in New York that I really got the solid training I needed. I learned to use myself at Circle Rep as a sort of emotional punching bag. I learned to use emotions like tools there. I remember acting exercises there

"An Interview with Jeff Daniels," conducted by Leigh Woods (March 1995).

where you had to break down completely, emotionally; and if you couldn't do that, you'd failed. That's a little different from doing *South Pacific*. Marshall taught that; and when you can do that with another actor onstage, you can do it in a film where the camera sits right over your shoulder. It's a lot harder to break down emotionally and project it in a larger theater.

L.W. Could you have grasped this approach to acting at an earlier age, or is there something about it that requires more maturity and life experience?

J.D. I never really thought I'd become an actor. I thought I'd stay in New York for ten years, never work, and then go back to my father's lumber yard or work as a teacher. There was a lot of personal stuff going on then and earlier, in my teens, that kept me from thinking about being an actor in any serious way.

L.W. To ask the question another way: Do you have to have your own life together to practice the sort of emotional approach to acting that you've described?

J.D. Oh, God, no, not for me. The more dysfunctional, the better. Or the more twisted, the more open to "Sybil-like" behavior, the better! I haven't gone into therapy, although many actors have. I'd be afraid that if I were in therapy, I'd actually start to understand why I'm the way I am and never be able to act again. At the same time, I know actors who've been married a long time and are just the most normal people, and they've done some incredible work. You can have your life together and be "normal" and still be a good actor.

L.W. When you went back onstage a couple of years ago in *Redwood Curtain* [on Broadway], did you find that you had to readjust to acting onstage?

J.D. I was most worried about having to perform eight times a week and at the same time keep the performance alive. I knew how to do that from before, when I'd done *Fifth of July* [in a long run] on Broadway. One way to approach the challenge is to become "the mule on the trail" and to make the same choices every night and give basically the same performance night after night, week after week, and month after month. You don't invest a lot of yourself that way, it doesn't hurt, and there's not a lot of pain. But I loved keeping it alive, as I felt I was able to do in *Fifth of July* with Richard Thomas [in the role of Ken Talley opposite Jeff as Jed]. Richard would spin something a little different way, and I'd be there with him and play it back, and we'd wonder, "Well, where's it going tonight?" It wouldn't differ all that much from night to night, but it would vary enough to keep us awake, and sometimes he'd really take off. So I went back to do *Redwood Curtain*, having done so much film in the meantime—which is more like a sprint, really, than the stage is, which is more like a marathon. Or to put it another way, film is more like a shotgun when it scatters, and it feels like you're emptying the chamber and then only looking up later to see what you actually hit. It's really spontaneous and alive. It's underrehearsed compared to theater, where you rehearse for weeks at a time, and then you're doing it eight times a week; and this routine has the effect of eating your performance out of you, and sometimes you can even come to feel that the routine is meant to do that. Some actors complain about the lack of rehearsals for films, but I look at this as a chance to bounce off the other actors with greater spontaneity and freedom. And that's what I'd been doing for the last ten years. So when I went back to do *Redwood Curtain,* I wondered whether I could be as spontaneous and present as I was used to being in films.

L.W. Could you?

J.D. Yeah, I was very pleased at being able to forget the previous day's show and not worry about tomorrow's. I could just concentrate on the show I was doing that night. I was able to do that. But then again, we ran for only five weeks, so it wasn't as great a test that way as it might have been.

L.W. Did any of the people who "matter" credit your ability to do that?

J.D. No, I don't think they did. It was just my personal goal.

L.W. It seems that you like film acting better in some ways than you do stage acting.

J.D. Well, in film there's no such thing as "wrong choices." I spent the first half dozen films I made thinking, "I've got to do it perfectly." What you see in *Terms of Endearment,* for instance, is an actor who's trying not to make any mistakes. I was aware of everything I did: every hand gesture, every inflection, every little thing. I just researched the hell out of that part. I still do research, but I learned from watching Jack Nicholson [in *Terms* and *Heartburn*] to simply walk into the action of the scene and go with whatever happens. He'll set himself up with the basics of the character and the situation, and then he'll just go with it. He's not afraid of making wrong choices. You can always throw away a particular take later on.

L.W. When you went back into film, then, after doing *Redwood Curtain,* did you find that your experience onstage had made any difference in the way you approached things in front of the camera?

J.D. No, it didn't. But that's because I'd spent nine or ten years entirely onstage before I started doing movies. So doing *Redwood Curtain* only reinforced what the theater had already given me. When you do a play eight times a week, there are always days when you just don't feel like doing it but you have to do it anyway. So, when there were shots in *Arachnophobia,* for instance, where it took twenty-five takes before the damned spiders would turn the right way, and I'd do my three lines over and over again twenty-five times, my stage training came in very handy. Then, on the twenty-fifth take, I could still make it look like it was happening for the first time. Without the theater, I don't think I'd have had the same consistency. In that sense, theater training has been invaluable.

L.W. Are there other film actors you admire besides Jack Nicholson?

J.D. There are countless people, actually. I steal individual moments from other actors all the time, or at least try to analyze what they're doing and why. There are people I admire from having grown up watching them on television: like Dick Van Dyke, for instance. I was also attracted to Jack Lemmon's work, and to Alan Arkin's, particularly the comedies. Or to John Cleese in *Fawlty Towers,* or to Peter Sellers, especially in the *Pink Panther* movies. These guys all did "big" comedy, but they also kept it real. You can't ever catch them going for the joke. So when I've done comedy, I've always wanted it to be believable, above all. Maybe this is my reaction to having done all that analytical acting work at Circle Rep, where we were always told that if we weren't being real, we should get out of the business. I wanted to be able to be funny and believable. And, I wanted to be able to do the sorts of things that Al Pacino did in *Dog Day Afternoon.* I saw that movie six times, because I knew from watching it that that was what I wanted to learn how to do. So when I started to do comedies, I never wanted to be like the *Saturday Night Live* guys, who were "just" comedians and not actors. I do think there's a difference there.

L.W. How easy is it to build a film career while straddling comedy and serious material? The people you've mentioned are some of the few, it seems, who've been able to do that. It seems as though it can be hard to cross over between serious films and comic ones.

J.D. It is, and especially since the advent of Dan Aykroyd and Chevy Chase and Bill Murray and Steve Martin. These actors have planted the sense in many people that what they do is the only kind of comedy that can be done. So when comic roles come up, the prevailing attitude is that we've got to get one of those guys to do it. They're very funny, too, in what they do, and I'd love to work with any of them. But I'm interested in finding more of a middle ground. I did a different brand of comedy in *Something Wild,* and if you put any of those other guys in it, it would have become a different movie. Hollywood likes to label actors, and then it's easy to get stuck in roles within that label. One of the things that interested me about *Dumb and Dumber,* for instance, was that I'd just done *Gettysburg*. I wanted to show that I could do something really different. But I've always been a little perverse that way, I guess, and I like to think about what I'm not supposed to be able to do; then I'll try to do that very thing, whether it's good for me or not. A while back, I spent three years working on independent movies because I liked the scripts, and I did this at a time when I was in demand for more commercial films. I learned a lot making those independent films, I loved the people I worked with, and I think I'm a better actor now because I did those films. Then down the road, I ended up getting some things that scored, like *Dumb and Dumber*. When that happens, everyone will tell you that they always loved your work, even when they may not have been going to see it.

L.W. Have you done more promoting with *Dumb and Dumber* than you've done before?

J.D. Well, I've made myself available and accessible with this film. I've gone everywhere and talked to everyone about it. When you have a movie that's a huge hit, you have to take advantage of that. Also, there have been a lot of people who've become very successful in films through television, and they've made it clear that you can use television to get into people's heads. So you do David Letterman and all the other talk shows, because that will translate into other roles and more opportunities.

L.W. What connection do you see, then, between the "business" side of film acting and of stardom and the "artistic" side? Does it lie in the range of choices that present themselves to you?

J.D. Well, I haven't always done as much publicizing and promoting as I've been doing recently. Sometimes you'll make a film and then just hate it, and you won't make yourself available in the same way.

L.W. Is it possible, or advisable, to keep the promoting side of the business separate from the acting side?

J.D. You always have to lead with your acting. I won't work hard on behalf of anything that I don't think is a good movie, or where I don't think I'm good in it. But if I think it's good, and that I am, I'll do everything I can for it. That can only work to my benefit. Also, I live in the Midwest, and it's important for me to remember that I'm working in a business and that it benefits me to do publicity for things I believe in as my part in being a good employee. What I'm not spending time doing, of course, is going to Spago's [restaurant] and to other people's premieres, and being seen in those places. I'm not spending all that time being famous, and being "out there." I'm not married to an actress, either. So when I'm not in a movie, or promoting one, I just disappear. That means that I have to look for ways of reminding people in the business that I'm still here, even when they can't see me.

L.W. Are there liabilities to living in a small town in Michigan? You've been living here now for nine years . . .

J.D. Oh, yes. You're out of the loop. But it's also hard to say. There may have been times when, if I'd gone to someone's party, they would have offered me a role while standing over the hors d'oeuvres. There are meetings in Hollywood I might have had that I didn't get. There are people in Hollywood, I've been told, who don't think that I take my career seriously enough because I'm not living there. And it's true that I haven't been working hard to become as famous as I can be. I sort of bailed out on that goal. And I told myself when I did that that I'd be happy playing supporting roles some of the time and leading roles some of the time, and that acting was something that I loved but that it would be just one of the things that I did with my life. I did choose some other things that were important to me then, like where I would be living, and how that would be for my kids, and my friends, and the chance to help run a live theatre. These are things I think I need to do in order to be able to stay in this business for the next forty years. There are elements to the film business that are so cutthroat and so dog-eat-dog, and that helps explain why you see a lot of families and marriages break up in Hollywood. So I chose to stop being part of that scene, rather than to keep on feeding the monster.

L.W. Are there any advantages to being away from that scene?

J.D. There may be. But your appeal as an actor really relates only to the gross for your most recent film. Living away from Hollywood has made me better as an actor, I think. I can't imagine that I'd be very happy living in Hollywood, and I can't play the game that you need to play in order to survive there. So I'm happier and healthier overall; and now, when I walk onto a set, I'm really happy to be there. When I walk into the 20th-Century Fox lot, I feel as though I can see Gable and Tracy and Bogart. Living in the Midwest maintains that kind of excitement for me. While I was living in Hollywood, and in New York, I couldn't see the ghosts of those people or feel the excitement that goes with them.

L.W. Is it possible to plan your career more than one film ahead?

J.D. Some people can. I can't.

L.W. Are you constantly receiving scripts?

J.D. Yes.

L.W. Are there many that appeal to you?

J.D. No.

L.W. Are there ever dry spells where you don't receive any scripts that appeal to you?

J.D. Yes. Again, that's tied to how much money your last movie made. I spent a couple of years doing independent films, like *Checking Out* and *Love Hurts,* and I had good roles in those films, and I loved the people I got to work with. And all of those films either went straight to cable or video—or they were released and did nothing, like *The House on Carroll Street.* It's a fact of life in Hollywood that if your last movie didn't make any money, then the next one had better do it. And if that one doesn't do it, then your opportunities begin to dry up. So you can find yourself flying to Los Angeles, after seventeen years in the business, taking five meetings (one of them for *Dumb and Dumber*), and you learn that you're going to have to read for the part. You can either throw a fit and say "How dare you?" or you can just do it—which is what I did. I knew that I wouldn't get *Dumb and Dumber* unless I read for the part. I wanted to work with [the film's star] Jim Carrey, and I wanted the range that it would give me compared to the other work I'd been doing. So I just asked them which scenes they wanted me to read.

L.W. Did you read with Jim Carrey?

J.D. Yes. But my attitude at those times is that I want the job all right, but also that the other actor has to stay with me through the reading. That's a good way to try and beat the nerves you feel at those times when you want a job very badly. If you can do that, then you won't necessarily subject the viewers to yet another nervous audition. So you try to flip the pressure over to the person you're reading with (who already had the job anyway, in this case). It was to Jim's credit that he'd said that he didn't want a comedian opposite him, but rather an actor who could react to him and to whatever he might do. That's largely the reason I got the job.

L.W. Do you ever choose projects based on factors other than the screenplay?

J.D. If it's not the first consideration, then it will always be a very close second. If you can't respond to the material, then you should probably just pass on the project. But very quickly, too, you have to find out who the director will be and which studio will produce and how much the budget is and how long the shooting schedule is; or is it a miniseries, like *Gettysburg,* which because it has to shoot in ten weeks means that you get only three or four takes for every scene. Or with *Arachnophobia,* Frank Marshall was directing for the first time, although Steven Spielberg was going to be right there with him. In that case, they also had plenty of budget, so that when they needed to build a house, they built a house; and all the production departments were the very best, too. So that kind of stuff can also influence the way you respond to the script.

L.W. I was impressed with *Gettysburg,* and with you in it. Was it rehearsed very little, or were there just very few takes?

J.D. It was both, actually. There was a week of rehearsal, but then they shot all the Confederate scenes first, and so rehearsal time was largely taken up with those [Daniels played Colonel Joshua Chamberlain, an officer for the Union army]. In that project, too, the shooting schedule was short in relation to the number of scenes that had to be set up, and that didn't allow time for many takes. In a film with a bigger budget, like *Arachnophobia,* you have a lot more time to set the camera up and to light the scenes. There was that kind of freedom, and those kinds of resources, around *The Purple Rose of Cairo,* too. In *Gettysburg,* it was more a matter of everyone doing the best work they could in the shortest time possible. But then that's what television is always like; you've got to move fast because you just don't have the money. If there were twice as much money, there would be twice as much time. Then there can be more takes, and the actors can try their scenes in more different ways. And then the editor has more versions of the scene to choose from. All of this stuff, though, you already know going into the shooting, and you just make sure that you've done the kind of homework you need to do in order to stay in step with the schedule, whatever it might be.

L.W. How were you able to get the sort of texture and richness that you found in *Gettysburg,* and under the less than ideal circumstances you've described around the shooting?

J.D. I got really interested in the guy I played in *Gettysburg.* He was a teacher, and he'd been in the army for only ten months. When I went up to Maine to research the role on his home grounds, people there told me that if I did nothing else—and they had no faith at all that Hollywood would feel any responsibility to the truth—could I at least show that this guy had the ability to think on his feet? People who had studied Chamberlain were all struck by this quality in him. This fed right into the moment-to-moment approach that I was comfortable with. So during the battle, Chamberlain found himself standing on Little Round Top [a hill], and he had ten minutes to get his troops ready before the Confederates came up the hill for the first time. So I made every-thing that happened there very present-tense. Woody Allen taught me to have the character get an idea on camera and then say the line that grows out of the idea. There's some of that kind of acting in *Speed,* too—as in the elevator sequences, for instance, where we're thinking our way through a situation.

But the emphasis there was on shoot-'em-up, on action, and so that was a different set of demands. There's not a lot of background work to be done.

L.W. Did you do a lot of research on the battle at Gettysburg?

J.D. Yes.

L.W. Was that true in general for the actors on that project?

J.D. Outside of Tom Berenger, who is a Civil War buff, and Ron Maxwell [the director], I don't think anybody else did that. On the other hand, nobody just came in and did the gig, you know.

L.W. No, it looked like the actors wanted to be there.

J.D. What was great about that was that everyone showed up ready to work. So that when I got in scenes with Kevin Conway [as Sergeant Buster Kilrain] or C. Thomas Howell [as Daniels' character's brother, Lieutenant Thomas Chamberlain]—and this was true for actors on the Confederate side, too—everyone brought their best work. Nobody sloughed off. People were trying to challenge each other with their best. And this was very positive energy; it wasn't competitive in a bad way. We started shooting the scene with Kevin under the tree before nine in the morning, and we did it in two takes. We had a little rehearsal beforehand, and Kevin really laid into it and nailed it, and it was so obvious that he was ready that I looked at Ron and he said, "I think we'll start with Kevin's closeup." That rarely happens, when an actor says "Let's go" like that. That's one of the purest scenes of film acting I've been part of.

L.W. The sort of commitment you describe was evident, I thought, throughout the film. Why doesn't that happen more often?

J.D. It's because the script isn't there, and because the characters aren't there as a result. This forces the actors constantly to be doing their own background work on the story, their own personal work to fill in blanks and simply justify even the most basic things that happen. There are a lot of scripts that get made, and it's not uncommon to have to ask very basic questions like, "Why would I do this, when earlier in the movie I did that [in contradiction]?" *Gettysburg* was based on *Killer Angels* [by Michael Shaara], which was a great book, and so the story and the characterizations were there already. Then the actors' jobs were to catch up with information that already existed, as opposed to creating our own.

L.W. Do you find yourself reading scripts differently now than you once did? Does the pressure you described for the success of films you act in to be successful influence your choices at all?

J.D. Yes, it does; but "commercial" isn't a dirty word either, any more than "comedy" is. I learned a long time ago that it's a matter of "One for you, one for them." Especially since I live in the Midwest, I couldn't keep doing projects that meant a lot to me personally but then didn't make any money. Occasionally, at least, you have to be in something that will make money. So that if you haven't been in something that's made money for a while, that becomes your focus. In the case of *Speed,* for instance, there were some people around that film who wanted me on the job, and others who didn't. And [the director] Jan De Bont went to bat for me and got me that job.

L.W. Was that because he knew your work?

J.D. They all knew my work. It's there for anybody to take a look at. But I was at a point where I needed a hit. So I did *Speed,* and then *Dumb and Dumber* came along. I actually chose between that and another movie. In fact, there were three or four projects in all that I was considering. But I thought that *Dumb and Dumber* had the best chance of doing well at the box office.

L.W. Do you solicit advice from other people about your choices of films these days?

J.D. Just my agents, at this point. I've had the same agent in New York for seventeen years—Paul Martino at ICM [International Creative Management].

L.W. Is that unusual?

J.D. Yeah, I think it's unusual. I think that a majority of actors move around from time to time. But I like Paul, and he was there for me when it hadn't happened at all, and he just kept sending me out [for auditions]. That lasted for two or three years before *Terms of Endearment* came along. Ever since then, things have been going pretty well. I also have a couple of guys in Los Angeles that I talk to. In fact, when I was choosing between *Dumb and Dumber* and this other movie, I got back home from a hockey game and my wife told me that they'd called from the coast to say that the other film had just tripled the offer to me up front and that I had to decide right then. I was already set for a wardrobe fitting for *Dumb and Dumber,* and so we had to set up a conference call where we talked the situation over.

L.W. Do you always have a clear idea about how you're going to play a role before you begin shooting?

J.D. I'm not very good at sitting down with the director and discussing the role for three hours. I'm an instinctive actor. So I find that if I try to talk it through, I only confuse myself and the director, too. But whenever it's possible, I'll ask the director what he wants. I'll listen to what he says, and take that and try to do it in my own way. Then, we'll both be heading in the same direction. When you're shooting, you don't really know what the hell you're doing. There's been little rehearsal, and there's a lot of guesswork involved. I also don't think it's good to walk into a scene that you're shooting with the attitude that there's only one way to play it. I heard Robert De Niro say once that an actor's only as good as his choices. So, if you make good choices, and if you guess right often enough, you're going to end up giving a good performance. If I've done some research, I know some basics, I have some skill and some craft, and the director and I agree about the character in a general way, then I try to give the director and the editor four or five different spins on each scene. That way, the director and editor can have a good time picking which one they want.

L.W. Do you watch rushes or dailies?

J.D. I have, but I don't anymore.

L.W. Why?

J.D. Part of it is laziness: it adds another two hours to the day. You're already working a twelve-hour day anyway, and it's hard to get ready for your big scene the next day when you're stumbling down at 10:00 P.M. to watch the rushes. By now, I know what my face looks like on film. It's very important to know what the muscles in your face are doing. So early on, I'd watch rushes more as a way of learning about that. When I made *Terms of Endearment*, [director] Jim Brooks wouldn't let me watch my own dailies, but I got to watch Jack Nicholson and Shirley MacLaine's, and particularly a scene in the kitchen when he was telling her about his pride at being an astronaut. I watched about ten takes of this scene, and in the first five or so, Jack was struggling for his lines and it was clear that he didn't have all the answers. But then in takes six through ten, he was able to put it all together, and each one was quite different from any of the others. This sequence left Jim Brooks wondering which take he would use. It was wonderful to see Jack rehearse on film, and to have the power and the clout in order to be able to do that. There are a lot of times when an actor, particularly if he has some experience and status, will discuss with the director which take will be used, or even which pieces of which takes will be used. Sometimes this can turn into a debate over artistic control.

L.W. Have you seen other actors who could rehearse on film?

J.D. Yes, I saw Meryl Streep do it in *Heartburn*. I've been able to do that, too, sometimes, especially when I was playing leading roles in some of the independent films I did. On the one hand, you don't want to get out there and just blow your way through the first few takes; that's not a good approach, and I would never do that. Sometimes, too, one of the first few takes will be the best, because there's a kind of spontaneity there when the scene is actually happening for the first time. And if you're acting with someone who is still struggling for lines in those takes, then in effect, you're being forced to wait until take four or five for the scene to really get going. You can lose some good stuff that way.

L.W. What makes an effective film director for you, as an actor?

J.D. The best ones can tell you what they want you to try in five words or less. That way, the actor is left to work out the details. It's as though they know how to handle you as if you were a feather, and they can just sort of waft you in the right direction. They give you gentle nudges.

L.W. Are there many directors who can do this?

J.D. Oh, yes. The best ones all know how to do this. They also know how to direct different actors in different ways, and that's another one of the qualities consistent among the best directors I've worked with. These directors will just tell me a little bit, and then they'll watch what I do; and maybe I'll get it wrong at first. And they'll tell me that I'm not quite doing what they had in mind, and then they'll let me try it again. Jonathan Demme can do this, and David Leland and Bud Yorkin and Robert Altman. These directors leave the acting up to you. It's certainly not that these guys don't know how to direct; but they do know how to give you the kind of freedom you need in order to figure things out for yourself. I've heard actors complain about directors who didn't direct them enough, and I've had experiences with other directors who'll tell you every little thing they want you to do, and then keep changing their minds about what they want. That can be frustrating.

L.W. What makes an actor you like to work with?

J.D. Someone who's alive—and that means behind the eyes. I like someone who doesn't have everything preplanned, either, so that they can react to what I do. That way you can draw energy from each other, and from what you're both doing. Actors have got to be able to listen. People sometimes talk about "chemistry" between actors; but in my opinion, all chemistry comes from two actors who are listening to each other. Listening can be very hard to do, because the business is set up in such a way as to make actors very aware of themselves as isolated individuals. Or as Laurence Olivier said, "Look at me, look at me, look at me." But the best work always comes out of giving and taking, and out of the ability to listen to the actor with whom you're acting.

L.W. Whom are you acting for when the camera's on? Or does that change? In the theater, you have a live audience, but what is there for you that way when you're acting in films?

J.D. There are different levels for different kinds of movies. In a movie like *Dumb and Dumber,* you've got to land the joke. Then, you want many people from different age groups all to laugh at what you did. In that case, the lens is really only a representative of the actual audience "out there." And there's a technique involved in landing jokes for that audience.

L.W. How can you tell when you've landed a joke?

J.D. You can't, really. That's film. You can go see the movie a year later and see whether they laugh. But you can feel it to some extent during the work, if you've been in the business long enough and you have a sense of comic timing. Now, more recently, I can also run to the monitor [just after shooting] and look at that. I don't look at dailies anymore, but if I'm really concerned about the way something is working, I can ask to see the playback. This kind of video playback has only been in use for the last eight years or so. Now, in fact, most directors will sit in front of a little television and watch the playback, whereas before, they'd sit directly behind the camera. Rarely do you see that now. Now, the director will sit in front of a television screen with the producer and some of the other technicians, so that he can watch the scene "through the lens." So this means that actors, when they're really concerned about something, can ask to see the videotape, too.

L.W. So in that case, you could say that you're acting for yourself?

J.D. In that case, you're acting to see whether you landed the joke. It's still partly guesswork, of course. In the case of *Gettysburg,* there were people out there who knew a lot more about Joshua Chamberlain than I could ever hope to find out. Then, I was acting for those people. The audience that's always there and that's the most reliable, of course, is the other actors, your peers. I'm among them, sitting out there and watching to see what people can do with what they're given. I talked before about stealing from other actors, and that's one thing you can get from watching. For instance, it's very hard to stop in the middle of a line of dialogue, or in the middle of a scene for that matter, and back up and spin around—Meryl Streep can do this, and Jack Lemmon can—and then start things up again. It's hard to do this and make it look real. On occasion, I've tried to do that kind of thing, just to see whether I could pull it off. But that was for me, and not for anyone else.

L.W. Are some actors more generous with their peers than others?

J.D. There are some actors who'll never like your work, no matter what you do. I used to be like that myself, but I don't think I'm that way now. There are still guys whose careers I look at even now, and I have no idea what's made them successful. It's beyond me. I do think that most actors know good acting when they see it, though. When I go see movies now,

I'm watching to see what kinds of choices the actors make. And it's not that I'm sitting there with this attitude that says, "It's going to take a lot to impress me." I'm just interested in what they do and how they do it, especially in cases where the actors are ones I've admired. These are people willing to take chances with their characters or their speeches by doing things in a way that nobody else would think of. On the other hand, I'll also notice actors when I can see them just sitting there, setting their jaws, and catching the light with their eyes and then speaking along in a monotone—and then finding themselves lauded as great stars.

L.W. Have you ever given a performance in a film that you really haven't liked?

J.D. There are pieces of performances I haven't liked. But to be honest, I don't watch my stuff much. On those rare occasions where I try to watch it, I usually turn it off right away. I just get bored.

L.W. When it's done, it's done?

J.D. I don't know what it is. Maybe I don't really want to see it. Maybe it relates to my not going to dailies any more. Or maybe it's that I have the feeling now that I can trust that I've got a performance going in the same way I did when I was standing on the stage of a theater. I don't want to mess with that feeling. I also trust directors to tell me what they need and whether they think I'm giving it to them. By now, I've been doing it long enough to have my own opinion about whether or not it's working, and about whether I'm doing what I want to be doing. I can usually tell what it looks like without actually seeing it.

L.W. Have there ever been times during the actual shooting of a film when you've felt that you weren't doing well or when you weren't pleasing yourself?

J.D. Yes, in *Terms of Endearment*. But then, I was just scared to death. Early during the shooting of *The Purple Rose of Cairo* I didn't feel very good, but that was because I'd gotten the part on a Thursday and then started shooting the following week.

L.W. Was it hard to move into that film so quickly?

J.D. Yes. I did a couple of the "actor's" scenes in that movie, and I felt fine in those. But I had a harder time with the guy in the safari hat. I was trying to do this Errol Flynn thing with it for a day or two, and Woody [Allen] told me that it just wasn't working. He asked me to just go back and do it as simply and honestly as I could. Back in the 1930s, of course [the period in which Daniels' character was based], they didn't have great depth and complexity in a lot of the characterizations. There were a lot of one-color portrayals, especially in the hands of actors who weren't very good. So then I tried to be a guy out of one of those bad 1930s movies, after I'd dropped the Errol Flynn thing.

L.W. Are you ever surprised now when a movie you've made looks and feels very different—or has a very different impact—than you'd anticipated while you were making it?

J.D. No. You never really know whether a movie will win a lot of awards or make a lot of money. I usually end the shooting with a pretty good feeling about whether we've done something good or not. In the case of *Speed,* I thought that we'd made a good action movie, and I knew that people on the set had loved the dailies. When the opening was moved from October back to June, though, because the movie had been testing through the roof, I realized that it might find greater success than I'd thought it would.

L.W. What in your career are you most proud of?

J.D. I'm very proud of *Something Wild* for a lot of reasons. The movie was ahead of its time, and it wasn't formulaic in any way. We used the script as an outline in that film, and I felt that that gave me a lot of freedom. I'd learned how to ad lib a bit on *Something Wild,* and I knew that it wasn't the easiest thing to do, because it's not just a matter of writing jokes when you do that. I'm proud of how that film turned out, even though it didn't do that well in its initial release. But people now treat it as a cult classic, and that's pleasing. People often come up and tell me that they can't understand now why the movie didn't do better. *Gettysburg's* a movie that I think will be around for a long time. I'm very happy at the success of what seemed to me a huge gamble I took in exposing the character to all the Chamberlain-lovers that I met. Those people could easily have said, "I don't think you portrayed him the way he really was." But they didn't say that, and it means a lot to me. And then in *Dumb and Dumber,* I'm proud that I was able to stay with Jim Carrey in a two[-actor] shot. He's very talented, he's a human tornado, he can go at a hundred miles an hour, and he can leave you eating dust. So I'm proud of that, too. In *The Purple Rose of Cairo,* working with Woody Allen meant a great deal, so much so that I named my theatre company after the film.

L.W. When you talk to aspiring actors these days, what do you tell them?

J.D. I tell them to make themselves into the best actors they can be. I tell them that if they just want to be stars and be famous, then they should go to Los Angeles and hope for good luck. But otherwise, they need to try to keep getting better and to learn something new, if they can, every year they stay with it. I also tell them that eventually they're going to have to deal with the fact that movies are a business. You can try to separate the acting and the art from the business part, but eventually you're going to need to find the way to combine these things if you want to stay in the business.

L.W. Is it hard to deal with the ebbs and flows in your career?

J.D. Yes, when you've got kids and a mortgage. The fact that I'm here after all these years is a kind of triumph, I guess. I feel like a survivor that way.

L.W. I once saw you talking to some theater students, and you were telling them about being out of work.

J.D. Yes, I give them the real deal.

L.W. And the real deal isn't always very pretty?

J.D. For me, now, the money is pretty important because I have these other commitments. And so I still get very upset when people in Hollywood will say that I'm not funny, for instance, because they haven't taken the trouble to rent *Something Wild* or *The Purple Rose of Cairo*. But that's the business; and that's what the kids don't see and don't know about. And we're not all Kevin Costners, or Tom Cruises, or now Jim Carreys, making $20 million a picture. There are only a handful of people like that. I'm doing just fine now, and this is a great time in my life. But things do go up and down, and you need to be ready for that.

The Method Revisited and Matters of Style

At its height in the 1950s, Method acting drew praise for capturing the starker qualities of postwar life. It found its clearest embodiment in films that disclosed brutal and isolating worlds on screens across America. In some measure, Method acting was a reaction against the increased emphasis on color and against the panoramic and often nostalgic images that film used to contest television, as that miniaturized, still black-and-white form found its first sweeping popularity. Certain elements of the Method have remained constant in American film acting ever since, though—including a characteristic inarticulateness and the resort to tears as proof of emotional depth. Gone, for the most part, is the Method's early credo of direct, one-to-one correspondence between actor and character.

Both the durability and the mutability of the Method may derive from the deep-seated suspicions of the arts held by many Americans, who demand sincerity in compensation for any measure of artifice. The Method may also owe its continual reconstitution to the visibility that American films gained abroad during the postwar generation. Furthermore, a method of some sort (if not *the* Method) may be a necessary hedge against the capriciousness of the film business, particularly after the loss of the order imposed by the studios. To the degree that most actors view chance as endemic to filmmaking itself—not to mention their own careers—they may require some methodical approach to help them deal with the accidents that happen by the day, by the hour, or by the minute, even, wherever cameras are rolling.

More recently, though, the American Method has come to be considered a style like others, contingent not so much on a timeless and universal notion of human nature as on historically and culturally determined factors. Now Method acting at its height seems nothing so much as an expression of American alienation at mid century, an encapsulation of states of mind resulting from the dawning of the nuclear age, the sometimes grudging sense of international obligation, and the particular struggles to maintain Hollywood's former glory in the face of changing conditions at home and abroad. Even though aspects of the Method still figure prominently, few will claim, as Lee Strasberg did while presiding over the Actors' Studio in New York City, that the American Method at its best offers a barely mediated reality, or even that it represents the whole range and complexity of Stanislavsky's theories about acting. Stanislavsky, for that matter, has himself come to be understood as subject to the pre- and postrevolutionary history that helped generate and advance his theories, first in Russia and later in the Soviet Union.

Stanislavsky and his disciples have been conspicuous in America since the 1920s. They were first influential at a particularly formative period of film acting, during the years just before the advent of sound. Ever since then, Stanislavsky's criticism of the vogue for stentorian and statuesque aspects of the nineteenth-century stage has generally found support among actors, who see film as a more intimate medium. A good number of American actors have joined the Soviets in contending that Stanislavsky's recommendations have been realized more fully in film than on the stage. Furthermore, certain characteristics of Method acting that have distinguished film acting in America—its casual narcissism, for instance, or its fixation on material reality— have worked to inspire its imitation elsewhere.

Reactions against the Method followed such visibility, though, and surface fairly often in the accounts that follow. Since the protest movements of the 1960s, film actors have more often sought to express the spirit of social activism rather than to project, with knitted brows, the nameless despair and lonely suffering affected by the Method school actors of the 1950s. Very often, too, a spirit of social engagement comes to the fore when actors consider how collaboration affects them in their own work or when they see that activism can overcome the strictures imposed by commercial filmmaking.

A good many of the actors in the section that follows want to influence the content of films they make and, unlike their predecessors at the studios, hope to do so independent of the industry that employs them. Among the actors who find greatest favor in Hollywood are some particularly effective subversives. In this connection, "style" can derive as much from an actor's sense of mission as from manner; most actors in this section show more interest in whom they work with, and on what, than they do in the more solitary and mechanical aspects of their craft.

Seldom has Jack Lemmon been regarded as a Method actor, and the comic roles in which he had his early successes are unlike the serious material generally associated with the Method. Yet Lemmon shows himself conversant with Method techniques as he weighs the value of external approaches over more internalized ones. He also talks about the elements of his own training, derived in part from the Method, that helped him adapt to the demands of the dramatic roles that came to him later in his career. His sense of the indeterminate nature of great roles is characteristic of Method actors' view of the dramatic text as incomplete, and of their necessary reliance on nonverbal means for conveying effects.

Marlon Brando stands foremost among Method actors in America in spite or perhaps *because* of the anomalous applications of the Method that have sprung from his maverick attitude toward Lee Strasberg and his dismissive distaste for any system at all. Brando's interest in spontaneity is extreme, although he paradoxically asserts that dramatic situations specified in the text predominate over any actor's efforts, or over any audience's response, for that matter. This interview, like the one with Marcello Mastroianni, may reveal more about Brando's quirky imagination and his perverse faith in the expressive capacity of evasiveness than it does about his actual ways of working.

Robert De Niro approaches the Method in much more conventional and, in a sense, old-fashioned terms. While underscoring its durability, De Niro explains how he has adapted the Method according to the particular demands of the role he is playing. As he does this, he shows himself as specific concerning the Method's uses as Brando is vague. He also espouses the postmodern notion that any character exists in moments and in glimpses, rather than in totality. De Niro's practice of the Method does not seem to have left him as isolated or as mistrustful of his collaborators as it has Brando.

Dustin Hoffman speaks passionately of his personal involvement in his roles. His identification with his characters stems in part from the Method, but his political perspective helps explain the number of roles depicting marginalized characters that he has chosen to take on. Unlike many actors associated with the American film industry, Hoffman feels responsible for even the slightest details in his films, and for the moral weight a work gains from the pains he and his collaborators have taken. He views contention among collaborators as a key element of filmmaking and as a model for his own approach to characterization.

Jack Nicholson adopts a surprisingly theoretical though nonetheless partisan view of filmmaking and emphasizes its difficulty and its distinctness from theatrical traditions. He considers the visionary nature of film acting and its ability not only to challenge the historical authority of literature but also to reflect social currents in subtle and eloquent ways. When he speaks of his willingness to subordinate himself to his directors, Nicholson invokes values usually associated with European actors and suggests the degree to which filmmaking is an international enterprise.

Finally, Lindsay Crouse conjures up a transformational style of acting that seems on the surface quite distinct from the traditions of the Method. Even so, she speaks of her need for deep personal involvement in her roles, and, ideally, in the aims of any film project as a whole. Crouse's call to broaden the base of production mirrors her conviction—and that of actors from other times and places—that films draw vitality from their capacity to enrich the lives of filmmakers and viewers alike. Her idealism, in the face of challenge and change, forms a fitting valedictory to *Playing to the Camera.*

Jack Lemmon Conversation with the Actor

NEWQUIST. How did you find your character in *Some Like It Hot?*

LEMMON. As far as the finding of a character is concerned there are two ways you can approach acting—at least as far as I can tell. One is the normal way, the Method or whatever you call it—it's like laying bricks. You start at the bottom and work up; actually I guess you start in the middle and work to the outside. You sweat and think and read until you get the various attributes of that character, the sum total of which makes you understand why that person behaves the way he does, why he says what he says and does what he does. Once you have this understanding and knowledge of the character you put the outside on, the mannerisms, the way he dresses and moves and looks. In other words, your makeup and your wardrobe stem from what the person *is*.

The other way to build a character is what would normally be called the wrong way—that is, to create a shell and crawl into it. To get the externals down first. The way the person dresses, looks, talks, behaves comes first—then you make the character a person who lives up to externals.

This is what I did. I purposely went the wrong way with *Some Like It Hot* for a very good reason: this was a comedy, and the bizarre character masquerading as a girl was going to be at least 50 percent of the visual comedy. So we experimented for days with wigs and makeup, and when I got what I thought was the right face, the right vacant idiot look with the eyes, and the beestung lips, and Billy agreed—only then did I make the character the kind of person that would behave openly in that manner. I found a shell and crawled into it, like one of those goddam crabs.

I did the last thing on a new picture, *The Great Race.* It's a two-parter—I play two roles, like I did in *Irma,* only I play two totally different people who happen to look alike. One is a fop prince, a Wildean character, not quite faggy but with a sort of shrewd weakness he affects on purpose. He's a lace hankie character, but the externals were important, so important I made him behave in ways that lived up to those externals.

In other words, the things you first learn as an actor can be disproved. I

Excerpt from Roy Newquist, "Jack Lemmon," *Showcase* (New York: William Morrow, 1966), 257–275. Text copyright © 1966 by Roy Newquist. By permission of William Morrow & Co., Inc.

Judy Holliday and Jack Lemmon in *It Should Happen to You* (1954)

went for result—saw what I wanted and made the character perform that way. But an actor has to have a great deal of experience to know how to do this. One of the plagues of actors in the old days of radio and television and movies (and it still happens today) is the bad directors—the result directors. Your direction can be stupid, and I'll exaggerate to make my point: "Be happy" comes on page eighteen. You can't play "Be happy"—it's not a specific, it's a result. It's a state of being, and you can't really play a state of being. You can play "to love," "to hate," "to anger" or "to provoke"—they're something definite.

In other words, acting doesn't have anything to do with listening to the words. (As you're first told in high school plays—"Listen, don't just wait for your cue, listen to what the other person is saying.") We never really listen, in general conversation, to what another person is saying. We listen to what they mean. And what they mean is often quite apart from the words. When you see a scene between two actors that really comes off you can be damned sure they're not listening to each other—they're feeling what the other person is trying to get at. Know what I mean?

Sorry—I get carried away with all this. Back to *Some Like It Hot*—you asked me about that hours ago. But it was one of those things I went at backward. (I hated directors, years ago, when I first began to learn this. There was a great fellow, a director our here now named David Alexander, who had a group class years ago. All of us were professional actors, working actors, and around twelve or fourteen of us would meet with him every week or two, and we'd do scenes—it was a scene study class with criticism on our craft level only. I learned a great deal from that class, and there again we were made so aware of result, of the traps of the superficiality of just playing for result rather than getting to something concrete.)

Now I want result direction. All I want to know is what result the director wants—I'll do the homework. I'll get the result. The interesting thing is that once I know *what* he wants I know there are possibly twenty ways to get the result, and the fun and delicious hell is trying to decide which way to do it. And the simplest way is the best—you don't need an hour of pseudointellectual imbibing and yapping about Method or any supposed deep-dish level of acting. Nothing is duller than somebody crying. And nothing is better than trying not to cry when the audience is crying.

Out of that class I also began to develop the approaches I now use as much as possible: counterpoint and obstacles. Dull scenes can certainly be made more interesting if you take them beyond routine. For example, a love scene staged out-of-doors: make it rain. You're trying to do a very tender love scene and you're sopping wet—at least it's more interesting.

I love obstacles because on the simplest level you have to achieve those certain things as an actor because they're there, they're written in. But now you try to put everything in the way of achieving what you must achieve and you frustrate the character. The frustration does two things. It creates a higher level of energy and dramatic conflict within the scene which therefore makes it more interesting and earns empathy. It gets empathy from the audience because they have frustrations and they tend to identify and so to understand and to care because of self-identification. I began to notice, in my reviews of recent years, that critics would say, "Lemmon again playing the put-upon guy who muddles through." This was totally unintentional on my part, but I realized that although I hopefully don't ever play characters the same there *is* one common characteristic: often the characters are frustrated.

A good example of this, from the directorial point of view, came in the introductory scene in *The Apartment*. Billy had to show that he had all these different people using the apartment, and he had them on the phone trying to juggle time. It was a long scene, about five pages of calling to change appointments. Hopefully, it would be amusing, but more than that it was necessary background to give the audience the plot. But Billy did a beautiful thing. He gave the guy a cold, and the scene worked because the poor son of a bitch had a temperature and a cold and was perfectly miserable and the audience knew how goddam lousy he felt and they loved the scene.

Another piece of Wilder's direction that I rebelled at, at first, but which made the scene, came in *Some Like It Hot*. (Honestly, I'll get back to it.) This is when Tony comes home and I've been out dancing with Joe E. Brown and I announce that I'm engaged and he says, "What the hell are you talking about?" and I say, "We're going to be married at Niagara Falls," and he says, "Why does a fellow want to marry a fellow for security, etc." Well, it's a great scene, but it was written straight, and when we came in to shoot it Billy handed me a pair of moochachas and said, "In between each line play them." I thought he was nuts—that he's really blown his lid—that I'd be ruining the scene. Well, without the moochachas the audience would never have heard anything beyond "I'm engaged" and the whole thing would have lasted twenty seconds. This way the scene took about a minute and a half, and it did a second thing, perfectly legitimate. I was so happy and ebullient about the whole thing that I got up and started dancing around with the moochachas. The scene was great. Billy Wilder was great again. And that's *Some Like It Hot*.

N. Have any other roles involved similar bits of business, or an external-to-internal characterization?

LEMMON. Billy and I had a time with the old man in *Irma La Douce*. Remember, Billy writes his script after he has the cast, a great way to work if you can get away with it, and he has a good idea of what his actors can and cannot do. Still, there are things to work out.

Take the old man's accent—once, unconsciously, I lifted my upper lip and Billy liked that touch of phony exaggeration so I got some false teeth I could slip over my own and played the part that way. Then there was his posture—I worried over it and Billy said, "I think I see him as exaggeratedly straight, if anything tilted backward," and that did it. I stood back like that—like I had breasts and was showing them—and the outward behavior of the man took shape. Same with the cane and gloves.

I can't explain how and why these little things, silly little things, can set a character, but they do—whether you're doing *Hamlet* or a comedy role. But I am firmly of the belief that it is not only legitimate, but a matter of duty, for an actor *not* to try to be honest about how a character should basically be played because I don't think honesty has anything to do with the theater. (I thought so, when I was very young.) An actor is there for only one purpose: to perform in front of people that must be amused on the highest possible level. And by amusement I mean *Some Like It Hot* or *Hamlet* or *Othello.* That audience is there to be amused. If you can legitimately bend a character, if you can make him behave in a certain way, as long as it's logical that he *could* behave that way, and if that way is dramatically or comically more exciting than standard behavior pattern, then I say bend that character. It's the actor's duty to find out the most exciting way a role should be played, then to play that role to the hilt. This could mean bits of business, like those we've discussed, it could be underplaying, it could be climbing up and down the walls, it could be chewing up the scenery, but if he doesn't give it hell, make his characterization as complete and compelling as possible, he isn't fulfilling his function as an actor.

. . .

N. Another world-in-a-nutshell question: Can you state your objectives as an actor?

LEMMON. For a long time I don't think I had a specific objective in mind—I'd wonder what the hell I was trying to accomplish but I could never state any objective beyond the fact that I wanted to act. I never thought beyond wanting to be a successful actor, a working actor. I never thought of being a star because I never thought of film. I guess I dreamed, like a kid dreaming of being a fireman or a policeman, of being one of the best stage actors in the world.

The only objective I have is to be the best actor I can possibly be, which means I'd like to be better than I am, now. I have great trepidations about it at times, and worry about it a great deal for reasons that never occurred to me when I was younger, but Christ! I can't let those get to me. There's a good deal of the child in most actors, I think. (This part will probably have no pertinence at all to the interview, but sometimes it would be interesting to go into this with an actor who would really be honest about what is an actor, what makes an actor; I'm convinced that a great part of it all involves childishness and egotism we don't want to admit.) Basically, the more I grow up, I think that the childlike qualit[y] inherent in many actors is just great. It's a shame that more people don't have it—that they can't daydream. They can't enjoy the real thing; they tell the boss off in front of the bathroom mirror or when they're on the freeway and it's all rather futile. But an actor can let it out, he can be somebody else and forget all his own frustrations. He can be a totally new character, and instead of that being a neurotic or unhealthy business it's beginning to dawn on me that it's healthy as hell, it's a great escape. I might very well be one of the people who happen to be an actor who is fortunate indeed to be working successfully at the trade. I haven't been analyzed, so I don't know a hell of a lot about myself, but I might very well be a neurotic mess if I was something else.

Yet acting isn't enough. If I don't play the piano every now and then I get a little stir-crazy. When I was a kid I used to bite my nails all the time, and the piano may be a more adult release of nerves and tension.

Sorry. I got sidetracked again.

Secretly, I would love to be called "the best actor." Who wouldn't? I think that desire is healthy—you should strive to be the best. One of the inherent problems of so-called success, however, is the definition, the ambiguity of terms. A man with five million dollars blows his brains out and they say, "Successful man kills himself." He wasn't a success—the poor bastard was a failure. The success was somebody else's opinion. The bloody fool was miserable.

At any rate, I want to be better than I am. I want to be called "a fine actor" as often as possible. I want to realize as much as I can of the potential I've got—which I think is big. If I don't walk away from things, if I keep getting good parts, and if I stretch to reach those parts, I'll continue to grow.

I said "stretch." If I look at a script, and I know precisely how to play a part, the hell with it. Why do it? If I don't know how to play the part, but respect the role and am intrigued by it, chances are it's a role I should do. A few minutes ago I mentioned the fact that success breeds problems. The worst one is this: The more successful you become the less you can do. I never realized this before. I just turned forty and I'm doing two pictures a year. Not too long ago, in a fairly short stretch, I did over 400 TV shows. I was growing by leaps and bounds and learning. Now, in England an actor is blessed by a setup which combines our star system with good common sense and great respect for acting, directing, and theater in general. You can play all kinds of parts without causing a hullabaloo. Here you can't. If I find a little gem, for example, that I'd love to do, but my role isn't the big one, I can't do it. Olivier can. Our public is as attuned as the industry is, and the minute I showed up in a character part they'd wonder what the hell happened to Lemmon, he must be slipping. It just isn't worth it.

The point I'm making is that by virtue of good fortune and hard work I'm a star, but I have to be more and more choosy. I was fortunate enough to get marvelous parts in pictures like *Some Like It Hot, The Apartment* and *Wine and Roses* to mention three in a row that were superb.

Naturally, you want to uphold that level and you start looking around for comparable parts and you don't find them, so you do a couple of other pictures in a row that aren't as good and people again wonder what the hell happened? What is Lemmon doing junk like that for?

Well, if you hadn't had those three great parts in a row they wouldn't call that "junk." They're just average pictures. You can't hope, really, to get two great parts a year, or even two in ten years, but you've got a problem that ties right up to the question of how good an actor you can become.

Basically an actor is more interpretive than he is creative. You have to work with the tools that are given you—the improvisations I talked about before are important, but the role has to be a good one to begin with. You are dependent upon the basic tools of the trade, the writing and the direction. Seldom will you see a memorable performance in a bad picture that's badly directed.

The trouble is, you can't get an *Apartment* or *Some Like It Hot* by calling your agent on the phone and ordering one or the other. So the problem with success is that you can't do just anything—and it's frustrating to have commitments to make pictures without having the right scripts for the kind of movies you really want to make. Right now, in two weeks of solid reading, I haven't found a damned thing that even remotely interests me. The kind of calluses I'm growing now have no relationship to my growth as an actor, and that's disturbing. Because you've got to grow, but in order to grow you've got to have the right parts.

N. What is your idea of the right part? We've talked about some of your films, but what do you look for in a role?

LEMMON. The answer has to be general.

To begin with, let me clear up one thing. I read everything and anything that comes along because I'm not looking for a comedy at one given time or a drama at another. Right now I'd like to find a drama because I've done four or five comedies in a row—I'd love to find the sort of thing that broke the routine when *Wine and Roses* came along. It was a great change of pace (a selfish way to look at it). If I said that I respect the writing, and the people involved in the project, and if I'm reading the script and am held by the story and by the character, and do not know how to play it, then I'm pretty well convinced that it is a good part.

When I say "don't know how to play it" that is 100 percent right. I don't think that any actor knows how to play a really good part. If he says he can read a script and grab the phone and say, "That's the part for me! I know this fellow, I can play him!" I say—baloney. He may want to play him, but if the part is really well-written he doesn't know how to play him. Oddly enough, the better a part is written the less clear it is. You might think that a very good writer would not include generalities and vagueness in his writing, that it would be explicit and clear and the character totally apparent, but that isn't true. It adds up to this: None of us are interested in people who are dull, routine, obvious and apparent. I've never met anybody interesting who was apparent. If you speak to someone for two minutes and know what kind of person he is, he's the dullest—he'll bore the bejesus out of you. He's a prototype. Now, this same thing applies to acting. Ninety percent of the acting we see isn't very interesting because a character-chewer is being created, not a character. The actor has the shell but he hasn't crawled into it. If there's depth and body to the character it's another story—and it's worth staying around for.

You know, a good psychoanalyst can take four years, perhaps, to get to the root of a problem in a patient he could be seeing three or four times a week. In many respects acting and analysis are similar. Both are the study of behavior in one human being at a time. Both are getting to the "why" of a character's actions and motivations. And once you know why, as an actor, you let the audience know what you've found out. Acting is the last step; 80 percent is analysis.

In other words, when you look at a good script you see an acre between each line. When you read it, if you're aware of that acre, there's something good—and you can't just pick the first thing that comes into your mind. You don't really know the character but you've got to get to know him. And it's a challenge, a big one.

Frankly, when I read *Wine and Roses* I was afraid of it. It's easy to protect yourself at times, to back away saying, "No, it isn't my cup of tea," when you're afraid, when you know you might fail in it. But you should do it, not back away, because only by doing it can you become a better actor. I was afraid of *Some Like It Hot* in some respects, too, but that was part of the reason why I said, "Yes, I'll do it." If I was afraid of it, and passed up the challenge, I'd be a complete fake, a charlatan, a living lie to everything I've said in this interview. I might fail, but screw it—I'd also learn a hell of a lot.

All these things add up to what makes me want to do a part. I don't mean that I'm afraid of every part I play (I've felt perfectly safe with lots of them) but if I *am* afraid of it there's an extra temptation to play it. But mainly if I'm excited and titillated by the part itself, and don't know how to play it, if it isn't routine, one of five thousand slight variations, then I'm for it.

Look at the parts I've had, though, and you see how very lucky I've been and how hard it is to play can-you-top-this when most actors don't collect a *Mr. Roberts, Some Like It Hot, Days of Wine and Roses, Irma La Douce, How to Murder Your Wife* and *The Great Race* in a lifetime. Take just *The Great Race*—if that isn't a great part it's nobody's fault but mine; it's beautifully written. I come out of six or seven months of work with three parts. As Professor Fate I'm the arch-villain of all time, the "corner-you-in-the-roundhouse-Nellie" takeoff. Then I'm the fop Prince from Europe confronting and playing scenes with the professor. Then I'm the first guy realizing the lookalike and imitating the Prince. This has got to be an actor's field day.

So now I sit and start to read scripts and nothing interests me, so I'll probably have to cool it for a couple of months and stop looking for great parts. My luck has been so fantastically great I probably deserve to sit it out for a bit.

Marlon Brando The *Playboy* Interview

PLAYBOY. Do you have a bad memory or is it that you feel remembering lines affects the spontaneity of your performance?

BRANDO. If you know what you're going to say, if you watch people's faces when they're talking, they don't know what kind of expressions they're going to have. You can see people search for words, for ideas, reaching for a concept, a feeling, whatever. If the words are there in the actor's mind . . . *Oh, you got me!* [*Laughing*] *You got me right in the bush.* I'm talking about acting, aren't I?

Actually, it saves you an awful lot of time, because not learning lines . . . it's wonderful to do that.

PLAYBOY. Wonderful not to learn lines?

BRANDO. Yeah, you save all that time not learning the lines. You can't tell the difference. And it improves the spontaneity, because you really don't know. You have an idea of it and you're saying it and you can't remember what the hell it is you want to say. I think it's an aid. Except, of course, Shakespeare. I can quote you two hours of speeches of Shakespeare. Some things you can ad-lib, some things you have to commit to memory, like Shakespeare, Tennessee Williams—where the language has value. You can't ad-lib Tennessee Williams.

PLAYBOY. But how does it affect an actor who is working with you if he's got your lines written out on his forehead or wherever?

BRANDO. It doesn't make any difference. They're not going to see the signs. [*Names a book title.*] I just saw a title on the bookshelf. You didn't see me looking for it, you didn't know that I was even doing that. I can do the same thing if I have . . . Well, anyway, it's more spontaneous.

PLAYBOY. So it is true that you no longer memorize lines when you act. But you did during the early stages of your career, when you were doing Williams and Shakespeare.

BRANDO. That's quite a different thing, because you cannot . . . Well, you're getting me. [*Laughs*]
. . .

PLAYBOY. Do you *like* acting?

BRANDO. Listen, where can you get paid enough money to buy an island and sit on your ass and talk to you the way I'm doing? You can't *do* anything that's going to pay you money to do that.

PLAYBOY. You do take acting seriously, then?

BRANDO. Yeah; if you aren't good at what you do, you don't eat, you don't have the wherewithal to have liberties. I'm sitting down here on this island, enjoying my family, and I'm here primarily because I was able to make a living so I could afford it. I hate the idea of going nine to five. That would scare me.

PLAYBOY. Is that what bothered you about acting in the theater?

BRANDO. It's hard. You have to show up every day. People who go to the theater will perceive the same thing a different way. You have to be able to *give* something back in order to get something from it. I can give you a perfect example. A movie that I was in, called *On the Waterfront;* there was a scene in a taxicab, where I turn to my brother, who's come to turn me over to the gangsters, and I lament to him that he never looked after me, he never gave me a chance, that I could have been a contender, I coulda been somebody, instead of a bum. . . ."You should've looked out after me, Charley." It was very moving. And people often spoke about that, "Oh, my God, what a wonderful scene, Marlon, blah blah blah blah blah." It wasn't wonderful at all. The situation was wonderful. *Everybody* feels like he could have been a contender, he could have been somebody, everybody feels as though he's partly bum, some part of him. He is not fulfilled and he could have done better, he could have been better. Everybody feels a sense of loss about something. So *that* was what touched people. It wasn't the scene itself. There are other scenes where you'll find actors being expert, but since the audience can't clearly identify with them, they just pass unnoticed. Wonderful scenes never get mentioned, only those scenes that affect people.

PLAYBOY. Can you give an example?

BRANDO. Judy Garland singing *Over the Rainbow.* "Somewhere over the rainbow bluebirds fly, birds fly over the rainbow, why, oh, why can't I?" Insipid. But you have people just choking up when they hear her singing it. Everybody's got an over-the-rainbow story, everybody wants to get out from under and wants . . . [*laughing*] . . . wants bluebirds flying around. And that's why it's so touching.

PLAYBOY. Had another person sung that song, it might not have had the same effect. Similarly, if someone else had played that particular *Waterfront* scene with Rod Steiger—a scene considered by some critics among the great moments in the history of film—it could have passed unnoticed.

BRANDO. Yeah, but there are some scenes, some parts that are actor-proof. If you don't get in the way of a part, it plays by itself. And there are other parts you work like a Turk in to be effective.

PLAYBOY. Did you know that *Waterfront* scene was actor-proof when you were doing it?

BRANDO. No, at the time, I didn't know.

PLAYBOY. Was it a well-rehearsed scene or did Kazan just put the two of you there to act spontaneously?

BRANDO. We improvised a lot. Kazan is the best actor's director you could ever want, because he was an actor himself, but a special kind of actor. He understands things that other directors do not. He also inspired me. Most actors are expected to come with their parts in their pockets and their emotions spring-loaded; when the director says, "OK, hit it," they go into a time slip. But Kazan brought a lot of things to the actor and he invited you to argue with him. He's one of the few directors creative and understanding enough to know where the actor's trying to go. He'd let you play a scene almost any way you'd want.

As it was written, you had this guy pulling a gun on his brother. I said, "That's not believable; I don't believe one brother would shoot the other." The script never prepared you for it, it just wasn't believable; it was incredible. So I did it as if he *couldn't* believe it, and that was incorporated into the scene.

PLAYBOY. Many actors cite your performance in *Reflections in a Golden Eye* as an example of superb improvisational acting. Did any of that have to do with the direction of John Huston?

BRANDO. No. He leaves you alone.

PLAYBOY. What about Bernardo Bertolucci's direction of *Last Tango in Paris*? Did you feel it was a "violation," as you once said?

BRANDO. Did I say that once? To whom? [*Laughing*] "As you once said."

PLAYBOY. What you said was that no actor should be asked to give that much.

BRANDO. Who told you that?

PLAYBOY. I read it.

BRANDO. I don't know *what* that film's about. So much of it was improvised. He wanted to do this, to do that. I'd seen his other movie, *The Conformist,* and I thought he was a man of special talent. And he thought of all kinds of improvisations. He let me do anything. He told me the general area of what he wanted and I tried to produce the words or the action.

PLAYBOY. Do you know what it's about now?

BRANDO. Yeah, I think it's all about Bernardo Bertolucci's psychoanalysis. And of his not being able to achieve . . . I don't know, I'm being facetious. I think he was confused about it; *he* didn't know what it was about, either. He's very sensitive, but he's a little taken with success. He likes being in the front, on the cover. He enjoys that. He loves giving interviews, loves making audacious statements. He's one of the few really talented people around.

. . .

PLAYBOY. What happens when you improvise and the actor you're working with wants to stick to the script?

BRANDO. If an actor can't improvise, then perhaps the producer's wife cast him in that part. You wouldn't be in the film with such a person. Some actors don't like it. Olivier doesn't like to improvise; everything is structured and his roles are all according to an almost architectural plan. . . .

PLAYBOY. Have you ever just walked through a part?

BRANDO. Certainly. Yeah.

PLAYBOY. Often?

BRANDO. No.

PLAYBOY. What about *A Countess from Hong Kong*, directed by Charles Chaplin?

BRANDO. No, I *tried* on that, but I was a puppet, a marionette in that. I wasn't there to be anything else; because Chaplin was a man of sizable talent and I was not going to argue with him about what's funny and not funny. I must say we didn't start off very well. I went to London for the reading of the script and Chaplin read for us. I had jet lag and I went right to sleep during his reading. That was terrible. [*Laughs*] Sometimes sleep is more important than anything else. I was miscast in that. . . .

PLAYBOY. What about when you direct yourself, as you did in *One-Eyed Jacks*? That was a first and last experience for you; did it cure your desire to direct?

BRANDO. I didn't desire to direct that picture. Stanley Kubrick quit just before we were supposed to shoot and I owed $300,000 already on the picture, having paid Karl Malden from the time he started his contract and we weren't through writing the picture. Stanley, Calder Willingham and myself were at my house playing chess, throwing darts, playing poker. We never got around to getting it ready. Then, just before we were to start, Stanley said, "Marlon, I don't know what the picture's about." I said, "I'll tell you what it's about. It's about $300,000 that I've already paid Karl Malden." He said, "Well, if that's what it's about, I'm in the wrong picture." So that was the end of it. I ran around, asked Sidney Lumet, Gadge [Kazan] and, I don't know, four or five people; nobody wanted to direct it. [*Laughs*] There wasn't anything for me to do except to direct it or go to the poorhouse. So I did.

PLAYBOY. Was it a new experience for you?

BRANDO. No, you direct yourself in most films, anyway.

Robert De Niro Dialogue with the Actor

QUESTION. In *Raging Bull* you don't so much play Jake La Motta as become him. Where do you usually start when you are developing a performance?

ROBERT DE NIRO. Well, everything I do is different. I could see someone in the street who has some sort of quirk or eccentricity, and that one little thing would be interesting to do in a film. It could be just that simple—say it's just right for the character. Usually, I read the script and I like the character and I can see things in it—or I get a picture in my mind of people I know or have seen. Then I start working on it and picking up things here and there.

QUESTION. What attracted you to *Raging Bull?*

DE NIRO. I was interested in fighters. The way they walk, the weight thing— they always blow up—and there was just something about Jake La Motta that was, for me, interesting. I wanted to play a fighter—just like a child wants to be somebody else. The fun of it is when you get into just experimenting. If you're lucky, you make good choices that will work. As Stella Adler used to say, "Your talent lies in your choice."

QUESTION. Did you have any trouble losing all the weight you gained?

DE NIRO. No. I just went back to my old eating habits. It was easy.

QUESTION. How did you gain sixty pounds?

DE NIRO. I'm answering this question for the six-thousandth time. It was very easy. I just had to get up at six-thirty in the morning and eat breakfast at seven in order to digest my food to eat lunch at twelve or one in order to digest my food to eat a nice dinner at seven at night. So it was three square meals a day, that's all. You know, pancakes, beer, milk.

QUESTION. In *Bang the Drum Slowly,* you managed to convince us you were a baseball player. What sort of homework did you do?

DE NIRO. I went down South with a tape recorder and got local people to go over the whole script with me. Then I was always watching for little traits that I could use. And then I did all the baseball. We practiced in Central Park for, I think, three weeks to a month. When I was in Florida, I practiced a lot, even

Excerpt from "Dialogue on Film: Robert De Niro," *American Film* 6 (March 1981), 39–48.

Robert De Niro (right) with
Michael Moriarty in *Bang the
Drum Slowly* (1973)

with the batting machines. I also watched ball games on television. You're
looking right at the catcher all the time, and you can see how relaxed he is, in a
sense.

The main thing is to make it appear as if you're throwing it away. I believe
in practice, just doing it over and over. If you do it over, then you can throw it
away. There was a scene in *Raging Bull,* one of the scenes where I went back
to the corner after knocking somebody down. I was doing too much because I
didn't know what to do, and it was the first fight scene that we shot. I was
jumping up and down a little too much. When you see actual fighters, they do
that. But they also just wait in the corner. It's like anything else. In the
beginning you learn the rules, and then you realize that the rules are there to
use or not to use and that there are millions of different ways of doing
something.

Even with *New York, New York* and learning the saxophone. It was just to
learn it so that I wouldn't look at if I didn't know what I was doing. I really
worked on it very hard. But I wonder if I should have saved a little more
energy for other things and just worried about what was going to be seen. I
worked like hell on that thing. But you either have to know it so well that you
can really do it or you have to find a way to do it so that you can know just
enough and still feel comfortable with it.

QUESTION. Do you sometimes look at dailies and say, for instance, "I'll
continue on that," or maybe feel that something was pushed too much?

DE NIRO. Oh, yes. I'll look, but then I'll realize I'm looking at myself in one
angle all the time. I know the director will see that, and if he's got any sense,
he'll cut away from the stuff that's not quite right. Or maybe he will feel that it's

OK, and it's me being self-conscious—I'll feel that it's not right, but actually it's OK. Professionals, say saxophone players, do the same things, but I'm watching so carefully that I have to lighten up and put it in its right perspective. Yes, looking at dailies you figure, "Well, next time I'll do this or do that." If they're really bad, you reshoot it.

QUESTION. But looking at rushes doesn't lead you to change your style of acting in a film.

DE NIRO. No. Some directors don't allow you to see them. Anybody who asks should be allowed to see them, unless they're "flippo" and they're going to watch themselves and go crazy and change their whole performance. I mean, you still have to walk from here to there to get to the other side of the street. If you see yourself, just maybe you walk a little this way, or change your style of walk slightly. But you have enough sense to know that you're not going to throw the thing out of whack, because then you're just screwing it up for yourself.

But I do want to do something where I never look at rushes, because you always get kind of disappointed. You know every foot of the thing; you've seen everything. So finally, it's hard to really be objective. I'd like to do one thing where I feel so confident about what I'm doing that I'll just do it and I won't look at any of the rushes. I'll just see the finished film.

QUESTION. What do you look for in a director—an ability to work with actors?

DE NIRO. Well, some directors—newer directors—know less about acting per se. Their tradition is not the theater, first of all. A director can have very good instincts but not know much about how to work with an actor. Kazan is someone who works very simply, but he is a wonderful director and he knows the theater and the movies, and works well in both. He gives you all the support that you need in a professional way—like a coach, you know.

Other directors, usually good ones, just have good instincts. They have an overall sense of how to make a film, but they don't understand actors and they don't have to. Some will let you alone. But they have good common sense and good taste. If they see that you're doing something wrong, they'll stop you, or they'll guide you this way or that way, depending on the overall thrust of the film and what they want to do with it and the reasons they cast you.

The worst thing is a director that tells someone how to do something. You know, some directors like results, and they'll tell you, "You do this and you go over and you smile." You say, "I've never been in this situation. What do you mean I go over and smile?" They don't understand that you could do it in another way and that it would be better for you. Not only better for you, but it would give you more confidence and more joy. And you would know that they trust you and your choice. It might not be the way the director imagined it. But in the long run it will have the same effect. So that's the most important thing, because you can break somebody's spirit very easily.

Then there's the opposite, where a director is intimidated. Say, in my position, if I'm with a director and he says yes to everything. That's ridiculous. I have to have somebody I respect and who respects me and who tells me, "No" or "That's OK, but try this." You have to have a give-and-take. If it's out of balance, then it won't work.

QUESTION. Should more directors have an acting background?

DE NIRO. It definitely would help. You can't lose by doing it.

QUESTION. Martin Scorsese had a small role in *Taxi Driver*. How did he come to play the part?

DE NIRO. Originally George Memmoli was supposed to play the part. What happened was, the day before he was supposed to come in, he fell and hurt himself really bad and he couldn't do it. So Marty decided to do it.

QUESTION. Do you think Scorsese wants to be in front of the camera more?

DE NIRO. I don't know. I know he was offered some parts he didn't want to do. He was offered the Charles Manson character for the television movie *Helter Skelter*. But he was a little paranoid. He figured they were going to come after him, too. But he might do something. If I ever directed a movie and I wanted him for one of the main parts, he would do it. I know he would do it.

QUESTION. Did the shooting script for *Taxi Driver* undergo significant changes during the filming?

DE NIRO. When you do a movie, it changes. You always make adjustments; you change when you're on the spot. Even if on paper it looks good, you know it won't be right if you shoot it that way. You get an idea, when you're on the set, to do this instead of that. What Paul Schrader does very well for us is give us a good structure. But in *Taxi Driver* there were a lot of things that weren't in the script that we would do.

When I walk up to Harvey Keitel and I shoot him, I don't know if that's the way it was written in the script. Now, if it was a director who was doing it by the book, he would say, "Why aren't you doing it the way it's written?" What's the difference how you do it? You've just got to do it, as long as it's right within the nature of the situation. I would say, offhand, twenty, twenty-five percent of the film is different from the screenplay.

QUESTION. Travis Bickle, the character you play in *Taxi Driver*, isn't easy to understand. How would you explain him?

DE NIRO. You know, everybody always says that you have to explain certain things. There are some things you can't explain. I used to ask Jake La Motta, "Why did you do this? Why did you do that?" The guy would answer me— and actually he did a very good job, because I couldn't do as well. He would tell me some answers that were insightful. If somebody asked me, I couldn't be that honest and straight. What I'm saying is that if you don't understand certain things about characters, it's all right. You don't have to spell it out. The movie is not a course on how to understand this character.

QUESTION. But *you* have to understand the actions of a Bickle.

DE NIRO. I make it work for myself, but I may not understand why this character would do this. I wouldn't do it. On the other hand, I can understand it in a way, and I have to find a way to make it work. Paul Schrader wrote the script ten years ago, I think. There was something about it that drew us to it— the loneliness of this guy.

QUESTION. Your character in *The Deer Hunter* isn't always easy to understand either. What do you think is going through his mind during the singing of "God Bless America" at the end?

DE NIRO. I felt he was going along with it, like you sing "Happy Birthday" at a party.

QUESTION. What was your own feeling about that ending?

DE NIRO. Some people, I heard, didn't like it. I thought it was OK. I thought it was nice. It wasn't a statement saying that these people were gung ho, sort of right-wing, whatever. It was just what it was.

QUESTION. How did you go about trying to understand your character?

DE NIRO. I went hunting and tried to shoot a deer with one bullet—no, I'm only kidding. That's what I liked about the script—I liked the characters. I liked that they didn't say much, that there wasn't anything that was conde- scending or patronizing toward them.

QUESTION. What problems did you have in doing the Russian roulette scenes?

DE NIRO. It's very hard to sustain that kind of intensity. I mean, we were really slapping each other; you sort of get worked up into a frenzy. It's a very difficult thing to do. It took a long time.

QUESTION. If the screenwriter is available, do you ever rely on him for building a character?

DE NIRO. A lot of times the writer doesn't know much more about the character than you. If it's a writer who writes very personally, you get the feeling he might be putting his personal feelings through a character. It could be a baseball player. He doesn't know the nature of the professional behavior of these people in a situation. Then you have to just go on your own, because you know he doesn't know it. In other words, it's up to you as an actor to make those details work for you.

It would be nice to get a writer who really knows a certain milieu, a certain life-style. Then you could ask him questions about it, and he would know all the nuances and everything. It's also good if you know a little bit about it, too, so you don't always have to rely on him. When we were doing the fight scenes in *Raging Bull,* Jake La Motta was always there. But then when we did the acting stuff in New York, we didn't want him around. He understood, because you don't want the guy to come over and say, "That's not the way I did it." You feel his presence and your energy is drained. You feel like you're doing it for the approval of someone else.

It gets back to the thing with directors. They have to validate what you're doing, and not say, "Very good," and tap you on the head, but just say, "That's right. It's moving in the right direction." You know yourself. But sometimes you know it and they don't know it, and that's a strange feeling. I've had that once or twice. You say, "I know this is right. I know it's right," and these people are saying, "It's wrong." But that was before, when I was in situations where I was hired as an actor and just did the work.

QUESTION. In those early days of your career, how did you go about choosing roles?

DE NIRO. Well, they chose me, I didn't choose. You get certain things and you make do with them; you're lucky to get a job. If it's a good part, you don't think about all the things that are wrong. But I turned down some things I knew were wrong. I also had what you'd call leads in movies. But then a director would come along and I'd want to work with him. It would be a small part, but I'd do it because I wanted to work with him or something.

QUESTION. What kind of criteria do you have now?

DE NIRO. A good script, number one. I usually have more to say now about the casting because I feel that it's very, very important that the movie is cast well. You know, I had somebody tell me once—he had done some films, but he didn't have that much experience—"You just cut away to this or that. You don't have to worry about the actors." But if you don't have anything that's interesting to watch, that's real or that grabs you, whether it be actors or real people, then no matter how beautiful the photography is or how great the editing, it's not going to make any difference. Like the Abscam tapes. All this blurry videotape stuff, but you're curious because of what it is. You watch it because you know a real thing is going on there.

QUESTION. You mentioned the changes that were made on the set of *Taxi Driver*. There's a scene in *New York, New York* where you're in a hallway and you hang up the phone. Suddenly, different thoughts go across your face, but you never say a word. Was that written in to the script?

DE NIRO. No, that was thought up on the sound stage. You don't know those things until you're on the set and you do them. You have to be flexible, because that means another setup, maybe another half a day, which then means money.

QUESTION. What *were* you thinking?

DE NIRO. I hate to disappoint you—I don't know. You probably thought I was really working. That's what I mean: It's very simple. Some people are able to do that more easily than others by being very simple. It's also what's been built in before. So you have to know that as an actor you don't overstate it and say, "Well, now I'm going to kvetch a little here to show them how I feel." The audience knows how you feel. The less that you show the better.

QUESTION. In *The Godfather, Part II*, was it difficult to portray a young man who had already been portrayed as an older man?

DE NIRO. Well, I was given certain things, and so I had to stick to those. In a way I didn't mind, because otherwise you have to think of it all on your own, you have to come up with something new. I was given Marlon Brando playing the Godfather. I had to play it in my way but connect it to him physically as much as I could, but not imitate or anything. So it was an interesting sort of problem.

QUESTION. In the films you've done with Martin Scorsese, have you had much opportunity to rehearse before shooting?

DE NIRO. In the few movies we've done together, we've rehearsed differently. I think rehearsal is important. Again, this is something that a lot of film-makers—newer filmmakers I think—don't think about. They don't think it's important to rehearse. There are all kinds of rehearsals. It's not like doing a play. Like for the next movie I'm going to do, I think it's important that we really rehearse for at least a month, because it really needs it. But it can also be sitting around a table and just getting familiar with each other. Sometimes you don't need much more, because the movie is maybe a couple of lines and a look from the character. So what are you going to rehearse? It's not like a play, where people say a lot and you literally have to learn the lines. Sometimes we videotape the rehearsals and get material that's even better than what's written and incorporate it into the scene.

QUESTION. Do you work through the entire script to get an overview?

DE NIRO. Right, right. Even when you read people for parts. You know, when you read with actors, you start getting a sense of how it sounds. If it's an actor who really latches into it and does it right, has the right rhythm of the character and the way it's written, then you see that it works. You see that it works, and probably that actor will get the part. Sometimes I read with actors and I think, For the next movie I'm not going to read until it's really down to a few people. I don't want to start getting into habits that are not like the character.

Actors always complain, "Well, they made me read with the casting director or the stage manager." When I'm there I feel a little bad if actors read with the casting director, because I know that I should read with them. But on the other hand, I don't want to get locked into anything. I kind of want to be outside of it. Otherwise, you're reading and you don't know who you are as a character yet.

QUESTION. You said you were preparing for something. What's your next film?

DE NIRO. I'm going to do a movie called *The King of Comedy* with Scorsese and Jerry Lewis. Some team. We're going to do that in the spring.

QUESTION. What is Lewis going to play?

DE NIRO. He's going to play a Johnny Carson-type character. I try to get on his show, and he's giving me the brush-off all the time. It's very well written, so I don't like to tamper with the dialogue too much.

QUESTION. Who's the writer?

DE NIRO. A guy named Paul Zimmerman. He used to be a film critic for *Newsweek*. I think he's a music critic now. But he wrote a very, very good script.

QUESTION. Are you interested in getting involved in other aspects of the business—directing, producing?

DE NIRO. Maybe directing. I'm thinking of that. But, you know, everybody wants to direct.

QUESTION. Is there an ideal part that you'd like to play in the future, some dream character?

DE NIRO. No, I don't think of anything at this point.

QUESTION. Are you going to stay with the same type of character that you've built on the screen?

DE NIRO. No, I don't want to. What do you think I should do? Does anybody have any suggestions?

QUESTION. The *King of Comedy* project may give you a chance to go in another direction. I'm assuming that it's lighter than *Taxi Driver,* unless you shoot Jerry Lewis.

DE NIRO. Yes. It is lighter. It's not a comedy the way we know comedies, but it's very funny.

QUESTION. What problems did you have doing *1900* for Bertolucci in Italy? Would you work for a European director again?

DE NIRO. Well, European directors I don't know much about. But I've heard about them. It's common knowledge that certain directors tell you what to do. I had that with Bertolucci, too. He would tell me what to do. We had some problems in the beginning. As a person I liked him very much, but as a director he has another style that for me wasn't as good as it could have been. So many of the greatest directors are Italian, but I've heard that they tell you, "Do this. You walk over here and do that." I don't know why they do that. They just don't look at it the way Americans do.

QUESTION. Hitchcock would tell the actors what to do rather than what to feel.

DE NIRO. But you see, now there it's a very specific type of style. The director should let the actors know what he's trying to do in the style. An actor understands, if you tell him. Then I would say, "Yes, you're right." I would only do that with people I respect very much and I want to work with, like Scorsese. I'll do anything that he wants just to see if it'll work. It's a lot of fun trying to make something stylized. Marty had a lot of that in the fight stuff in *Raging Bull.* For him I would do it. I'd do it for others, too. But it's important to be one on one and give the actor the confidence and explain to him what the thing is, especially if he asks. Not to say, "Do it."

QUESTION. But there are lazy actors.

DE NIRO. Yes, OK. There are, and people tell them what to do. It depends on who you cast. If you use a lazy actor, an actor who doesn't care—I don't see that person in anything that I even want to be involved with.

QUESTION. In *1900,* how did you develop the character you played?

DE NIRO. It was hard. It's not my culture, so I spent a lot of time there before it was shot to get a sense of the place and the people and so on.

QUESTION. Did everybody speak English?

DE NIRO. Everybody spoke their own language. In Italian movies you just speak what you want and they dub it all in later. But actually, this one was direct sound, because it was an American-financed project, a big thing. That's a mistake, I think. As soon as some European directors get the three-picture deal over here, that's the end for them, more or less. Very few can really make a movie here and make it work. They all gear it to the American audience— "Will it make it in America? Will it make it in America?" You can't think of it that way. You've got to make it for yourself, and if it makes it in America as an art film, then that's what it is. But at least people have respect for you.

When I'm in Italy, they give me scripts and they ask me if it will work in America. "I don't think so," I say. But they shouldn't be thinking that. The best directors—Bergman, Buñuel—they don't worry about that. You know, I read somewhere that Fellini said, "I don't even know what kind of tie a person would wear in America. How could I do a movie there?"

QUESTION. You've talked about the script changes that take place on the set. Are some of those changes in the way of editing, tightening?

DE NIRO. You know, you find that when you do a movie, you can overstate something. You can say it three times when all you have to do is say it once. And that one time is more powerful than all the others; each time it diminishes it more and more. You can edit a script and you think you have it. But when you get out there and then you see it finally on the screen, you can edit even more. It's hard to visualize.

Some people have a very good knack at doing that, and some I think don't. Some people, like Hitchcock, plan everything. That doesn't mean that they don't give actors freedom within all that exactness. Sometimes, like with Scorsese, I'll do something off camera, or something that I'm sure is going to be cut out and then what he'll do is leave it in. You know, it's a little out of character and he likes it, so he keeps it. So now I have to be more careful.

QUESTION. Are there any particular actors or actresses that you've especially enjoyed working with?

DE NIRO. I don't want to sound like Mr. Nice Guy, but I've enjoyed working with most of the people I have worked with. I enjoyed working with Joe Pesci, who plays my brother in *Raging Bull*. He's very good. I like to see an actor who is good. That's a real turn-on, because you know when people are good the whole thing is going to be good.

QUESTION. How important is a camera angle on your acting, particularly if you know that it will make the moment more dramatic?

DE NIRO. Scorsese, say, will put it at a certain angle because he knows that that will make it more dramatic and that's what he wants. It won't affect me. But I'll get off on it. I'll understand what he's doing. We joke about one scene in *Taxi Driver* where I'm over the fire. We call that the Charles Atlas scene. I didn't know it was going to be like that. I don't know if he intended it that way.

I'm curious to see how it's all going to turn out, so I get off on doing whatever we have to do.

QUESTION. He looks to camera angles to bring out something more than is in the script.

DE NIRO. Yes. Well, he knows what he thinks it will be, and then maybe when he gets on the set, he'll change something. Scorsese does a lot of storyboards; he does little drawings and everything. The fight stuff in *Raging Bull* was all choreographed and storyboarded. I think he had in one fight—the last fight I have—about sixty setups.

QUESTIONS. Have you been concerned, by the way, about Jake La Motta's reaction to *Raging Bull*?

DE NIRO. He knows it's a movie. He knows you can't be literally this and that, even with the fight stuff. He was with us enough to know what it takes. You know, we all worked hard on it, so he hopes that it does well. He'll know by the feedback that he gets from people. If they tell him bad things, then he'll come looking for me.

QUESTION. You and Scorsese have worked together on four or five films now. How do you work and communicate together?

DE NIRO. A lot of times I used to like to talk to him in private, in front of no one. I like sometimes to be very personal with the director. He can say whatever he wants to other actors, but when we talk, it's with each other and that's it. We've worked so much with each other now, we trust each other. Not that we didn't trust each other before, but I think now if there's another person around, we can still talk. We have solid communication. But even so, a lot of times I still like to just talk to him on the side so nobody hears. Maybe it's something I'm going to try, and I want to prepare him for it so he can cover it. It might get a reaction from the other actors, so he has to be ready for it.

QUESTION. Does he get specific with you? Things like, "Give me more."

DE NIRO. He likes to orchestrate. I can see Marty if he was over there and we're doing a scene here, he'd be doing this, "Keep it down." [*Motioning with his hand.*] It's not like he's telling me and I should be aware of what he's telling me. It's half-and-half. But it's not intrusive. I see him doing it when he's watching other scenes, like to himself. It's really just orchestrating, leading.

QUESTION. Do you go into the editing room?

DE NIRO. No, I don't. I'll see a rough cut after a few months. I'll look at it again and again, and I'll just make notes and tell them what I think.

QUESTION. Obviously, you trust Scorsese enough to know that he's not going to ruin your performance or ruin the story.

DE NIRO. No, he's not. We disagree on things. I tell him this or that. All I can do is say it, because it's his movie. If I was directing something, I would feel that same way. I would want input from people, and I would want to know what they felt. But in the long run I have to make the final decision. But we don't disagree strongly about stuff, because we think very much alike.

QUESTION. Does your approach to a role change from director to director?

DE NIRO. Well, I did *The Last Tycoon* with Kazan, and we used to do "improvs" on the nature of being a studio executive. They were very simple, and he was very supportive all the time. You wouldn't feel that it was laborious; it was more fun. He's very easy. It's like he takes it trippingly. If you want to do it again, he'll do it. I sometimes like to do it again and again and make sure it's right. His method of improvisation doesn't mean improvising on the screen. It means improvising behind the scenes, like on a situation to find other colors.

That's the way it's meant in the theater—to loosen you up and find behavioral things. Because in a play, what the author writes is written in stone. You can't get one word changed most of the time. The lines are there, and this is what it is. So you find other ways physically of doing things through improvs. But those are working improvs. In movies improvising means something else. It means you ad-lib, which can be OK too.

So with Kazan we stuck very much to the script, practically word for word, because Kazan promised Harold Pinter that he wouldn't change anything. I frankly think that a script should be changed; you have to make adjustments. In movies especially, you have to make the adjustments, or it becomes something rigid. With Scorsese we would improvise another way. He would videotape it, and then we would look at it after.

QUESTION. Did Coppola, for instance, give those freedoms?

DE NIRO. Yes, Coppola does. He respects actors. In my experience, he lets them do what they want. He gives you the support. He wants you to be comfortable. I think he does that with all the people who work for him. That's the first thing—to allow people to feel that they're contributing and that they're not being held down all the time and can't express their own ideas. But he picks people who understand him, too, so they have some common ground.

QUESTION. But some actors, on their own, are inclined to "push" a scene.

DE NIRO. It happens more in movies because movies are more subtle. An actor feels he's not doing enough, so he overcompensates for it. It's like what I was saying when I was in the corner in *Raging Bull*. I was jumping up and down too much. What I try to do as an actor is be aware of those things so that

I can work on them, so that I can feel relaxed in that situation. That's why when I prepared for *Bang the Drum Slowly,* I saw in every baseball game how relaxed the players were. I could just pick it up. I could practice in my room watching them do nothing.

That doesn't mean you should be flat. You still have to be thinking. It's like people who talk about their families. Their mother was hit by a car and killed and so on, and they kvetch and moan and groan and all that. And other people—one guy told me how his wife was murdered, and he just told me blank. Of course, the feeling I got was that it was over, it was a past thing. Now if he was telling somebody in a more immediate situation, he might have broken down; in this situation he didn't. But an actor might tend to feel, Gee, this is a powerful, emotional scene. I have to give a little more. As soon as he gives too much, the audience gets turned off.

QUESTION. How does a director pull back his actors?

DE NIRO. You can give them an object—not a cigarette, because that's the oldest crutch in the world—but something to take their minds off the fact that they want to overdo it. Or just give them what you call an "as if"—imagine that you're talking to a dog or whatever. Anything that they can use to take their minds off it.

QUESTION. If you have to repeat an emotional scene, say to cover another angle, what tricks do you use to work yourself up again?

DE NIRO. It's hard to get worked up. If it's a very emotional scene, it's very hard. That's why I like to use a few cameras. Otherwise, I have to get myself worked up again. I might have somebody say something to me that will get me started. I might see one person, and if I associate something with that person—say somebody in the crew—I might ask him to say something to me or to do something. They might think I'm a little crazy, but they know and they'll do it. You get them to do it realistically. It could be anything to get started or back into it. It's hard.

QUESTION. You've been mentioning the theater. Do you have any desire to go back to the theater?

DE NIRO. I want to do a play.

QUESTION. You studied with Lee Strasberg, who's trained a number of stage actors.

DE NIRO. Yes. I studied mainly with Stella Adler. I used to do off-off-Broadway plays. Some of them were comedies. I traveled around the South and did some dinner theaters—Neil Simon type of comedy and stuff like that. But I haven't done a play in six or seven years. Time goes by. But I want to do a play. I've been seeing plays in New York. I don't know when, but I will. I have two films I want to do; then I'm planning on doing something.

QUESTION. Would one of those films be a Western?

DE NIRO. No. I wouldn't want to touch a Western. They've been done so often, and who wants to be out in the middle of the desert for three months? Forget that.

QUESTION. Do you still enjoy what you're doing as much as when you first got into it?

DE NIRO. Yes, yes, I do. When I'm working, I do. There are other things that come along with it, but I do enjoy it. I can get sidetracked here and there, but the most important thing is to keep my mind on what I'm doing. You know, I have a little time off now before I do the next movie. I always wanted the time off. Now I have it and it's like I don't know what to do. I get a little depressed almost. What am I going to do with myself?

Dustin Hoffman Interview with the Actor

MITCH TUCHMAN. You've said that your role in *Tootsie* took longer to put behind you than other roles.

DUSTIN HOFFMAN. I don't know why it was harder to drop emotionally. Some of it may have had to do with my mother, who I had spent a great deal of time with since she had a stroke in the last year and a half of her life, which was at the same time that I was working on the script with Murray Schisgal and then Larry Gelbart. My brother Ron felt that Dorothy Michaels is, in fact, at least in spirit, our mother. (She, as a matter of fact, is the reason that the movie is called *Tootsie,* because when I was a kid, she called me Tootsie).

TUCHMAN. Any other reason?

HOFFMAN. Anytime you feel that a portion of your life is wasted because of a way of thinking that you have had, and you think that now you understand

Excerpt from "Dialogue on Film: Dustin Hoffman," *American Film* 8, no. 6 (April 1983), 26–28, 69–72.

something, there's a sadness in having wasted so many years. Growing up in Los Angeles in the forties and the fifties and then moving to New York City in the late fifties, I was a product of the time when I was raised. It was the *Playboy* center fold mentality, which still possesses me, and still works. I'm still taken by that fantasy girl. When I tried to become this character, Dorothy Michaels, I couldn't become as pretty as I wanted to become, and we tested for over a year, because I felt that I should try to look as attractive as I could, just as I want to be as a man.

It suddenly occurred to me after doing Dorothy for a while that if I'd met her at a party, I'd never so much as condescend to talk to her, because physically she was a write-off. It's a shallow attitude, certainly, to judge people by the way they look, and I think that is what started to make me sad.

TUCHMAN. For all the opportunities that had been missed?

HOFFMAN. For all the interesting women that I didn't spend time with because of the way they looked. Also, I think I realized that if I wasn't going up to these women, in a sense I was rejecting myself. I was a male Dorothy. In high school, girls passed me over for the same reasons.

Dorothy was able to accept the way she looked; I couldn't. She was able to have a tremendous amount of self-respect, and I guess, for that reason, it was hard to lose her.

TUCHMAN. How did you get the idea for the role?

HOFFMAN. It started with *Kramer vs. Kramer.* At the end of the movie, I wanted to feminize that character more. We improvised a lot in that movie—we improvised a courtroom scene, and at one point I had a good emotional thing going. The judge said, "Why should you have the child?" I said, "Because I'm his mother." And I didn't know I said it and I couldn't get Bob Benton and Stanley Jaffe to use it in the cut—they thought it was gilding the lily.

So when the film was over, I was very excited about a new feeling—what makes a man, what makes a woman, what is gender? I had a lot of conversations with Murray Schisgal, over what masculinity is, what femininity is, the difference between homosexuality and femininity in men. Suddenly he asked me this question: "What kind of woman would you be if you were a woman?" And I said, "What a great question."

So we started to experiment. I was so concerned with looking like a woman and not like a man in drag, and sounding like a woman and not a falsettoed camp thing, that I couldn't concentrate on the character. After a year, when the day came when I looked and sounded like a woman, then I made a crucial decision: I'm not going to try to do a character; I'm just going to be myself behind this and see what happens. And that's all I did. I had to assume a southern voice because it held my voice up.

TUCHMAN. You developed this character before you created a story?

HOFFMAN. No, at the same time. While Murray was writing drafts—and after that with Larry Gelbart and Elaine May.

. . .

This was *my* project—I was the producer. Pollack's refusal to see me in any role but that of an actor was somewhat paternalistic, just the way the agent sees Michael. I think that some directors are close minded about what an actor can contribute. You'll hear directors say sometimes, "Yes, I got a performance out of that actor; I had to push him. I had to push him further than he thought he could go." Well, there are probably a lot of uncredited occasions where actors have pushed directors into areas that they haven't gone into before, and I think there have been more than a few occasions where a picture is better because of the actor who is in it. They will say, "The actor is subjective—only cares about his own part." Not so. An actor is as capable of considering "the whole" as the director, and often does. Sure we care about our own parts, but we have a responsibility to the entire film also, and I don't think many of us ignore that responsibility. And, believe me, I know some very subjective directors, who focus mostly on covering their ass. Yet actors generally are thought of as somehow less intelligent or responsible or aware of what film-making is about than the director or the producer.

I think Brando once said it—we're housewives, we're these emotional creatures. They say, "We're going to make you look good, just don't argue. Don't try to make the big decisions. Leave that to us. Leave that to the daddies, the husbands." It doesn't have to be that way. I think there should be a real partnership, not the classically imagined situation where a supposedly "solid, objective" director simply "handles" a "neurotic, subjective" actor.

TUCHMAN. This business of you and Pollack having to agree on everything— was that a stipulation he made?

HOFFMAN. No. It's one *I* made. He said, "If I'm going to direct this, I'm going to produce it." I said, "But you're taking away all the controls I've earned over the years I worked on the project." He said, "Well, I won't do it otherwise." So we bargained, and I had to give him final cut. But even that was with an agreement that I would get script and cast approval and that I would go into the cutting room, see it as it was being cut, and be able to disagree and even show alternatives.

What's on the screen is the result of our discussions, our arguments, our fights. If I had not argued, I think the film would be fifty percent different. I'm not saying it would be worse or better, but it certainly would be much different.

TUCHMAN. I've heard that Shelley Winters sometimes builds up a maelstrom of tension on the set and then works out of that somehow. Is fighting really necessary for your performance?

HOFFMAN. No. I heard Sydney say on television that he thought I was neurotic, that he thought I needed to work out that kind of thing, and it's not true. I didn't work that way with Bob Benton in *Kramer,* and I haven't worked that way in most of the films I've done. I've done about fifteen films, and I think I've had a rough time with about three or four directors; Sydney is one of them. Sydney and I had a rough time together, and I wish that he could find it in his mind to see it as it really was, and not the picture he has painted for himself, which is, "I'm the normal, healthy, rational director, and he's the neurotic actor, and I had to sit on him."

I like to be very prepared, and I feel that the success or failure of a film is many times determined before you start principal photography. I wanted rehearsal very much. I was promised two weeks and was grieved that I didn't get it, and that we followed the risky course of starting to shoot with a screenplay that wasn't completed, because Sydney had decided to rewrite the script I had approved. And I think that created a tension that never eased. Never dissipated. We should have had all those disagreements out in a rehearsal room someplace, before we started to shoot, like I did with Benton, and we should have locked in the script before we started. That way we could have avoided most of the delays and arguments during shooting.

The trouble with movies is that it's such an intimate experience, especially for the principals. You get married when you start working together, before you become friends. I don't think Sydney and I ever had a chance to become friends. I don't even know if we would have; I don't know if we're the type of personalities that blend together well.

If you want to get down to the facts of the accusation that I'm "difficult," simply talk to the many directors that I've worked with, and I don't think you'll find more than three or four who would say I gave them a rough time. That doesn't mean I don't "fight" in the sense of questioning decisions—battling if I think they're wrong—but it's not that I "love" fighting or get off on it.
. . .

TUCHMAN. What are the specific reasons you fight with directors when you do?

HOFFMAN. I've done fifteen films now in fifteen years, and I'm learning what does work, what doesn't work. I'm learning about how much self-deception goes on amongst the creators themselves and how many critical errors are casually made—the lack of thought glossed over with glib, pat phrases—"Don't worry about that, it's not important, we don't need that shot." Those "little" mistakes cost the movie, collapse the movie. That's why I fight. I want to know *why* we don't need that shot. If you can convince me, OK, but don't give me unreasoned platitudes.

Somebody told me Picasso said a painter walks around for months with a movie of images in his mind and he winds up with *one* image on canvas—imagine the tension, because he's got fifty million images he's rejecting. Every new stroke destroys the painting before. That's exactly the way a movie is, because we can work on a screenplay, we can work on a structure, we can work until we're blue in the face, then look at the first day of rushes and it's different. It's either worse or it's better, but it's not what it was on the page. You've got to be led by what's on the screen, and yet you work with people sometimes who are not led by that—it's like they're blind. It's not translating from the page, yet they want to stick with it anyway, and you go crazy because you see how little it takes to hurt a film. Another painter once said, "I'm so afraid when I'm painting, because the slightest little thing, the slightest little move, one stroke, collapses the tension of the canvas."

TUCHMAN. What is the appropriate division of labor between the actor, the director, and the producer?

HOFFMAN. I think that the best working relationship I've ever had on any film was *Kramer*. The producer was Stanley Jaffe, the director-writer was Bob Benton. I had this part that was central to the story, and the three of us worked on the script for months and we brought forth our own experiences. We argued, we talked, we fought—and out of it, I think, came a somewhat personal film, by the three of us. I thought it was ideal. We even fought during the filming of it. You can't not fight. I'm not saying what Pollack says—that I live to fight or need it emotionally. I don't. But when you think the film may succeed or fail depending on the decision you're fighting about, it's essential to fight, to question. That's how you get the best out of each other.

Sometimes, I don't think film is set up to get the best work out of anybody. In a sense, it's set up for you to fail, by virtue of the fact that you're told what amount to create every day. And implicitly it's stated that you can't go home again—you're usually not going to get another chance to do retakes, which are very expensive.

Woody Allen told me that he has written in his contract that he can come back during postproduction to shoot maybe twenty, thirty percent of the film, and in that way do what a writer or a sculptor does—you go back and you keep working on it till it's right. Most movies aren't that way. They always say, "Don't worry about the sets; they'll be there." And then they're not there. Studios are funny that way. They don't want you to go back again. Woody Allen told me, "I never shoot sets. That's why I shoot Rockefeller Center, because I know it's going to be there."

That's why I think preparation plays such a major part. But you live in a kind of Looney Tunes atmosphere sometimes in this business. If you say that you spent two or three years on a screenplay, they think you're crazy; why, I don't know. A book can take ten years. But with a screenplay, there's something wrong if you're working on it more than a few months. Yet if you take your time and get it right before you start shooting, you'll save time and money and have a far better film.

TUCHMAN. We hear a lot about "collaborative filmmaking" these days. Is that a concept you approve of?

HOFFMAN. Yes, I like collaborative filmmaking. I like to go on a set and have everyone feel that they can be a part of that film. There is a caste system that exists in filmmaking that I think a few people are trying to break down. No one should just have a job. No one should be told that they're "just" the costumer, just do the costumes, or they're "just" the makeup man, just do the makeup.

You're working with people who are really first-rate in their work, and who do many more films than the directors, the producers, or the stars. The crew members go from one film to another—their credits are triple or quadruple what ours are, and they get a smell of whether the work is fraudulent or real. Some of the best ideas I've ever seen that result in the finished film have come, when allowed, from somebody on the crew. Tommy Priestley, the camera operator on *Kramer*—he was going through the same thing the character in the film was, and he would say, "Jesus, this is right out of my life." And I'd go up to him and I'd talk to him and I'd say, "Tell me. Tell me." And he did. And it's on the screen.

I think it's a family, and I think it can be an emotional, spiritual experience. It still means you have a director—you have someone who has final say—but it doesn't mean that you have an atmosphere where people are afraid to open their mouths. There's no better feeling in the world than to hear a crew laugh at something on the set or to have them applaud or to have them come up and say, "Good take" or to have them *involved* in it. I don't think Dorothy Michaels would be on the screen as she is now without the crew's love for that character. They pulled for her. They wanted her to work. And a great deal of the credit for how well she works is theirs.

TUCHMAN. Given that this sort of familylike situation or noncaste situation is beneficial for filmmaking, you still have talked quite a bit about wanting control.

HOFFMAN. When you see the same mistakes being made year after year, you have to be an idiot not to speak up. Suddenly you're no longer a virgin; you know a couple of things.

To have control means that you can set up an atmosphere. If I initiate a project, I would certainly want to control its destiny. But if a director comes to me with his baby, no, I don't expect to have control of it. At the same time, I've found that I work best when I work in a collaborative way.

I'm not saying that you give a script out to everybody and say, "Tell me what you think." A few key people work on it, and *then* it begins to open up. The art director comes into it, the cinematographer comes into it, the costume-wardrobe people, the editor, etc.—those key people expand it, and all start to add input. You don't want to stifle that. I once read that Ingmar Bergman wrote a letter to his entire crew and cast before he started, saying, "Now that we're starting production, now that we have the script, please feel that this is a family—it is *our* film."

Interestingly enough, what doesn't get any press is that *Tootsie* had a terrific crew and cast. Very close and very warm, and there was a lot of hard, first-rate work on the set every day, and a great spirit.

TUCHMAN. If I were to make an analogy between what you do and something else, it would be Paul Muni. Even when he played a role that was a contemporary person, he seemed to play it as a character actor.

HOFFMAN. After *The Graduate*, everyone said, "Well, Mike Nichols has got this guy who's just playing himself." I got so upset when I read that, I couldn't wait to prove it wrong, and when I chose to do *Midnight Cowboy*, Nichols called up at one point and said, "Are you sure you want to play Ratso Rizzo? It's not even the star role. You're secondary and it's such an unattractive role and you could kill the career that you established with *The Graduate*—you should play Joe Buck." But I was out to show that I was a character actor— and, in fact, Benjamin was as much a character as any part that I had done— and that I was not just this nebbish kid that Nichols found.

I was very affected by Lee Strasberg when I studied with him; he would say over and over again, "There is no such thing as a juvenile or an ingenue or a villain or a hero or a leading man. We're all characters." I was maybe twenty-one years old, I'd just come to New York to study, and it hit me very strong, because I was a victim of casting. Even today, casting people can kill you. Because you sit down, and before you say a word they're going to look at you and without knowing anything about you tell you, "Well, you're not a leading man. You're not a juvenile. We'll cast you as a doctor, or a scientist, maybe." What's much more fun is to get to know someone, and then to see a way of casting that most people wouldn't cast them as. You start to see something coming out that is what they are underneath.

When I was a younger actor, I kept being told I was a "character juvenile"—they meant juvenile delinquent. I was always told by people, "Once you mature, once you get into your forties, you'll start to get character roles." Now, I think that, like everybody else, I want to stay young-looking as long as I can. Aside from my own narcissism, I want to keep the range open. I want to keep that range as wide as I can. One of the reasons I did *Marathon Man* is because I said to myself, This is my last chance to be in college. I just could feel it. I was closing in on forty at that time.

TUCHMAN. How do you prepare?

HOFFMAN. I have a disagreement with some directors—I say actors shouldn't have to "act"; the scene should be constructed in such a way that you don't have to. When I did Ratso Rizzo, an actor told me, "Once you get the limp right, why don't you put rocks in your shoe? You'll never have to think about limping. It will be there; you won't have to worry about it." And I think that's one of the greatest things that anybody ever said, 'cause you shouldn't have to "act." It should be there, like butter—all the work should have been done beforehand—so you don't have to sit there and start jerking up emotion. It should flow.

Brando went out and did research in *Mutiny on the Bounty* and found out that when you die from burns you die from shock, and he found out what shock was like. It was like being encased in water. So when he came to do the shot, he put himself in a bathtub on the ship. When it got time for the close-up, he was in the bathtub filled with ice. So he didn't have to "act" it. That's an extreme example. But I admire his imagination.

God knows I've done enough crap in my life to grow a few flowers, but one of the things that constantly hits me is that when I go outside on the street, what I see is not what I see on the screen, and I never stop thinking about that. I turn on the television, and what I see on the screen is not what I see in real life. It bothers me. I want to get closer to what I see in life. I love to see hair out of place. I love to see people without makeup, or at least with their own blush showing, their own pimples, and their own specific behavior. It's like when you go to New York to shoot, everyone says, "We've got to get the real life of New York City." Well, the minute you rope off a street, you alter it. Movies tend to take out life, and then put back a substitute for it. I think television news has had an incredible impact on film. You see every human emotion in any twenty-four-hour period.

When you turn on the television sometimes, you say, "Is this a documentary?" That's the way you want it to be on film. But, at the same time, you don't want it to be pure documentary, because it's art; you want it to be condensed, subtly heightened. Fellini took background and made it foreground, and once he did that, I was in love with him. He does two things, in other words, at his best: He shows you life the way it really is, and yet as we don't always see it.

Movies are not plays. With plays, you sit in the audience, and the first five rows of the orchestra really get to see the actors, like in a movie. Outside of that, no one gets to see anything. The words are carrying you. In a movie, everyone has a front-row seat, so the words, in a sense, become secondary. Generally speaking, this is a very young art form. We're constantly playing with it. In *The Graduate*, some of the most wonderful moments were accidents. The same is true in *Midnight Cowboy, Tootsie, Kramer*—they're accidents. It's interesting to me what an audience remembers. They don't remember anything differently than they remember from their own lives. What do you remember of your life? This incident, that one, boom, boom—these vivid colors—the rest is like a blur. Of the films that I've done, by and large, people point to the same moments all the time, and they don't remember the rest of the film. They just remember these moments. And a lot of them were improvised, a lot of them were accidents. Banging on the taxi in *Midnight Cowboy,* "I'm walking here," that was an accident. That was a hidden camera, and it was a cab that almost ran us over. Schlesinger left it in, but many directors wouldn't have.

TUCHMAN. Are you hopeful for better-made movies out of this system?

HOFFMAN. If you have truth, if you have honesty, if you do your work beforehand, if they give you the money—and if you get very lucky—how are you ever going to miss making a good film?

You study acting until you're blue in the face and you go out there and it's got nothing to do with what you studied: "Here's your script, here are your lines, here's your mark, hit that, hit that, do this—and that's it. Good-bye and good luck." And you say, "What did I learn? What was I spending ten years learning for?" But, you know, it's not our money; it's their money. If only they would give you the time—but they don't. It seems too expensive. I understand; but I wish it were different. I wish I could convince them that it doesn't have to be more expensive; that rehearsal isn't a dirty word, but a concept that can save money; that rewriting doesn't mean the picture will never be made, just that it will be built on a solid structure; that doing your work *in advance*—even if that preparation takes longer—will save time and money in the end and, more important, will give you far better odds of success. Well, who knows, maybe someday we'll convince them—whoever "they" are.

TUCHMAN. If making movies is frequently a frustrating process that ends up with a disappointing result, where is the gratification?

HOFFMAN. I have great gratification and satisfaction on the finished product of *Tootsie*. I also do with *Kramer*. I do with a lot of films that I've done.

But you always want to go back and change certain things. It's like taking an easel out—you've been looking at this countryside, and one day you take your easel out, and you find a spot, and you put it out there, and you've got your canvas up, and you've got your palette, and you start painting. You're now three hours into it, and suddenly you happen to look down and you hear a noise far off, a train—you look down, and you've put your easel on a railroad track, and you start painting it just a teeny bit faster, and the train now is coming a little bit faster, and you don't want to paint faster, but you have to. And suddenly the train's getting faster and you're painting faster and faster so that just before the train hits, you jump off with the easel, and the canvas and the palette knife go flying all over, and you're just holding on to that canvas as the train rushes past you, and that's the movie.

Jack Nicholson "The Bird Is on His Own"

Tell me about your beginnings.

I got out of high school a year early, and though I could've worked my way through college, I decided I didn't want to do that. I came to California where my only other relatives were; and since I wanted to see movie stars, I got a job at MGM, as an office boy in the cartoon program. For a couple of years I saw movie stars, and then Al Triscone and Bill Hanna nudged me into their talent program. From there I went to the Players Ring Theatre, one of the few little

Excerpt from Beverly Walker, "The Bird Is On His Own" (interview with Jack Nicholson), *Film Comment* 21, no. 3 (May–June 1985), 53–61.

Jack Nicholson in *Five Easy Pieces*
(1970)

theaters in L.A. at the time. I went to one acting class taught by Joy Flynn before Judson Taylor took me to Jeff Corey's class.

Up until then I hadn't cared about much but sports and girls and *looking* at movies—stuff you do when you're 17 or 18. But Jeff Corey's method of working opened me up to a whole area of study. Acting is life study and Corey's classes got me into looking at life as—I'm still hesitant to say—an artist. They opened up people, literature. I met Robert Towne, [Carole] Eastman, [John] Shaner, and loads of people I still work with. From that point on, I have mainly been interested in acting. I think it's a great job, a fine way to live your life.

. . .

What was your first professional engagement?

Tea and Sympathy at the Players Ring. I made $14 a week. During the run I got my first agent, as well as some work on *Matinee Theatre,* a live TV daytime drama. Ralph Acton helped me a lot. . . . During the interim between jobs, I got a part in a play downtown. At the time, the only professional theaters in L.A. were road companies, but there were a lot of little theaters where you were paid about $20 a week. However, in this theater there were too many seats and it couldn't come under a little-theater contract, so I was paid $75 a week.

While I was doing this, I got the lead in my first movie, *Cry Baby Killer.* Jeff recommended me. I read for it just like every other actor in town. I screamed and yelled—I know I gave the loudest reading, if not the best. And when I got the part I thought: "This is it! I'm made for this profession." Then I didn't work for a year.

Still, it seems that you didn't have too difficult a time getting started.

But what I'm talking about covers a three-year period. For the next few years I got a couple or three jobs a year, mostly with Roger Corman, and one or two TV shows. My problem in those days was that I didn't get many interviews. I always got a very good percentage of the jobs I went up for, but the opportunities were few and far between.

It's been said that you gave yourself ten years to become a star. Is that true?

No. Corey taught that good actors were meant to absorb life, and that's what I was trying to do. This was the era of the Beat Generation and West Coast jazz and staying up all night on Venice Beach. That was as important as getting jobs, or so it seemed at the time. I don't reckon it has changed today—but I don't know, because I don't go to classes much.

At the beginning, you're very idealistically inclined toward the art of the thing. Or you don't stick because there's no money in it. And I've always understood money; it's not a big mystical thing to me. I say this by way of underlining that it was *then* and is *still* the art of acting that is the wellspring for me.

In that theoretical period of my life I began to think that the finest modern writer was the screen actor. This was in the spirit of the Fifties where a very anti-literary literature was emerging—Kenneth Patchen and others. I kind of believed what Nietzsche said, that nothing not written in your blood is worth reading; it's just more pollution of the airwaves. If you're going to write, write one poem all your life, let nobody read it, and then burn it. This is very young thinking, I confess, but it is the seminal part of my life. This was the collage period in painting, the influence of Duchamp and others. The idea of not building monuments was very strong among idealistic people. I knew film deteriorated. Through all these permutations and youthful poetry, I came to believe that the film actor was the great "literateur" of his time. I think I know what I meant. . . .

The quality of acting in L.A. theater then was very high because of the tremendous number of actors who were flying back and forth between the East Coast and Hollywood. You could see anybody—anybody who wasn't a star—in theaters with 80 seats. But it always bothered me when people came off stage and were told how great they were. They weren't, really, in my opinion. It was then I started thinking that, contrary to conventional wisdom, film was the artful medium for the actor, not the stage.

The stage has a certain discipline. But the ultimate standard is more exacting in film, because you have to see yourself—and you are your own toughest critic. I did not want to be coming off the stage at the mercy of what somebody else told me I did.

Did you develop any concise image of yourself as an actor? Leading man? Young character actor? And how did your awareness of yourself as a potential commercial commodity square with your anti-structure bias?

I never thought in terms of typing myself, because I wasn't that successful. After an actor has done a few pieces of work, his naiveté is the part of the craft he has to nurture most. You don't want to know it all as an actor because you'll be flat. As a means of supporting that experiential element in film, once I begin to work on a particular movie I consider myself to be the tool of the director.

At about that same time, I had started writing—first with Don Devlin and then with Monte Hellman. I thought of myself as part of the general filmmaking effort. And as my scope broadened, I began to think about directing. I wanted to be the guy who got to say whether the dress is red or blue. I'd still like to make those ultimate decisions. It's like action painting. It's not a question of right or wrong about red or blue, but that only one guy gets to say it—and if you don't get to, you're doing something else. The craft of acting interfaces with this idea.

As an actor, I want to give in to the collaboration with the director because I don't want my work to be all the same. The more this can be done with comfort, the more variety my work has had. I think this is inherent to the actors' craft. It is a chosen theoretical point of departure.

That's a very European attitude.

That's why I've worked with more European directors than the average actor has. They somehow understand that this is where I am coming from. And I'm not doing it to get employment. I'm doing it because I just know that sameness, repetition, and conceptualizing are the acting craft's adversaries, and it seems more intelligent to start off within a framework where those things are, to some degree, taken out of your hands. That doesn't mean I don't exercise my own taste, criteria, and forms of self-censorship; but those elements have to do with who I choose to work with, on what and how it relates to the moment I start and finish. All those factors come into play, but they come into play *before* the action of acting.

Once you've started a film you don't become a wet noodle. You must have that conflictual interface because you don't know, and they don't know. It's through conflict that you come out with something that might be different, better than either of you thought to begin with.

There is one thing I know about creative conflict: once my argument is exhausted, I am not going to be unhappy—whether it moves in my direction or away. That's what the structure does for you. In the real world there's an after-effect of disappointment if you lose an argument. But if, to begin with, you're set up *not* to have this particular autonomy, then you're not disappointed.

I have never felt brutalized as an actor. Many actors do, sometimes, but I've never had that experience. If I'm not happy with the balance, I just won't work with that person again.

You obviously saw Easy Rider *before knowing the critical and public response. Did you have any clue it would become such a bombshell?*

Yes, a clue. Bob [Rafelson] and I were involved in writing *Head* when Dennis [Hopper] and Peter [Fonda] brought in a twelve-page treatment. I felt it would be a successful move right then. Because of my background with Roger Corman, I knew that my last motorcycle movie had done $6 to $8 million from a budget of less than half-a-million. I thought the moment for the biker film had come, especially if the genre was moved one step away from exploitation toward some kind of literary quality. After all, I was writing a script [*Head*] based on the theories of Marshall McLuhan, so I understood what the release of hybrid communications energy might mean. This was one of a dozen theoretical discussions I'd have every day because this was a very vital time for me and my contemporaries.

Did you think it would make you a star?

When I saw *Easy Rider* I thought it was very good, and I asked Dennis and Bert [Schneider] if I could clean up my own performance editorially, which they gracefully allowed me to do. I thought it was some of my best work by far, but it wasn't until the screening at the Cannes Film Festival that I had an inkling of its powerful super-structural effect upon the public. In fact, up to that moment I had been thinking more about directing, and I had a commitment from Bert and Bob to do one of several things I was interested in. Which I did. Immediately after *Easy Rider,* I directed *Drive, He Said.*

But at Cannes my thinking changed. I'd been there before and I understood the audience and its relative amplitudes. I believe I'm one of the few people sitting in that audience who understood what was happening. I thought, "This is it. I'm back into acting now. I'm a movie star."

You really said that to yourself: "I'm a movie star."

Yep. It was primarily because of the audience's response.

How did it feel to wake up the next morning and know definitively that your life had changed—in terms of financial security, creative and other life options?

It didn't happen quite that way—in one big zap. Because of Bob's and Bert's interest in me as a director, I felt on a big upswing before I arrived in Cannes. The screening there was part of a feeling that things were going well for me. Oh, I got an enormous rush in the theater. It was what you would call an uncanny experience, a cataclysmic moment. But you must understand that Dennis was there, Peter was there. We were in the boat together, so I didn't feel the success pointed so singularly at myself.

So I didn't wake up saying, "Gee, my life is going to be different." I still don't wake up that way. I don't leap too easily to results. I'm very suspicious and wary in my way, and still get stung by people who feel I shouldn't even be working. I always expect something horrible next.

Would you care to speculate what about you the public responded to?

It's hard for me to know. I wasn't a babe in the woods. I'd watched a lot of stars, from James Dean to Brando, and I'd seen everybody alive work at MGM. I had a certain old-timer's quality, even though I was young and new, and drew on what I believed before I made it.

You've got to be good at it, number one, and sustain it. There are no accidents. Any kind of sustained ability to go on working is because something is valid in the way you work. The star part is the commercial side of the business—and, frankly, no one knows anything about that. The economic side is really statistical. It's not based on the fact they think you're going to do something good; it's because their economics tell them this is a very good capital venture investment.

From a Jungian concept of archetypes, why is it that certain people become icons for their culture?

I believe that part of the entire theatrical enterprise is to undermine institutions. What did I know? I went from *Easy Rider,* where I played a Southerner effectively enough for a lot of people to think I *was* a Southerner, to *Five Easy Pieces,* where the guy pretends to be a Southerner in the first half but in fact turns out to be from a sophisticated classical-music family.

The other part of the answer is that I am reflective of an earlier audience who didn't find the movie conventions of their time entertaining any longer—who, frankly, found them quite repressive. These same conventions were shortly thereafter flung off by the society as a whole. And once you're rolling, you stay right there in a surf-ride on that sociological curve. The minute your theoretical meanderings aren't valid, your work won't be well received.

For an actor, style comes last. You first have to implement the whole thing, but your style comes from the subconscious, which is the best part an actor brings to his work. These conscious ideas are only the springboard for what you hope will be the real meat from the unconscious.

I see where characters I've played are influencing the culture we live in. Henry Miller wrote an essay called "On Seeing Jack Nicholson for the First Time" about my character in *Five Easy Pieces.* I believe Jules Pfeiffer's writing for *Carnal Knowledge* was very influential. And half the people in the world still call me Randall Patrick McMurphy.

Since Easy Rider *by what criteria do you select projects?*

I look for a director with a script he likes a lot, but I'm probably after the directors more than anything. Because of the way the business is structured today, I have sometimes turned down scripts that I might otherwise have accepted had I known who was directing them. *Witness,* for example.

You've taken more risks with subject matter, supporting roles, or directors than any American star of recent memory. Is the director central in your taking risk?

Yes. There are many directors in the middle range who've made mostly successful pictures, and then there are a few great directors who've had some successes and some failures. I suppose my life would be smoother if I wasn't almost totally enamored of the latter category. My choice pattern hasn't really changed. There were Hopper and Rafelson and, before them, Monte Hellman and Roger Corman. Of course, in that period I had no choice; these are the people who wanted me.

You've definitely been in the vanguard of people interested in serious films, films that made statements. If you'd been in New York in the Fifties, instead of out here, your interest in European cinema and existentialist angst wouldn't have been so unusual. Where do you think your taste came from, and how did it develop?

I imagine that somewhere out in America right now is a guy lookin' at movies and saying: "I can't believe this shit. I'm in high school. I don't have any of these fuckin' lame-o parties and a bunch of lame-o bullshit. I got serious things to do in my life. *Why are they making these movies?* All right, if it's a dog picture, but don't pretend to be makin' this shit about me." That's where I think taste starts to get formed. The desire . . . *not to be insulted.* Right. . . .

Many auteurs are more fascinated by individual stars. They sense something in the star they want to use, like a color on a palette.

Oh, have I found that out! And I'll tell you why: because a star is not a manipulated image. Nobody can prove that better than I. Only that audience out there, that audience which I'm not a terribly affectionate person toward, as you know, makes a star. It's up to them. You can't do anything about it, or I never would've got anywhere. Stars would all be Louis B. Mayer's cousins if you could make 'em up.

And that's what those directors love, because they've studied or written every type of scene from every angle. I've been over every goddamned type of scene, either by myself or with somebody, and I don't want to make a nice movie that's like a great play. I want to make "that other thing." Rafelson's shooting the goodbye scenes; the wind blows, and a bird flies through. It's the oddest thing of all time. Not planned. The audience may not realize it consciously, but somehow they know that is what made the scene right. The written scene is "I love you." The bird is on his own.

Lindsay Crouse "Acting Has to Be *About* Something Else"

L.W. Is it common for actresses in your age-group to be making this many movies?

L.C. I don't really know. Actresses can get very isolated from each other, and so I don't know a lot about what's happening with other actresses. I do know that for women in their forties, there's not a lot of challenging writing. Women, it seems to me, still want to be rescued, appointed, elevated. It's a lot more magical to have the male head of a studio say "You" than to roll up our sleeves and go to work on our own, writing, directing, and creating our own films. We might have to take small salaries and start with something on a small scale which has to do with our own lives and with what we really want to say. We might have difficulty marketing such films at first, and distributing them, and it may be a long ride before we realize this plan. But ultimately if our goal is to tell different kinds of stories, to tell stories that are more internal, maybe to handle these differently in visual terms, maybe to use a different sense of time in such movies, too—then we have to can the titillation and work with each other, make the decision that that's what's necessary and move forward and do it.

"Acting Has to Be *About* Something Else": an interview with Lindsay Crouse, conducted by Leigh Woods (June 1995).

Lindsay Crouse in *The Verdict* (1982)

L.W. I believe that you've founded a production company [Spoolabosch Films] in order to help realize such a plan?

L.C. Well, I started a few years ago to make a documentary, and I'm still in the process of doing it. As a single mother raising two children, I can't always make a beeline toward the things I want to do. I think women's lives are composed more of pieces than they are of simple curves. But I am keenly interested in making my own films. I believe that film is a very, very young medium, and that it's become formulaic in this country. Every once in a while, I'll go to a festival of short films, and it'll absolutely knock me for a loop. There are so many possibilities that we've never even considered. Because films are so costly, experimentation is very limited. Because people tend to go only through certain channels, they don't use their imaginations as much as they might when they're trying to get a film done.

L.W. Do you find yourself getting more involved in other areas of filmmaking besides acting these days?

L.C. I'm less involved in film production right now than I am in teaching and fostering a group of people who can generate work on their own. I am in a workshop at UCLA in creative writing for the spoken word. And I am in acting class myself. I want to help actors change the way they see themselves, help them come up with new definitions of what it means to be an actor. One of the things I'd like to change, in fact, is an old way of thinking that makes actors believe that they're beholden to others as the source of inspiration for their own creative work. I don't think that's true at all.

L.W. And if it is true, it doesn't put you in a very good position as an actor. You're always waiting for someone to hire you.

L.C. It's lousy. As you get older, it's undignified. Sanford Meisner [at the Neighborhood Playhouse], who was one of my acting teachers, said that it takes twenty-five years to make an actor. He was right. It takes at least that long. I'm sure acting's not the only art where a master would say that to an apprentice. Acting is the art of self-revelation, so you not only need the skill to act—you need to know yourself in order to reveal yourself. This takes real maturity. It can take years to begin to have some idea of who you are.

L.W. Let me get back to the idea of "transformation" for actors that you mentioned earlier. It seemed to me that you used the word to mean two different things: the first of those applies to ways in which you think that acting—and the business of characterization—involves transformation, and the other involves your thoughts about the different roles you feel actors might need to take with regard to production. In the first connection, I've been impressed at your ability to change so much in your acting from film to film. How do you account for this quality, or ability, that you seem to have?

L.C. One of my heroes is Alec Guinness, whom I've always identified as the *character* he was playing rather than the person he is. I think that if you have real compassion for the character you're playing, you can "disappear" yourself into the character's world. I think that's the great art of acting. The problem many actors face in this country is that they receive a lot of ratification for being stars. They become logos, commodities. This can be so destructive, because it inhibits an actor from "disappearing" and inhibits an audience from losing themselves in an imaginary world. My interest lies in this kind of character acting. Also for me, acting has always been an extension of my education. So I was thrilled [in *Places in the Heart*] to play a beautician in Texas in 1929 or [in *The Juror*] to play a prosecuting attorney in an important Mafia trial. I've never been to law school, but I don't have to get the degree. I get to *do* that, it's an extraordinary thing. It's a continual education.

L.W. Alec Guinness is British, of course. How much of this acting do you see happening around you in America?

L.C. I don't see much of it around me at all. I think that actors, apart from those in the theater, haven't developed a very strong work ethic in this country. Too many don't consider that they have to practice acting, or train themselves as actors. I don't mean to be judgmental, because film acting does require a certain kind of spontaneity. But if actors have a story to tell, or a text to deal with, they need some kind of control and preparation. I couldn't have done a film like *The Verdict* [in which she played a key supporting role] if I hadn't spent hours on that part. And it's not that I had a huge speech to learn, either. In fact, most of my text consisted of Yes and No. But to achieve some kind of variety, and not be monotonous in what was surely a pivotal scene in the movie, and when I was given only Yes and No to say . . . Anyone who's watched the O. J. Simpson trial knows how boring it is to listen to people saying Yes and No over and over again. So the challenge for me in *The Verdict* was to find the real drama of the scene, and explore the circumstances around it. That took a lot of work.

L.W. Can the sort of acting you describe, and that you admire, be taught?

L.C. Sure. There's such a thing as mastery; and in no way am I calling myself a master. But there are certain things I know, and certain distinctions that must be made for actors, especially because they're always using themselves. This takes a real technique, so that they can be very accessible emotionally and at the same time understand that they're not actually Jesus Christ or Madame Defarge [from Dickens's *Tale of Two Cities*], because otherwise they can damage themselves along the way. So actors need very clearly defined ways of working. Even to get back to being a child with an active imagination—this is something we get away from pretty quickly in our educations. Kids as young as five or six will come home from school and say, "I cannot draw a horse," and that's never been an issue before. They get intimidated by someone's having told them that there's a particular way it should be done. And from that moment on, any teacher's job is to get people to overcome this conditioning. Most actors have to be taught that it's all right to return to the point before such conditioning took over, when children still thought of themselves as unlimited. I once heard Lillian Gish say in an interview that acting can't be taught. I respect what she meant in suggesting that if someone doesn't have sense enough to pit themselves against imaginary circumstances, there's nothing that any acting teacher can say to them. But there are a lot of very talented people who have blocks, or who've been mistaught, or who're just confused or overly intellectual, and these people *can* be taught. An acting teacher told me only last week that I had no right to an interpretation I'd made of a scene that he'd seen a cold reading of. This teacher said that the right of interpretation belonged to the audience in such a situation, and not to me. I disagreed really strongly with this. As I've had more success, I've come to feel that it's my *obligation* to have an interpretation. I'm *supposed* to interpret the material in some way.

L.W. There is an old tradition, based in literary sensibility, that says that a scene can "act itself," and so regards the actor more as a medium for the written word than as an independent interpreter. I've heard this applied to Shakespeare, in particular, a lot.

L.C. I'm really starting to examine the word "interpretation" in the classes I teach. How much of "interpretation," I wonder, lies in protecting yourself against real vulnerability? How much of it is ego? If an actor's job is self-revelation, then what has to be gotten out of the way to achieve that? Acting's really an amazing art, and I've come to respect it more and more with the years. I almost wish that at this stage of my career, I could take time out and be in class every day, five days a week for a year, and get back to first principles. I've done this before in my acting career [see the *Post Script* interview]. One of the great things about being a dancer is that no matter what you're performing at night, the next morning you always start with a *plié*, and so you're always getting back to the very first thing you ever did as a dancer. So [Rudolf] Nureyev is doing a *plié*, and you're doing a *plié*, and everyone else in the class is doing a *plié*. This is a way of getting yourself back to first base all the time, and there's something very profound about that. I think that actors, on the other hand, often get shot out a cannon and experience some kind of meteoric success, and this director or that director wants them for this role or that role; and there are very few stations along this path where you can stop and ask yourself what it is, exactly, that you'd like to symbolize to a group of people. Do I want to take parts that are violent, or do I not? Do I want to take my clothes off, or do I not? Do I want to represent all of humanity—women who strip, women who shoot, women who steal or kill—is that my job? What *is* my job, exactly, and what should my relationship be to an audience? This is such a big question that my students and I can spend entire classes on it.

L.W. In the *Post Script* interview, you talked about the other people on the set serving as your audience.

L.C. That's so true.

L.W. Does that audience vary a lot from set to set?

L.C. It varies in its quality. I just did an afterschool special, a beautiful piece about breast cancer, as it happens. I played a mother with breast cancer who has to deal with her teenaged daughter. After one scene the cameraman wiped off his eyepiece, and he said, "You got me on the wide shot." I said, "That's the nicest thing that anyone's ever said to me!" His remark was totally un-solicited. When the crew says it's good, you know it's good. They've seen a lot of acting, and there's no reason for them to get emotionally involved in it; they have their own work to take care of. If you can hook them, you know you've done your job.

L.W. Are there any other images of audience you use to draw energy or inspiration from?

L.C. I like to think of the audience as myself. I feel that any other assumption is ultimately arrogant and separatist. After all, I go to movies. This year, in my classes, we've been trying to come up with some new definitions of the relationship between the actor and the audience. I ask my students, "Is acting a leadership position?" I believe that it is. Many actors have never thought about this question, or they've assumed that the real leaders are the directors or the producers or the writers. I can't agree with this. I'm very interested in what an actor's intrinsic work in the world is. What are we here to do? Even when we don't have a job, it's important to consider what it is we're doing as actors each day. What if an actor's work were "to acknowledge people when they least expect it?" After all, actors are good at speaking up, and they're very aware of what's really going on between people. I asked my students, "What if the goal of a production were to acknowledge an audience when they least expect it?" By this I don't mean having the actors come to the lip of the stage and say, "What a wonderful audience you are." I mean that what the production stands for would effectively acknowledge the audience, perhaps as listeners, perhaps as people searching for a higher good or as people who should be credited for simply coming to the theatre, or maybe as people who recognize the value of beauty or who commit random acts of kindness, or as fellow adventurers, as explorers, as people furthering their own education. If we dedicated a production to this kind of acknowledgment, it could create a very interesting relationship between the actors and the audience. If we refer to the audience as friends, then we start to think about "them" in a different way—we start to think about "them" as "us." Hollywood promotes the idea of testing films before audiences in artificial and isolated circumstances. I think it's a travesty to take something that's been developed over a year or more by the artists involved, and to grant editing powers to a random group of people who will react to this scene or that in the most superficial way. It's a lark for them. Such a group doesn't comprise a natural audience, because they know that they're coming to perform this particular function, and they find excitement in the power they have to influence a film. It reminds me of the Romans in the Colosseum. Thumbs up or thumbs down. It can be a sick thing, in my opinion.

L.W. I want to get back to your other use of the word "transformation"—the one involving your notion of producing or generating or working on films in a different way than happens generally in Hollywood.

L.C. I worked on a film called *Chantilly Lace* at [Robert Redford's film institute at] Sundance, where we were just seven women. It was an improvisational film; there was no script. We started with a circumstance, which involved a group of women meeting for the fortieth birthday of one of the group. And we created all of the characters and relationships out of this single circumstance. We started by improvising a "first scene," which was very powerful. And then after that, each woman went to Linda Yellen [the director] and recommended very specific events based on the group's initial work. Of course, our ideas of what should happen were very different. We filmed this entire project in only six days, with no one getting paid; but about halfway through it, we found Linda weeping in the basement. She said that she felt like a novelist whose characters had escaped from her. She said that we were all so passionate and involved and there were so many possibilities that had come out of the single scene we'd improvised, that there was no way she could be true to all of us in the space of only six days. It was just amazing how much stuff we [Lindsay, Jill Eikenberry, Martha Plimpton, Ally Sheedy, Talia Shire, Helen Slater, and JoBeth Williams] got out of that one situation. We could have made movies for years to come out of that group and that situation. There were things that each of us would have changed, of course. But we started with an impossible challenge, and what we came up with was good. One of the most amazing things about this is that actors can become very authentic when they have no obligation to speak. And in this project, there was no obligation to speak; it was liberating. Acting teachers will always tell you not to speak until something moves you to do it. But if someone could really direct based on this principle, they could get something extraordinary. This is partly what I meant when I said that film is a very young medium. There are so many things still to be done.

L.W. In the *Post Script* interview, you told Carole Zucker that you thought, "Film is light that you're looking at. You're very transparent when you're on film." Can you elaborate at all on what you meant?

L.C. People think of film as a very documentary medium. They think that life unfolds and you just hold the camera up and capture that. But film is really a very subjective, rhetorical, and poetic medium. If you spend any time on a set watching the director of photography (and you should really read Sidney Lumet's book, just out, called *Making Movies* [Knopf 1995] for its chapter on the director of photography), you'll see how the f-stop [lens opening], the exposure of the film, the filters, the speed of the film, the level of the light, the color of the light, all that happens in the developing process when they're either lifting or reducing the colors, when they're burning the negative or not—you'd be amazed at how *manipulated* that product is. It reminds you of the sort of experimentation the Impressionists did, painting at different times of the day and juxtaposing pigments in different ways. If you look at films from this point of view, your eye would start to show you how different from "real life" they are. The audience is apt to think of what they see as reality, unless they're watching an animated cartoon, but that's not true at all. People who have a good conceptual vision could make extraordinary films, quite unlike anything we've seen before.

L.W. How could an actress make herself a figure of light?

L.C. I think that acting is a delicate art. Its power on a stage is very raw, whereas its power in film is highly refined. In the theatre, an actor is a kind of force field; but in film, it's as if that force is so amplified, it's like shooting sound through a microphone—all you need is a very light kiss. I was just making *The Juror,* and I had a moment as a prosecuting attorney when I stood up and looked at Demi Moore. In that moment, the audience had to see me realize something about her relationship to a mafioso in the courtroom. And then I was supposed to turn my head as the camera panned from me to him and followed him as he left the courtroom and stopped before a statue signifying Justice. A "button," as we call it in the theater. This scene had to serve as an end to the introduction to the film. It was a tricky moment, because on the one hand I had to be very controlled physically, while something had to be really happening inside me. The cameraman came up to me and told me that we'd have to work very carefully together, because he wanted to keep my head on the right side of the frame for the first part of the shot, and then on the left side of the frame for the rest of the shot. As we all know from reading, we give different weights to the left and the right sides of the page. So when he was framing, the cameraman had these values in his head. The analogy to the stage would lie in ways of blocking the actors and placing them on different parts of the stage according to what they need to do and what impression you want the audience to take away from their actions and interactions. This is an elaborate way of saying that there's a visual refinement in films that everyone's working on together. In the theater, you just sort of gouge things out, whereas in film the acting needs a much finer touch. This can represent a real challenge for someone who's come from a background in the theater, because while the process for the actor is the same, the images derive from a different sensibility. I was working with Demi Moore the same way I would in the theater, but there were many more physical restraints when I was shooting the scene for film. There were angles of my face where the light looked better, and so there were certain ways that I couldn't turn my head. There's the demand for a coordination of factors that makes film a very refined art.

L.W. Do you get back to the stage now and again?

L.C. Oh yes. I worked in not-for-profit theater all last year here in Los Angeles.

L.W. Is there any relationship between this kind of theater and the sort of films you have in mind to work on?

L.C. No. I just love working in the theater.

L.W. Does this seem to make any difference in your film work?

L.C. Yes. Film is always "pulled down." So if you get the chance to do something big, it's always going to help you. There's also a lot of fear involved in film work. Movies are always such a big deal, and so they're scary as heck to do. Your tendency is always to pull in a little bit. So the theater gives me a chance to get out there and work on things in a bigger, freer way. I worked on a big melodrama called *The Tavern* by George M. Cohan. I played an orphan who's totally wacko: she accuses every man she meets of being the person who ruined her life. It was the most fun ever.

L.W. Was it a comedy?

L.C. Yeah, I hope so!

L.W. As someone who was born and bred on the East Coast, do you feel you have to live near Hollywood in order to have the kind of career that you want?

L.C. Yes, because film directors don't go east to cast anymore. When I started out in the movies, directors would come to New York and they'd see you in some stage performance, and then you'd get a call asking you to interview for some film they were doing. Film directors themselves were doing the casting. Now casting agents do the casting, and so everybody's here. Also, the economic situation has changed a lot in the last twenty years, so that many actors can't afford to live in New York on theatrical salaries any more. The year before I moved out here, I did three plays in New York, and they were three of the nicest experiences I've had. But you could hardly call it making a living, and I couldn't have paid for even one of my children's schooling. Theater now is something that you do because you love it, unless you can work on Broadway all year—and of course there's never any guarantee of being able to do that.

L.W. Do you think about doing other jobs in film besides acting?

L.C. I'd love to direct.

L.W. Where do the costs lie with the sort of career you've chosen?

L.C. It can cost you with your children. Mine have regularly wished that I were "normal," so that, for instance, I could actually *plan* to be at their

Christmas play. Shirley Knight and I were talking one night and exchanging stories of the incredible efforts we'd made to get to some performance or other by some small child, when our getting there had depended on our hitchhiking, or taking the Concorde, or twisting the arm of some producer so that we could be shooting on this day instead of on that one. You just can't plan anything. And as you get older, you might really like to study a language or take music lessons or study karate, or maybe you'd simply like to raise your children in one town; but then, suddenly, you get a picture that's three months on location—in the *Arctic*! Or even if you're living out here, in Los Angeles, you might get three months on location in Boston. Then you have to say: "OK, I'll do the two films, and I'll take my children out of school, and I'm going to transport them across the country, and I'm going to put them in another school." And the kids get totally messed up, because the curriculum is different, and they're doing the math this year that they did last year in school. So there are many decisions you have to make along the way in trying to control the cost of the business. Do you take a stand that your children are going to stay in school, and you'll go off alone and only take them out of school for a bit, or do you uproot them? It's disorienting for the kids either way. It can also wreak havoc in marriages, because the spouse is not the priority. Your career is. And so if somebody's mother dies, or he's going through a period of depression and needs support, and you're off on location, it can get rough. People think of the film business as very glamorous, but it has a terrific cost on actors' lives. You get up for work, and you're being driven somewhere at 4:30 in the morning in the freezing rain to a dirty trailer somewhere in Nyack, New York, and the generator's not on so there's no heat or water. You can't use the bathroom. There's mud outside the trailer, and there's nobody there yet with umbrellas or capes, and you have to get to the makeup trailer and you're soaked and freezing. It can be really, really hard.

L.W. Well, with all of this, can you say that you're having the sort of career you want to have?

L.C. It's a deeper question than you might think, because who knows why they're having the sort of career they're having? I think that I'm more excited now about acting and the possibilities around it than I've ever been before. I'm also happier that I chose to be an artist than I ever have been. I feel less competitive than I ever have; I feel less inclined to worry about success than I ever have. I'm so interested in the work of acting and the fun of it and the exploration that goes with it. And through all the difficulty, then, I find myself just trying to keep my sense of humor. When that goes under, then I'll know

I'm in big trouble. I think my children would tell you that I do pretty well around them, at least.

L.W. Does all this mean that it's harder for women to work as film actors than it is for men?

L.C. Well, the business can be hard on women if they have strong opinions, which often come with experience. This is partly why more strong roles aren't written for older actresses. In spite of the women's movement and the declared right of women to have a voice, the reality is slow to take effect. I'll give an example. In almost every role I play as an authority figure, I am told by the "higher ups" in production that I must wear a jacket. If the character seems comfortable and is working on her own turf, I might ask to wear a sweater or a soft blouse. No, the answer comes back, she's working in a man's world; she can't afford to give an inch. Oh dear, I think, doesn't this character *have* the job?

L.W. Are you excited about upcoming projects?

L.C. First I have to finish up my work on *The Juror,* and then I'm not really sure what I'll be doing next.

L.W. Does it happen often that you don't know what you'll be doing next?

L.C. All the time. I'm learning to surf.

L.W. Literally?

L.C. No, it's a metaphor, one I think about since moving out here. [laughter] Uncertainty doesn't bother me as much as it used to but I'm a very industrious person and I like to be working. I also take class, I teach, I have my writing workshop, and I have my children. It's a very full life.

L.W. What have been your impressions of the effects of celebrity on movie-making, particularly since you've been living on the West Coast? Is this something that's affected you? Does it have larger effects on filmmaking in general?

L.C. I couldn't begin to tell you what creates actual celebrity. I know from firsthand experience that celebrity and talent are not always synonymous; but everyone knows that already. If, in your life, you shoot for celebrity, what are you really doing? For me, the only reason to play on a world stage is to have the chance to play with world-class players. That's the fun of it. I did my second movie [*All the President's Men*] with Robert Redford and Dustin Hoffman and my third [*Slap Shot*] with Paul Newman. That was pretty heady, and it gave me a taste of what the pros were like. But to me, it doesn't really matter what "stage" you're on, because you can have an extraordinary experience even in a small off-Broadway house. Right now, the scene is confusing for some of the same reasons that professional sports are. Some actors are bathing in champagne, and others can't support their families. This set of extremes hurts the team, and movies are a total team sport. When everyone's value is recognized, the set is charged with creativity.

L.W. Has the business changed much in the twenty years you've been making movies?

L.C. Yeah, it's changed a lot. It's referred to now as "the industry." Not an evocative word, very different from "filmmaking." It's easy to feel as if you're working for Mattel Toys. It's hugely corporate.

L.W. Does this demand compromise?

L.C. You have to take things step by step and moment by moment. Each film that comes up is a separate case, and you have to consider it on its own merits.

L.W. Do you get sent a lot of good scripts?

L.C. No. Some. There are not a lot of good scripts around.

L.W. Why is that?

L.C. I think it's because there's no place for the writers to write. Even in the old studio system—which I'm sure could be real hell sometimes—there were people hired as writers. They wrote a certain number of films a year, and they were put on a salary to write those films. Now there's such a struggle to get any screenplay put on that I wonder why any writer would ever be motivated to write another one. The atmosphere either nourishes and promotes writers, or it doesn't. And here, it doesn't. The theater is the same way. You can't have the *New York Times* condemning every play that comes along and then expect there to arise a new generation of playwrights. It just isn't going to happen. Playwrights will try it once, and then they'll slink away. Maybe it would have taken them ten plays before they could write a good one. I was home the day that [Lindsay's former husband] David Mamet wrote *Glengarry Glen Ross.* He wrote it in four hours. He went upstairs, I heard the typewriter going, and he didn't stop for four hours. When he came down, he said to me: "I don't know what I just did. Would you take a look at this?" But it was the preparation from what he'd written during *years* before that allowed him to go upstairs and just shoot that play through his system. He really didn't know what he had; it just came through him. The creative process can be like that. You go through all kinds of pushing and pulling and striving and struggling; and you can do maybe five projects where you're criticizing yourself the whole way, saying "I didn't like that, . . . I want to do this better." Then all of a sudden, because of all that awareness, something comes sailing through you. You may not even take credit for it when it happens. For most of my best work, I can't even feel that I really did it. Instead, I'm apt to feel that I got lucky, or that I prepared well, or whatever. You just want to get there again. But then you have to get back to self-criticism and this process of pushing and pulling again. You get it wrong, you overact, you underact, you push too hard, or you get railroaded by a director. It never stops.

L.W. When you consider the roles you've done on film, can you identify one that's been the most difficult?

L.C. I think *House of Games* was pretty difficult, because it was so restricted.

L.W. It's surely one of the most stylized American films I've seen.

L.C. People have asked me whether it was fun to make. It wasn't fun. I wouldn't use that word for it. It was like threading a needle all the time.

L.W. Did you feel that you were able to do most of what you wanted?

L.C. Yes. I had different ideas of what I wanted to do than David [Mamet] did. But it was his first film, and he had written it and was directing it. He wanted to realize his vision of the film, and I respected that. I think that *Daniel* was hard, too, because I really wanted to do justice to a Jewish woman of that time and place [New York City in the 1940s and 1950s, during the McCarthy period]. I felt a tremendous moral obligation to speak for a character [Ethel Rosenberg, executed for spying for the Soviets] who was dead and therefore mute. I wanted to do that part justice, because I felt that Ethel Rosenberg had been so submerged in the hysteria of the times that she never was allowed her own voice.

L.W. You spoke about the Cohan comedy you did on stage. Have you done any film comedies?

L.C. Well, I just did *Bye Bye, Love*. I've done a lot of comedy on stage, but most of my films have been dramas. I'd love to do more comedies.

L.W. Are there any movies that you've made that cause you pain when you watch yourself in them?

L.C. No, but I'm always critical. I don't like to go to dailies unless the director asks me to look at something in particular. Sometimes, a director will say that he wants me to see the effect I'm making, because he may think that it's different from the one I'm after or he's after. I'll take a deep breath then, and look at dailies. But I think it's very hard to judge yourself in something while you're participating in it.

L.W. So can you imagine ever directing yourself in a film?

L.C. Sure. But how would I complain about the director? [laughter] I think I'd rather direct other actors.

L.W. If you could cast a film yourself, could you choose happily from among people you know?

L.C. I could cast fifteen movies tomorrow. Not only do I know a lot of people, but none of them are working. [laughter] I know a lot of really talented people. SAG [the Screen Actors' Guild] can give you percentages of people who are working at any given time, and it's not a pretty picture.

L.W. What's your favorite among your own performances?

L.C. I like *The Verdict*.

L.W. Was that only the one scene for you?

L.C. It was really two, but there was mostly the one big one.

L.W. You were at the turning point in that movie, as I recall.

L.C. Yes. What a gift that part was! It was a very small role, but everything hung on that trial scene. Very dramatic. I felt enormous pressure doing it. My husband had written the film, and my favorite director was directing me. On the day of the shooting he saw my fear, and as I took the stand, he leaned over and whispered, "Kaitlin, just talk." Calling me by the character's name was such a vote of confidence. I loved doing that film.

L.W. Wasn't *All the President's Men* like that, too?

L.C. Yes, but the scenes weren't so pivotal. There's a beautiful supporting cast in that film, and we all had wonderful scenes. It's one of the things that lends the film its fine quality.

L.W. *Eleanor and Franklin* was made for TV?

L.C. Yes.

L.W. And released later as a feature film?

L.C. I'm not sure. I played only a tiny role in it, as one of Eleanor Roosevelt's old friends from school.

L.W. Have you done much television?

L.C. Yes, a lot.

L.W. Is it distinct from the stage and film?

L.C. Oh, my God, yes. Here's television: You get a call in New York on a Saturday night that you're being hired to do three episodes of *Hill Street Blues,* and you're going to start on Monday. So you scramble around and somehow fly out to the coast on Sunday, and nobody's around then. So you get on the set and they throw you into your uniform, and they slap your gun belt and your nightstick on you and you walk about like an idiot with those things on. And somebody says "Go," and you do it. And about the second shot in, you get introduced to the director. [laughter]

L.W. When do you get the script?

L.C. Somewhere around Sunday night. I did an episode of *LA Law* where I had a summation speech to a jury, and the final version of the speech came in at about 9:00 P.M. the night before shooting. It was a long speech, and they wanted to shoot it in one shot so there was no way to learn half of the speech before lunch and the other half for the afternoon. That was another time when I started to shake. In fact, that was one of the few times I've caught sleeping sickness; I started to pass out as soon as I got handed the script because there was so much pressure. And in that case, the lateness of the script was for the best of reasons, because the writer wanted to feel really good about what he was giving us. But the long and short of it is that in television, there's no rehearsal, there's no discussion, and you just plunge in. When you're working on a series, then there's more time. You're working with the same people day in and day out, and you work closely with the writers. Under those circumstances you have some breathing room to develop a character.

L.W. Were you on *Hill Street Blues* for a while?

L.C. I did only a few episodes.

L.W. Were you able to settle in?

L.C. I felt that by the last episode, I was ready to start. That's how it is with pilots, too. Often, by the last day you feel that you're just about ready to begin work on the character.

L.W. Does television work to keep you away from acting in films?

L.C. Yeah, but it's also a matter of where I'm placing my attention right now—trying to get as much movie work as I can.

L.W. What would draw you back into television?

L.C. A great series would. And that would mean a wonderful character to play. Or a children's show for television. And of course any drama for T.V.

L.W. How would you recognize the prospect for a good series, before it went into production?

L.C. In a pilot, you need to see a character that you really want to portray, and see that character in a set of circumstances that appeals to you. For instance, if someone offered me the role that I played in *Hill Street Blues* as a series, I'd do it in a minute. The character was a gay cop, and she had a lot of interesting issues to deal with. Her romantic interests would have been unusual, the group of people that she would be speaking for would be interesting, and the issues involved with her being in a position of authority would be complex. It would be fun to do that.

L.W. Do you choose film projects in the same way? Do screenplays lay out characters with ready-made qualities about them that you can identify?

L.C. Yes. I look for either a character or a story that interests me.

L.W. Do you ever trust to the film director, in a case where the screenplay might be rough or sketchy?

L.C. Yes, because screenplays are often very sketchy. A screenplay is such a living organism that it's sometimes hard to tell anything from the version of the screenplay you read at first. I once signed on for a script that changed so much between the time I expressed interest in it and the time I got the job, that it was almost unrecognizable to me.

L.W. What would be the other variables you might weigh if the screenplay didn't bowl you over?

L.C. I'd weigh who the writer is and who the director is. If it's a studio, which one? And if there's an audition, what kind of atmosphere prevails? Are people willing to say that they're aware that there are problems with the screenplay? Are the problems being work on? Has the writer just been fired from the project? Is there a new writer coming in? Is there someone great to play opposite?

L.W. Can you tell while making a movie whether you're going to like it or whether it will be received well?

L.C. There are certain things you can glom onto. If it's a children's film with special effects, you can pretty well say that if the studio will push it and it has a wonderful story, then it will probably be a successful film—if the actors don't mess it up. But then again, there are films and series that I wouldn't have bet a nickel on, and they turned out to be absolutely extraordinary. Very often my agent says to me, "Lindsay, just *go* [to the audition or interview]." Because you do not know, sometimes, especially with a pilot, what might happen with it.

L.W. How else have you supported yourself when you're not doing films?

L.C. I coach actors. I've done voices for cartoons. I do a lot of books for tape. And I do a lot of narration. I really like doing these things, too.

L.W. Have you done commercials?

L.C. No.

L.W. Would you?

L.C. They would have to be very special commercials for products that I'd really like to get behind. I've auditioned for some commercials, because I really liked what the commercials were going to represent. But going up for commercials becomes its own little mini-career, and it takes a lot of time, so I haven't done it much.

L.W. Have you ever been away from acting for an extended period?

L.C. No. Even when I had my kids, I was able to keep acting.

L.W. Is this unusual, in your experience?

L.C. I don't really know. Most people in the business have hiatuses and downtimes. But I like to work, so I'll often take small parts—like this after school special I just did, or public service announcements. I'll do little things as well as bigger ones.

L.W. What sorts of changes can you envision in moviemaking over the next few years?

L.C. The business is getting very top-heavy. The good that might come out of this is that we would return to . . . nothing. Those who aren't getting much at all from the business will return to nothing. And then, they'll start to create from nothing. You might see more oddball little movies sprouting from some play or from someone's passionate interest in something or other or from a group of actors getting together and organizing something on their own or from a new studio that might get created from the grass roots upward.

L.W. Are there any signs that this is beginning to happen?

L.C. It's not so much that there are signs as that it's logical that it should happen. It's in the air. People will stop counting on the profession to be there for them, and then they'll turn to their own resources. Most of the actors at my level in the film business are not just acting any more. They're doing other things, like writing, for instance. Many of them are interested, as I am, in working on a smaller scale with people they like. And it's good for everybody when that happens.

L.W. Do you think that Hollywood as we know it will eventually dissolve?

L.C. I don't know. But it doesn't really matter, either.

L.W. Doesn't it matter if you want to keep the house and the pool?

L.C. The house and the pool can go. That would be OK. I've never objected to Hollywood in that sense. It's like what kids say: "Let the cheaters play." Hollywood's corrupt, it's crazy, it's without any priorities that people who are artistic can really understand. But that's what it is, and it's certainly allowed me to do some work that I never could have done otherwise. So when you ask me whether my career is what I'd like it to be, I could give you an entire fantasy of what I'd like my career to be that it isn't. But I don't grind my teeth all night over this, either. I just have to recognize what Hollywood's values appear to be, and know that those values are different from mine.

L.W. How do your ideal-career fantasies run?

L.C. If I had my druthers, I'd make three or four independent films a year. And if I didn't get to do that many films a year, I'd work in the theater. But doing at least two independent films a year would make me so happy. I say "independent" to include films made by people who are passionate or concerned about something, and where everyone's there to tell a story and they're not primarily interested in the money or their own billing—or where, at least, these motives are not paralyzing or determining entirely the film that gets made.

L.W. What sorts of things do you find yourself saying in your workshops? Do you have a "mantra"?

L.C. It's just that sometimes we get so stuck with the way things are that we don't see what's possible right in our own backyard. We overlook very talented people who are near us, and who could provide us with a resource. And we often sit around complaining. If we just shifted our attitudes a little bit, we could be at work that very afternoon. I've seen a lot of discouragement and despair on the part of a lot of very, very good people who feel helpless around the problem of beginning something they think will be worthwhile. I think that could change overnight, if we could become more practice- and less product-oriented, if we could be more devoted to the adventure of the work and not think of how much money we're making or how much credit we might receive. Acting has to be *about* something else. It's a life that allows for tremendous heart and extraordinary opportunities. I don't just say this in my workshops, but to myself as well, every day. I think, too, that it's really important to be creative in broad terms. I use the other arts a lot in the workshops. I teach my classes to visual artists, to musicians, to sculptors, and to singers; these things are all interrelated.

L.W. I heard [playwright and screenwriter] Arthur Miller say once that he thought there would be great theater in the United States —and he may have been including films, too—when America found itself in crisis, as it did during the Depression.

L.C. Those are the times when people are forced to draw on their own resources and when they're reminded of what's really valuable to them. If this whole tower that's called Hollywood falls over, things will grow from the debris. Film, like the other arts, will never disappear entirely. People were painting in caves a long time ago. I don't worry about whether or not it will continue.

Biographies of Film Actors

Arliss, George (*b.* George Augustus Andrews, Apr. 10, 1868, London; *d.* 1946). Arliss made his London stage debut at eighteen. In 1902 an American tour brought him great success and he stayed for twenty years, to appear in many Broadway productions and films. He was particularly popular for his stage portrayals of such historical figures as Voltaire, Richelieu, Disraeli, and Alexander Hamilton, a specialty he was later to transfer to the screen.

In 1921 he made his first film appearance in *The Devil*, an adaptation of the Molnar play, in which he had appeared on Broadway in 1906. That same year he repeated another Broadway success in a silent film version of *Disraeli*. A sound version of the same film brought him an Academy Award for 1929–30.

Arnold, Edward (*b.* Gunther Edward Arnold Schneider, Feb. 18, 1890, New York City; *d.* 1956). He was a character star of Hollywood films who grew up on New York's Lower East Side. In 1907 he appeared on the stage with Ethel Barrymore in *Dream of a Summer Night*. In 1915 he was engaged by the Essanay studio in Chicago as a cowboy star and appeared in some 50 silent two-reel action pictures before returning to the stage in 1919. In 1932 he returned to the screen and become one of Hollywood's most versatile and convincing character actors, specializing in authoritative roles—judges, senators, uncompromising businessmen—as well as in roles of amiable scoundrels. In all, he appeared in some 150 pictures. Best remembered for his leading roles in *Diamond Jim* (1935) and *Sutter's Gold* (1936) and in Capra's *You Can't Take It with You* (1938) and *Mr. Smith Goes to Washington* (1939).

Astor, Mary (*b.* Lucille Vasconcellos Langhanke, May 3, 1906, Quincy, Ill.; *d.* 1987). Astor was a delicately beautiful star of silent and sound films. Driven by a career-minded German-immigrant father, she entered a beauty contest at fourteen and films at fifteen. After playing an assortment of small roles, she coasted to stardom in 1924 as John Barrymore's leading lady in *Beau Brummel*. She remained an important screen personality through the remainder of the silent era and through the 1940s. A secret affair with playwright George S. Kaufman, Hollywood's most publicized scandal of the 1930s, almost ruined her career, but she quickly returned to the screen, typically playing elegant, sophisticated, often bitchy women-of-the-world. After 1949 she was seen in films only occasionally, in character parts.

Barrymore, Lionel (*b.* Lionel Blythe, Apr. 28, 1878, Philadelphia; *d.* 1954). The son of Maurice Barrymore (Herbert Blythe) and Georgina Drew, and brother of Ethel and John Barrymore, he made his stage debut with his parents while still an infant but did not act professionally on a regular basis until his late teens. By 1902 or 1903 he was playing lead roles on Broadway.

The first Barrymore to appear in films and among the first legitimate stage stars to actively seek a screen career, he joined Biograph in 1909 and began playing leading roles in films two years later. He appeared in many of D. W. Griffith's early films, including *The New York Hat, The Informer, The Musketeers of Pig Alley* (all 1912), and *Judith of Bethulia* (1914). In 1915 he appeared in the Pearl White serial *The Exploits of Elaine* and its sequel, *The Romance of Elaine,* and later played leading roles for various studios.

Barrymore continued appearing regularly on the Broadway stage until 1925, when he finally abandoned the theater completely to devote his talents exclusively to acting in films. In 1926 he signed with MGM, a studio with which he remained associated for the remaining twenty-seven years of his film career. He continued playing leading-man roles for several years but gradually moved into character parts and in the 1930s and 1940s became established as one of Hollywood's foremost character stars. In all, he played some 250 screen roles of varied character and range. He won an Academy Award for his performance in *A Free Soul* (1931). In the late 1930s and early 1940s he was popularly identified with the role of Dr. Gillespie, which he played in all 15 films of the *Dr. Kildare* series.

Brandauer, Klaus Maria (*b.* June 22, 1944, Altaussee, Austria). A graduate of the Academy of Music and Dramatic Arts in Stuttgart, he became famous throughout the German-speaking world for his distinguished performances on the German and Austrian stage. He was virtually unknown elsewhere, however, when he stunned moviegoers with his extraordinary portrait of a moral coward in István Szabó's Hungarian-German film *Mephisto* (1981). Named Best Actor at Cannes for this performance, he went on to play character leads in many other international productions. He was nominated for an Academy Award as Best Supporting Actor for *Out of Africa* (1985).

Brando, Marlon (*b.* Marlon Brando, Jr., on Apr. 3, 1924, Omaha, Nebr.). He attended the Dramatic Workshop in New York for one year and, following a season of summer stock on Long Island, made his Broadway debut in 1944 as Nels in *I Remember Mama.* In 1947, Brando exploded into Broadway stardom with his forceful portrayal of Stanley Kowalski in Tennessee Williams' *A Streetcar Named Desire.* His naturalistic style of acting and his casual, mumbling delivery also heralded the arrival of the Method as a fashionable style of acting. In the late 1940s he became one of the early members of the Actors' Studio, a workshop for professional actors.

In 1950, Brando brought his Actors' Studio training and his magnetic, rebellious personality to the screen. In his film debut he played an embittered paraplegic in Stanley Kramer's *The Men*. He was nominated for an Academy Award as Best Actor four successive years: for his performance in the film version of *A Streetcar Named Desire* (1951), for the title role of *Viva Zapata!* (1952), for his Marc Antony in *Julius Caesar* (1953), and for his portrayal of Terry Malloy in Kazan's *On the Waterfront* (1954). He won the Oscar for the 1954 effort and also received the New York Film Critics Award and the Cannes Film Festival prize for his work in *On the Waterfront*.

In the 1960s, unable to find proper roles and unwilling to cooperate with most directors, he played in a succession of unsuccessful movies. But he made a remarkable comeback in the early 1970s with superb performances in two extremely diverse roles. His powerful portrayal in the title role of *The Godfather* brought him a second Oscar. He won another Oscar nomination as well as unanimous acclaim for his study of middle-age sexuality in Bernardo Bertolucci's controversial *Last Tango in Paris*. Although he has chosen to limit his screen appearances in size and frequency, Brando has remained a charismatic film personality, capable of commanding huge fees even for cameo roles.

Brooks, Louise (*b*. Nov. 14, 1906, Cherryvale, Kans.; *d*. 1985). She began her professional career at age fifteen as a dancer with the Ruth St. Denis company. Appearances in George White's Scandals and the Ziegfeld Follies led to a Hollywood contract and a 1925 film debut in a bit role. A pretty, shapely brunette with a boyish bob hair style, she was cast at first in routine flapper comedies but gradually emerged as a talented actress in such films as Hawks's *A Girl in Every Port* and Wellman's *Beggars of Life*. But her true worth as an artist was revealed in Germany, where she gave remarkable performances for director G. W. Pabst in *Pandora's Box* and *Diary of a Lost Girl*. She gave another sparkling performance in a French film, *Prix de beauté*, then returned to Hollywood, where she was offered minor roles in minor films.

Unable or unwilling to reacclimate herself to the film colony, she retired from the screen in 1931. In the mid-1950s she was rediscovered by film cultists when some of her old films were rescreened in Europe and the United States. In 1956 she settled in Rochester, New York, at the urging of James Card, curator of the George Eastman House collection. There she studied film and devoted herself to writing for film periodicals.

Chaplin, Charlie (Sir Charles Spencer Chaplin, *b.* Apr. 16, 1889, London; *d.* 1977). When he was seventeen he took the first important step of his career when he joined the successful Fred Karno company. It was with Karno that Chaplin acquired his basic comic skills and the rudiments of the style that was to be immortalized in his films.

Chaplin went on a U.S. tour with one of the troupes in 1912, and it was during this tour that Mack Sennett, the boss of Keystone, caught a glimpse of him. In December 1913, Chaplin joined Keystone. In early films for Keystone he played mainly in support of such established comedy stars as Fatty Arbuckle and Mabel Normand. After less than three months as a screen actor in eleven one- and two-reel films, Chaplin was seized with an urge to direct. He now began shaping the character of Charlie the Tramp.

Chaplin made thirty-five films during his year at Keystone, many of which he also wrote and directed. By the end of the year he was a popular screen comedian, and he went on to sign with Essanay in 1915. The Essanay period saw the full bloom of Charlie's screen character, the invincible vagabond, the resilient little fellow with an eye for beauty and a pretense of elegance who stood up pathetically yet heroically to overwhelming odds and somehow triumphed.

Chaplin made *The Kid* (1921), his famous first feature-length film, for First National. *The Kid* revealed Chaplin's growing tendency to inject sentiment into his work. In 1919, Chaplin had founded United Artists Corporation in partnership with Mary Pickford, Douglas Fairbanks, and D. W. Griffith. Through United Artists he released *The Gold Rush* (1925). Considered by many to be his masterpiece, it is a poetic culmination of Chaplin's film art that contains some of the most memorable moments of comedy and pathos in his entire body of work.

Despite his continued success and popularity in such pictures as *The Circus* (1928), *City Lights* (1931), and *Modern Times* (1936), Chaplin was evidently uncomfortable with the requirements of the feature-length format and the inevitability of dialogue. His sound-era features were spaced years apart and became appreciated more for vignette highlights than for their total impact as fully integrated productions. *The Great Dictator* (1940) featured his last appearance as the little tramp, and to many of his fans it signified the end of an era in film comedy.

Chekhov, Michael (*b.* Aug. 29, 1891, St. Petersburg; *d.* 1955). Nephew of playwright Anton Chekhov and a noted stage actor and director in Russia and Germany, he worked in close association with Konstantin Stanislavsky and Max Reinhardt. He emigrated to England, where he founded the Michael

Chekhov Theatre and a drama school. He later settled in the United States, founded another acting school, and appeared in character roles in Hollywood films from 1944 until his death. He was nominated for an Oscar for his performance in Hitchcock's *Spellbound* (1945).

Cherkasov (also Cherkassov), Nikolai (not to be confused with Nikolai P. Cherkasov, or Cherkassov, also known as N. Cherkasov-Sergeiev, who played the title role in Pudovkin's *General Suvorov* (1941) and leads in other Soviet films; *b.* July 27, 1903, St. Petersburg; *d.* 1966). A graduate of the Leningrad Theater Institute, he first appeared on the stage in 1926 and made his film debut the following year. One of the USSR's most commanding actors, he was cast in leading roles of heroic proportions in many outstanding Soviet films, notably the title role in Eisenstein's two-part *Ivan the Terrible* (1944–1946).

Compson, Betty (*b.* Eleanor Luicime Compson, Mar. 18, 1897, Beaver, Utah; *d.* 1974). She started out in vaudeville at fifteen, billed as the Vagabond Violinist. A stunning blonde, she broke into films in 1915 as the heroine of Al Christie's comedy shorts. She appeared in dozens of these during the next three years, then emerged as a dramatic star in *The Miracle Man* (1919), opposite Lon Chaney. She was one of Hollywood's top stars during the 1920s, appearing in numerous silent films from Paramount and other studios. She closed out the silent phase of her career on an upbeat note by playing two of her most memorable roles in Tod Browning's *The Big City* and Josef von Sternberg's *The Docks of New York* (1928). She made a smooth transition to sound and for a while continued to play leads, but she gradually slipped into minor productions and supporting parts and finally retired from the screen in 1948.

Crawford, Joan (*b.* Lucille Fay Le Sueur, Mar. 23, 1904, San Antonio, Tex.; *d.* 1977). As Billie Cassin (her stepfather's name) she appeared in night spots in Detroit and Chicago and was in a Broadway chorus line when she was spotted by MGM for a Hollywood contract.

During the flapper era of the late 1920s she rivaled Clara Bow as the personification of Charleston-dancing flaming youth. In the socially conscious 1930s she was the incarnation of the Depression-wise working girl reaching out for the top. Later in the decade and in the early World War II years she represented Hollywood glamour at its shiniest. In the 1940s, following the termination of her MGM contract after she was written off as "box-office poison," she bounced back as a superstar at Warner Brothers, in a new image, playing the suffering heroine of pulp melodramas and winning a 1945 Academy Award for her performance as the sacrificing mother in *Mildred Pierce*. During the 1950s she played mature femme fatales, and in the 1960s, when again she was considered through in the business, she came back triumphantly in the horror genre as the co-star of her former rival, Bette Davis, in the surprise box-office hit *What Ever Happened to Baby Jane?* (1962).

Cronyn, Hume (*b.* July 18, 1911, London, Ontario, Canada). He made his stage debut with the Montreal Repertory Theatre in 1930 while still a student. By 1934 he had reached Broadway and soon gained a reputation for excellence and versatility. He became especially adept at portraying ordinary people—at times fanciful, at others pathetic, and on occasion quite despicable. In 1942 he married Jessica Tandy, who acted with him in many plays. Cronyn's screen career, although secondary to his stage work, has been consistently impressive for memorable supporting parts of a tremendous range. He has appeared in such films as *Shadow of a Doubt* (1943), *The Postman Always Rings Twice* (1946), *Conrack* (1974), and *The World According to Garp* (1982).

Crouse, Lindsay (*b.* May 12, 1948, New York City). The daughter of playwright-librettist-screenwriter Russel Crouse (1893–1966), she began her performing career as a modern and jazz dancer, then moved on to acting on stage and television and in films. While appearing in more than a dozen films, such as *The Verdict* (1982) and *House of Games* (1987), she has maintained a career as a stage actress on both American coasts, in classic and contemporary plays.

Daniels, Jeff (*b.* 1955, Georgia). This placid leading man of Hollywood films who often plays young professionals in conflict, trained at Central Michigan and Eastern Michigan Universities and at the Circle Repertory Company in New York City. Daniels played stage roles at the Circle Repertory beginning in the mid-1970s, won an Obie Award for his solo performance there in *Johnny Got His Gun,* and acted for the first time on Broadway in Lanford Wilson's *Fifth of July*. He began his film career with a small role in *Ragtime* (1981) and has since appeared in films at a rate of more than one per year, including *Terms of Endearment* (1983), *The Purple Rose of Cairo* (1985), *Something Wild* (1986), and *Gettysburg* (1993).

Davis, Bette (*b.* Ruth Elizabeth Davis, Apr. 5, 1908, Lowell, Mass.; *d.* 1989). After some light experience in school productions and in semiprofessional stock, she enrolled at John Murray Anderson's drama school. In 1928 she appeared with the off-Broadway Provincetown Players and the following year made her Broadway debut. In 1930 she was tested and signed by Universal.

After appearing in a number of indifferent roles in routine productions, she attracted favorable attention as George Arliss's leading lady in *The Man Who Played God* (1932). This was the first of Davis's long succession of films under a long-term contract with Warner Brothers. She did, however, have to fight for her right to star (on a loan-out to RKO) as Mildred, the nasty, selfish waitress in John Cromwell's *Of Human Bondage* (1934). She finally got the role and responded with a sterling performance. Still Warner Brothers continued offering her mediocre vehicles, mostly routine crime melodramas and tearful soap operas, but she capably survived the worst of them, and critics constantly praised her acting while panning her films.

In 1935 she won her first Oscar for *Dangerous,* an inconsequential tearjerker. The following year she had a meaty role in *The Petrified Forest,* but her subsequent two scripts were again of poor quality. She refused another unsuitable role, with the result that Warner Brothers finally began treating her with greater respect and offering her roles to suit her temperament and talent.

Davis appealed most strongly to female audiences, who not only were more attuned to the romantic flavor of her films but also identified with her screen image as a willful, liberated woman who managed to remain spitefully independent in a world dominated by men. In 1938 Davis won her second Academy Award, for *Jezebel.* Her stature grew with every film she made in the early 1940s; but by the end of the decade she seemed headed for oblivion. The indomitable Miss Davis then countered with one of her greatest performances, in *All About Eve* (1950). Late in the 1950s her career again faltered, but she emerged triumphant in the early 1960s, this time with a couple of made-to-order horror films, *What Ever Happened to Baby Jane?* (1962) and *Hush Hush . . . Sweet Charlotte* (1965).

De Niro, Robert (*b.* Aug. 17, 1943, New York City). Trained for the stage by Stella Adler and Lee Strasberg, he appeared in off-Broadway productions and with touring companies before entering films in the late 1960s. He gave interesting characterizations in several low-budget Brian De Palma films but attracted little attention until 1973, when he etched a sensitive portrayal of a dying baseball player in John Hancock's *Bang the Drum Slowly* and gave an incisive performance as a simple-minded small-time hood in Martin Scorsese's *Mean Streets.*

The following year he won an Academy Award as best supporting player for his portrait of the young Vito Corleone in *The Godfather, Part II.* He topped these achievements in 1976 with a memorable performance in the role of a psychotic cabbie alienated by the moral and physical squalor of New York in Scorsese's *Taxi Driver,* affirming his position as one of the finest American screen actors of the 1970s. He was nominated for an Oscar for *The Deer Hunter* (1978) and won a second Academy Award, this time as best actor, for his portrait of boxer Jake La Motta in Scorsese's *Raging Bull* (1980). An intense, perceptive performer, he has remained a forceful figure on the American screen in the 1980s and 1990s, in a variety of roles.

Donat, Robert (*b.* Mar. 18, 1905, Withington, Manchester, England; *d.* 1958). He began taking elocution lessons at eleven to overcome a stutter and developed an exceptionally fine and versatile voice that was to make him a leading actor of British stage and films. He made his stage debut at sixteen and played a variety of Shakespearean and classical roles in repertory and with touring companies before appearing in his London debut in 1930. Tall, handsome, and romantically dashing, he was soon noticed by film producers. After turning down a Hollywood offer by Irving Thalberg, he accepted a contract with Alexander Korda and became internationally famous as the romantic lead in *The Private Life of Henry VIII* (1933). He was rushed to Hollywood to star in *The Count of Monte Cristo* (1934) but didn't like the town or the prospect of becoming a conventional movie star. Returning to England, he established himself as a highly respected and popular actor of both stage and screen.

He played the leads in some of Britain's finest films of the 1930s and early 1940s, ranging from Hitchcock's adventurous *The 39 Steps* to René Clair's comedy-fantasy *The Ghost Goes West,* in which he played the title role. He won an Academy Award for his performance in *Goodbye, Mr. Chips* (1939). But Donat's career was severely hampered by a lifelong struggle with chronic asthma, as well as by nagging insecurities and self-doubts. He turned down more screen roles than he accepted and never fulfilled the magnificent promise of his early years. He was seriously ill during the production of his last film, *The Inn of the Sixth Happiness* (1958), and died at fifty-three before the picture was released.

Finney, Albert (*b.* May 9, 1936, in Salford, England). He trained for the stage at the Royal Academy of Dramatic Art and made his debut in 1956 with the Birmingham Repertory Theatre. During the late 1950s he appeared almost exclusively in Shakespearean roles. But in 1960 he burst forth as a dynamic personification of rebellious youth in *Billy Liar* on the London stage and in Karel Reisz's film *Saturday Night and Sunday Morning.* He rapidly rose to prominence in plays and films written by John Osborne and directed by Tony Richardson. In 1961 he received the best actor award at the Théâtre des Nations international festival in Paris for his performance in *Luther,* a play he subsequently brought to Broadway, and in 1963 he soared to international popularity with his boisterous performance in the film *Tom Jones.* In 1965 he formed his own production company, Memorial Enterprises, and in 1967 he directed himself in *Charlie Bubbles.* He was nominated for Academy Awards for *Tom Jones, Murder on the Orient Express, The Dresser,* and *Under the Volcano.*

Fonda, Henry (*b.* May 16, 1905, Grand Island, Nebr.; *d.* 1982). In 1925 he was asked to play the leading role in an amateur production at the Omaha Community Playhouse; he stayed with the company for three years. In 1928, while he was playing a lead in New England summer stock, his path crossed that of a group of young theater aspirants who formed their own company, the University Players. Fonda joined the group, which included Joshua Logan, Margaret Sullavan, and James Stewart.

In 1934, Fonda played his first important Broadway part; the same year he reaped enthusiastic notices for the title role in *The Farmer Takes a Wife,* then went to Hollywood to repeat the role on the screen (1935). Fonda's rise in films was meteoric. Within a year or two the shy young man was an established star and by the end of the decade internationally famous.

Fonda's engaging sincerity, natural style of delivery, and characteristically "American" personality proved ideal for the screen. He reached the peak of his early Hollywood career with *Young Mr. Lincoln* (1939) and *The Grapes of Wrath* (1940) and then demonstrated his versatility by playing comic roles in *The Lady Eve* (1941), *The Male Animal* (1942), and *The Magnificent Dope* (1942).

Fonda returned to Hollywood experienced and matured after naval service in World War II, and the change was evident in his first postwar roles, in John Ford's *My Darling Clementine* (1946), *The Fugitive* (1947), and *Fort Apache* (1948), and in Anatole Litvak's *The Long Night* (1947). In 1948 he scored his greatest stage triumph, playing the title role in Broadway's *Mister Roberts.* He did not return to the screen until 1955, when he repeated his stage role in the film version of *Mister Roberts.*

From the mid-1950s on, Fonda alternated between screen and stage. Gravely ill during the production of his last film, *On Golden Pond* (1981), Fonda was paid homage during the Oscar ceremonies that year (for 1980) with an honorary Academy Award. Just months before his death the following year, he won the Oscar as Best Actor for his glowing performance in the film.

Garbo, Greta (*b.* Greta Louisa Gustafsson, Sept. 18, 1905, Stockholm; *d.* 1990). At the Royal Dramatic Theater training school in Stockholm Garbo was discovered by Mauritz Stiller, who, with Victor Sjöström, dominated the Swedish cinema during its golden age. Stiller was looking for a young actress to play the second lead in his forthcoming film, *The Saga of Gösta Berling.* The four-hour-long *Gösta Berling* (1924) scored well with European critics and launched Garbo as a promising new screen personality.

In 1924, MGM production chief Louis B. Mayer offered Stiller a contract to work in Hollywood. Reluctantly, Mayer was forced to accept the director's condition that his discovery, Greta Garbo, would also be put on the MGM payroll. Not until they saw the daily rushes of Garbo's first MGM film, *The Torrent,* did studio brass realize what a prize possession they had signed. When the film was released in 1926, the critical and popular acclaim was unanimous: a new superstar was born and the Garbo myth began.

The resources of the entire MGM machine were invested in enhancing the Garbo legend. When she appeared in her first talkie, *Anna Christie* (1930), the slogan "Garbo Talks!" filled much advertising space. When she appeared in her first comedy, *Ninotchka* (1939), the ads screamed: "Garbo Laughs!"

Garbo was twice named best actress by the New York film critics, for *Anna Karenina* in 1935 and for *Camille* in 1937. In 1941, following the release of the disastrous *Two-Faced Woman,* Garbo suddenly announced her retirement from films. True to character, she never explained why.

Gish, Lillian (*b.* Oct. 14, 1896, in Springfield, Ohio; *d.* 1993). The actress who is widely recognized as the "First Lady of the Silent Screen" took her first steps on the stage when she was five, in a melodrama, *In Convict Stripes.* Lillian Gish's big chance came in 1912, when she ran into an old friend at the offices of Manhattan's American Biograph Company, to which she had gone to seek work. The friend, whose name was Mary Pickford, introduced her to director D. W. Griffith.

Lillian was a made-to-order Griffith heroine. Her deceptive fragility, masking a great spiritual vibrance that could surge forth unexpectedly as physical strength, was perfectly suited to the Victorian sentiment of his dramas. She remained with Griffith until the early 1920s, when they amicably parted ways over a salary dispute. Until then he had directed nearly all her films, most notably *Broken Blossoms* (1919), *True Heart Susie* (1919), *Way Down East* (1920), and *Orphans of the Storm* (1922).

Miss Gish then starred in several major films of minor companies that gave her control over scripts and choice of directors. She received the same privileges when she joined MGM in 1925 and chose King Vidor and Victor

Sjöström to direct her in *La Bohème* and *The Scarlet Letter,* respectively. Both films were highly successful. But her subsequent films for MGM did not fare well commercially, and with Garbo emerging as a star, the company could afford to let Lillian Gish go in 1928. She acted in her last screen lead in a Paramount film released early in 1934. From the early 1940s on, she kept returning occasionally to the screen in character parts but devoted more of her energies to the stage and later also to television and lecture tours.

Graham, Charles. He took part in some of the Vitagraph and Hepworth productions he describes in "Acting for the Films in 1912." In *The London Stage 1910–1919,* he is recorded as Polixenes in Harley Granville-Barker's production of *The Winter's Tale* at the Savoy in October 1912 and as Lorenzo in Johnston Forbes-Robertson's production of *The Merchant of Venice* at Drury Lane in May 1913. At the time of his writing of "Acting for the Films in 1912," Graham was acting in the repertoire of plays with which Forbes-Robertson made his three-year farewell tour of the United States and Canada.

Hale, Louise Closser (*b*. Oct. 13, 1872, Chicago; *d*. 1933). A character player of the Broadway stage and Hollywood early talkies, on the screen she typically played tyrannical matrons. Her films include *Daddy Long Legs* (1931), *Rebecca of Sunnybrook Farm* (1932), *The Shanghai Express* (1932), and *Dinner at Eight* (1933).

Hepburn, Katharine (*b*. Nov. 9, 1907, Hartford, Conn.). Drawn to the stage at an early age, she later gained experience in college dramatics. She made her professional debut in 1928 in a stock production of *Czarina*.

Strong-minded and outspoken, she was hired for the leading part in Broadway's *The Warrior's Husband* (1932), in which she scored her first critical success. RKO offered her a film contract. Her screen debut in *A Bill of Divorcement,* opposite John Barrymore, was an unqualified hit. She appeared in a mixture of good and mediocre productions for RKO, then capped her screen achievements of the 1930s with sparkling performances in the hilarious screwball comedy *Bringing Up Baby* and the film version of the Broadway hit *Holiday* (both 1938, opposite Cary Grant).

After turning down several projects, Hepburn agreed to play the lead in the Broadway play *The Philadelphia Story*. It enjoyed tremendous success, and the MGM film version (1940) brought Hepburn the New York Film Critics Award.

Her next film at MGM, *Woman of the Year* (1942), brought into her life the man who was to become a lifelong intimate friend, Spencer Tracy; they formed a remarkable screen team in nine films.

Two memorable portrayals of spinsters, in *The African Queen* (1951) and *Summertime* (1955), as well as a remarkable performance as a Southern matriarch in *Suddenly, Last Summer* (1959), highlighted Hepburn's career in the 1950s.

Hepburn and Tracy were reunited on the screen for the last time in *Guess Who's Coming to Dinner* (1967). Hepburn won her second of four Academy Awards for her performance in that film. Undaunted by deteriorating health, she continued appearing in occasional films into the 1990s.

Hoffman, Dustin (*b.* Aug. 8, 1937, Los Angeles). This antiheroic, unlikely superstar of Hollywood films took acting classes at the Pasadena Playhouse and began acting at nineteen. He went to New York, hoping for a career on the stage; but it wasn't until 1965 that he was able to act off Broadway. He received much critical praise in 1966 for his performance in a British farce, *Eh?* Director Mike Nichols, who saw the play, insisted that the then-little-known Hoffman play the lead role in his upcoming film *The Graduate* (1967).

The great commercial success of *The Graduate* catapulted Hoffman into instant stardom. Hoffman returned to the screen in John Schlesinger's *Midnight Cowboy* (1969), and gave a memorable performance as the pathetic Ratso Rizzo. He has since demonstrated a remarkable range of screen characterizations. He played a white man adopted by Indians who ages on screen from adolescence to 121 in *Little Big Man* (1970), portrayed a doomed, ugly little Frenchman on Devil's Island in *Papillon* (1973), impersonated tragic comedian Lenny Bruce in *Lenny* (1974), and was *Washington Post* reporter Carl Bernstein in *All the President's Men* (1976). He won his first Oscar for his role as a beleaguered, custody-battling father in *Kramer vs. Kramer* (1979) and a second for a stunning performance as an autistic brother to Tom Cruise in *Rain Man* (1988).

Lemmon, Jack (*b.* John Uhler Lemmon III, Feb. 8, 1925, Boston). He was educated at Harvard, where he was active in the Dramatic Club. After serving in the Navy as an ensign, he began the uphill climb toward an acting career, playing piano in a New York City beer hall, appearing on radio and off Broadway, and finally on T.V. After a brief Broadway exposure, he was introduced on the screen in two successive Judy Holliday vehicles. Shortly after, he scored a personal triumph as Ensign Pulver in *Mister Roberts,* for which he won an Academy Award as Best Supporting Actor, and was on his way to stardom. He won the Oscar for Best Actor for his performance in *Save the Tiger* (1973). The brand of comedy he has made famous sadly mocks the frustrations of a well-bred, well-meaning individual in a world governed by impersonal superstructures. Lemmon is capable of a broad range of portrayals, from slapstick to deeply moving drama. Lemmon's Oscar nominations reflected his versatile mastery of characterization, spanning the gamut of thespian emotion in films from cynical comedies like *Some Like It Hot* (1959) and *The Apartment* (1960) to sincere dramas like *Days of Wine and Roses* (1962), *The China Syndrome* (1979), *Tribute* (1980), and *Missing* (1982). He was named Best Actor at Cannes for *The China Syndrome* and *Missing*.

Marsh, Mae (*b*. Mary Wayne Marsh, Nov. 9, 1895, Madrid, N.M.; *d*. 1968). In 1912 she went to New York and after a couple of appearances in Kalem films joined D. W. Griffith's stock company of players at Biograph. Like Lillian Gish, she made an ideal Griffith heroine, at once youthful and mature, physically frail and spiritually strong. As the "Little Sister" she provided some of the most tender and moving moments in *The Birth of a Nation*.

The following year, Marsh surpassed her achievement with a superior dramatic performance as Robert Harron's grief-sticken wife in the modern episode of *Intolerance*. In 1916 she left Griffith to sign a lucrative contract with Goldwyn. But her roles for this and other studios in the United States and Europe rarely did justice to her talent. It wasn't until she returned to a Griffith film, *The White Rose*, in 1923 that she had the opportunity to give another memorably intense dramatic performance. Except for an occasional role, she retired from the screen in 1925 but returned in the early 1930s as a character actress and appeared in numerous talkies through the early 1960s, including *A Tree Grows in Brooklyn* (1945), *The Robe* (1953), and *Donovan's Reef* (1963).

Mastroianni, Marcello (*b*. Sept. 28, 1923, Fontana Liri, Italy; *d*. 1996). After the war he went to Rome, where he worked as a clerk in the accounting department of the British Eagle-Lion Italian office and, in the evenings, began acting with a group of university players. In 1947 he made his screen debut in an Italian version of *Les Misérables* and the following year joined Luchino Visconti's stage stock company. Gradually he built himself a reputation among Italian audiences as a talented and fetching leading man both on stage and in films. By the mid-1950s his reputation was international, and after starring in such films as Visconti's *White Nights* (1957), Fellini's *La dolce vita* (1960), and *8½* (1963), Antonioni's *La notte* (1961), and Germi's *Divorce, Italian Style*, he was established as one of the world's leading screen personalities, in a wide range of finely delineated dramatic and comic roles, enjoying universal popularity as a prototype of the modern-day urban European male. The British Film Academy named him Best Foreign Actor for *Divorce, Italian Style* and *Yesterday, Today, and Tomorrow* (1963); and Mastroianni won the Best Actor Prize at Cannes for *The Pizza Triangle* (1970) and *Dark Eyes* (1987).

Nicholson, Jack (*b*. Apr. 22, 1937, Neptune, N.J.). He made his first film appearance in 1958 as the lead in a Roger Corman cheapie, *The Cry Baby Killer,* and subsequently appeared in other horror, motorcycle, and action films. Nicholson got his big break when he was called in to replace Rip Torn in *Easy Rider* (1969). He made the most of the small role of a dropout lawyer and for his effort received the first of several Oscar nominations.

In the ensuing years, Nicholson emerged as one of the American screen's most intriguing personalities. He turned in an exceptional, complex performance in Bob Rafelson's *Five Easy Pieces* (1970), then went on to display uncommon acting skill in such disparate films as Mike Nichols' *Carnal Knowledge* (1971), Hal Ashby's *The Last Detail* (1973), Roman Polanski's *Chinatown* (1974), and Michelangelo Antonioni's *The Passenger* (1975). He won the Oscar for Best Actor for his performance in Miloš Forman's *One Flew Over the Cuckoo's Nest* (1975), in which he played a free-spirited individualist whose arrival in a hospital's mental ward catalyzes the patients' lives.

Nicholson went on to register memorable performances in many other films, including *Reds* (1981), *Prizzi's Honor* (1985), *Ironweed* (1987), *A Few Good Men* (1992), and *Terms of Endearment* (1983), for which he won the Oscar for Best Supporting Actor.

Olivier, Laurence (*b*. May 22, 1907, Dorking, Surrey, England; *d*. 1989). Olivier was a brilliant performer on the British and American stage and screen. The son of a strict Anglican clergyman of Huguenot ancestry, he made his acting debut as a schoolboy of nine. He subsequently joined the Birmingham Repertory (1926–28) and made his first appearance on Broadway in 1929. His British screen debut was in 1930 and his Hollywood debut the following year.

Within just a few years, through a succession of memorable Shakespearean roles on stage and several romantic portrayals in Hollywood films, Olivier emerged as one of the most exciting and versatile actors in the English-speaking world. Through such heartthrob roles as Heathcliff in *Wuthering Heights* (1939), de Winter in *Rebecca* (1940), Darcy in *Pride and Prejudice* (1940), he was establishing himself in the banner years 1939–40 as a glamorous Hollywood star, when World War II broke out. In 1944 he was discharged from service and appointed co-director of the Old Vic Theatre. While supervising the restoration of the distinguished theatrical institution to its prewar glory, Olivier began his first film as a director, *Henry V.* His second film, *Hamlet,* won the Academy Awards for Best Picture and Best Actor (Olivier) as well as a number of other Oscars. His continued appearance in occasional films and in numerous plays demonstrated his virtuosity in a wide range of roles.

In 1963 he became the director of England's National Theatre Company. He played his final role on stage in 1974, the year in which he was stricken with dermatomyositis, a crippling muscle disease. Nontheless, he continued appearing in films and on T.V. in roles large and small, with amazing frequency.

Poitier, Sidney (*b.* Feb. 20, 1924, Miami, Fla.). Poitier was the American screen's first prominent black star. Raised in the Bahamas, he dropped out of school at thirteen and worked at a variety of menial jobs and served in the Army. He then joined the American Negro Theater and made his Broadway debut in the 1946 all-black production of *Lysistrata.* Beginning in 1950, he rapidly became Hollywood's number one black actor, and by the 1960s he was established as a popular screen star with charismatic personal appeal and the ability to tackle an ever-widening range of roles. He won the Academy Award for Best Actor for his role in *Lilies of the Field* (1963). His success helped pave the way for the entry of other black stars into the mainstream of the American commercial cinema. Poitier reached a peak of popularity with magnetic performances in three superior films of 1967, *In the Heat of the Night, To Sir with Love,* and *Guess Who's Coming to Dinner.* With his acting career slipping in the early 1970s, he turned to directing, first his own films, then those starring others. In 1992 he became the first black recipient of the American Film Institute's Life Achievement Award.

Portman, Eric (*b.* July 13, 1903, Yorkshire, England; *d.* 1969). This distinguished character actor of the British stage starting in 1924 and the British screen starting in 1934 played leads early in his film career, typically as a haughty, cynical aristocrat, then reverted to character parts, often villainous. His films include *The Prince and the Pauper* (1937), *We Dive at Dawn* (1943), *The Deep Blue Sea* (1955), and *Freud* (1962).

Pudovkin, Vsevolod I. (*b.* Feb. 6, 1893, Penza, Russia; *d.* 1953). In 1920 he enrolled at Moscow's State Institute of Cinematography; in 1922 he joined

Lev Kuleshov's "experimental laboratory" and soon distinguished himself as the teacher's most brilliant pupil and assistant.

With *Mother* (1926) and his two subsequent silent films, *The End of St. Petersburg* (1927) and *Storm Over Asia* (1928), Pudovkin took his place alongside Sergei Eisenstein and Aleksandr Dovzhenko at the summit of Soviet cinema and in the forefront of world cinema. Pudovkin's basic creative tool, like Eisenstein's, was montage. But where Eisenstein juxtaposed separate shots to achieve conflict and collision, Pudovkin used them as building blocks; while the masses were Eisenstein's collective heroes, Pudovkin's heroes were individuals, sometimes idealized figures, who personified the masses. By emphasizing narrative and characterization, Pudovkin was able to involve his audiences emotionally, while driving home the same revolutionary message that Eisenstein approached intellectually.

During the filming of *Mother,* Pudovkin began writing his theoretical pamphlets, which were eventually published as *Film Technique* and *Film Acting.* In 1928 Pudovkin joined Eisenstein and Gregory Alexandrov in a manifesto advocating audiovisual counterpoint as a basic technique in sound films. Of his sound films, only *Deserter* (1933) and *Suvorov* (1941) lived up to Pudovkin's reputation. Much of his later work was hampered by the limitations imposed on Soviet film directors by party officials.

Redgrave, Michael (*b.* Mar. 20, 1908, Bristol, England; *d.* 1985). An eminent leading man and character star of the British stage and screen, Redgrave was the son of British actor Roy Redgrave (1872–1922), who appeared in Australian silent movies. He made his stage debut in 1934 and before long became one of England's most distinguished and versatile players. Specializing in cerebral roles, he appeared in numerous films starting in 1936, reaching the peak of his screen career in the late 1940s and early 1950s, when he appeared in such films as *The Captive Heart, The Browning Version,* and *The Importance of Being Earnest.* He was nominated for an Oscar for his performance in *Mourning Becomes Electra* (1947) and won the Best Actor prize at the Cannes Festival for *The Browning Version* (1951). His marriage to actress Rachel Kempson produced Vanessa and Lynn Redgrave, both of whom went on to become stage and screen stars in their own right.

Sothern, Edward H. (*b.* 1859, New Orleans, La., and educated in England; *d.* 1933). Sothern was primarily a stage actor. He first appeared in New York at the Park Theatre in 1879 and in London at the Royalty in 1881. Sothern was associated with New York's Lyceum Theatre from 1885 to 1898 but appeared at many other theaters throughout the United States, Canada, and

England, often in leading roles in Shakespeare's plays. *The Chattel* (1916) and *The Man of Mystery* (1917) are two Vitagraph films in which he acted. He published his autobiography, *My Reminiscences,* in 1917.

Stewart, James (*b.* May 20, 1908, Indiana, Pa.; *d.* 1997). After graduating from Princeton in 1932 with a degree in architecture, he was persuaded by classmate Joshua Logan to join the University Players at Falmouth, Mass., whose members included such future stars as Henry Fonda and Margaret Sullavan. Stewart and Fonda were roommates when they both took their first steps on Broadway later that year and also when they first arrived in Hollywood in 1935.

A gawky, gangling young man with a slow, hesitant drawl and a shy country-boy manner, Stewart was an oddity among Hollywood's leading men and a challenge to casting directors. But the oddity was soon revealed as a unique asset, when Stewart's clod-kicking embarrassment and pleasantly nasal delivery were put to work in W. S. Van Dyke's *It's a Wonderful World* (1939) and in Frank Capra's sentimental social comedies *You Can't Take It with You* (1938) and *Mr. Smith Goes to Washington* (1939). He won the New York Film Critics Best Actor Award for the last of these three films. The following year, 1940, he won an Academy Award for *The Philadelphia Story* and took his place among Hollywood's leading stars. After the war, Stewart's screen personality matured, and he played detectives, Western heroes, and other masculine types and only occasionally returned to the shy, absent-minded characters he had played in the past.

Stewart was cited again by the New York Film Critics in 1959 for his performance in Preminger's *Anatomy of a Murder.* His career as a leading star extended into the early 1970s.

Streep, Meryl (*b.* 1951, Basking Ridge, N.J.). Streep is a radiant, expressive, talented leading lady of the American stage and screen. She developed an interest in acting while attending high school and began playing leads in school productions. She later majored in drama at Vassar, and went on to do graduate work at the Yale School of Drama. After playing leads in several productions of the Yale Repertory Theater, she went to New York and appeared successfully in a number of Broadway plays. In 1976 she joined the New York Shakespeare Festival and in the following year made her screen debut in *Julia.* She won the National Society of Film Critics Award for her role in *The Deer Hunter* (1978). Streep won the Oscar for Best Supporting Actress for her work in the divorce drama *Kramer vs. Kramer* (1979). She then won Best Actress for her role in *Sophie's Choice* (1982) as a Polish woman who must choose which of her children lives. Throughout the 1980s Streep tackled a wide variety of dramatic roles, becoming well known for her uncanny ability to mimic accents. She turned to comedic roles in the late 1980s and early 1990s in *She-Devil* (1989) and *Death Becomes Her* (1992).

Swanson, Gloria (*b.* Gloria Josephine Mae Swenson, Mar. 27, 1897, Chicago, of Swedish-Italian descent; *d.* 1983). A chance visit to Chicago's Essanay studios in 1913 resulted in her employment as an extra player and her move to Hollywood in 1919, where she was paired with Bobby Vernon in a series of romantic comedies for Keystone.

Swanson soon tired of comedy and starred in a succession of tearful dramas for Triangle beginning in 1917. In 1919 she moved over to Cecil B. De Mille's unit at Paramount and rapidly rose to top stardom in a series of slick, suggestive bedroom farces. By the mid-1920s she ranked among Hollywood's reigning queens of the silent screen.

Swanson remained with Paramount until 1926, specializing mostly in drama. During the period of transition to sound, Swanson proved she could not only talk effectively but even sing. Her early talkies were mostly unsuccessful, however, and in 1934 she retired from the screen.

She came back for one comedy, opposite Adolphe Menjou in 1941 (*Father Takes a Wife*), then made a memorable second comeback in 1950, giving an outstanding performance in *Sunset Boulevard,* in the role of a neurotic, faded silent screen star. Swanson returned to the screen once more in 1974, in a key character role in *Airport 1975.*

Trintignant, Jean-Louis (*b.* Dec. 11, 1930, Fiolenc, France). He left law school at twenty and went to Paris to study acting. Overcoming personal shyness and a thick provincial accent, he made his stage debut in 1951 and has since appeared in many plays. He made his first screen appearance in 1956 in a supporting part and became known to international film audiences later that year for his role as Brigitte Bardot's timid husband in Vadim's . . . *And God Created Woman.* He has since remained one of the leading personalities of the European cinema, a star whose appeal seems to stem largely from his economy of expression and the sense of ambiguity and mystery he projects on the screen. He garnered wide praise for his performance in such films as *A Man and a Woman* (1966), *My Night at Maud's* (1969), and *The Conformist* (1970). In 1969 Trintignant won the Best Actor Award at Cannes for *Z.*

Ullmann, Liv (*b.* Dec. 16, 1939, Tokyo, to Norwegian parents). Ullmann is an outstanding dramatic actress of Swedish and international films whose splendidly expressive face and subtle acting have figured prominently in several Ingmar Bergman productions. After completing her high school education in Norway, Ullmann joined a provincial theatrical group and several years later gained prominence on the Oslo stage and in Norwegian films. She achieved international fame in the late 1960s and in the 1970s as the emotional strained protagonist of such Bergman films as *Persona* (1966), *Hour of the Wolf* (1968), *Shame* (1968), *The Passion of Anna* (1969), *Cries and Whispers* (1972), *Scenes from a Marriage* (1973), *Face to Face* (1976), and *Autumn Sonata* (1978). Ullmann's radiant beauty and her reputation as an actress of extraordinary emotional range brought her offers of starring roles in international productions, including Hollywood's musical *Lost Horizon* and comedy *40 Carats* (both 1973), in both of which she was woefully miscast. She has also starred on Broadway and the European stage.

Ure, Mary (*b*. Feb. 18, 1933, Glasgow; *d*. 1975). She was a leading lady of the British stage and infrequent films. Ure first came to prominence in the film of John Osborne's play *Look Back in Anger* (1959) and was nominated for an Oscar for her role in *Sons and Lovers* (1960). She died at forty-two, hours after opening a new London play, of a mixture of alcohol and barbiturates.

Zetterling, Mai (*b*. May 24, 1925, Vasteras, Sweden; *d*. 1994). Trained at Stockholm's Royal Dramatic Theater School, she made both her stage and screen debuts at sixteen and subsequently pursued successful careers in both dramatic forms. On the screen, she attracted attention in 1944 in Alf Sjöberg's *Hets* (known as *Torment* in the United States and *Frenzy* in the United Kingdom), a landmark film of Swedish cinema, from a script of Ingmar Bergman. Her sensitive portrayal of a simple girl victimized by a sadistic professor brought her international fame, and in 1946 she was invited to Britain to star in the film *Frieda*. She subsequently appeared in many other British films, as well as in several American productions.

In the early 1960s she decided to switch to the other side of the camera. She directed several feature films in Sweden, the themes of which often dealt with the position of women in modern society and which have been noted for their intense dramatic sense, fluid visual style, and explicit sexuality.

Select Bibliography

Abbott, Leslie. *Acting for Film and TV.* Belmont, Calif.: Star Publishing, 1994.

Adams, Brian. *Screen Acting: How to Succeed in Motion Pictures and Television.* Beverly Hills, Calif.: Lone Eagle, 1987.

Affron, Charles. *Star Acting: Gish, Garbo, Davis.* New York: Dutton, 1977.

Agnew, Frances Scheuing. *Motion Picture Acting.* New York: Reliance Newspaper Syndicate, 1913.

Albertson, Lillian. *Motion Picture Acting.* New York: Funk and Wagnalls, 1947.

Andrews, Cyril Bruyn. *The Theatre, the Cinema, and Ourselves.* London: Clarence House, 1947.

Ankerich, Michael G. *Broken Silence: Conversations with Twenty-Three Silent Stars.* Jefferson, N.C.: McFarland, 1993.

Antonioni, Michelangelo. "Reflections on the Film Actor." *Film Culture* 22–23 (summer 1961), pp. 66–67.

Arvey, V. "How Music Has Helped the Stars." *Etude* 50 (Oct. 1932), pp. 693–694.

Atwan, Robert, and Bruce Forer, eds. *Bedside Hollywood: Great Scenes from Movie Memoirs.* New York: Moyer Bell, 1985.

Au Werter, Russell, et al. "Special Report: The Director-Actor." *Action* 5, no. 1 (Jan.–Feb. 1970), pp. 11–26.

Babson, Thomas W. *The Actor's Choice.* Portsmouth, N.H.: Heinemann-Methuen, 1996.

Baker, Fred, and Ross Firestone, eds. *Movie People: At Work in the Business of Film.* New York: Douglas Book Corp., 1972.

Banks, I. "Acting for the Screen." *Movie Maker* 12 (Jan. 1978), pp. 36–37.

Bara, Theda. "How I Became a Film Vampire." *The Forum,* 61 (June 1919), pp. 715–727.

———. "The Curse of the Moving-Picture Actress." *The Forum,* 62 (July 1919), 83–93.

Barkworth, Peter. *The Complete "About Acting."* London: Methuen, 1991.

Barr, Tony. *Acting for the Camera.* Boston: Allyn and Bacon, 1982.

Barry, Iris. "Acting." In *Let's Go to the Movies.* New York: Payson and Clarke, 1926, pp. 87–99.

Bellais, Will. "Acting for Film and Television." *American Film Institute Newsletter* 3, no. 4 (Mar.–Apr. 1980), n. p.

Benner, Ralph, and Mary Jo Clements. *The Young Actor's Guide to Hollywood.* New York: Coward-McCann, 1964.

Bergman, Ingrid. "On Rossellini: Interview with Robin Wood." *Film Comment,* 10, no. 4 (July–Aug. 1974), pp. 12–15.

Bermel, Albert. "Culture Watching: Do Film Actors Act?" *New Leader* 69 (22 Sept. 1986), pp. 20–23.

Bernard, Ian. *Film and Television Acting.* Stoneham, Mass.: Butterworth-Heinemann, 1993.

Blakeston, Oswell, ed. *Working for the Films.* London: Focal Press, 1947.

Blue, James. "Pier Paolo Pasolini" [his use of actors—interview]. *Film Comment 3,* no. 4 (fall 1965), pp. 25–32.

———. "Satyajit Ray" [his directing of nonactors—interview]. *Film Comment 4,* no. 4 (summer 1968), pp. 4–17.

———. "Susumu Hani" [handling untrained actors—interview]. *Film Comment 5,* no. 2 (spring 1969), pp. 24–25.

Blum, R. A. "Acting for the Camera." *Cinema Canada,* no. 45 (Mar. 1978), pp. 31–32.

Blum, Richard. *American Film Acting: The Stanislavsky Heritage.* Ann Arbor, Mich.: UMI Research Press, 1984.

Bonica, Joe, comp. *How Talkies Are Made.* Hollywood, Calif.: J. Bonica and Co., 1930.

Brandes, D. "Roman Polanski on Acting." *Cinema Papers,* no. 11 (Jan. 1977), pp. 226–229.

Braudy, Leo. "Film Acting: Some Critical Problems and Proposals." *Quarterly Review of Film Studies* 1, no. 1 (Feb. 1976), pp. 1–18.

———. "Nobody's Perfect: Method Acting and '50s Culture." *Michigan Quarterly Review* 35, no. 1 (winter 1996), pp. 191–215.

Braun, Eric. "Where Have All the Stylists Gone?" *Films and Filming* 13, no. 8 (May 1967), pp. 50–55; 13, no. 9 (June 1967), pp. 38–43; 13, no. 10 (July 1967), pp. 12–16; 13, no. 11 (Aug. 1967), pp. 10–14; 13, no. 12 (Sept. 1967), pp. 12–16.

———. "The Changing Patterns in Stardom on the British Screen." *Films and Filming* 19 (Sept. 1973), pp. 34–40; 20 (Oct. 1973), pp. 32–40; 20 (Nov. 1973), pp. 31–40; 20 (Dec. 1973), pp. 28–40.

Briskin, Sam. "Training Talent for the Movies." *Literary Digest* 123 (30 Jan. 1937), pp. 23–24.

Britannicus, Cato. "Why the Stars Shine." *Films in Review* 6 (Oct. 1955), pp. 369–376.

Brophy, P. "Read My Lips: Notes on the Writing and Speaking of Film Dialogue." *Continuum* 5, no. 2 (1992), pp. 246–266.

Brundidge, Harry T. *Twinkle, Twinkle Movie Star!* (31 interviews). New York: Dutton, 1930.

Brustein, Robert. "Are Britain's Actors Better than Ours?" *New York Times* (15 Apr. 1973), sec. 2, p. 1.

Bucquet, Harold S. "Have You a Screen Personality?" *Christian Science Monitor Magazine,* 15 Jan. 1936, p. 5.

Burton, Hal, ed. *Acting in the Sixties.* London: British Broadcasting Corp., 1970.

Butler, Jeremy G., ed. *Star Texts: Image and Performance in Film and Television.* Detroit: Wayne State University Press, 1991.

Cagney, James. *Cagney by Cagney.* Garden City, N.Y.: Doubleday, 1976.

Caine, Michael. *Acting in Film: An Actor's Take on Movie Making.* New York: Applause, 1990.

Callow, Simon. *Being an Actor.* New York: Grove, 1988.

Campbell, Russell, ed. *The Velvet Light Trap,* no. 7 (winter 1972–73), 60 pp. (entire issue, "The Film Actor").

Cantor, Eddie. *My Life Is in Your Hands.* New York: Harper and Row, 1928.

Caron, Leslie. "Dialogue on Film," *American Film Institute Publications,* Nov. 1971.

"The Cast: The First Principles of Film Acting and the Stars of Three New Films." *Cinema* (Calif.), 1, no. 6 (Nov.–Dec. 1963), pp. 24–30.

Caster, Paul. "Thoughts on Film Acting." *Films in Review* 12, no. 9 (Nov. 1961), pp. 513–518.

Cawelti, J. G. "Performance and Popular Culture." *Cinema Journal* 20, no. 1 (fall 1980), pp. 4–13.

Ciampi, Yves, et al. "Film Acting." *Film* no. 13 (Sept.–Oct. 1957), pp. 5–9.

Ciment, Michel. *Kazan on Kazan.* London: Secker and Warburg/BFI, 1973.

Clien, Harry. "The Reel People." *Show,* 9 July 1970, pp. 14–19.

Cohen, M. S. "Film Noir: The Actor; Villians and Victims." *Film Comment* 10, no. 6 (Nov.–Dec. 1974), pp. 27–29.

Cole, Toby, and Helen Krich Chinoy, eds. *Actors on Acting.* New York: Crown, 1949.

Cole, Tristan de Vere. *A Guide to Actors New to Television.* Longmead, Dorset: Element Books, 1985.

Cook, B. "Why TV Stars Don't Become Movie Stars." *American Film* 1 (June 1976), pp. 58–61.

Cox, Warren, ed. *The Theatre and Motion Pictures.* London: Encyclopaedia Britannica, 1933.

Coxhead, Elizabeth. "A Film Actor." *Close Up* 10, No. 1 (Mar. 1933), pp. 47–49.

Curtis, Thomas Quinn. "Movie Acting." *Sight and Sound* 16, no. 62 (summer 1947), p. 68.

Damico, J. "Ingrid from Lorraine to Stromboli: Analyzing the Public's Perception of a Film Star." *Journal of Popular Film* 4, no. 1 (1975), pp. 3–19.

Dangerfield, Fred, and Norman Howard. *How to Become a Film Artiste.* London: Odhams Press, 1921.

De Cordova, Richard. "The Emergence of the Star System in America." *Wide Angle* 6, no. 4 (1985), pp. 4–13.

De La Roche, Catherine. "Stars." *Sight and Sound* 22, no. 4 (Apr.–June 1953), pp. 172–174.

Dmytryk, Edward, and Jean Porter Dmytryk. *On Screen Acting: An Introduction to the Art of Acting for the Screen.* Boston: Focal Press, 1984.

Dougan, Pat. *Professional Acting in Television Commercials.* Portsmouth, N.H.: Heinemann-Methuen, 1995.

Dyer, Richard. *Heavenly Bodies: Film Stars and Society.* New York: St. Martin's, 1986.

Eidsvik, Charles. "Perception and Convention in Acting for Theatre and Film." *Post Script: Essays in Film and the Humanities* 8, no. 2 (1989), pp. 21–35.

Eisenstein, Sergei M., and G. V. Alexandrov. "Doing Without Actors." *Cinema* 1 (June 1930), pp. 18, 56.

Ellis, John. "Stars as a Cinematic Phenomenon." In *Visible Fictions: Cinema, Television, Video.* London: Routledge and Kegan Paul, 1982, pp. 91–108.

Eustis, Morton. *Players at Work: Acting According to the Actors.* New York: Theatre Arts, 1937.

Farber, Manny. "The Decline of the Actor." In *Awake in the Dark,* ed. David Denby. New York: Vintage/Random House, 1977, pp. 340–349.

Feist, Gene. "Stage and Film Acting: The Growing Dichotomy." *National Forum* (the journal of Phi Kappa Phi) 70, no. 3 (summer 1990), pp. 19–20.

"The Film Actor: A Series of Interviews." *Seventh Art* 2, no. 1 (winter 1963), pp. 9–16.

Fox, Julian. "Casualties of Sound: Part One." *Films and Filming* 19, no. 1 (Oct. 1972), pp. 34–40.

———. "Casualties of Sound: Part Two." *Films and Filming* 19, no. 2 (Nov. 1972), pp. 33–40.

Freeman, K. "A Celebration of the Craft." *Screen Actor* 23, no. 1 (1981), pp. 2–3.

Fridell, Squire. *Acting in Television Commercials for Fun and Profit.* New York: Crown, 1987.

Funke, Lewis, and John E. Booth, eds. *Actors Talk About Acting.* New York: Avon Books, 1961. 2 vols.

Gable, Josephine Dillon. *Modern Acting: A Guide for Stage, Screen, and Radio.* New York: Prentice-Hall, 1940.

Gallagher, T. "Flashback: Acting for John Ford." *American Film* 11 (Mar. 1986), p. 16.

Gardin, Vladimir. "On Soviet Film Art." In *Soviet Cinema,* ed. Alexander Yakovlevich Arosev. Moscow: VOKS, 1935, pp. 253–254.

Gardner, P. "Bette Davis: A Star Views Directors" (interview). *Action* 9, no. 5 (Sept.–Oct. 1974), pp. 10–17.

Gerassimov, Sergei Apollinarievitch. "Out of the Factory of the Eccentric Actor." In *Cinema in Revolution: The Heroic Era of the Soviet Film,* ed. Luda Jean Schnitzer and Marcel Martin. New York: Hill and Wang, 1973, pp. 109–123.

Gies, M. "Directing Actors: The Method Approach." *Filmmakers' Monthly* 13 (Aug. 1980), pp. 24–30.

Gledhill, Christine, ed. *Stardom: Industry of Desire.* London: Routledge, 1991.

Goldstein, Laurence. "Familiarity and Contempt: An Essay on the Star Presence in Film." *Centennial Review* 17 (summer 1973), pp. 256–274.

Goodell, J. D. "Programming the Future: Computer-Created Actors." *Screen Actor* (Aug. 1984), pp. 68–73.

Gordon, George M., and Irvin A. Falk. *Your Career in Film-Making.* New York: J. Messner, 1969.

Griffith, D. W. "What I Demand of Movie Stars." *Moving Picture Classic* 3 (Feb. 1917), pp. 40–41, 68.

Griffith, Richard. "The Function of the Actor." *Cinema Quarterly* (Edinburgh, Scotland) 3, no. 3 (spring 1935), pp. 139–142.

———. *The Movie Stars.* Garden City, N.Y.: Doubleday, 1970.

Guy, Rory. "The Character Actor: Going, Going, Gone." *Cinema* (Calif.) 2, no. 2 (July 1964), pp. 14–18.

Hadleigh, Boze. *Conversations with My Elders.* New York: St. Martin's, 1986.

Hardy, Karen, and Kevin J. Koffler. *The New Breed—Actors Coming of Age.* New York: Holt, 1988.

Harman, Renée. *The Actor's Survival Guide for Today's Film Industry.* Englewood Cliffs, N.J.: Prentice-Hall, 1984.

Harris, Roy. *Conversations in the Wings: Talking about Acting.* Portsmouth, N.H.: Heinemann, 1994.

Harris, T. "The Building of Popular Images: Grace Kelly and Marilyn Monroe." *Studies in Public Communications* 1 (1957), pp. 45–48.

Hart, William S. "Living Your Character." *Motion Picture Magazine* 13 (May 1917), pp. 71–72.

Herman, Hal C., ed. *How I Broke into the Movies.* Hollywood, Calif.: Hal C. Herman, 1928.

Herring, Robert. "But Something Quite Different Is Needed." *Close Up* 7, no. 2 (1930), pp. 90–97.

Higson, Andrew. "Film Acting and Independent Cinema." *Screen* 27, nos. 3–4 (1986), pp. 110–132.

Hinsdell, Oliver. "What It Takes to Get into the Movies." *American* 122 (July 1936), pp. 20–21.

Hinson, H. "Some Notes on Method Actors." *Sight and Sound* 53, no. 3 (1984), pp. 200–205.

Hirsch, Foster. *A Method to Their Madness: The History of the Actors' Studio.* New York: Norton, 1984.

———. *Acting Hollywood Style.* New York: Harry N. Abrams, 1991.

Hope-Wallace, Philip. "Acting." *Sight and Sound* 19 (Dec. 1949), p. 22; 19 (Mar. 1950), pp. 30–31; 19 (June 1950), p. 167; 19 (Nov. 1950), p. 289; 19 (Jan. 1951), p. 375; 19 (Mar. 1951), p. 443; 20 (June 1951), p. 51.

Holtzman, W. "Towards an Actor-Icon Theory." *Journal of Popular Film* 4, no. 1 (1975), pp. 77–80.

Hornsby, Richard. "Understanding Acting." *Journal of Aesthetic Education* 17, no. 3 (1983), pp. 19–37.

———. *The End of Acting: A Radical View.* New York: Applause, 1992.

Howard, Leslie. "The Actor." In *Behind the Screen: How Films Are Made,* ed. Stephen Watts. London: Arthur Barker, 1938, 78–90.

Hyland, Wende, and Roberta Hayens. *How to Make It in Hollywood.* Chicago: Nelson-Hall, 1975.

Jacobson, L. "Character Actors: Hollywood's Unsung Heroes." *Hollywood: Then and Now* 25, no. 1 (1992), pp. 12–17.

Jaffe, Ira S. "Chaplin's Labor of Performance: *The Circus* and *Limelight.*" *Literature/Film Quarterly* 12, no. 3 (July 1984), pp. 202–210.

Janowska, Alma. "Truth Behind a Mask." *Films and Filming* 8, no. 2 (Nov. 1961), p. 10.

Jansen, P. "The Acting Profession." *Lumiere* no. 33 (Apr.–May 1974), pp. 4–5.

Jeffri, Joan, ed. *The Actor Speaks: Actors Discuss Their Experiences and Careers.* Westport, Conn.: Greenwood Press, 1994.

Joels, Merrill E. *Acting Is a Business.* New York: Hastings House, 1955.

———. *How to Get into Show Business.* New York: Hastings House, 1969.

Johnston, William Allen. "The Silent Stage." *Harper's Weekly* 53 (13 Nov. 1909), pp. 8–9.

"The Journal Looks at Hollywood's Star System." *Journal of Screen Producers' Guild* (Dec. 1962), pp. 3–28.

Kalter, Joanmarie, ed. *Actors on Acting: Performing in Theatre and Film Today.* New York: Sterling, 1979.

Keane, Marian. "Dyer Straits: Theoretical Issues in Studies of Film Acting." *Post Script: Essays in Film and the Humanities* 12, no. 2 (winter 1993), pp. 29–39.

Keil, M. "On Acting." *Motion* (Sept.–Oct. 1974), pp. 35–36.

Kennedy, Joseph P., ed. *The Story of the Films.* New York: A. W. Shaw, 1927.

Kerr, Paul, ed. *The Hollywood Film Industry.* London: Routledge and Kegan Paul, 1986.

Kindem, Gorham. *The Live Television Generation of Hollywood Film Directors: Interviews with Seven Directors.* Jefferson, N.C.: McFarland, 1994.

King, Barry. "Articulating Stardom." *Screen* 26, no. 5 (Sept.–Oct. 1985), pp. 27–50.

Kirkman, Larry, et al. *TV Acting: A Manual for Camera Performances.* New York: Hastings House, 1979.

Klaw, Irving. *How to Become a Movie Star.* New York: Klaw, 1946.

Klumph, Inez, and Helen Klumph. *Screen Acting: Its Requirements and Rewards.* New York: Falk, 1922.

Knox, Alexander. "Acting and Behaving." *Hollywood Quarterly* 1, no. 3 (Apr. 1946), pp. 260–269.

———. "Performance Under Pressure." *Hollywood Quarterly* 3, no. 2 (winter 1947–48), pp. 159–168.

Kobal, John. *People Will Talk.* New York: Aurum/Knopf, 1986.

Kuleshov, Lev. *Kuleshov on Film,* ed. Ronald Levaco. Berkeley: University of California Press, 1974.

Lambert, Gavin. "Actor on Cinemascope." *Sight and Sound* (Oct.–Dec. 1953), p. 70.

Lewis, Robert. "The Actors' Studio and Beyond." *Screen Actor* (Aug. 1984), pp. 39–41.

Locher, M. "The Actor's Life Unmasked." *Screen Actor* (Aug. 1984), pp. 104–113.

Lowenstein, Harold. "Can Children Act?" *Sight and Sound* 6, no. 21 (spring 1937), p. 17.

Luchting, Wolfgang. "Profound Banality in the Film." *Journal of Aesthetics and Art Criticism* 17 (Dec. 1958), pp. 208–213.

Macklin, F. A. "'Film to Me Is Another Art': An Interview with Stanley Kauffmann." *Film Heritage* 8, no. 1 (fall 1972), pp. 16–36.

March, Sibyl. "To Be, Not to Understand." *Seventh Art* 1, no. 2 (spring 1963), pp. 8–9.

Mariani, J. "Models Turned Actresses. Or How Hollywood Chooses Its New Talent." *Millimeter* 5 (July–Aug. 1977), p. 12.

Marsh, Mae. *Screen Acting.* Los Angeles: Photo-Star, 1921.

Mason, James. "Stage vs. Screen." *Films and Filming* 1, no. 2 (Nov. 1954), p. 5; 1, no. 3 (Dec. 1954), p. 7.

Mast, Gerald, ed. *The Movies in Our Midst: Documents in the Cultural History of Film in America.* Chicago: University of Chicago Press, 1982.

McArthur, Benjamin. *Actors and American Culture, 1880–1920.* Philadelphia: Temple University Press, 1984.

McArthur, Colin. "The Real Presence." *Sight and Sound* (summer 1967), pp. 141–143.

McBride, Joseph, ed. *Filmmakers on Filmmaking.* Los Angeles: J. P. Tarcher, 1983. 2 vols.

McDonald, Gerald D. "Origin of the Star System." *Films in Review* 4 (Nov. 1953), pp. 449–458.

McGilligan, Patrick. *Cagney: The Actor as Auteur.* South Brunswick, N.J.: A. S. Barnes, 1975.

––––––. "Actors Directing." *Focus on Film.* no. 36 (Oct. 1980), pp. 4–7.

McKenna, Pat. "Camera, Action, Let's Pretend!" *Cinéaste* 1, no. 3 (winter 1967–68), pp. 18–19.

McVay, Douglas. "The Art of the Actor." *Films and Filming* 12, no. 10 (July 1966), pp. 19–25.

––––––. "The Art of the Actor." *Films and Filming* 12, no. 11 (Aug. 1966), pp. 36–42.

––––––. "The Art of the Actor." *Films and Filming* 12, no. 12 (Sept. 1966), pp. 44–50.

––––––. "The Art of the Actor." *Films and Filming* 13, no. 1 (Oct. 1966), pp. 26–33.

––––––. "The Actor and the Star." *Films and Filming* 13, no. 2 (Nov. 1966), pp. 26–33.

Meeker, D. "Actors as Directors." *Film,* ser. 2, no. 4 (July 1973), p. 24.

Mekler, Eva, ed. *The New Generation of Acting Teachers.* New York: Penguin, 1987.

Merritt, R. "The Griffith-Gish Collaboration: A Tangled Affair." *Griffithiana* 14, nos. 40–42 (Oct. 1991), pp. 101–103.

Meyerson, Harold. "The Case of the Vanishing Character Actor." *Film Comment* 13, no. 6 (Nov.–Dec. 1977), pp. 6–15.

Miles, Bernard. "The Acting Art." *Films in Review* 5, no. 6 (June–July 1954), pp. 267–282.

Milne, Tom. "How Art Is True?" *Sight and Sound* 31, no. 4 (autumn 1962), pp. 166–171.

Mitchell, John D. *Actors Talk: About Styles of Acting.* Midland, Mich.: Northwood Institute Press, 1988.

Mitchell, T. "The Construction and Reception of Anna Magnani in Italy and the English-Speaking World, 1945–1988." *Film Criticism* 14, no. 1 (fall 1989), pp. 2–21.

Monod, Roland. "Working with Bresson." *Sight and Sound* 27, no. 1 (summer 1957), pp. 30–32.

Moore, Dick. *Opportunities in Acting: Stage, Motion Pictures, Television.* New York: Vocational Guidance Manuals of the City of New York, 1963.

Morin, Edgar. *The Stars,* trans. Richard Howard. New York: Grove, 1960.

Morris, G. "Actors and Directors." *Bright Lights* 1, no. 2 (1975), pp. 29–30.

Muni, Paul. "The Actor Plays His Part." In *We Make the Movies,* ed. Nancy Naumburg. New York: W. W. Norton, 1937, pp. 131–133, 135–142, et passim.

Musser, Charles. "The Changing Status of the Film Actor." In *Before Hollywood: Turn-of-the-Century American Film,* ed. Jay Leyda et al. New York: Hudson Hills Press, 1987, pp. 57–62.

Naremore, James. "Film and the Performance Frame." *Film Quarterly* 38, no. 2 (1984–85), pp. 8–15.

————. "Expressive Coherence and the 'Acted Image.'" *Studies in the Literary Imagination* 19, no. 1 (spring 1986), pp. 39–54.

————. *Acting in the Cinema.* Berkeley: University of California Press, 1988.

Naumberg, Nancy, ed. *We Make the Movies.* New York: Norton, 1937.

Newquist, Roy. *Showcase.* New York: William Morrow, 1966.

Noose, Theodore. *Hollywood Film Acting.* New York: A. S. Barnes, 1979.

O'Brien, Mary Ellen. *Film Acting: The Techniques and History of Acting for the Camera.* New York: Arco, 1983.

O'Neil, Brian. *Acting as a Business.* Portsmouth, N.H.: Heinemann-Methuen, 1993.

Orme, Michael. "Stardom vs. Acting." *Illustrated London News* (7 Nov. 1931), p. 722.

"Our 'Wild-Flower' Talkie Actresses." *Literary Digest* 110 (1 Aug. 1931), p. 19.

Oumano, Ellen. *Film Forum: Thirty-Five Top Filmmakers Discuss Their Craft.* New York: St. Martin's, 1985.

Parry, Florence Fisher. "Are Movie Stars Actors?" *Delineator* 123 (Sept. 1933), p. 4.

Pate, Michael. *The Film Actor: Acting for Motion Pictures and Television.* South Brunswick, N.J.: A. S. Barnes, 1970.

Peck, Stephen Rogers. *Atlas of Facial Expression.* New York: Oxford University Press, 1987.

Pichel, Irving. "Character, Personality, and Image: A Note on Screen Acting." *Hollywood Quarterly* 2, no. 1 (Oct. 1946), pp. 25–29.

Potamkin, Harry A. "The Personality of the Players." *Close Up* 6, no. 4 (1930), pp. 290–297.

Prendowska, C. "Marlon Brando as the Auteur." *Literature/Film Quarterly* 7, no. 2 (1979), pp. 120–125.

"Private Lives." *Films and Filming* 5, no. 6 (Mar. 1959), pp. 27–28.

Probst, Leonard. *Off Camera: Leveling About Themselves.* New York: Stein and Day, 1975.

Prouse, Derek. "Notes on Film Acting." *Sight and Sound* 24, no. 4 (spring 1955), pp. 174–180.

Pudovkin, V. I. "Film Acting: Two Phases." *Theatre Workshop* 1, no. 1 (Oct. 1936), pp. 53–67.

————. *Film Technique and Film Acting,* trans. Ivor Montagu. New York: Bonanza, 1949.

Quayle, Anthony. "Society and the Actor." *Films and Filming* 3, no. 10 (July 1957), p. 6.

Redgrave, Michael. *An Actor's Ways and Means.* London: Heinemann, 1953.

————. "I Am Not a Camera." *Sight and Sound* 24, no. 3 (Jan.–Mar. 1955), pp. 132–137.

Reed, Rex. *Conversations in the Raw.* New York: New World, 1969.

Richardson, Tony. "The Method and Why: An Account of the Actors' Studio." *Sight and Sound* 26, no. 3 (winter 1956–57), pp. 132–136.

Robinson, David. "The Players' Witness: Notes on Some Early Acting Performances Preserved in the National Film Archive." *Sight and Sound* 29, no. 3 (summer 1960), pp. 148–151.

Robinson, David, et al. "Twenties Show People." *Sight and Sound* 37, no. 4 (autumn 1968), pp. 198–202.

Rogosin, Lionel. "Interpreting Reality: Notes on the Esthetics and Practices of Improvisational Acting." *Film Culture* no. 21 (summer 1960), pp. 20–28.

Rosenbaum, Jonathan. "Improvisations and Interactions in Altmanville." *Sight and Sound* 44, no. 2 (spring 1975), pp. 90–95.

Ross, Lillian, and Helen Ross. *The Player: A Profile of An Art.* New York: Simon and Schuster, 1962.

Roth, Lane. "Actor-Icon Theory and the Horror Film." *Midnight Marquee,* no. 28 (Sept. 1979), pp. 34–36.

Rumens, S. "The Forgotten Art of Film Acting." *Film Making* 14 (July 1976), pp. 13–17.

————. "The Step from Stage to Screen." *Film Making* 14 (Sept. 1976), pp. 35–37.

————. "The Formula: Film Acting Made Easy." *Film Making* 14 (Oct. 1976), pp. 53–55.

Sarne, Mike. "How to Handle Directors." *Films and Filming* 11, no. 7 (Apr. 1965), pp. 41–43.

Sarris, Andrew. "Acting Aweigh!" *Film Culture,* no. 38 (fall 1965), pp. 47–61.

———. "The Actor as Auteur." *American Film* 2, no. 7 (May 1977), pp. 16–19.

Satariano, C. "This Way to Better Movies: Actors and Acting." *Movie Maker* 14 (Nov. 1980), pp. 826–828.

Schickel, Richard. *The Stars.* New York: Dial, 1962.

Schultz, E. "Can Real People Look and Sound Real on Camera?" *Making Films in New York* 8 (Apr. 1974), pp. 38–39.

Searle, Judith. *Getting the Part.* New York: Simon and Schuster, 1991.

Shaffer, Lawrence. "Some Notes on Film Acting." *Sight and Sound* 42, no. 2 (spring 1973), pp. 103–106.

———. "Reflections on the Face in Film." *Film Quarterly* 31, no. 2 (winter 1977–78), pp. 2–8.

Shelley, Frank. "Psychology of the Actor." In *Stage and Screen.* London: Pendulum, 1947, pp. 9–19.

Shtraukh, Maxim. "On Soviet Film Art." *In Soviet Cinema,* ed. Alexander Yakovlevich Arosev. Moscow: VOKS, 1935, pp. 256–262.

Sklar, Robert. *City Boys: Cagney, Bogart, Garfield.* Princeton, N.J.: Princeton University Press, 1992.

Slattery, W. J. "Acting or Experience?" *Audience* 5 (Feb. 1973), pp. 5–8; 5 (Mar. 1973), pp. 7–8.

Slide, Anthony. "The Character Player." *Films in Review* 41 (Mar. 1990), pp. 130–138; 41 (Apr. 1990), pp. 204–211.

Smith, Frank Leon. "Trade Secrets." *Films in Review* 10 (June–July 1959), pp. 381–382.

Stanbrook, Alan. "Towards Film Acting." *Film,* no. 17 (Sept.–Oct. 1958), pp. 15–18.

Steele, William Paul. *Acting in Industrials: The Business of Acting for Business.* Portsmouth, N.H.: Heinemann-Methuen, 1994.

Steen, Mike, ed. *Hollywood Speaks: An Oral History.* New York: G. P. Putman's Sons, 1974.

Steiger, Janet. "The Eyes Are Really the Focus: Photoplay Acting and Film Form and Style." *Wide Angle* 6, no. 4 (1985), pp. 14–23.

Steiger, Rod. "The Truth About 'The Method.'" *Films and Filming* 3, no. 7 (Apr. 1957), p. 7.

———. "On Acting." *Cinema* (Calif.) 3, no. 6 (winter 1967), pp. 18–19.

———. "On the Actor." In Fred Baker and Ross Firestone, eds. *Movie People: At Work in the Business of Film.* New York: Douglas Book Corp., 1972, pp. 101–122.

Sterling, Anna Kate, ed. *Celebrity Articles from "The Screen Guild Magazine."* Metuchen, N.J.: Scarecrow, 1987.

Swift, Clive. *The Job of Acting.* London: Harrap, 1976.

Taylor, Malcolm. *The Actor and the Camera.* Portsmouth, N.H.: Heinemann-Methuen, 1994.

Tembeck, R. "Expressing. Acting: A Dialogue on Communicating Experience." *Motion* (July–Aug. 1974), pp. 40–41.

"The Ten Greatest One-Scene Performances in the History of the Cinema." *Film Comment* 29 (Sept.–Oct. 1993), p. 74.

Thompson, F. Grahame. "Approaches to 'Performance.'" *Screen* 26, no. 5 (Sept.–Oct. 1985), pp. 78–90.

Thompson, John O. "Screen Acting and the Commutation Test." *Screen* 19, no. 2 (summer 1978), pp. 55–69.

———. "Beyond Commutation—A Reconsideration of Screen Acting." *Screen* 26, no. 5 (Sept.–Oct. 1985), pp. 64–76.

Thomson, D. "Acting English." *Film Comment* 18 (May–June 1982), pp. 7–14.

Thomson, D. "The Look on the Actor's Face." *Sight and Sound* 46, no. 4 (1977), pp. 240–244.

Tibbetts, John C., ed. *Introduction to the Photoplay: Contemporary Account of the Transition to Sound in Film.* Los Angeles: National Film Society, 1929.

Toback, J. "Notes on Acting." *Film Comment* 14 (Jan.–Feb. 1978), pp. 34–35.

Tomlinson, Doug, ed. *Actors on Acting for the Screen.* New York: Garland, 1994.

Tucker, Patrick. *Secrets of Screen Acting.* New York: Routledge, 1994.

Turner, David Steele, comp. *Actors About Acting, Loving, Living, Life.* Hollywood, Calif.: Stanyan, 1972.

Viera, Maria. "Using Theatrical Acting Techniques in the Production of Short Films." *Journal of Film and Video* 46, no. 4 (winter 1995), pp. 13–23.

Villagra, Nelson. "The Actor at Home and in Exile." In *Cinema and Social Change in Latin America: Conversations with Filmmakers,* ed. Julianne Burton. Austin: University of Texas Press, 1986, pp. 211–219.

Vineberg, Steve. *Method Actors: Three Generations of an American Acting Style.* New York: Schirmer, 1991.

Von Sternberg, Josef. "Acting in Film and Theatre." *Film Culture* 1, nos. 5–6 (winter 1955), pp. 1–4.

Wagenknecht, Edward. *The Movies in the Age of Innocence.* Norman: University of Oklahoma Press, 1962.

Walker, Alexander. *Stardom: The Hollywood Phenomenon.* New York: Stein and Day, 1970.

Watts, Stephen, ed. *Behind the Screen: How Films Are Made.* London: Arthur Barker, 1938.

Weaver, Tom. *Interviews with B Science Fiction and Horror Movie Makers: Writers, Producers, Directors, Actors, Moguls, and Makeup.* Jefferson, N.C.: McFarland, 1988.

———. *Science Fiction Stars and Horror Heroes: Interviews with Actors, Directors, Producers, and Writers of the 1940s Through 1960s.* Jefferson, N.C.: McFarland, 1991.

———. *They Fought in the Creature Features: Interviews with Twenty-Three Classic Horror, Science Fiction, and Serial Stars.* Jefferson, N.C.: McFarland, 1995.

Weis, Elisabeth, ed. *The Movie Star: National Society of Film Critics on the Movie Star.* New York: Viking, 1981.

Welsch, Janice R. "Actress Archetypes in the 1950s: Doris Day, Marilyn Monroe, Elizabeth Taylor, Audrey Hepburn." In *Women and the Cinema: A Critical Anthology,* ed. Karyn Kay and Gerald Peary. New York: Dutton, 1977.

Wexman, Virginia Wright. "Kinesics and Film Acting: Humphrey Bogart in *The Maltese Falcon* and *The Big Sleep.*" *Journal of Popular Film and Television* 7, no. 1 (1978), pp. 42–55.

———. "The Rhetoric of Cinematic Improvisation." *Cinema Journal* 20, no. 1 (1980), pp. 29–41.

———. *Creating the Couple: Love, Marriage, and Hollywood Performance.* Princeton, N.J.: Princeton University Press, 1993.

Wexman, Virginia Wright, ed. *Cinema Journal* 20, no. 1 (1980). Special issue on film acting.

Wilson, Ivy Crane. *Hollywood in the 1940s: The Stars' Own Stories.* New York: Ungar, 1980.

Winick, Charles. "The Face Was Familiar." *Films and Filming* 11, no. 4 (Jan. 1965), pp. 12–17.

Wright, C. "How Not to Direct Children!" *Popular Photography* 48 (Jan. 1961), pp. 90–91.

Yacowar, Maurice. "An Aesthetic Defense of the Star System in Films." *Quarterly Review of Film Studies* 4, no. 1 (1979), pp. 39–52.

———. "Actors as Conventions in the Films of Robert Altman." *Cinema Journal* 20, no. 1 (1980), pp. 14–28.

Yampolsky, Mikhail. "Kuleshov's Experiments and the New Anthropology of the Actor." In *Inside the Film Factory: New Approaches to Russian and Soviet Cinema,* ed. Richard Taylor and Ian Christie. New York: Routledge, 1991, pp. 31–50.

Yoakem, Lola G. "Casting in Contemporary Theatrical Motion Pictures and Filmed Television Programming." *Film Quarterly* 12, no. 2 (winter 1958), pp. 36–42.

Young, Stark. "Note: Moving Picture Acting." *The New Republic* 72 (21 Sept. 1932), pp. 150–151.

Zanussi, K. "The Actor and Information Theory." *Young Cinema and Theatre,* no. 1 (1974), pp. 43–48; no. 2 (1974), pp. 45–48; no. 4 (1973), pp. 37–39.

Zolotow, Maurice. "The Stars Rise Here." *Saturday Evening Post,* 18 May 1957, pp. 44–45.

Zucker, Carole. "Some Observations on Sternberg and Dietrich." *Cinema Journal* 19, no. 2 (spring 1980), pp. 17–24.

———. "The Illusion of the Ordinary: John Cassavetes and the Transgressive Impulse in Performance and Style." *Post Script: Essays in Film and the Humanities* 11, no. 2 (1992), pp. 20–26.

———. "The Concept of 'Excess' in Film Acting: Notes Toward an Understanding of Non-Naturalistic Performance." *Post Script: Essays in Film and the Humanities* 12, no. 2 (winter 1993), pp. 54–62.

_____. *Figures of Light: Actors and Directors Illuminate the Art of Film Acting*. New York: Plenum, 1995.

_____, ed. *Making Visible the Invisible: An Anthology of Original Essays on Film Acting*. Metuchen, N.J.: Scarecrow, 1990.

Zucker, Carole, ed. "Special Issue: Film Acting." *Post Script: Essays in Film and the Humanities* 12, no. 2 (winter 1993). Includes Zucker's "Interview with Lindsay Crouse," pp. 5–28.

Index

Cukor, George (director), xi, 98, 228, 229, 231
Czinner, Paul (director), 101–102

Dall, John, 203
Dandridge, Dorothy, 235
Daniel, 321
Daniels, Jeff, 86, 222, 247–262, 332
Darwell, Jane, 215
Davis, Bette, 174, 175, 177–185, 245, 332–333
Davis, Ossie (director, actor), 237
Day, Doris, 209
Days of Thunder, 242
Days of Wine and Roses, 273, 274, 275
Dead of Night, 104
Dean, James, 307
De Bont, Jan (director), 256
Deer Hunter, The, 284
De Forest, Lee (inventor), 226
Delsarte, François (theorist, acting teacher), 6
DeMille, Cecil B. (director, producer, screenwriter), 200
Demme, Jonathan (director), 258
De Niro, Robert, 257, 265, 280–293, 333–334
Detective, The, 218
Dewhurst, Colleen, 245
Diamond Jim, 75
Diary of a Lost Girl, 47
Dick Tracy, 242
Diderot, Denis (theorist), 1, 10–11
Die Hard 2, 242
Dietrich, Marlene, 46, 50, 51–52
Docks of New York, The, 52, 66
Doctor and the Devils, The, 105
Dog Day Afternoon, 250
Donat, Robert, 85, 89–93, 334
Don Juan, 186
Dreyer, Carl (director), xi
Drive, He Said, 306
Dumb and Dumber, 250–251, 253, 256, 259, 261

Duse, Eleanora, 27

Eastman, Carole (a k a Adrien Joyce, screenwriter), 303
Easy Rider, 306–307, 308
Edison, Thomas (producer, inventor), 31, 226
Edison Company (production company), 5, 50
Eikenberry, Jill, 315
Eisenstein, Sergei M. (director), 10, 119–120, 121, 128, 138, 139, 142, 147
Eleanor and Franklin (film made for television), 322
Emigrants, The, 161
Entertainer, The, 107, 117–118
Evans, Edith, 98

Fail Safe, 217
Fairbanks, Douglas, Jr., 189, 192
Falconetti, Renée, xi
Famous Players (production company), 16
Farrell, Charles, 58
Fawlty Towers (television series), 250
Fellini, Federico (director), 157, 289, 301
Ffrangçon-Davies, Gwen, 101
Field, Shirley Anne, 108
Fields, W. C., 50
Fifth of July (play), 248
Film d'Art (production company), 16
Finney, Albert, ix, 86, 107–116, 334–335
First Artists (production company), 232, 239, 240
Five Easy Pieces, 303, 307, 308
Fleming, Rhonda, 139
Fleming, Victor (director), 213
Flynn, Errol, 260, 261
Flynn, Joy (acting teacher), 303
Fonda, Henry (actor, producer), xi, 175, 204, 210–219, 335
Fonda, Jane, 218
Fonda, Peter (actor, screenwriter, producer), 306, 307